WANDERING

My Pursuit of God and Music

By
Ray Last

Melinda - Experience the
presence of Jesus.

Doug

TABLE OF CONTENTS

FOREWORD

I have purposed in the beginning chapters to build a foundation for the thrust and emphasis of this book. The influences and experiences of my childhood and teen years truly formed my deep desire for God and music.

Destiny is often 'crazy' driven. It's Loco-Motion.

CHAPTER 1

RAMBLINGS

I t was my Aunt Jenny who said to me quite a few years ago, "Ray, all these things you've done are so fascinating—you should write a book."

Since then, others have encouraged me in a similar way, so I took their suggestions to heart.

By the way, Aunt Jenny makes the best apple pie. She makes them from those big yellow baking apples that grow near the house on their farm "Up North." Here in Wisconsin, most any place north of where you are is "Up North," though their farm is truly in the northern part of the state.

My grandpa Kulczyski immigrated to the United States from Poland around 1908 and made his way to the upper Midwest. Determined to be a farmer, he laboriously cleared the rocks from the land and settled into this mostly Polish community. My mother, being one of his seven children, ventured down to Grafton in southeastern Wisconsin looking for factory work during World War II, as did one of her brothers and several sisters.

I grew up in Grafton, a small farming and factory town about twenty miles north of Milwaukee. During the summer of 1961 when I was only 11, I'd ride my bike to a small pine forest on the south end of town just to sit in that peaceful setting among the pines so that I could talk to God. This was just months after my mom died. I supposed that I was trying to adjust and needed to be alone. My two best friends, Peter Gramoll and Dick Buchholz, still had both their parents, and they didn't seem to know how to act around me after my mother's death.

April 26, 1961, will probably always be vivid in my mind. At noon that day, I rode my bike home from school to eat lunch as I always did. As I walked into our house, I was shocked to find my mother lying on the bed unresponsive. I nervously called a neighbor for help. An ambulance took my mother away, and four hours later she died. I never really knew what she died from until twenty-five years later when I stumbled upon the medical records. It seemed that I was almost too young to grieve, unable to understand just what had really happened. The pine forest became my place of solace. Having the desire to build a fort there, I chopped down my first tree. After hacking away at this thirty-foot pine with my axe, I finally saw it sway and heard the crack. Whoosh! What a sound it made when it finally came down. I was truly taken aback when I saw what I had done to this beautiful tree. Still and silent, alongside the tree, I stood as if in mourning. Many of the boughs were used to help build the fort. Feeling certain that God existed, I sat inside this pine-scented shelter and freely chatted with Him.

Being so proud of building this fort, I just had to tell my dad. He drove down to the forest with me in his '57 Rambler and brought along his faithful Brownie box camera to take pictures. When we got there, I was greatly dismayed and angered to find that someone had completely destroyed it. This made no sense to me. My dad took pictures anyway: pictures of me looking sad and dejected.

Grafton was not a very big town during my boyhood years, with maybe two to three thousand people. The Milwaukee River that moseyed through and the reassuring sound of the railroad nearby were just a block from my house. I never did care to fish but instead preferred to sit on the bank of the river and watch the sun sparkle off that dingy, brown water. Legend has it that the native Sauk Indians called it "Stinking Yellow River." The river lent itself to easy, pleasant thoughts. In winter I'd skate upriver just to enjoy the peace and seclusion of this winding, tree-lined ice way. My friend, Tommy Schwenner, and I fashioned a raft out of boards, logs, and inner tubes and just lazily floated around during the heat of the summer. Boy, when I think of it now— yuck—we used to swim in that filthy water. We'd dive off the old concrete bridge; you'd have to bring a box of Morton Salt along just to get the bloodsuckers off your feet. Some guys (and girls) were sissies, and they wore tennis shoes. My Great uncle Artie's house and cottage were right next to the old stone bridge on the river. He always loved to sit on the porch in his wicker rocker and watch us swim. I'm sure that he laughed often, remembering when he also swam there as a boy.

I vividly remember the odd things that he had in that one-room cottage. One of them was a stuffed porcupine on a tree branch. I now have this prized possession.

My Uncle Artie, whose last name was Rose, really played the accordion beautifully. After my mom died, I took lessons from him for a few years. I excelled, and my dad had great hopes of me being on stage with him and his band, playing all the favorite polkas and waltzes. My dad played sax and clarinet and did a really good Louis Armstrong imitation. Much of my childhood was spent in local taverns on Saturdays and Sundays with my dad while he enjoyed life, his music, and his friends.

I didn't mind playing the accordion then, and my grade school friend Danny Swoverland and I would often get together and goof around. He played drums. We'd make up songs as we practiced for hours in his bedroom. Well, anyway, something was lacking in the accordion. I mean, it just wasn't in me to bring it out on the front porch to try and attract girls. I never did care to read music, but I always pretended to read in front of Uncle Artie. I'd memorize songs instantly, like "Whispering," "Red Roses," and "Melody of Love." I didn't have the heart to tell Uncle Artie that I hated to read. I wonder if he ever knew.

CHAPTER 2

BACK TO THE FARM

I cherished the two weeks during the summer throughout the 1950s and early '60s when I would be able to stay on my Uncle Peter and Aunt Jenny's farm up north. Their farm was a half-mile from the nearest paved road. As my dad's Rambler—he always drove Ramblers—would near the farm, the first thing visible was the picket fence that never did get painted. My cousins, Pat and Lorraine, would run out to greet us, Aunt Jenny hugged and kissed, while Uncle Peter calmly smiled, and Blackie the dog barked. (Blackie lived to be twenty-three years old.)

My memory comes alive with the sights and sounds of that little town. I easily recall the hard-working people, houses, shacks, cabins, barns, broken blacktop and dirt roads, wooden bridges, train whistles, pigs, cows, chickens, horses, dogs, cats, church bells, and forests laden with pine, maple, birch, and oak trees. Most of the people were of Polish descent and about as lively and colorful as can be. They did come up with the polka songs and dances, you know. I don't mean to get sidetracked here, but I'd love to make you aware of my dad's side of the family. They were German. I lived in two extremes. The Polish folks were always busy and wired while the Germans were laid back and easy going. I'm a mix of both, wired on the inside and mellow on the outside.

Uncle Peter and Aunt Jenny owned over several hundred acres of beautiful land up there. A creek ran through their property, as did the railroad tracks. What a comforting sound it was: hearing the train and its whistle echoing for miles. It's as if the train was talking to the forest.

Early in the morning after Peter and Jenny milked the forty or so cows, the milkman would come to pick up the cans that sat in the ice cold water in the milk house. Those cans were heavy, and he picked two up at a time as he heaved them on his truck. I got to ride with him one morning up to LaChapelle's farm. The thought of spending a day with my friend Billy LaChapelle was exciting. I was nervous and uncomfortable sitting next to this milkman, though. He was so free and easy, sure of who he was.

That's how it was with most everyone up there and certainly with Billy LaChapelle and his family. Billy was about a year older than me (and still is). I had a hard time believing that someone like Billy would like me without my proving myself to him first. As the milkman pulled up into the barnyard, my smile was shaky and my words unsure, but there was Billy waiting for me.

He must have sensed that I was uncomfortable and seemed extra kind to me. He took me around their farm and showed me what kind of chores he did. He thought maybe I'd feel better if we played catch with a baseball. He had an extra glove. To my surprise it was a nice one and left-handed, too (I'm very left-handed). Finally, I felt like I could take charge here and show him how good I was at baseball. After all, this is what I did best. Well, we tossed the ball around a little, and I threw it back to him as hard as I could to impress him. He suggested that maybe we could take turns pitching to each other.

"Sure, you pitch first," I said.

Well, he threw the ball so fast, that my right palm and index finger just burned. I said nothing, just quietly grimaced and thought, "How did this farm boy ever learn to throw like that?"

He threw a sinker, and I couldn't catch it. I didn't even see it sink. I didn't even know what a sinker was! I was afraid to catch his pitches and needed to tell him so or else find myself with a hardball embedded in my head. He was so superior to me in many ways.

When it came time to eat the noonday meal with the LaChapelle family, I was terrified. I knew they were Catholic, and I guess I was, too. Sure enough, here we were, I mean this whole happy family: brothers, sisters, mother, father, maybe even some grandparents, and they all stared at me and asked me things like, "Are you having a good time?"

I made it through the meal, and actually had some mundane conversation as if I sort of fit in.

My dad came in the late afternoon to pick me up at the LaChapelle's farm. He seemed relaxed with these people. I said good-bye to Billy.

His family waved from wherever they happened to be. I never went back again though I did write him a few letters.

Have you ever heard the old farm theory that if you carry a calf every day after it's born, you'll eventually be able to carry it when it's a full-grown cow? Well, we planted a little two-foot cedar tree in our backyard in Grafton. My thinking was that if I jumped over it every day, then I would eventually be able to jump over a very tall tree. Well, the tree is now about thirty-five feet high. I guess I must have missed a few days of jumping throughout the years.

I was really a loner and preferred being by myself than being with my cousins. I mean, we liked each other a lot, but I just wanted to be by myself. I would walk by the old outbuildings and machinery, sit in those antique retired cars, and walk around by the chickens and pigs just to be alone. Did you ever see a chicken run around with its head cut off? That was really strange, almost frightening. You know, I guess I always thought that if your head was gone, that was it. But not so with chickens. They don't know any better. They don't even know that they're dead.

There were many hours that I'd just sit in the hay barn. I'd climb way up on all those bales of hay and just think. Some like-minded cats would snuggle up to me next to a recluse chicken egg or two. It was always extra cozy up there when it rained. A beautiful peace was present. What a racket the rain made as it pelted down on the roof.

One brave morning I climbed on top of the chicken coop to see what it would be like to jump on a cow and ride it. Shh, quiet, here comes one typical black-and-white meandering beast. I leaped down on its back. Whoa! It's a bull! He threw me about twelve feet over the fence. I looked around to make sure that Uncle Peter didn't see that and got up, putting on an air of grace as I walked back to the house.

I always looked forward to getting the cows in at night. Pat, Lorraine, myself, my older brother Donald, and Blackie the dog would venture out down the cow trail.

"Here boss! Here boss!" Pat would call as the herd came waltzing back home.

We always listened for the cowbell to find out where they wandered to in the woods. Blackie would fetch them out, we'd open the gates and cross the tracks, close the gates, cross the tracks again, and follow the cow path home.

On occasion, we'd drive up north to the farm in the dead of winter. Did you ever get up at two o'clock in the morning in ten-degree below zero weather, put on your clothes, and run twenty yards to the outhouse? If you were blessed enough to be of the male gender, you could usually do your duty standing up. They didn't get indoor plumbing until sometime in the 1970s. They never had a hot water heater, either. We took baths in a washtub behind a curtain, heated the water on the wood stove, and made quick business of it. Now it's all so mysterious. You turn on a faucet, switch a knob, pull a plug, and watch it all happen. I still can't figure out how water goes uphill and comes out a faucet, much less how a light comes on by the press of a button or flick of a switch.

There was an old Ukrainian man who lived about a quarter mile down the road in a valley. His name was Grandpa Pukacz. He was tall and thin with broad, protruding jawbones. He was truly a kind, humble man, who spoke little English. He lived alone in a two-room shack that he had built; Grandpa Pukacz made powerful ice cream, the kind that's so cold that it splits your forehead open.

One day, Aunt Jenny asked me to go down to his house and get some sugar and flour. She briefed me on what Ukrainian words to say, such as please, thank you, and good-bye. I went over and over these words as I slowly walked down the hill. I was nervous and a little frightened as I tapped on his door. All the time his bull that wasn't fenced in kept eyeing me up. "At least I can run fast if I have to," I thought.

Grandpa Pukacz opened the door, and with a huge smile he welcomed me in. His floor slanted on about a seven-degree angle. I excitedly told him in his language what I wanted. He chuckled and asked me if I would stay for some ice cream. Aunt Jenny already told me to say yes when he asked. He opened up a little refrigerator and dished out some homemade ice cream. We sat down at his rickety handmade table, two aliens just getting sugared out together. Sure enough, my forehead started to split. I smiled and in a monster type voice said, "Gooooood!"

He must have thought that Frankenstein taught me how to talk. Well, I took the sugar and flour and said good-bye. He told me not to worry about the bull because he was tied up. Relieved, I walked back up the hill, victorious.

I always thought that Grandpa Pukacz was seven-feet, one-inch tall and lived to be over one hundred years old. My story about the legendary Grandpa Pukacz became widely known among my friends and their friends. I even wrote a song about him. Well, the truth is that he was really about six-feet, one-inch tall and lived to be sixty-eight years old. Aunt Jenny set the story straight when my wife and I were visiting her for the first time as newlyweds. Well, I don't care; I still remember Grandpa Pukacz as a boyhood legend.

I brought my accordion up north with me several times. Everybody was tickled to hear me play all those polkas. I even yodeled for them! I've gotten very good at yodeling and use it in many of the songs I've written—it's sort of a "Scat Yodel."

Around 1967, my Uncle Peter decided to give up dairy farming. He just couldn't keep up with all the new state and federal regulations for milk production. He and his family moved down to Grafton, where most of my mother's brothers and sisters had already relocated. I can still hear those words echoing down the hall at Grafton High when my cousin Lorraine would call me, "Cousin Raymond!"

We were both juniors together in the same high school, and when she saw me walking down the hall, she'd yell out my name in a piercing, shrill voice. I got so red from embarrassment I nearly hid in my locker. She was very forgiving, and we laugh about it now, but at the time we were worlds apart. She was an honest, friendly farm girl, and I was a seventeen-year-old potential rock-and-roll star with an image to guard.

Aunt Jenny doesn't make as many apple pies anymore. I usually have to butter her up by saying things like, "You look so pretty today. You haven't changed in twenty years!"

Then that rosy, rounded face with the broad, open smile gets a little flushed, and she asks me, "How many would you like me to bake?"

"Two, if it's not much bother," I usually tell her.

Somehow being on that farm up north was what living was all about. You'd work, see the fruits of your labor, and live at peace with yourself and all that's around you. These farm people were all brought up to share, to make due with little, to be kind and loving, to bear one another's burdens, and to thank God for the day. It was simplistic and good!

CHAPTER 3

MUSIC IS ME

My dad was one of the first people in our town to have a tape recorder in his home. He had an old Revere with a red light that flickered when you got too loud. I've used this tape recorder thousands of times myself. He also cut his own 78 rpm records in the 1940s and early '50s. I have about seven or eight small 78 records that he pressed of my birthday parties, Easter, and Christmas gatherings from 1948–1953. My dad recorded me singing "You Are My Sunshine" and other favorites when I was only three years old. I couldn't pronounce the words so well, but I was on key.

Around 1954, we had a dark brown wooden box radio on top of our Westinghouse refrigerator. That's where much of the music I heard bounced out of, including programs like "Fritz the Plummer's Polka Show" and various big band dance music. One Saturday afternoon as my dad and I collected around the refrigerator, listening to the radio, I sang along with the song that was playing. At the end of the song, the announcer came in with an exuberant, "Very good, Ray!"

I was floored. I thought he actually knew that I was singing along. My dad laughed and told me that the bandleader's name was Ray. Funny how certain things are captured in the memory.

A local television show, "Joe Schotz and the Hot Shots" was also a favorite at noon. It featured polkas, waltzes, and whatever was happy music. My mother put life on hold at noon to watch this. I loved to sing, and as years went by, I sang songs like "Bye-Bye Love" by the Everly Brothers, "Peggy Sue" by Buddy Holly, and many of Elvis Presley's first songs. My older brother Donald usually bought the records, but I ended up listening to them and copying their styles as best I could. I recall listening to the radio while driving on a back road with my dad in the spring of 1959. Buddy Holly's song "That'll Be the Day When I Die" was playing, and I loudly sang along. When the song was over, my dad made me aware that Buddy Holly had recently died in a plane crash. The bad news was so strange and depressing as I thought, "How could he sing a song about dying and then die?" I felt like I couldn't sing his songs anymore because he wasn't alive.

In the early '60s, weeks before Christmas would come, I'd sit on a kitchen chair, put my feet on the big hot-air register, lean back, and belt out all those beautiful Christmas songs. My brother would scream at me to shut up. I loved to sing. We had a big wooden bass drum, and I'd beat it with a wool mallet while singing my guts out. The drum has this cute little decal of a blond haired boy, "Little Squirt," holding a bottle of Squirt soda water.

I used to get so embarrassed and bashful around the age of seven or eight when company would come over and request to see me do the hootchie-kootchie. I usually gave in, got limber, shook my hips, danced, sang, and made my parents proud. I guess when you're a child you have to do that stuff.

At an early age I sang many of the old standards like "Sentimental Journey," "Whispering," "Blueberry Hill," "Red River Valley," and "Beautiful Blue Eyes." Those melodies are enchanting. I could be found singing all the time. I sang when I made toast in our toaster that had the two flaps. When you saw smoke, it was time to flip the bread over. I sang when I threw garbage into the tin kitchen garbage can with the foot pedal that opened it. No one has improved on those cans. I'd hum when I would open up a penny carton of milk. I'd sing the same note that the spinner doorbell made on my great uncle Elroy's outside door. Yes, I sang a lot, and I bet I got some of it from my dad. He was a crowd pleaser and half a comedian on stage with his band.

In the summertime, during the local American Legion and Fireman's picnics, they'd set up a huge beer tent and spread sawdust on the ground. Spilt beer and dirt makes for good mud (That's why the sawdust). My dad and his little band, who were known by whatever name was handy at the time, would play well into the morning hours under those beer tents. The tents held up to three hundred people, who usually got very wild. They loved his music. My friends and I would sleep outside in our tents on the evening of a picnic. About four or five o'clock in the morning, we'd go down to the park and walk around with our flashlights, looking for money around the carnival rides and under the beer tent. We usually found up to ten dollars each in change. Quarters were my favorite. We'd even find a few people who had danced too many polkas, sang too many songs, drank too much beer, and were now eating too much sawdust. The song's lyrics live on: "Roll out the barrel, we'll have a barrel of fun." and "In heaven there is no beer, that's why we drink it here, and when we're gone from here, all our friends will be drinking all the beer," as the crowd shouts the chorus, "E-I-E-I-E-I-O!"

What a crazy mix: Germans and beer.

CHAPTER 4

RAMBLINGS PART II

These small town, carnival-type picnics played a large part in my memories of summer. They were held in towns with names like Newburg, Saukville, Fredonia, Cedarburg, Waubeka, Boltonville, Port Washington, Thiensville, Slinger, and West Bend. It was a very German area. In fact, many storekeepers throughout the 1950s still had to speak German.

I know I've already mentioned that I love to play baseball, and of course, my favorite team was the Milwaukee Braves. I collected hundreds of baseball cards and still have quite a fine collection from 1953–1962. I also put together an impressive Milwaukee Braves scrapbook.

In October of 1988, I had the great opportunity to meet and sit with Hank Aaron, who at that time was still the all-time home run king. He was in Port Washington, Wisconsin at the grand opening of his Arby's Restaurant. He actually seemed somewhat impressed with my Milwaukee Braves scrapbook and baseball card collection, and graciously autographed his 1955 card for me. What a nice man.

Boy, I can't describe the excitement of watching the Milwaukee Braves in the World Series against the Yankees in 1957 and seeing the Braves winning. I was privileged to watch it at home in color. The first twelve-inch color television was introduced to the public on March 25, 1954, by RCA. We were one of the few people to have a colored television then.

There was a program that was on around 1954 or 1955. I think it was called *Quiziack©*. You could order a colored plastic sheet to tape over your black and white TV so that you could see their show in color. Well, we ordered one of these magic sheets, and all you saw was green on the bottom, red in the middle, and blue on top. Does anyone remember this?

There are so many other television shows and characters from the '50s embedded in my memory such as Captain Kangaroo, Roy Rogers, Dale Evans, the *Mickey Mouse Club©*, *Romper Room©*, Howdy Doody, Buffalo Bob, Clarabelle, Paul Winchell and Jerry Mahoney, *Sky King©*, Hopalong Cassidy, Wild Bill Hickock and Jingles, George Burns, Jack Benny, Edgar Bergan, and Charlie McCarthy, Shari Lewis and Lambchop (I had a crush on her), the Hardy Boys, *Ding-Dong School©*, Gene Autry, *I Love Lucy©*, Dick Clark's *American Bandstand©*, *Dragnet©*, Amos and Andy, Jackie Gleason's *Honeymooners©*, Ozzie and Harriet, the Lone Ranger and Tonto, Kukla, Fran and Ollie, Farfel the dog that did those Nestlé's commercials—"N-E-S-T-L-E-S, Nestlé's makes the very best . . . Chocolate."—Gabby Hayes, Jimmy Durante, and Jan Murray's game show *Treasure Chest©*.

There was a game show that displayed serial numbers from one-dollar bills on the television screen. If yours matched, you'd win big. My mom always made Wally, who delivered our milk, go through his stack of one-dollar bills to see if they won. They never won, and Wally probably ran late for his next delivery.

I loved to figure skate and even won a figure skating trophy in 1962 during the Jaycee's first annual winter carnival. That's the winter that the horse-drawn hay wagon tipped over with about thirty people on it. I was one of those on the wagon. No one was injured.

Around 1960, I became a young anti-pollution activist pioneer. While swimming with my friends in the Milwaukee River off a small sand bar in Millpond Park, we saw this grayish-green murky cloud come out of a drainage pipe. We were very disturbed and decided that our little band of nine- and ten-year-olds would go to every factory in Grafton and find out who was polluting the water. The receptionists and company presidents greeted us with a raised brow and an expression that said, "Aren't they cute?" The president of one of the companies bought us all a Coke and assured us that it was not his company doing this. He patted our little behinds and wished us well.

Then we met with another company president who thought we were little Communist spies being paid by his competitors to uncover his top secrets. He gave us each a dollar and made us promise never to tell anyone what we saw inside his factory. Strange fellow.

I got scolded once in kindergarten—yeah, really, me. The milkman came in with a crate of those eight-ounce penny milk cartons, and I started singing a song about him. The teacher, Mrs. Kliner, became furious with me and told me to stand outside. Well, I thought she actually meant outside, so I went out on the playground and started to swing on the swings and play on the teeter-totter. All those dear five-year-olds were watching me with envy from the window. Mrs. Kliner came running out screaming my name, "Raymond Last! You get in here!"

She grabbed me by my left ear (which is why I think it sticks out more than my right) and told me she meant that I should stand outside the *door* and not outside on the playground. Many of the children laughed at me.

I was transferred to the Catholic school for the first, second, and third grades. I'm sure you've heard some frightening stories about Catholic nuns and their means of discipline. Most of the nuns were quiet and kind, but there were a few who weren't what I envisioned as gentle servants of the Lord.

Before fourth grade started, my parents decided to put me back in the public school. My first day in fourth grade found me having to fight the class toughie as a form of initiation. I fought him during recess on the playground; many boys and girls eagerly watched, forming a circle around us and cheering him on. If it weren't for the experience I had of constantly fighting with my older brother, I probably would have been hospitalized. Instead, to my surprise, I held my own to this guy, and everyone stood in a hush wondering what he would do to me for this. He smiled, said I was tough, shook my hand, and welcomed me into his gang. We're good friends to this day, Dennis King and me.

Grade school was actually fairly good to me. My fifth-grade teacher, Mrs. Hansen, was so kind and understanding, knowing that my mother had recently died. I clung to her. A real boost came to my ego in seventh grade as I was voted king of the class and began breaking out of my shy little shell. I became popular and well liked; I even dated some girls at birthday parties.

Before my mom died, I spent my Sunday mornings going to the Catholic church in Grafton. The church was a huge stone building with all the stained glass depicting death and suffering. The overwhelming cloud of incense was often almost too much for me to bear. I was so frightened to go there and just dreaded Sunday mornings. There were so many rituals and rules. Sit, kneel, repeat this, follow this, and try to keep up with the mechanics of worship, in Latin yet. I had the impression that God was either angry or dying. All these rituals and laws seemed so stiff, cold, and frightening. I had pictured God as warm, understanding, and graceful. The religious structure of this church, and the God that I openly talked to, didn't quite match.

Confession at church on Saturdays was scary and seemingly ridiculous. The people there were required to kneel in front of a black veil, and confess to the priest all the sins that they had committed that week. I recall walking past a photo studio in Grafton and seeing a picture displayed in the window of women in bathing suits. Shortly after staring at this photo, I had fearful thoughts that this sin would send me burning in hell. Just in case this could be true, I surely confessed it next Saturday at "Confession." The priest mumbled something about saying two Hail Marys and four Our Fathers as penance. I knelt by the oak pews with all the other sinners and repeated my prayers. Afterward, my friends and I would compare how many Hail Marys and Our Fathers we had to say. My recollections of these religious practices are still dark and frightening. Men in Black.

You know, even at the age of about ten, I questioned this religious tradition. Somehow, I couldn't believe that God really worked this way. How could a priest, being a common man, forgive my sins? Well, this didn't prevent me from talking to God about my problems and worries. I still prayed to Jesus when I was alone and believed that God loved me and watched over me.

After my mother died in 1961, my Aunt Delores, her sister who lived next door, earnestly encouraged me to go to church. I appreciated her efforts and concern, but unbeknownst to her, I'd go to church, put my fingers in the holy water, get a Sunday bulletin, and walk down to Millpond Park, hang around for an hour there, and go back home. I usually made sure that she saw me walking home with the bulletin. This made her feel good.

CHAPTER 5

HIGH SCHOOL – MUSIC TAKES FORM

The Beatles emerged big time during the winter of 1963–1964 when I was in eighth grade. Often I would stand in front of the mirror in my bedroom with my Beatles wig on, strumming my dad's Dobro Hawaiian-type steel guitar. As I pretended to be Paul McCartney, I envisioned myself on stage in front of thousands of girls screaming at me. I had a little blue record player with pictures of people doing the twist on it. Stacking it full of 45s, I'd crank it up to where the little five-inch speaker was pleading for mercy, as I sang my lungs out.

We had a variety/talent show in eighth grade. Danny Swoverland, Kim Gruetzmacher, Tony Modra, and I put on our guitars and Beatle wigs and pantomimed along with the newly released Beatles songs "I Want to Hold Your Hand," "She Loves You," and "I Saw Her Standing There." The sixth, seventh, and eighth grade girls all started screaming. It was unreal. The entertainment fever hit, and I knew then that I wanted to play the guitar and start a band. We easily won the contest and had our photos in the local paper. I guess I was supposed to be Paul McCartney because I held the guitar left-handed.

In the summer of 1964, I yearned to have a guitar. My dad didn't take me seriously. My accordion case sat in my closet along with the music stand and sheet music. Lawrence Welk was struggling to hang on to his audience while Ed Sullivan was trying to contain the screaming girls. There was no stopping the English music invasion.

A friend of mine who lived down the block had an acoustic guitar. He even knew a few chords. I was awestruck. He said that I could use his guitar for a while. I couldn't believe it. I mean, just to hold a real guitar and to take it home, too. Well, all I could really do was look at it. It was made for a right-hander, anyway. They all were. I gave it back after two weeks and resigned myself to just singing along with the records.

High school started, and I was a freshman, a short one at just five-feet, two-inches. It must have been a long summer for many of my friends because they really grew. I didn't.

Erv and Elmer Thom opened up a little music store in Cedarburg, just two miles southwest of Grafton. They actually sold electric guitars, amplifiers, and microphones. My dad knew Erv, who was only about nineteen years old at the time. Having a chance to see this store with my dad, I just gazed at all those shiny guitars with the chrome knobs and bent my head to the side while studying all the settings on the amplifiers. Erv and Elmer were both very likable and quite daring to open a store catering to rock 'n' rollers. Most adults felt that it was just a passing fad, and in a few months we'd be crying for our accordions again. All I could do was look and dream. We went home, I went to school, and the music kept coming: music from the Rolling Stones, Gerry and the Pacemakers, the Searchers, the Animals, Manfred Mann, Dave Clark Five, and of course, the Beatles.

Christmas was coming, and my dad didn't want to hear any more talk about guitars. I was only fourteen years old. I couldn't make enough money to buy one, and my hope diminished. Christmas Eve came and, as others before, I was home alone. My brother was gone, and my dad was out playing his sax somewhere or maybe playing Santa Claus. I usually decorated the tree because no one else had an interest in it. I loved looking at that Scotch pine at night with its ornaments and lights. Well, I just sat there wishing that I had a normal family, a peaceful happy family without all the drinking and arguing.

The family gatherings always started out with big, happy smiles, but as the alcohol kept pouring, they got louder and meaner, and people started screaming at one another. Doors slammed, families broke up, and I stood off in a corner just wanting to get away from it all. I know I cried a lot, pleading to go home. That Christmas, I was old enough to stay home, and I did.

About ten o'clock Christmas Eve, my dad came home with Tony Skiris, a guitarist friend of his. I couldn't believe it as I saw my dad walk in with a guitar case and a small Gibson amplifier. Dad said, "This is your Christmas present."

I undid the shiny latches and slowly opened the case. It was a beautiful, very red, double cutaway electric guitar. The brand name was Harmony. I gently lifted it out of the case with astonished eyes. I didn't even know how to hold it. Tony Skiris propped it up on my lap and started to show me how to make a C chord. I nervously looked at him and said, "But I'm left-handed."

Tony snickered, "You're right-handed now."

Until that evening I would just goof around with my dad's Hawaiian steel guitar, picking and strumming with my left, fingering with my right. Now I'd have to think backwards.

Tony and my dad left for the evening, and I just sat with my guitar. We became friends. Several weeks later, I bought some Mel Bay Easy Method Guitar books. You know, the kind that starts out by telling you which is your left hand and right hand. I felt advanced because I already knew this. I just wanted to get on with it. I practiced chords and learned how to tune the guitar, and where to find the notes. Gary Matthew, a friend's brother, taught me a few simple guitar licks. He knew how to play "Rumble" by Link Wray and "Raunchy" by Bill Justis. Wow! He sounded just like the record. Then a great moment came. He began to show me how to make barr chords, saying that I would use them a lot. In order to make a barr chord, you have to stretch your index finger (first finger) over all six strings and squeeze real hard with all you've got while at the same time placing your second, third, and fourth fingers on various strings and frets. I thought, "Impossible! I can't do it; my fingers are too small. I'll never do it. I may as well give up! I'll never play the guitar with short hands."

I practiced and practiced, and my thumb got terrible cramps. That big muscle below the thumb became so hard from cramping that I thought my skin would split open. Sometimes it took up to ten minutes for the pain to subside. My fingertips throbbed and actually bled. Blood was on my guitar strings. But I was persistent beyond pain. I wanted to play—badly. One evening as I sat practicing in the very same spot where I first opened my guitar case, I finally made a barr chord. All six strings made a facsimile of noise. I nearly cried. I disciplined my body, and I heard the results. I was on my way to becoming a guitarist. With my bedroom door locked, I sat down on my bed and started to learn songs off of the records I listened to. Through the years I've come to learn about five hundred songs right off the record.

Stereo speakers came out around 1965. It was strange listening to a rhythm guitar in one speaker and the lead vocal in another. This stereo separation really did help in my ability to figure out guitar and harmony parts. Of course, I just had to learn the themes from *Bonanza* and *Twilight Zone*.

It was around March of 1965 when Danny Swoverland and I had begun practicing music together in his bedroom. It was around this same time that a casual friend and classmate of mine, Butch Kostrewa, also began to play the guitar. I asked Butch if he'd be interested in starting a band with Danny and me. Butch said, "Sure, I even sing a little. I was a choirboy at St. Joseph's Catholic Church."

We found out weeks later that our fathers were very good friends and even sang together in big bands.

One day during lunch in the school cafeteria, I noticed a new student sitting all alone. He must have transferred from another world because he was wearing a suit and tie. It had to be his first day here, I reasoned. He looked scared, nervous, and lonely. I walked up to him and introduced myself. He gave me a hesitant smile and told me his name, "Bob Greene." His family had just moved here from Rockford, Illinois, and his dad was part owner of a machined spring company that had opened in Grafton. We talked for a while, which helped put him at ease. As the weeks passed, we became friends, and often his mother would pick me up, and I'd spend the day at his house. They had a beautiful new ranch home about three miles north of Grafton. At first I felt uncomfortable in their gorgeous home, but quickly his mother, Lucille, made me feel at home. She was very kind and always willing to listen to my problems about girls and growing up. She even laughed at my jokes.

So, Danny, Butch, and I were still looking for a bass guitarist, and I asked Bob if he had any music ability and did he think he'd like to play bass. He quickly responded, "No, I don't know anything about music, can't even hold a note. Sure, I'd like to play bass."

"Great," I thought, "His parents will probably buy him a good guitar and big amp, and we might even be able to practice in their nicely finished basement."

A week later, his dad took us all to a music store in Milwaukee where he bought Bob a very expensive blue Fender jazz bass guitar and big Fender amp. The amp was nearly as tall as I was. Danny, Butch, and I moved our stuff into the Greene's basement and started to blast out some musical noise. His older sister held her ears and grimaced, his mother chuckled, and we had fun. We called ourselves the Ekkos and make a cardboard sign to put over Danny's bass drum. I tutored Bob on bass guitar, and he slowly came along. Butch got better, Danny got the girls, and I joyfully spent my time figuring out songs and arranging guitar and vocal parts. This was one of the greatest pleasures I ever knew. We got better and better, and our song list increased.

The following is a somewhat exhaustive list of songs that we worked out and performed from 1965 to June 1968:

"Lucille"	Everly Brothers
"Carrie Ann"	Hollys
"Empty Heart"	Rolling Stones
"Wooly Bully"	Sam the Sham
"Here Comes the Night"	Them
"Brown Paper Sack"	Gentrys
"Time Won't Let Me"	Outsiders
"Midnight Hour"	Wilson Pickett
"Nowhere Man"	Beatles
"Mister, You're a Better Man Than I"	Yardbirds
"Land of 1,000 Dances"	Cannibal and the Headhunters
"Well Respected Man"	Kinks
"Don't Let the Sun Catch You Crying"	Gerry and the Pacemakers
"1941 New York Mining Disaster"	BeeGees
"To Love Somebody"	BeeGees
"I'll Go Crazy"	James Brown
"Please, Please, Please"	James Brown
"Yellow Balloon"	Yellow Balloon
"Hanky Panky"	Tommy James & The Shondells
"Never My Love"	Association
"Can't Do That"	Beatles
"Honey Don't"	Beatles
"Torture"	Everly Brothers
"Peggy Sue"	Buddy Holly

"I Can't Get No Satisfaction"	Rolling Stones
"Hound Dog"	Elvis Presley
"Hold On I'm Comin'"	Sam and Dave
"Michele"	Beatles
"If I Fell"	Beatles
"I'm So Glad"	Cream
"Sunshine of My Love"	Cream
"Hang On Sloopy"	McCoys
"Your Ma Said You Cried"	Turtles
"She's About a Mover"	Sir Douglas Quintet
"Live For Today"	Grass Roots
"Tell Me Why"	Beau Brummels
"All Day, All Night"	Kinks
"Sgt. Pepper" (the complete album)	Beatles
"Louie, Louie"	Kingsmen
"Wipe Out"	Safaris
"Let There Be Drums"	Sandy Nelson
"Teen Beat"	Sandy Nelson
"House of the Rising Sun"	Animals
"Get off My Cloud"	Rolling Stones
"19th Nervous Breakdown"	Rolling Stones
"As Tears Go By"	Rolling Stones
"Mr. Moonlight"	Beatles
"Why Do You Love Me?"	Dave Clark Five
"Have I the Right?	Honeycombs
"King Midas in Reverse"	Hollys
"For What It's Worth"	Buffalo Springfield
"Eve of Destruction"	Barry McGuire
"I'm So Lonesome"	B. J. Thomas
"October Country"	October Country
"Up on the Roof"	Cryin' Shames
"All Shook Up"	Elvis Presley
"I'm Gonna Love Ya, too"	Hulla Balloo's
"Happy Together"	Turtles
"Boots Are Made For Walkin'"	Nancy Sinatra
"I'm Telling YOU Now"	Freddy and the Dreamers
"Do the Freddy"	Freddy and the Dreamers
"Little Red Book"	Love

"I Fought the Law"	Bobby Fuller Four
"Rain"	Beatles
"Purple Haze"	Jimi Hendrix
"Don't Let Me Be Misunderstood"	Animals
"Gloria"	Them
"Brown-Eyed Girl"	Van Morrison
"Runaway"	Del Shannon
"Words of Love"	Beatles
"Money"	Beatles
"Lady Madonna"	Beatles
"Roll over Beethoven"	Beatles
"Kansas City"	Beatles
"Magical Mystery Tour"	Beatles
"Hello, Good-Bye"	Beatles
"Pretty Flamingo"	Manfred Mann
"Light My Fire"	Doors
"Round and Round"	Rolling Stones
"Baby, You Can Drive My Car"	Beatles
"It's Cold Outside"	Choir
"I'm a Believer"	Monkees
"Girl"	Beatles
"Love Me Tender"	Elvis Presley
"Rapid Transit"	Robbs
"Turn, Turn, Turn"	Byrds
"Mr. Tambourine Man"	Byrds
"Paint It Black"	Rolling Stones
"This Boy"	Beatles
"Kind of a Drag"	Buckinghams
"Stop and Listen"	Shaggs
"Could Be We're in Love"	Cryin' Shames
"Stagger Lee"	P. J. Proby
"Help"	Beatles
"Ticket to Ride"	Beatles
"Hide Your Love Away"	Beatles
"'Till There Was You"	Beatles
"And I Love Her"	Beatles
"Slow Down"	Beatles
"Good Day Sunshine"	Beatles

"Love Me Do"	Beatles
"Twist & Shout"	Beatles
"Boys"	Beatles
"P.S., I Love You"	Beatles
"Do You Want to Know a Secret"	Beatles
"Act Naturally"	Beatles
"Yesterday"	Beatles
"We Can Work It Out"	Beatles
"Day Tripper"	Beatles
"My Girl"	Temptations
"Slaughter on 10th Avenue"	Ventures
"I Walk the Line"	Johnny Cash
"In My Room"	Beach Boys
"Barbara Ann"	Beach Boys
"Mellow Yellow"	Donovan
"Who'll Be the Next in Line?"	Kinks
"Rainy Day Women"	Bob Dylan
"Tired of Waiting"	Kinks
"Little Red Riding Hood"	Sam the Sham
"Do Wah Diddy"	Manfred Mann
"Pied Piper"	Crispian St. Peter
"Like A Rolling Stone"	Bob Dylan
"Respect"	Aretha Franklin
"You've Lost That Lovin' Feeling"	Righteous Brothers
"World without Love"	Peter and Gordon
"Trains, Boats, and Planes"	Billy Jo Royal
"Monday, Monday"	Mamas & Papas
"Little Children"	B. J. Kramer
"Gimme Some Lovin'"	Spencer Davis
"The Letter"	Boxtops
"Needles and Pins"	Searchers
"Wild Thing"	Troggs
"She's Not There"	Zombies
"Papa's Got a Brand New Bag"	James Brown
"Good Lovin'"	Young Rascals
"Summer in the City"	Lovin' Spoonful
"Young Girls"	Mamas & Papas
"Jet Plane"	Mamas & Papas

"Fire"	Jimi Hendrix
"You'll Never Walk Alone"	Gerry and the Pacemakers
"We Can Fly"	Cowsills
"Sunday Will Never Be the Same"	Spanky & Our Gang
"Foxy Lady"	Jimi Hendrix
"Hey Joe"	Jimi Hendrix
"Wind Cries Mary"	Jimi Hendrix
"Liar, Liar"	Castaways
"I Feel Free"	Cream
"Steppin' Stone"	Paul Revere & the Raiders
"Question of Temperature"	Balloon Farm
"I Just Want to Talk to You"	Jimi Hendrix
"Think about It"	Yardbirds
"Incense, Peppermint"	Strawberry Alarm Clock
"I Can See for Miles"	Who
"Mrs. Brown"	Herman's Hermits
"Silhouettes"	The Rays
"Over, Under, Sideways"	Yardbirds
"Sounds of Silence"	Simon & Garfunkel
"The Last Time"	Rolling Stones
"That's How Strong My Love Is"	Rolling Stones
"Play with Fire"	Rolling Stones
"Bits & Pieces"	Dave Clark Five
"Glad All Over"	Dave Clark Five
"Time of the Season"	Zombies
"Mercy, Mercy"	Buckinghams
"Hurdy Gurdy Man"	Donovan
"Heart of Soul"	Yardbirds
"We Ain't Got Nothin' Yet"	Blues Magoos
"Everyday"	Buddy Holly
"Darling, Be Home Soon"	Lovin' Spoonful
"Come A Little Bit Closer"	Jay & The Americans
"Go Now"	Moody Blues
"Twine Time"	Alvin Cash & The Crawlers
"Birds & the Bees"	Jewel Akens
"Sha La La"	Dave Clark Five
"Mustang Sally"	Young Rascals
"On Broadway"	Drifters

"Something's Burnin'"	Kenny Rogers
"Memphis"	Johnny Rivers
"Sunday Morning"	Spanky & Our Gang
"Just a Little"	Beau Brummels
"Stop Get a Ticket"	Clefs Of Lavender Hill
"Pretty Woman"	Roy Orbison
"Words"	BeeGees
"Your Were on My Mind"	We Five
"Crying in the Chapel"	Elvis Presley
"Shelia"	Tommy Roe

We started out in the early summer of 1965, playing for parties in garages, basements, barns, Legion halls, and we eventually advanced to school gymnasiums. We joined the Milwaukee Musicians Union, Local #8, and played in bars when we were only fifteen. Our parents usually drove us there and patiently sat and listened. Lucille, Bob's mother, actually began to enjoy our music. Our hair got longer. Mine was nearly one-inch over my ears.

Boy, the excitement was at an all-time high weeks before the Beatles came to the Milwaukee Auditorium in 1965. My classmate and friend, Chris, offered to get me a ticket to see them. For some dumb reason I said, "No thanks." This was my first regret in life. I was overly excited in just knowing that they were only miles away in Milwaukee. The four of us, as the Ekkos, did see the Rolling Stones, though. It was quite thrilling just to be standing in the streets in downtown Milwaukee with thousands of others, hoping to peek at their limousine. The most memorable thing about this concert was when Butch stood up on his folding seat, and it folded in. He couldn't get his foot out and panicked. We roared with laughter. Finally, an usher got a crowbar and pried the seat back. Butch was limping for a few days. Mick Jagger never even noticed him (Mick's loss).

We did figure out the Rolling Stones song "I Can't Get No Satisfaction" the same day it premiered on WOKY radio in May of 1965. I taped it off the radio, figured it out with my Gibson fuzz tone, and we performed it that weekend. I, along with millions of others around the country, had attacks of impatience and anticipation whenever rumors spread that a new Beatles album would be released soon. I kept going to the stores daily and was told, "No it's not in yet." However, when it came in, word hit like fire. I would rush to buy a copy just to gawk at the cover. Wow! My own album. I would listen to that album fifteen to twenty times the first day. Usually I grew to love almost every one of their songs. In 1966 we decided to change our band name to the "4 Dimensions." We had our drivers' licenses by now, and Danny's parents pretty much gave us their Volkswagen van to use. We painted it lavender and had the name "4 Dimensions" professionally painted on both sides with an electric guitar. Talk about big time.

Speaking about drivers' licenses, I have a long-buried secret about how I learned to drive. When I was fifteen, my dad took me out in his '63 Rambler station wagon. (What a Rambler man, the first one he had was a 1950 Nash) Anyway, he pulled over on a dirt road east of Grafton and said, "Do you want to drive this?" I had never driven a car before, not even in our driveway.

I hesitated and squeamishly nodded, "Okay."

He got out, and I scooted over. He pointed to the knobs, park, drive, and the brake. I put it in drive and goodness alive, this car was moving! Whoa, I was in control. I was nearly a quarter mile down the gravel road doing a good thirty miles per hour when a sharp curve came up. My dad sternly told me to slow down. I thought, "Naw, I'll make it easy." He screamed, I hit the brakes, I hit the curve, I lost control, and the car flipped on its side.

I yelled to him, "Are you okay?" I thought he was dead or hurt badly.

He very quietly whispered, "I'm okay."

This was unlike my dad. Did he hate me that much? Did he feel sorry for me? Did he think it was his fault? My fault? Why wouldn't he say anything to me? We climbed out through the driver's side window. My dad said he knew the farmer down the road, and we'd have to get his tractor to tip the car over and pull it out. This was the first walk that I remember taking with my dad. It was a nice day, weather-wise, but every second was terrible. All I heard was his breathing, my heart, the crickets, wind against the wheat, the shuffling of our shoes on the gravel, and my thoughts of agony. He never said a word to me. The farmer was standing right there in his barnyard as if this was planned. He got the car out with a big red tractor, and my dad thanked him. There was very little damage; only the right front fender was caved in. We drove away (my dad drove). The car seemed to be okay. I was so relieved. My dad said, "Don't tell anybody about this. I'll get it fixed. No one has to know."

I told him over and over again that I was sorry; I had no idea that driving on gravel could do that. He never said a word. The next time he took me out, I had my temporary driver's permit.

Now, keep in mind that my dad raced stock cars at Cedarburg's quarter-mile dirt track back in the late 1930s and '40s. It was a month or two later on a Sunday afternoon, and he let me drive around a little. I did okay. He started to feel better about his number two son who wasn't into auto mechanics, just music. We came to Cedarburg's Fireman's Park where the dirt racetrack was. He drove in. I quickly questioned, "Why are we going in here?"

My dad shadily answered, "The gates are always open. I'm gonna drive around the track."

I wanted to get out. I pleaded, "No way, dad, let's go home. What if somebody catches us?"

He only chuckled with a childlike grin. He started driving around the track with his '63 Rambler. Whoa, he was going faster. Then he said, "Watch me take this curve at eighty-five miles per hour." He looked demonic, possessed by speed.

I shouted, "No, let me get out—kill yourself!"

I really felt that we'd both die or be seriously injured. We came into the curve; I clenched the door handle and braced myself with my other arm. Good night! He actually controlled this car, brought the back end in from a tailspin. The two left wheels were nearly off the ground. "Well," he said, "I just wanted to show you how to correct a skid."

I mumbled, "Oh."

"Now you do it," Dad said.

I pleaded, "No, Dad, I don't want to drive here. It's illegal" (as if I cared).

He made me do it. He insisted that I take the north curve at a really fast speed. I told him I wouldn't, and I didn't. I went into it at about fifty miles-per-hour. He was satisfied. We closed the gate and went home. I could probably drive anywhere now. He still didn't say much to me, and I had to guess as to how he felt and what he was thinking.

One day, Butch took us all on a luxury cruise up Hwy. 32 in his mom's fully loaded Chrysler. When the speedometer hit 119 mph, we all shouted, "That's fast enough!"

The first car that I owned was a 1961 Ford Fairlane. When I was sixteen years old, I worked a summer job just down the block at a factory, the F. W. Busch Company. I saved money working there to buy that car. The F. W. Busch Company was an old factory with relic-type punch presses fifteen feet high and spot welders everywhere. There was always the constant throb of the presses punching out quarter-inch steel and an ever-lingering stench from the welding which created a filthy blue cloud.

My daily chores included sweeping the floors with a red compound, cleaning the toilets and urinals, and washing the stained coffee cups in the office. At the end of my work day, I took out and burned the garbage. Because of my "long" hair which by then was nearly covering my ears, I had to face and tolerate constant heckling from many of the workers. I often heard worn-out remarks such as, "Hey, did your barber die?" I hated this job, and was only paid $1.30 an hour. At the end of the day, I felt grimy and wiped out. Still, I forced myself to practice at night with the 4 Dimensions.

This job was for me an ugly awakening as to how people can hit a miserable dead end and just shrug their shoulders and say, "What's the use? Whatcha gonna do?"

I felt so sorry for most of them. They were trapped until they retired or died with no dreams, hopes, or ambitions. They just put in their forty or fifty hours per week, got paid, watched TV, drank beer, and had fleeting moments of happiness. They grumbled their way out of bed on Monday mornings, and started it all over again for another week. The drone of the presses, the pot-bellied T-shirts burned full of holes—it never changed. Piece work, it was all piece work. Lose a finger, lose an eye—it was all part of the job. Sometimes I had to degrease and paint those punch presses. I could paint them any color as long as it was factory gray. On one of those *degreasingly* romantic outings, the grimy punch press split in half while the woman was still working on it! She just kept working, no down time there. Piece work, it was all piece work. Factory work was hard and exhausting.

I quit the job after three months, toward the end of the summer, just before my junior year in high school. I was willing to stay on and work just two hours every day after school, but I wanted $1.50 per hour, a twenty-cent raise. My boss said absolutely not. We had a bad argument, and I walked out. I was relieved to get out of there and back to something more sane like music and school.

In 1961, Glenn at the Standard Gas Station would let me wash cars and sometimes pump gas. He still had the old floating ball-type gas pump. He'd buy me sodas and give me a couple of dollars once in a while. Glenn was a nice guy. He was like a father figure to me until his wife had a baby. Then he no longer paid attention to me.

When I was sixteen, I acquired a job delivering the *Milwaukee Journal*. The rural route that I drove was eighty-five miles round trip. But because my driver's license had been suspended for speeding, one of my friends would have to drive my car when I did the route. I once threw a paper right into the box at forty-five miles per hour. I think I ripped up a lot of people's *Milwaukee Journals* this way.

Only a few months had passed after the first time I lost my driver's license, and then it was taken away again, this time for six months and one year's probation. I was caught with four cases of beer in the trunk of my car, which a friend purchased illegally.

When I was only thirteen years old, a small gang of us took a glass-cutter and cut a small hole in the window of a tavern's liquor storage room. We were able to release the latch to open the window. The scene was set, a nice dark alley, a cold October night, and a bunch of boys with no guidance and nothing to do. Yep, I was the one who opened the window, crawled in, and quickly handed out the bottles of hard liquor. Just as I was crawling out and closing the window, the barmaid came in to get a few bottles. We ran fast and never got caught, but we sure did get drunk and sick—good times?

The remainder of my high school years would find me in and out of the courtroom. A very rebellious character was forming in me. I organized a protest against the closing of our youth center in Grafton. Admittedly, it was a hangout, but it kept us contained. We played pinball, pool, and foosball. The youth center had live rock bands, and we played there several times. It was our social and activities center. But the Grafton Village Board and Police department decided it was best to close it down. We had a large sidewalk protest with placards and slogans. About forty people showed up, and, of course, the newspapers covered it. This was all to no avail because they closed it down anyway. We were very bitter toward the police and all who were behind this. What would a hundred local teenagers do now? Teens run in packs like dogs. Eventually we created a new hangout, and we did it to an unsuspecting restaurant. I think we destroyed their business.

I hated the law. I hated being told what to do, and I needlessly argued with teachers and sassed back at the judge on a few occasions. I associated with dead-end friends; some of them are in jail this very day for serious crimes. Word got around in this small town that Harvey Last's boy was no good, a juvenile delinquent! I was determined to defy authority.

We stole phonograph records from stores and more bottles of alcohol from liquor stores while, at the same time, being void of any guilty feelings. Somehow, we justified it. We even broke into the biology room at school and stole a handful of some pink pills, which were a form of amphetamine, real speed. We'd pop one or two of these, get buzzed, get drunk, smoke dope, and just rip up the area. We destroyed mailboxes, slashed tires, and scraped the finish off cars.

Because it rained on the night of the high school's homecoming parade and bonfire, the bonfire was never lit. So the next evening, seven of us poured gasoline on the school's homecoming bonfire pile and on the junior class float. Quickly they ignited. We ran like terrified deer through the fields and through the woods. The flames shot fifty feet in the air that cool October night. Fire engines sounded; police cars raced around, and the rendezvous car, which was mine, picked us up about a mile down the road. We all laughed, talked big, and tried to make sure we had our stories straight about what we were doing that night. Well, the next day in school, one of the guys involved started getting loud and bragging about it. By nine o'clock that morning, at least ten of us were taken to the police station in police cars. We were very scared while being accused of arson and destruction of private property. The guy who brought the gallon of gasoline, lit the match, and bragged about it, told the police that he was innocent and that he saw me do it. When the court date was set, our stories conflicted. He was found partially guilty because he was there. I was found guilty because my car was used as the getaway car even though I wasn't driving it. My license was still suspended at the time. The judge advised all the others involved not to associate with a troublemaker like Ray Last.

Well, I had to pay fifty dollars to the farmer whose wagon was burned, and the other guilty party also paid fifty dollars. The shop class at school built a new hay wagon for the farmer as a project. The local papers reported this wonderful human-interest story, and the group of rowdies I associated with were made to look even worse. Our classmates no longer admired us; they scorned us. All I really wanted was to be accepted and liked. I yearned to have friends. This was the turning point. I stayed away from those so-called buddies of mine and focused on music instead.

CHAPTER 6

MISERY SONS

In the fall of 1965, some people who were well trained vocally, suggested that I take voice lessons to improve my range and power. My first reaction was, "You're kidding." Then I thought, "Me? Voice Lessons? I don't need voice lessons. That's for people who can't sing. I can sing."

Well, as I sometimes do, I overreacted. A few days later, after much thought, I found myself looking in the Milwaukee Yellow Pages under vocal instruction. I called the Mark Steger Studios and talked in length to Mark himself. He had a deep, rich, articulate voice that intimidated me. I sort of quivered and told him that I wanted to sing rock and roll. He chuckled. He even had a deep, rich chuckle. I didn't know why I was wasting my time with a square who laughs at rock and roll. I figured he probably sang opera, anyway, and he probably even talked that way out in public. After talking to him at length on the phone, he helped me to realize that I possibly knew little about singing. I mean, aren't rock and rollers supposed to be self-taught? Hmm, maybe not. He gave me a list of famous vocalists that he had instructed. I was impressed.

That day, I pleaded with my dad to let me take voice lessons. It was $3.00 per lesson, but the catch was that he was located on Keefe and Green Bay Avenues in Milwaukee. I couldn't drive yet, and my dad had to pay for the lessons and drive me. I brought it up to my dad three of four times that week, and finally he consented. "Okay," Dad said, "just try one lesson." Boy, I was going to show this Mark Steger guy how good I was; he'd be impressed.

We drove down to Mark's studio on a Wednesday evening. Ooh, his studio was located in a somewhat "bad" neighborhood. I walked up to the second floor while my dad took off to one of the bars in the area where they often had live jazz bands on weeknights or at least jazz on the jukebox. Mark had a welcoming, cozy, and carpeted waiting room, even a nice couch to sit on. Very unlike the typical studio waiting rooms with hard wooden chairs and bland walls. Big Mark came out. I stood up with a Charlie Brown grin and whimpered, "Hi, I'm Ray Last, I have a …"

"Well, good evening, Ray. I'm Mark Steger."

The volume of his voice nearly knocked me through the wall. "I'll be with you in ten minutes. Sit down and relax."

Ten minutes later, his door opened. A lady with a partial smile came out. She was bad. I could hear her through the door, struggling to sing on key. I felt like telling her to hang it up.

I walked into a fairly large living-type room. Mark sat down behind a black grand piano and said, "Okay, let's see what you sound like. Sing these scales with me. Do, re, mi, fa, so, la, ti, do."

"Oh, come on," I thought, "Do, re, mi? This guy can't teach me anything. What a rip-off."

Well, right away he told me that I was breathing wrong and not pronouncing my vowels correctly. He spent that whole half hour getting me to breathe and push out from my abdomen, my diaphragm. I labored with facial contortions to get my tongue placed properly on certain vowel sounds. A, E, I, O, OO. Mark said, "Very good, Ray. Practice this at home. See you next week." He was so sure of himself. I thought he probably didn't even know who Paul McCartney was. Maybe I wouldn't go back. I waited outside on the street for my dad, who was consistently late. At least he was consistent.

I noticed a record store right next door and moseyed on in. There were a lot of black people there. Up to this point, I had very little exposure to anything other than typical white people from European descent. As I stepped into the store, they all began to stare at me, probably wondering to themselves, "What's this guy doing in here?" "What a weird record store," I thought. They didn't have any Beatles or Stones, Kinks, nothin' like that. It was all music and groups I had never heard of. How could this store stay in business? This was really my first encounter with the Black culture. I was amazed to realize that something other than white middle class existed.

My dad finally came to pick me up. We had some good conversation during the nearly hour-long ride back. I had no idea that he was so familiar with this area. For one of the first times in my life, he started to open up and tell me about his life and his past. My dad began to mildly boast of how he sat in on saxophone with some of these jazz greats in the late 30s and 40s, even Louis Armstrong. I was very impressed by this and finally felt proud of my dad.

Well, back in Greene's basement, all the other guys were laughing at me as I practiced my new vocal techniques. Day after day, I seriously worked at it for hours in front of a mirror. I went back every Wednesday night, provided that my dad was available and didn't forget. I probably took about fifteen lessons over a period of five months. All Mark Steger seemed to do was drill me to perfection on my breathing and vowels. My voice and range improved tremendously, and this technique actually became second nature. I am very grateful to him for setting me straight and grateful to my dad for giving up some of his leisurely Wednesday nights to drive me down there.

While writing this memoir around 1990, I thought I'd look in the Milwaukee Yellow Pages to see if he was still listed. Sure enough, he was still in there, Mark J. Steger Music Studio. He moved to a better location, though. It was almost twenty-five years since I've talked to him. Well, I decided to give him a call.

"Hello," a man said.

"Mark?" I asked.

"Yes," he answered.

"This is Ray Last. Remember me? I took voice lessons from you in 1965."

"Yes, Ray, I do remember you," Mark Steger answered.

"Wow," I thought, and got all excited. He was still alive. I told him that I was beginning to write a book and got to the part about voice lessons, and I just had to call. What a warm conversation we had! We were so happy to hear from each other. I was almost in tears after that phone call. He was eighty-one years old then, still active, and recently had completed a vocal training study course on cassette tape. What an encouragement! The physical check-up that he had showed that he was in fine condition. See, it's the breathing, I bet. He was very interested in what I had done musically and was genuinely happy for me. We found it hard to say good-bye and kept prolonging the conversation.

Finally he said in his much slower, somewhat frail octogenarian voice, "Okay, boy. Bye now." You know, I hadn't thought about it until now, but he never did teach me to sing rock and roll.

Our group, The 4 Dimensions, with the addition of a lead singer, changed its name to the "Misery Sons." By the beginning of my senior year in 1967, we became one of the most popular bands in the state. We broke several long-standing attendance records at local auditoriums. One night, we had over a thousand people crammed into a gymnasium while several hundreds of others stood outside, hoping to get in. They came to see the show. I wanted so much to have straight hair that I started using gunky, smelly, straightener which only held for a few hours.

Ron, a new high school acquaintance of mine, moved to Grafton from New Jersey. His dad was transferred here. Well, Ron was very introverted, and one day during a class that we had together, I asked him if he had a driver's license because I needed someone to drive my car home. He was absolutely tickled and honored that someone wanted him to do them a favor. As he was driving me home, I found out that he was very adept at electronics. Well, we needed some repair work done on our guitars and amplifiers and also wanted portable stage lights built. He was thrilled to be able to help us out. That evening at Greene's house, Ron met all the guys.

Ron spoke the language of electronics, and we unanimously asked him to join the band to run our sound system and lighting. He happily accepted. Soon, very soon, he was to become very popular and have many friends. His electronic genius was in demand. Erv at the music store hired him to be an all-purpose repairman. Ron was in. He was somebody. We nicknamed him "Wolfman" because he became so engrossed with what he was working on that it looked like he was madly eating it. Plus his hair was red and wiry in a natural Afro. He looked wild. We became best friends, talked about our love lives, worked on songs and stage effects together, and laughed a lot.

We now had a solid band comprised of bass, drums, rhythm guitar, lead guitar, lead singer, plus Danny, Butch, and I held our own on vocals and harmonies. We doubled on several other instruments and Ron completed the show with sound and lights. We played greasy bars like the Pit in Kenosha in southeast Wisconsin. It was called the Pit because it sat on the edge of a sand pit. Fights often broke out between bikers and greasers. People were slashed with broken beer bottles. Women would wrestle on the floor, scratching faces, and pulling hair. Once our speaker cabinets were accidentally smashed, but we kept playing because everybody liked the band. I was always hoping that this place would be shut down when we got there so we wouldn't have to set up and play.

There was a time during the Legion picnic at Mill Pond Park in Grafton when my dad suggested, "Just get your equipment and set up on this band shell. Who would care?"

Well, the five of us huddled together and said, "Sure, let's do it."

One hour later we were all set up and hundreds of people were crowding around. We played two and one-half songs when suddenly the county Sheriff cut the power to the band shell. My goodness! The crowd started booing at the police. We packed up and got out of there. No contract, no music.

Many of the disk jockeys from several Milwaukee radio stations would be the MC where we played. It was a big draw and great publicity for us over the radio. Ron rigged up a twenty-foot rain gutter filled with flash powder. On a particular cued note during Jimi Hendrix's song "Purple Haze," we would all turn our backs on the audience, close our eyes, and he'd flip a switch and ignite this powder. That was literally an awesome incredibly bright flash, but, oh, did it stink! We could hardly breathe from the dust, and our mouths became cotton dry. Ron also had several soup cans filled with flash powder set in inconspicuous places around the stage. With the flick of a switch, there'd be a loud noise and a brilliant flash. One ballroom owner told us never to use that stuff, but Ron became annoyed at him and blew the rain gutter off anyway. The owner immediately cut our power, told us to get out, and shouted to the eight hundred or so people, "Go home! It's all over!" What a mess! In retrospect, I don't blame him at all. It stunk and left a dusty film on everything.

We blew a ceiling apart because of the twenty-foot rain gutter. The ceiling came crashing down on our amplifiers. Our lead singer was knocked out when a large wood ceiling beam came down right on his head. We kept playing, anyway. It's only rock and roll, you know.

We often spent more money on special effects than we were paid. There was a very embarrassing moment during a packed house at an auditorium when Ron accidentally bumped the switch that blew off a can of flash powder that the disk jockey, Tony Carr from WOKY, was standing over. He was thrown or blown about five-feet away. He wasn't hurt, just very embarrassed. All of us felt sorry for him and told him so, but he never mentioned us the next day on his radio show.

We also gave a girl in the audience twelve stitches in her forehead. Copying the rock group, The Who, we smashed cheap guitars over a concrete block. Big thrill, huh? Butch smashed a guitar and a splinter viciously flew about fifteen-feet striking this girl in the forehead. It caused a big scene among the one thousand teens packed into the high school auditorium. Her dad wasn't very happy about it. We told him and her that we were sorry. She recovered and came to hear us on many other occasions, keeping her distance though. Well, that's show business.

Yes, we had a strobe light, bubble machine, and weird water projectors. It was all part of the psychedelic '60s.

One of the forty-five minute music sets that we did, consisted of dressing up in old red band uniforms that we acquired from the high school for the purpose of performing all the songs from the Beatles' "Sgt. Pepper" album. The audience stood nearly breathless and silent throughout the whole set.

Leonard DiForte, a local businessman originally from the east coast, became very interested in the Misery Sons. We asked him to be our manager, as we just couldn't handle all the affairs of being locally famous. Advertising and promotion now became big business, and we were still in high school. He was a well-rounded Italian man with graying hair, a big cigar, three-piece suit, and a Boston accent. We couldn't lose.

We entered ourselves in a battle of the bands and were one of the ten bands to be accepted. We practiced and practiced the four or five songs we were going to perform, and Ron got his lighting system all set up. This was one of the most memorable evenings of my life. The Battle of the Bands was held at the Belgium Community Center about ten miles north of Grafton. The excitement was at a zenith high as the bands began to set up and hundreds of people started filtering in. The noise sounded like musical chaos as the guitars and drums tuned up and sound systems were checked. Everyone was eyeing up the competition. We decided to wear our matching blue sequined shirts for this special night. When it was our turn to perform, we did an excellent job of our songs. At the end of the evening, everyone anxiously waited to see who the winner was. To our astonishment, we received ninety-four percent of the judge's vote and about ninety-seven percent of the popular vote. We were ecstatic. That very same evening, my dad drove up right after we had won the battle of the bands, and he gave me an envelope. My driver's license finally came back to me after six months revocation. It was a big night.

Leonard DiForte was proud of his boys and through him we became booked in the Chicago area. This was the scary big time — mafia stuff, maybe. Who knows? Leonard had set up an audition for us on a weekday afternoon at a club called Like Young in Old Town Chicago. Unfortunately, we had to skip school to do this. Our parents consented to it, so we packed the big blue school bus we now owned and drove the one hundred ten miles down to Chicago. We experienced severe anxiety to the point of nausea.

When we finally made it to Old Town, we were absolutely amazed when we saw the streets filled with hippies and freaks. Marijuana and other drugs were being sold openly. Milwaukee's east side was a hippie haven, but nothing like Old Town Chicago. It was a weird abstract world. Beads, long hair, sandals, paisley prints, and anything goes. People were chanting with tambourines, and long-haired girls were dancing with flowing gowns like gentle fairies right in the middle of Chicago traffic. Love and peace. My eyes were fixed on the first sitar (an East Indian stringed instrument) I'd ever seen, perched in the window of a freak store, a "head shop." That's what the little shops were called that sold drug paraphernalia, psychedelic posters, beads, tie-dyed shirts, and an odd assortment of counter-culture stuff.

Ron and I spent an hour in a record store looking through obscure albums that we couldn't find in Milwaukee. One of these albums was by an English group named Cream. We bought the album, which was entitled "Fresh Cream." Shortly after we got back home, we listened to this album and just loved most of the songs, especially a song called, "I'm So Glad." We soon learned several songs off this album and immediately began performing them live, months before the radio stations began playing their songs. Eric Clapton and Cream went on to iconic fame. We even had a pending contract to be their backup band when they performed in Milwaukee.

Well, anyway, our audition at Like Young in Chicago went lousy. Our lead singer wandered the streets, having gotten quite stoned, and showed up late. He didn't look well. We had let Leonard DiForte down and also got expelled from school for skipping out. It became a whole ordeal at school with our parents having to meet all at one time with the principal. Well, to our surprise and relief, all our parents supported what we did and firmly told the principal so. We were admitted back into school but expelled again because our hair was touching our ears. Leonard DiForte was prepared to take this to court under the premise that long hair was part of our professional attire.

I was even told that I could no longer be on the track team in high school unless I got my hair cut. I was very good in track and held the high school record for the long jump at twenty-four feet, nine inches in an unofficial meet. I chose music over sports and quit the team. The school administration hesitantly accepted our long hair, and we became the first high school boys in the area allowed to have long hair. We thought we had a great victory. Within months, this appearance rule was dropped and many other guys started growing their hair.

Through Leonard DiForte, who we called "Studley," we did eventually play quite a few clubs in Illinois and the Chicago area. One very famous club, which held around eighteen hundred people, called, the Wild Goose, was in Waukegan, Illinois. Only national acts played there, and often we were contracted to back them up. One evening, after we performed before the main act came on, the crowd kept cheering for us. The main act came on stage, but the crowd started booing them and chanting, "Misery Sons!"

We heard all this backstage and thought it was fantastic. The manager of their group began arguing with Leonard DiForte and the owner of the Wild Goose. He was outraged that the Wild Goose chose such a good group like ours to back up one of his national acts. To save whatever face he had left, he pretended that there was an electrical shortage, cut the power, and pulled his group off-stage. Well, shortly thereafter, we were booked at the Wild Goose as the main act.

I wrote two songs while in the Misery Sons in high school. "Responsible" in 1966 and "Opalescent Merry-Go-Round" in the spring of 1968. "Opalescent Merry-Go-Round" was a piece I composed for Creative Writing class in high school, which I won some award for. It's simply all about clouds going by. I cut a record of this song, and it received some radio airplay but quickly faded. The *Rolling Stone Magazine*, August 1988 issue, inadvertently overlooked my record while researching the top one hundred singles in the past twenty-five years. I mean, I sold over twenty copies in the first year alone.

Opalescent Merry-Go-Round

An opalescent merry-go-round swirls through a cala-colored chamber.

Juxtapositioned ships float, on a circular ocean,Luminous celestial body glides, as you watch the skies go over.

No joy, little fun, pleasure's gone, hide the sun.
Swoop, sway, stagger, and stoop on your azure dance floor.

Cadmium, cameo, come and go.

A luminous celestial body glides as you watch the skies go over.
Juxtapositioned ships float, on a circular ocean.

No joy, little fun, pleasure's gone, hide the sun.
Swoop, sway, stagger and stoop on your azure dance floor.

Come with me; come and see.

A luminous celestial body glides as you watch the skies go over.
Juxtapositioned ships float, on a circular ocean.

June, 1968, came around, and we were all soon to graduate. No one in the band had any plans for going to college; we'd just keep on as we were, I guess. I had some troubling decisions to make concerning my future with the Misery Sons. Much of the new music that we were playing just didn't interest me. The other guys seemed to be drifting towards more hard acid rock like that of Jimi Hendrix. I preferred more melodic music filled with vocal harmonies. The foundation of the group's popularity was built on this. Working out extremely tight four-part harmony was very difficult and disciplined work. I guess for most of them, it had become more work than fun.

At the same time that I was struggling with this contrasting musical direction, I was also experiencing increased tension with my girlfriend. She felt that I was giving too much time to music and very little time toward her. Well, I was very serious about her; being eighteen and responsible I thought that maybe I should get a job and eventually marry her. In the middle of June, 1968, just one week after we graduated, I decided to leave the group. The news was broken to the group all at once in Greene's basement. I gave my reasons. The guys responded with resentment and shock. A week after I left the group, my girlfriend dropped me for another guy, an organist in a local band. Now I was empty, sad, and extremely depressed.

CHAPTER 7

COME AS YOU ARE

Just two weeks out of high school, I was hired as a commercial artist apprentice. I guess I felt that I needed to be doing something respectable other than music. A suit and tie was required, yuk! I even had a clean haircut. Why was I doing this when it was music that burned in my heart? Working as an apprentice at the Phillip Litho Company in Grafton proved to be a nowhere job. I pasted up pickle labels and painted file cabinets while earning $1.65 per hour. In March of 1969, I quit this job. I knew that music was me.

While still employed at Phillip Litho, I spent many weekday evenings and weekends working on multi-track recordings of songs I was writing and arranging. Randy Liska, a grade school friend of mine, played drums and percussion. Ron played a small compact Farfisa organ. Mike Haupt, a new acquaintance, played clarinet, and Dan Burgard, known as Bogey, occasionally sat in on bass. Several other musicians I encountered played various horns—trumpet, trombone, French horn, and so on. All this stuff, along with my guitar and recording equipment, was set up in the upstairs bedroom that I still had at my dad's house. It was cramped and cozy, just the way I liked it.

Recording fever hit us, and Len DiForte offered to rent a studio in Chicago and pay for the session time with hopes of this new, full, and exciting music catching on. Len and his family had at this time moved to the Chicago area, and his wife offered to have us stay over the night before the session to save us the two-hour ride in on Saturday morning. So, at about six o'clock at night on an early February evening in 1969, we packed two cars and drove down.

A terrible, wet snowstorm hit and traffic on the old Highway 141 crawled along at about twenty-five miles per hour. All the exit signs were covered with snow, and we hardly knew where we were driving. We had to ask a man in one of the Chicago toll booths just how many exit signs to look for before we were to get off. He grumbled and said, "Two."

We finally found our way close to the DiForte's house and called them at a pay phone to come and guide us. Well, it took us over four hours to go about ninety miles, squinting and swerving down this white-on-white highway. We were exhausted. Mrs. DiForte made us some fine snacks, and we bedded down, unable to sleep. Anxiety bites deep.

We all got up early, ate a beautiful breakfast, and got to the studio by eight thirty in the morning. It was pretty exciting, but I had pictured a bigger studio with fancy equipment. They had trouble finding more than two microphones, and those were preset for accordion and saxophone. The carpet was old, dirty, and torn, and the walls were a shade lighter than factory green. There were only two one-hundred-watt light bulbs hanging from the ceiling. This made for nice, dreary shadows. The man in the control room seemed rude and impatient. He constantly winced and grimaced when Randy played his "loud" drums. These conditions along with that of being nervous and scared, made for a very poor recording session. After about six hours of laboring over only three songs and dozens of takes, we called it quits. The trumpet player lost his *embouchure* (his lips failed). Some of the harmonies were off, and we had no zip left. Quite disappointed, we packed up and headed into the cold, slushy Chicago street. Leonard didn't say much. I said I'd call him in a couple of days. We got in our cars and drove home very defeated. We didn't talk much and only had a few reserved laughs among us. This recording session meant a lot to me, and I knew we had to try again soon, definitely in a better studio.

After I left Phillip Litho in March of 1969, Ron, Randy Liska, Mike Haupt, and I became enthusiastic about renting an apartment in Chicago with the hope of making it big in music. It was my desire to start a new band called, "Come As You Are, a Burlesque Theater Band." We thought that in Chicago, we could easily find the other musicians we needed to complete the group. Len DiForte lived down there, and we were ready to go. Well, one by one, each one of us came to our rational senses and dropped the idea. We had no money, no jobs, just dreams, so we stayed in Grafton.

In April of 1969, I got a job in Grafton at Power Products, a small engines manufacturer, where my dad worked. All I did eight hours a day was wash lawn mower crankshafts in a tub of kerosene. It was probably the worst job I ever had, but I got paid $2.85 per hour. I even cleared $100.00 a week! I hated it, but the money bought me things like my azure blue 1969 Camaro for $2,400.00 and more musical equipment, so I stuck with it.

During the thirteen months that I labored at Power Products, I also took jazz guitar lessons from Bob DeBley in Milwaukee. He helped me tremendously with fingerings and techniques. I quickly became faster and more versatile, practicing forty to sixty hours a week; fanaticism engulfed me. On Fridays after work, I'd cash my check, go home, and go to bed by five o'clock in the afternoon. The alarm was set for one o'clock in the morning. Yes, one o'clock in the morning! At times I thought I was nuts, but I got up anyway, washed up, made a lot of coffee, and began practicing my guitar and working on original songs until about ten o'clock at night. Exhausted, with a tremendous feeling of accomplishment, I'd go to bed, get up by six o'clock in the morning, and do it all over again until ten o'clock Sunday night. Every weekend I saw the gains that I had made. I kept getting better on my guitar and singing. Similarly, my original songs increased and improved. A year passed. I had kept this disciplined schedule for an entire year. I actually cried some Monday mornings because of hating my job so much. Devotion to music was my greatest desire.

As I practiced my forty to sixty hours a week, I also came to appreciate and admire the styles of certain guitarists such as George Harrison, Eric Clapton, and Djano Reinhardt, the romantic French gypsy jazz guitarist. I copied the guitar style of two native people from Northeastern Brazil called Los Indios Tabajaros. They had several hit records in the late '60s, "Marie Elena" and "Jungle Dream." I had the great opportunity to see Andrea Segovia, the legendary classical guitarist, in 1969 at the Performing Arts Center in Milwaukee. What a quiet, humble master of the classical guitar he was. He continued to perform until his death in 1987 at the age of around ninety-four. I credit all these unique guitarists with helping to influence my own style.

I was still living with my dad, but in the summer of 1969, four of us rented a fourteen-room ranch house on Bonniwell Road about fifteen miles southwest of Grafton. It was very secluded. I still can't figure out why this farmer would rent to a bunch of long-haired, irresponsible rock and rollers, but he did, and we managed to get up the two hundred dollars a month to pay him. By this time, around July '69, I had found other musicians to fill the void and "Come As You Are" became a practicing group in the basement of this ranch house. Bill Knutson, who everyone called *Dag*, was a trumpet player from Kenosha Wisconsin. I met him through a crazy, fun-loving middle aged lady who we called, Ma Swatco. Ma Swatco followed the Misery Sons wherever they played. She hand-embroidered band uniforms for us and invited us to her Kenosha Home for a great feast whenever we played in the area. Ma Swatco was a very large woman with a huge heart for teenagers. Several keyboardists auditioned for Come As You Are. The only member missing was Ron, who was drafted into the Marines. Yes, drafted.

The military draft lottery came to be in 1969. My number was two hundred fifty-six. It was a high number, but still I was worried as was everyone else. The stories about Viet Nam were horrifying. During my high school years, I daily lived the fear of having to go to war as soon as I graduated. I know that all my friends felt this way, but we just didn't talk about it much. There was enormous confusion and controversy about why we were there. It wasn't a matter of patriotism. The daily newspaper and the three big networks all had such scary, negative reports. It couldn't possibly have been likened to World Wars I or II, or Korea. There was such great pride then in serving our country and such honor in returning. This wasn't the picture in Viet Nam. Two million seven hundred thousand men and women eventually served there.

My fears of going always became greater at night. Who could be blamed for questioning Viet Nam? I didn't burn my card, and I respected the flag. The Legion Post in Grafton was even named after my great-uncle Fred Rose, who died in England during World War I. I knew that there was a tremendous heritage among my relatives that had served in these previous wars. Many people made the ultimate sacrifice so that this country would remain strong and free. I pray that those who had loved ones that died there and those that have deep emotional or physical wounds from active duty would be healed. God bless those who willingly fought for freedom. The following is a letter that I wrote to the local papers after attending a ceremony in Grafton on Monday, August 29, 1988. The Wisconsin Viet Nam War Memorial statue came through briefly on a visit of fifty towns in the state before eventually settling in Kneilsville, Wisconsin, at the High Ground Memorial site.

It was a somewhat cool, overcast afternoon in late August. As they gathered, the conversation was solemn but warm. There was unity. Flags blew boldly, and uniforms were pressed.

I was the least of anyone there. I had been terrified of going to Viet Nam. My draft number was high, and I watched the war on TV while sitting in a cozy chair.

But now, my insides were weeping. I felt honored to be standing among men and women who had served our country, especially those who were in Viet Nam.

The four-figured, life-size statue pulled up on a gooseneck army trailer. People stood in awe. Cameras clicked, the pledge was said, speeches were made, and applause was given.

The truck pulled out after its proud hour. I wanted to cheer, but the reverent silence overcame me.

Finally, the people of the United States of America were giving honor and glory to the Viet Nam veterans.

God . . . give them strength and meet their needs.

Ron was drafted in the spring of 1969; they lined them all up at the induction center in Milwaukee, and every seventh man went into the Marines. I couldn't believe that he had to go. This reality hit me hard. We had great plans to pursue together. Saying good-bye to Ron, my only close friend was awkward and grievous. Ron still managed to chuckle about it.

Living in this big ranch house on Bonniwell Road was very lonely. Usually no one else but me was home, working on songs and being alone. I was still very heartbroken more than a year later after my high school sweetheart found another. That, combined with Ron's absence and working a bummer job, drove me to being extremely depressed and suicidal. One Wednesday evening in July of that year, I truly felt I would take my life. But first, I had the urge to drive to Kenosha to weep on Ma Swatco's shoulder. I tried calling her, but she didn't answer. I got in my car to drive to Kenosha and wept most of the way there. Such sorrow and emptiness was upon me. I drove up to her house; the lights were out. I knocked on the door. She wasn't home. I just stood there at her door with a heart and a mind that was breaking down. Was there no one left in the world that I could turn to? It was one of the darkest, most lonely evenings of my life. No one would care if I killed myself, I thought. The drive home didn't seem to exist. I went to bed, went to work, came home, and wondered where my life was going. For what reason should I be living? At nineteen years old, I was alone. All I wanted was a girlfriend, music, and a few close buddies. I held the God of my childhood at a distance; oddly enough I never even called on him.

Days and weeks went on. The group sort of stumbled along. There wasn't much commitment, mostly partying. The keyboardist turned out to be a thief, stealing much of our equipment one day while we were gone at work. I called the police, whom I hated to have involved. They told me that this guy had quite a criminal record. Late that same evening, the police drove him out with all the stolen equipment. He just mumbled that some friends helped him move out, and they took some things by mistake.

Well, it looked like Come As You Are couldn't be held together, as everyone else had moved out of the house, and I was left alone paying two hundred dollars a month. No, thank you. I moved back in with my dad, back upstairs.

I started to toy with and delve into the occult. Fascination with the supernatural was gripping at my mind. I had an interest in this ever since the days I spent with my great-uncle Artie. At twelve years of age, just a year after my mom's death, he told me that he was receiving letters from her from beyond and invited me to call her up on the Ouija Board. Boy, this seemed eerie and crazy, but I went along with him. Sure enough, the peg moved on the board. It told us that it was my mother. Was this really happening, or was my uncle making it move? Artie perceived that I had an interest in these matters and proceeded to share with me all about his out-of-body experiences and how I could have them. He did readings on me from my coffee-cup grounds and encouraged my flirtation with déjà vu. Whoa, I've done this before. He ate it up.

I never did feel comfortable playing with the occult, but I felt myself having an interest in this upstairs at my dad's. I literally freaked my friends out with ESP, clairvoyance, and trance-like states that I fell into. Many times I would stare into a mirror without blinking in a dimly lit room until my face would disappear. I went to a lady astrologer several times in Milwaukee. She played the part right out of the crystal ball, candles, and gypsy wagon. This lady was very confused and tense. I couldn't take her seriously, but she had no problem taking my money. The fad eventually wore off, but I knew that I had probably reached another dimension. Could it be useful? Could it be developed?

It was also during that summer that we heard rumors about an outdoor rock festival in Woodstock, New York. Supposedly, anyone who made it there could play a couple songs on stage, and maybe some people from record companies would hear. Well, Randy Liska and I were ready to go. We planned to take off that Friday afternoon for New York, but my boss at Power Products said that if I wasn't back to work on Monday morning at seven o'clock, I'd be fired.

He somehow heard that I had intended to go to New York. Common sense got the best of me. I needed the job, I needed the money, and I didn't go. You know, I still think I should have gone just to say that I was there. This became the second regret in my life.

They would call it the Woodstock Nation, Associating Woodstock with free sex, drugs, love, liberation, and music. Years after the dust settled, America discovered that the Woodstock Nation was a disaster that began to infect this country. Aimless burnouts with dissent and disloyalty were created. Free sex turned into noncommitment and illegitimate children yearning for parents. Marriage had worked quite well for thousands of years: husband, wife, father, mother, an unconditional commitment for life. Now it was purposely being broken down. Drugs never liberated anyone. Now it's one of the greatest problems the United States of America faces, along with suicide, mental breakdown, demise of family, and an inability to be responsible and cope. Drugs played the paradox and became a prison. Much of the music has turned into absolute trash; it deceives many by glorifying wickedness. Yet people buy it. Sick minds get sicker. The great revolution of the late '60s has turned into a vulgar mess.

I wasn't at Woodstock, but I was very much a part of that culture. I got nowhere, year after year, following this loose philosophy. I got nowhere. Nowhere has its limits. It produces many questions with few answers.

In the fall of 1969 I met with Len DiForte, and we found a new studio in DeKalb, Illinois. I rounded up most of the same musicians that I had previously recorded with, and we spent a Saturday putting down the basic tracks for about six songs. Things went very well with a new studio, and the owner/engineer really liked my music. We accomplished a lot that day and felt great. I went back two more Saturdays to dub in all the harmony parts and some miscellaneous instruments and to finally mix it all together. The final work was beautiful. I still get a thrill out of listening to these recordings.

As I mentioned earlier, I cut a record of "Opalescent Merry-Go-Round," and Leonard tried to get airplay in Chicago. I tried earnestly in the Milwaukee area, and Tom Roy a high school friend of mine made it number one in Grafton, West Virginia where he worked as a disc jockey. Well, the record died after about three weeks, and I quickly began to experience the way of the record world. Producers, promoters, disc jockeys, BMI, ASCAP, record labels: they were all too complicated for me. I was just a musician/singer/songwriter looking for the right avenue to travel.

I know that I became very discouraged, but I continued to write and arrange songs. I wrote the "Sheepherder's Song," a guitar instrumental. As I daydreamed about being a sheepherder in Scotland, basking in the setting summer sun, laying in a field surrounded by hills with hundreds of baying sheep and a couple of herding dogs. It was really peaceful.

"Come As You Are" (To the Night Time) was written as a defense for those who had prejudice cast against them, such as the handicapped, elderly, blacks, and people who weren't physically comely. The song pictured all these people in a field under a dimly lit night sky. Nobody saw anyone else as different, just accepted and equal.

"Decrease" (In the Hearts of Men) was another song I wrote having deep sorrow for all those that left for the Viet Nam war. "My Good Friend," was a fictitious song about a dog being my best friend.

In 1969 after traveling down to Grafton, West Virginia to see Tom Roy, I wrote a song called "Glory's Town." Small mountain towns moved and inspired me to write this piece about a Utopian village with perfect, friendly, and honest people, that was heaven on earth.

I was still on a girlfriend search, and it seemed that the only way to meet a girl was through frequenting the bars. I wasn't interested wasting my life hanging around a tavern, and anyway, I no longer drank alcohol ever since the day at seventeen years of age when I had a party at my house while my dad was gone. We got so drunk from hard alcohol that it took three days for me to recover. I was in bed for nearly a day and a half. Alcohol left a bad taste with me after that.

While working at Power Products, I became good friends with Gordie. He opened up a nightclub in the late '60s on Milwaukee's east side called the Avant-Garde. It was a quaint, nonalcoholic coffeehouse with good live music. In 1968 and 1969, Ron and I would go there often and just be amazed at how unique the atmosphere was in this second-story loft with round tables, dim lights, candles, and a menu of drinks all in French. It was *avant-garde*.

Gordie often told me about his exciting weekend excursions to New York City. He was instrumental in persuading me to go there to pursue music. I recall his strong warning, "Ray if you don't make it by the time you're thirty, you'll probably never make it."

In February of 1970, my heart was stirring, my mind was excited, and I could no longer contain what was erupting within me. It was possible not to live in Grafton for the rest of my life working in a factory and dreaming. I was free to go. I had no very special friends, no family that I would miss, no money—whoa, no money. Car payments, too. Well, I'd save what I could in two months, maybe sell some musical equipment, and in the end of April 1970 move to New York. People thought I was nuts; I couldn't just do that. What did I, a hick from Grafton, Wisconsin, know about a big scary city?

I met with Ron's stepfather on several occasions to talk about New York City. He was from New Jersey and had been to New York City many, many times. He was an enthusiastic encouragement to me, giving me maps and introducing me to the scheme of the subway system. As he shared his joy of the theaters, museums, and Broadway, I was itching all over to go. My month's notice was given at Power Products, and at the end of April, 1970, I left for New York City with three hundred fifty dollars and a pocketful of well wishes such as,

"See you on the Ed Sullivan Show," and "We'll look for your name in *Billboard* magazine."

I drove my azure blue '69 Camaro, and Gary, a casual friend of mine, came along for the ride. I was scared, and Gary was goofy.

CHAPTER 8

MANHATTAN, NEW YORK

We drove a thousand miles straight through Wisconsin, Illinois, Indiana, Ohio, Pennsylvania, and New York. It was a very flat ride except for parts of Pennsylvania. About twenty-five miles into New York state, the highway patrol pulled me over. I had no idea what I did wrong. This big guy got out and started walking toward my car. The patrol uniform was ominous. He told us, "Get out! I'm going to search the car."

There was a steady rain with a thirty-mile-per-hour wind. He wanted everything out of the car, trunk, and all. I had my Fender guitar and amp, tape recorder, microphones, and all my clothes. There it sat, neatly piled on the shoulder of the road, getting soaked. After a complete search of us and the car, he mumbled, "Okay," as he drove off.

Gary and I looked at each other somewhat amazed and said, "Wow."

Have you ever noticed that words like *wow* have withstood the test of time?

About one hundred miles further we were pulled over again by some local police. I had no idea why. Two police cars with sirens and lights going sandwiched me in on the side of the road. Three police got out. I really don't remember what I was thinking, but they weren't happy thoughts. This police guy probably ate some gravel and then barked, "Okay, buddy, follow us. We're takin' you in."

I thought, "How hospitable of them!"

Into the police station we went. Gary was told to wait in the car. They booked me on suspicion of driving while under the influence of drugs. I sort of pleaded, "We're clean! We don't have any drugs."

The officer looked at the sergeant and snickered, "They were laughing in the car. I saw him in his rear view mirror."

I bounced to my defense, "We're just happy, that's all."

Poor defense. I was put behind bars with a ten-dollar bail. I took out my wallet and said, "Here is ten dollars. Can I go now?"

Somebody bellowed out, "You can't pay your own bail. Your friend has to."

So shortly after this stimulating conversation ended, someone went out and brought Gary in. I slipped him a ten-dollar bill, and he handed it to the guy behind the counter. You know, the guy with all the official paperwork. They unlocked the jail door, I was free to go. I should have said, "My uncle is Barney Fife. You'll be sorry!" (No, I didn't say that but, I should have)

The guy that pulled me over kindly said, "We never wanna see you again around here."

Three or four guys started chuckling and probably got on the phone to the local pizza place and ordered the ten dollar "highway special" to go.

I didn't feel so good at this point about New York. Gary and I drove out of their town frowning; that'll show 'em.

Well, after seeing numerous highway signs informing us as to how many miles it was to New York City, we were finally sucked into the Lincoln Tunnel. The eagerness of the traffic was tremendous. I had no idea where I was going with three or four lanes zipping by me as the Camaro cautiously putzed along. When I pulled over at a gas station to look at my map, my '69 Camaro was hit near the back end while I was parked. The guy that hit me just yelled something profane and drove away. I thought, "Man, I should be yelling at him."

Gary and I found our way down to Lower Manhattan where Greenwich Village is. With bums on park benches and hippies everywhere, I parked my car by Tompkins Square on the corner of Avenue A and 7th Street. We walked around, wondering what to do next. Whoa, just like that, some rock group set up in a band shell and started to play. People merged on them out of nowhere. Apparently, this was common throughout the Village, to just set up and play. We walked a few blocks to 2nd Avenue and St. Marks, the focal point of the hippie movement.We saw Bill Graham's Fillmore East, with headliners Sly and the Family Stone, Electric Light Orchestra, Chicago, Laura Nyro, Janice

Joplin, Jimi Hendrix, Blodwyn Pig, Grateful Dead, Crosby, Stills, Nash and Young, Alvin Lee and the Winter Brothers, Johnny and Edgar. On and on went the names on the marquee and posters. Hells Angels were everywhere with their Harleys, black leather jackets, and skuzzy looks, but they seemed passive, even friendly. Boy, it seemed that everywhere there were head shops with psychedelic posters and drug parapher-nalia, weird T-shirts, and beads. The city was still talking about what had happened last summer at *Woodstock*. It was strange, especially at night. Greenwich Village people had their own world down there. Most major cities had an area like this during the late '60s, early '70s, but Greenwich Village had no rival. The rock clubs were painted with flu-orescent orange and green with black doors dimly lit and light shows going on constantly. Wavy Gravy and his "Earth People Bus" would pop up and park for a while and then move onto another area.

The Bowery, populated with hundreds of bums, was just a block away; it seemed to be a mile long—peace, love, and the weirder the better. There were drugs I'd never heard of and young people patheti-cally lost and burned out sleeping in the streets, alleys, and condemned buildings. It certainly was a radical revolution; people were lying in their own blood and vomit. Hardly anybody cared. Self-survival in this city was a number one concern. Skuzzy alley cats seemed to have it better. People would pick old pizza crusts and apple cores out of the steel mesh garbage containers; siren screams and gunshots became background music. It wasn't the New York City that could be seen in the movie *Love Story*. Thousands had great hopes, dreams, and aspi-rations. Few ever saw the taste of recognition and success.

Why was I here? I thought this over and over on my first night. Gary didn't come to stay, just to visit. I came because I was led to believe that this was where I'd have a break in music. The nation and the world would hear of Ray Last and his music. I would go and sac-rifice a lot toward that goal, being driven by an insatiable desire to be recognized for my talent and wit. I wanted to be a star and still show everyone that I was a regular guy unstained by fame. This, my first night in the mythical city, exactly 1,000 miles from home, found me stirring with excitement. I had about three hundred dollars left, so Gary and I slept in my car.

Our first evening in the car by the park wasn't too bad for me being five-foot four and three-quarters inches tall, but Gary's knees hit the roof. We managed a few good nervous laughs like unsure conquerors. About eleven that night someone knocked on my window. My mind raced as I thought, "Window's up, the cars locked, God, he's going to kill us. No, maybe he's a cop, and we can't park here. I know. We'll pretend we're sleeping. No! Gary, don't sit up! Oh, man, he knows we heard him." I rolled my window down two inches and boldly said, "Yeah?"

He bolted out with excitement like a stray dog come home, "Are you from Wisconsin? I've got friends in Madison."

I thought, "How did he know?" Of course, my license plates. Relaxed and in control I quickly said, "Yeah, just north of Milwaukee. My name's Ray, and this is Gary."

"Hey, I'm Bob. You just get here? Need a place to stay? Let me show you around, I'll buy you a meal. Keep your car here, let's walk."

"But," I cleverly responded, "I've got a lot of stuff in this car. I don't want it stolen."

He assured me, "It's safe down here."

We got out and felt more calm about this place. I mean he wanted to be our friend already. We followed him all around the East and West Village, which encompasses an area of approximately fifteen square blocks. He bought us pizza, Coke®, and hot dogs. (The staple diet around there.) He talked and talked and talked. We laughed a lot. This guy was friendly. We finally got back to the car, which I was relieved to find was still there. He said he'd catch us tomorrow as he said, "Goodnight." We actually slept about four hours total. Not bad.

We got up about six o'clock in the morning and went to a nearby gas station wanting to wash up in the station's lovely bathroom. You've heard of them, perhaps you've seen one. Brown crud all over the walls, autumn colored cold water, and a toilet that puts a thousand flushes to rest. I know that there once was a light bulb in here because there's a remnant left of where the light switch was. We decided we were better off not to wash up. I asked the guy working at the station if he had a good map of the area. I couldn't understand everything he said with his broken, foreign English accent, but I understood him to mean, "If you don't want gas, get out."

I found out that day what hard core "New Yawkers" were like. Chicago seemed tame in comparison.

I spent a good part of the day looking through the counter-culture weekly newspaper, *The Village Voice*. There were pages and pages of places to rent, and I made at least fifty phone calls. It seemed that everything was taken. How could that be? The paper just came out two days ago. Boy, anything that I could afford was already rented. We wandered the village and took the subway. I said that rather casually, didn't I? Took the subway—aagh! Man, you get on, you get pushed in; it's like being sucked into a vacuum. You have to know just where the leak in the vacuum is in order to get off. I couldn't believe that this little island, which is only twelve by two miles, has over ten million people roaming during a given working day, and they all know how to get in and out of the vacuum.

Well, I finally got off somewhere underground but Gary missed the stop. I can still picture his forlorn eyes waving good-bye. He was destined to ride forever. It took me several hours and numerous subway tokens and transfers to get within reason of where the East Village was. I ended up walking about forty blocks. At least I knew I was going in the right direction. "It" finally released Gary, and we met up again in Tompkins Square in the late afternoon.

I saw parts of uptown Manhattan, the CBS building, Times Square, Broadway, 42nd Street, Macy's, and, of course, the Empire State Building. In fact, I believe that it was that day in late April, April 22, that the first Earth Day was held in New York; I just had to get in on it and see what it was all about. The city closed some of its streets down, and it seemed that literally millions of people were marching right down the pavement carrying signs, dressed goofy, and chanting things. It all had something to do with Earth Day, which I didn't understand. Well, I thought it would be really neat to go to the top of the Empire State Building and look down at all these little people. So I walked to the Empire State Building and took the elevator all the way up to the top. I'm not even sure how many floors it is anymore—one hundred and twelve stories or something like that. I actually got to walk outside on the very top. It was a beautifully clear day, but there was around a forty-mile-per-hour wind kicking against me. I walked over to the edge by the railing and became nauseous. I was hoping to look down to see all these people marching, but to my disappointment, all I saw was more buildings. I couldn't even see any cars. Well, I looked out and out and out as someone said to me that you could see for eighty miles on a clear day. I wobbled back into the elevator and down the street. It was good to be back on earth for Earth Day. They were just starting construction on the World Trade Center at that time; otherwise, I probably would have gone to the top there also.

I wrote an editorial for several local newspapers in commemoration of the twentieth anniversary of Earth Day, April 1990. It read as follows:

To the Editor:

So, we're hearing a lot about the 20th anniversary of Earth Day. Well, on April 22, 1970, I was in New York City—just my second day into a 1½-year stay.

Wandering about near 52nd Street and the Avenues of the Americas, I stumbled upon a million-plus people marching in the streets.

I thought, "Is this what they do in New York City? Far out!" Mimes were out in full force and clown costumes abounded. Signs waved joyously: "Save our planet" and "Earth Day, U.S.A."

It seemed like a neat idea to go to the top of the Empire State building to observe all this hoopla.

Let me tell you, the express elevator has no mercy. Most of my insides were thrust down to my feet. It took two days for my blood to catch up.

As I left the elevator, I was met by a 45-mph wind daring me to maneuver about on the open-air platform.

A man with an invigorated smile said that on a clear day you could see 80 miles. Well, it was a clear day, but I just preferred clinging to the rail than gazing out.

With a bold curiosity, I peered down the 112 stories to take in the full scope of Earth Day activities. All I saw were buildings overshadowing other buildings.

Rather disappointed, I took the express elevator back down in hope of equalizing my internal organs and blood flows.

I can't think of a better place to kick off an ecology movement like Earth Day than New York City.

Okay, I've finally burned that story out of my system. Now, what were you doing on April 22, 1970?

Ray Last
Port Washington

Our friend, Bob, showed up around six o'clock in the evening and offered to take us around again. This time I drove. I told him all about my desire to start a band and get a recording contract. He asked me if I wanted to sell my amplifier and guitar knowing that I really needed the money. I hesitantly told him that I'd sell my amp for about three hundred fifty dollars. He quickly responded and told me that a good musician friend of his probably would buy it. His apartment was about eight blocks from here on around 4th Street and Avenue C, a rugged neighborhood. The evening was dark and drizzling. We pulled over in front of what appeared to be or should have been a five-story brownstone. Brownstone brick was the common material used in apartment buildings, side by side, alongside thousands of others. There were old boards over the windows, a door hanging by one hinge, garbage everywhere, street lights, or at least they were broken out, and a foul stench from a late April smog-drenched rain. Bob told me he'd carry my amp in and show it to this guy. I had nicely cared for the 1966 Fender Vibrolux amp with a custom fifteen-inch Lansing speaker. I didn't take well to his idea and at least smartly said, "Let me go in with you and meet this guy first. Gary, wait in the car." We cautiously walked into this totally dark hallway.

Bob yelled something like, "It's me. I've got a friend."

"Well," I thought, "I'm really special to be his friend and be able to enter this creepy sanctum unharmed."

Bob held me back with one hand and said, "Stop." He bent down and felt around on the dirt floor and pulled a heavy throw rug back. There was a pit dug about four feet in diameter, and China knows how deep. He laid a conveniently placed board over it and walked over, telling me to follow. We went through a maze of doors and hanging rugs until we came into this dimly lit room with about four people barely existing, eyeing me up.

Now, you don't have to be a pharmacist to know when you're around drugs. These people looked bad, a girl and three guys. One guy was squirming on the floor in real pain holding his right arm with blood oozing out of it. Bob calmly asked, "Is he going to be okay?"

Somebody muttered, "Yeah."

Bob assured everybody that I was cool (dumb is a better word) and told them I had an amp to sell for three hundred fifty dollars. "Ya wanna buy it?"

Some guy said, "Yeah, I'll look at it. Bring it in."

Well, all this while I was scheming as to how to get out of here. I told Bob that I'll go out to my car and get it, but "You've got to help me find my way out."

This, my second night in New York City and I'm already learning to con. He led me out to the door. I ran to my car, which felt like home, got in it quickly, started it, and told Gary, "We're gettin' outta here!" and took off. The wipers were going, my heart was going, my mouth was going, and Gary was still trying to find a decent radio station.

Well, back in Tompkins Square, we indulged in a large slice of pizza and a Coke® at this now-familiar open-air counter. A thirty-cent slice included free grease and wax paper. Oddly enough, it always tasted good, and I never got sick.

The next day Gary and I split up in the morning. He became a low-budget tourist, and I pursued a place to rent. I met a lot of people and saw the apartment on Bleeker Street where Bob Dylan was living, walked past Jimi Hendrix's recording studio, Electric Ladyland, and bumped into Richie Havens at a strange record store. He assured me that he didn't do drugs anymore; it almost killed him. I wondered why his teeth were missing. Quite frankly, I didn't know who Richie Havens was at the time. He told me that he played local clubs often, and I should come and hear him. He seemed like a nice guy with a big left thumb. Over the years I've had occasion to see him play the guitar and he really uses that thumb to play the lower strings. Boy, Greenwich Village in its entirety was full of irregular people. Nobody even noticed my long hair, beard, and dirty Levis.

Gary and I met up again late afternoon. He had a brown bag and told me to open up my trunk, "Quick!"

Obviously, I asked why. He said he bought a pound of marijuana for eighty dollars.

I couldn't believe it and exclaimed, "We're running out of money, and you spend eighty dollars on dope? I don't want it in my car!"

Gary tried to convince me that he'd sell it easily for three times that much.

"To who?" I asked.

We opened it up to inspect it. Being around a lot of weeds in my day, I immediately smelled that it was catnip. "Gary, this is catnip. Smell it."

Gary's face grew long. Out eighty bucks. I was somewhat relieved to know I wasn't carrying drugs. This was going to be an expensive high for some beat-up alley cat.

New York wasn't being very good to us yet. The next day in the late morning, we met up with Bob again. He wondered why I took off so fast. I shrugged my shoulders and mumbled that it just didn't seem right. He was very excited for us because some friends of his were moving out of their apartment, and we could have it. It was only eighty dollars per month and an eighty-dollar security deposit. "Do you want it?" Bob asked.

I paused for about four seconds and yipped, "Yeah, let's see it!"

It was relatively nearby; I think it was on West 3rd Street, a little into the more desirable West Village. The day was sunny, the streets were clean, the bottom entryway was open, and very artsy people dominated the area. We walked up to the fourth floor. Bob had the keys and let us in. It was a two-room cozy place; I loved it. "When can I have it?" I asked.

"Today," Bob gleamed. He mentioned that I had to sign a small lease, but it was best I stay here and he would get the lease and pay the eighty dollars rent and security deposit to the landlord. He told me that the manager downstairs wasn't very friendly and might ask me a lot of questions if he saw me.

"Well, okay," was my hesitant response. I gave Bob one hundred sixty dollars cash.

He said, "Wait here. I'll be right back with the lease."

I waited and waited. Nearly fifteen minutes went by in this partly furnished apartment. I reasoned out many things in my mind and finally went down to the manager's place to see what was going on. I knocked on the door that had the small letters "manager" scribbled under the number three. Well, I knocked again and again and finally a hard-sounding man yelled, "Whada ya want?"

I told him my name and that I was waiting for Bob and that I just rented apartment twelve on the fourth floor.

He cracked the door about five inches, and there stood an obese slob about forty-five years old with a stained T-shirt, four days growth on his face, and a cigar that could chew all by itself. He barked at me, "I don't know nuttin'. Go away."

This guy Bob baited me for five days and finally got my money. Gary and I were very bummed out. We basically gave away two hundred forty dollars, and we had only thirty dollars left. It didn't take long to make the decision to get out of here and go back to Grafton. Therefore, I stuck my tongue out at New York City, and we drove the thousand miles straight through nonstop in fourteen hours. Very depressed, with bloodshot eyes, we entered Milwaukee at sunrise. The well-wishers' haunting phrase, "See you on Ed Sullivan," kept going through my mind. Friends and relatives would be hard to face; it would be hard to explain this failure.

CHAPTER 9

MANHATTAN ATTEMPT

I was determined to go back and have a crack at it. I sold about six hundred dollars of my musical equipment. During the week and a half that I was back in Grafton, I wrote three songs pertaining to the experience I had in New York City. The first song was called, "When You're Down and Out, Don't," and basically it was about not committing suicide when you're extremely bummed out. The second song was called, "There's a Lot of Hard Times Coming Now," and the third song, which I felt described my experience in New York City, was entitled, "Mad Dog Fight."

So, after ten days of living back upstairs at my dad's, Randy Liska, my drummer friend, drove me to Milwaukee's Mitchell Field Airport. I had just two suitcases this time and a little more wisdom. I landed at JFK International and didn't have the vaguest idea how to get anywhere. I'd never been on an airplane. It was rather boring.

I asked and asked how to get to Manhattan, the city. New York City is actually made up of five boroughs—Manhattan, Bronx, Yonkers, Brooklyn, and Queens, although Manhattan is commonly referred to as New York City. Finally, I saw a bus that said *Manhattan*. I asked the driver, while yelling through his opened door, "How much?"

He snapped back, "Quarta."

A lot of people snap back there. Try buying a newspaper at a newsstand, you almost feel like you're asking a big favor of them. Always have correct change.

The bus ride was tight and crowded; you didn't have to worry about falling over when the bus took off or stopped; you couldn't move, it was all bodies. Two suitcases didn't help, either. Well, I didn't know you had to pull the string to ring the bell before your next stop, but I eventually got close to St. Marks and 2nd Avenue. I had some of my money rubberbanded to my feet. Yes, I had shoes on. It was the middle of May, and the weather was delightful. I started to whistle. Finally, people noticed me. Nobody whistles.

I rented a room at the St. Marks Hotel for around $8 a night, a lousy place, right on the corner of St. Marks or 8th Street and the Bowery. St. Mark surely would have questioned why this was named after him. The clerk was friendly to me when he saw that I was a Midwesterner—part scared, part humble, but always smiling. It felt really neat having my own room in New York City. The room was about eight by five feet. The sheets were yellowed and stained, and I had to use a common bathroom down the hall. My room was right next to the clerk's desk. I heard a lot of lively conversation out there. One night a lady had a fight with a man in the room next to mine; she was screaming and swearing, and he stabbed her and fled. She collapsed in front of my door. The clerk took care of her, and paramedics took her away.

Certainly not all of New York City is like this, but you'd need a fair amount of money to live in the secured lovely areas. After about a week of living in this hotel, the awe and excitement of being in the fabled city started to wax low. I became very, very lonely. A friendless depression set in. I thought about this close acquaintance of a girlfriend I knew back in Grafton. I desperately needed to talk to someone. I called her collect, and she seemed very surprised and overjoyed to hear from me. Words spewed from my mouth about things that went on here and how I'd been looking for a cheap apartment and some kind of tolerable job. I even told her about how I answered an ad for a roommate. When I went to his apartment on the west side, it was very lovely and well kept, and the man asked me if I was gay. "Well," I told him, "Yes, I'm a happy guy." He sort of kindly laughed and explained to me that he meant whether I was homosexual or not.

I became extremely uncomfortable and embarrassed saying, "No I'm not."

He sadly mumbled, "Well, I don't think this will work out between us."

I left, a bit bedazzled now knowing that there was a different definition for the word *gay*.

Well, my lady friend Shelly and I talked to the point where we felt it would be good for her to move out there with me. She had very few friends in Grafton and only a boring future. In about two weeks she arrived with her suitcases, approximately $500, and a very baffled expression. We found an apartment in the lower East Village on Houston and Forsythe. The rent was okay, but as is the custom in New York, the tenant advertises a unit and charges a fee to move in. Landlords and rental agreements were bypassed. I bought the right to live at 208 Forsythe Street, Apartment 9, for $400, and I only paid $42 a month rent. All I had to do was send the next rent check with my name on it, and if they cashed it, I became the legal tenant.

The people that were moving out of the apartment were native New Yorkers with guts, purpose, and a pioneering spirit: two common hippies into natural foods and a more natural lifestyle. They left New York City for the Yukon with about $2,000 and all they owned in their backpacks. This couple had a desire and determination to buy some land up there and become self-sufficient. I really admired them. Their last name was Russo. If you see them gnawing on bark somewhere, say hello for me. The Russos gave me my very first exposure to natural food and vitamins. I was even invited to have a vegetarian dinner in the building next to that one with their friends. I accepted. It was okay, but I felt out of it. I mean, I was used to drinking a quart of Coca Cola®, smoking one and a half packs of Marlborough® cigarettes, and eating gray hamburger and beans every day. I didn't even know what lentils were. I thought it was a Jewish holiday. I didn't know that apples were sprayed with poison and that Vitamin C is good for you. You can even legally buy it.

Well, the day came when the Russo's moved out and we moved in, inheriting a scrawny cat. It meowed all night and wouldn't even let a sweet guy like me pet it or anything. After about three days of listening to this obnoxious cat, I decided to take it outside and let it go. I picked the pretty little kitty up, opened all the locks on the door, and started my mission down four flights of stairs. The cat freaked out; he obviously was never outside this two-room apartment before. He squirmed out of my arm and thrust his claws in my back. Running down the stairs, I thought he might kill me. When I got to the street, the only thing I could do to get him off my back was to smash my back into the concrete wall. I did this two times, and he took off out into the street. My back looked like I used a jagged razor blade on it; it was bad. But kitty was gone, looking for a new home. Since then I have come to own, nurture, and enjoy a number of cats.

I started to slowly tame New York, and even became a graceful subway hopper, got some odd jobs, and pursued music. I tried out as a guitarist and backup vocalist in the popular group *Brooklyn Bridge*. I would have passed the audition, but I had no musical equipment of my own. It was left back in Grafton at my dad's. Because I had no money to buy a guitar and amp, my only option was to rent from a pawn-shop. The guy wanted $50 rent and $100 security deposit on a Gibson guitar. I paid him the $150 so that I could try out for a few other groups and some jingle commercials. In about two weeks when I brought the guitar back to his pawnshop, I handed him the receipt showing that I had $100 in security deposit coming back. He grabbed the receipt, tore it up, put it in his pocket, and coldly told me he didn't know "nuttin' about it." I was shocked as I asked, "How can you do this to me? You stole my money?"

He threatened, "Get out or I'll call the police!"

Life has some surprises.

Gradually I started to learn that to survive here I'd have to be ruth-less. On one occasion when a panhandler asked me if I could spare a nickel, I just snapped, grabbed him by the neck, and viciously threw him into a parked car, screaming at him, "Get off my block!"

I did make a few casual friends like Doug, the photographer who lived in apartment #8 next to me. He had really long hair and a ponytail. (Mine was getting there.) Doug was quiet, friendly, always alone, and obsessed with doing a portfolio on Thelonius Monk, the jazz musician. A Puerto Rican family also lived on the same floor. I think that in the fourteen months that I lived there we never said a complete sentence to each other, just smiled and nodded a lot. They did teach me how to get rid of cockroaches, though. If this ever got around, it would put exterminators out of business. They toasted a piece of bread, put butter and sugar on it, placed it in a corner and soon twenty to thirty cockroaches would be crawling all over it. Then a pair of shoes quietly walks towards the corner and steps on them. There, all done. And now you have jam with your toast.

You know, as I write this I realize that every day in New York was a short story. My mind is rushing with memories, like the long walks I took at night up to 57th and Park Avenue, over to Broadway. I would easily cover one hundred city blocks a night; the average city block was six hundred feet long, one hundred seventy five feet wide. I usually walked eight to nine miles a night.

The stores in the area were always changing. Window shopping was at its finest. I'd see movie stars getting out of their limousines with Afghan dogs, sex derelicts on 42nd Street, colored lights and signs everywhere, and millions of people. Everybody seemingly had a reason for being there. I bought guitar picks and strings at Mannings' Music located around 47th and Broadway. All the famous musicians went there. Hundreds of photographs were displayed on the walls. I was impressed.

A unique irregular regular on the corner of 52nd Street was Moondog. A long-haired, bearded poet-musician dressed in Viking attire with spear, helmet, and horns. Moondog always had abstract poetry to recite or a song to sing. Often I would stand and listen to him. I had a curious admiration for his creative boldness. He was blind and in a class by himself. Moondog disappeared from New York streets in 1974 and at the age of 57 was assumed dead. *People* magazine writer Peter Mikelbank unearthed his story in 1989, finding him alive and well in West Germany. He was active as ever with great musical endeavors under his Norseman's belt and great dreams before him. He may very well be one of the best hidden musical geniuses of the 1900s.

Floundering with a definite musical direction, I auditioned for other groups and sang for commercials but never had a plan or a goal. So far, I was just there getting training and experience as I attempted to make sense of this place. I still wonder whether that city has a system for functioning or whether it operates on motivation and desire. After about two months, going into July, I reasoned that I was really there to promote myself and my music. This renewed revelation felt great.

With an eager enthusiasm, I took my tape of the six original songs I recorded to various major record companies like Atlantic, Columbia, Reprise, Capitol, and many others. I usually left the tape at the desk, hoping that someone would listen, love it, and sign me to a recording contract. The closest I came to this was when Reprise said that if I had a group they would consider signing us. Another company wanted to buy the rights to my song "Glory's Town" and have Marianne Faithful record it. I wouldn't sell the rights as I had intended to record this song myself, and I would just have to buy it back. Atlantic wrote me a nice letter telling me that they weren't interested at this time. I kept the letter hoping that someday I'd be able to display it on a competitor's album jacket.

Without question, my next move would be to actually start a group, rehearse, write originals, and perform. This became my day-long drive. I wrote many unique sounding ads and ran them in *The Village Voice*. It was very costly, but I received a lot of responses from musicians. I was looking for a drummer, bass player, pianist, trumpet player, trombonist, and saxophonist. I ran at least one ad a week and received about twelve hundred phone calls over a three-month period. Musicians are interesting people. Sometimes we make up what we would like reality to be. I weeded out most of the calls and actually auditioned about one hundred twenty-five people. Many of them came to my apartment, as I'd have them listen to the half-hour tape of my original, fully arranged songs. We'd talk a lot if they were talkative, and I'd hear them play. They were almost always very good. Some of these guys put me to shame; they had so much experience having played with major groups such as The Benny Goodman Band, Sly and the Family Stone, The New York Philharmonic, and Miles Davis. Some of these guys even played at Woodstock the previous summer. Some were sought after studio musicians. Some were lousy. We got together, and they almost always showed me respect. It seems that everyone liked my music and arrangements.

Often I would take my 1965 Fender Jaguar guitar, which my dad finally sent me, and go to their apartments. My guitar weighed about twenty-eight pounds so it got a little heavy after walking numerous city blocks, and switching busses and subways. I think my left arm was stretched longer from this. I had a pad sewn on the guitar case handle so it wouldn't dig so deeply in my hand.

On one occasion I auditioned a trumpet player who lived near 125th Street. It was a long ride, and I got off the subway, walked up to street level, and sort of noticed that everybody was black. It was hot, and they were all on the steps, sidewalks, and street. There I was this cute little hippie with his guitar. People stared at me like I was diseased. Boy, they called me names and stood in my way. I really put on my tough uninterested look and kept walking, head down. All this hostility toward me was weird. I got to the guy's house (he was white) and told him where I had walked to get to this place. He became whiter, quite amazed. He exclaimed that I had just walked through the heart of Harlem—and with a guitar yet. Really! I didn't even know what Harlem was. I mean, I knew the song "Harlem Nocturn" and I even saw the Harlem Globetrotters at the Grafton High School, so what was so special about Harlem? He just shook his head in amazement and proceeded to tell me stories about his friends being stabbed and how he was beat up in daylight and had his trumpet stolen. "Don't ever go back there again," he advised.

"Okay," I sheepishly said.

I keep remembering this Japanese guy out in Brooklyn. He had a nice spacious lower flat, I was happy for him that he had room and even a little yard with a tree. He played a mediocre keyboard, and he sang "Maybe I'm Amazed" by Paul McCartney. His voice was okay, but it seemed so out of place hearing someone from Japan singing a Beatles song. But, greater still than my impression of this guy was the size of his dog. I really thought it was a stuffed bear lying on the floor; it never moved. Once it groaned, and I nearly lost an eyeball. He assured me that the dog (the dog?) was very gentle and was from China, mainly used as a beast of burden to pull carts. He told the dog to stand up; I begged him not to. This was obviously no easy task for the big black furball. He finally managed to get his whole body up after a lot of grunting. I'm not kidding; this dog's body stood three feet high, and his head was about forty-two inches up from the floor, the biggest dog I'd ever seen. It made a St. Bernard look like a puppy. I touched him, and he looked at me. "Perhaps he can play trombone," I thought.

The auditions went on and on, and I made friends with a really tall trombonist from California named Jon Johnson. Although he never became a member of the group, at least we did become friends, and I kept it in mind that he was from California. I decided on a drummer from the Bronx, his name was Bob F. I haven't been able to get in touch with the people who played in my band, so I'm only using their first names. I came to his apartment in the nearly completed projects on Pelham Parkway. He lived with his parents who were very nice people. His drum set was in the living room, taking up half their space. He was still sleeping when I got there, and his mom woke him up. He hardly knew who he was much less why I was there. I played him my tape, and then he said he'd like to warm up before playing for me. His warm-up session on the drums was the best I ever heard. I wanted this guy in the band, which I still called Come As You Are (a burlesque theater band), it was to be a burlesque theater band because of the comedy I had in mind. We talked a lot, and he decided to join and hang in there until the group was complete. I understood that he was a drummer in the original Vanilla Fudge and Nice groups.

A pianist I auditioned named Elliott lived right across from the CBS building on 52nd and Madison. He was exceptional and had the style of Herbie Hancock. He wanted to join and was quite taken aback by the big voice that came out of my little body. I always had to warn people that sometimes I sing loud. It reminds me of this old black man talking on a Spanky and Our Gang album. He says, "You kin play as loud as you wan' as long as you playin' good."

Bob, Elliott, and I started to work songs out. A bass player named Carl happened to call from my ad as a lark. We became interested in each other, got together, and he joined. He lived about eighty miles out of the city in Brewster, New York. I couldn't imagine why he wanted to hang out in New York while living in the country. Carl was a big guy with a big mustache, very friendly, and good humored; I felt like his friend.

I auditioned numerous horn players, and by then Come As You Are was an actual group. We rented rehearsal space for around fifteen to twenty dollars an hour. Goodness, this was foreign to me, having to rent a space to practice. But, over the next year, we would go from one studio to another, always paying for it.

We decided on an alto sax player named Al from Secaucus, New Jersey. He played sax, clarinet, flute, and oboe. He was a thin guy, always smiling and usually funny. The trumpet player Gene lived in Brooklyn and played with the New York Symphony. He was good at what he did but felt out of place with rock and jazz, though he grew to like it and even started to jam a bit. The trombonist's actual last name was Daddio*; his hair was slicked back, and he talked lewd, but he fit in, and we got along. What a weird group! I felt like the least of them as a musician, but I was a strong vocalist and wrote the songs. No one in the group ever knew it, but I lied about my age by four years. I was only twenty years old, the youngest in Come As You Are, but for fear of not getting respect, I said that I was twenty-four.

On occasion we would practice up at Carl's house in Brewster. It was a very relaxing break for me taking the train out of Grand Central Station, seeing trees, fields, clear skies and open space again. Carl picked us up at the train depot. I would always embarrass Elliott in the train by mocking the conductor when he'd come through and call out the names of the towns. He'd bark out, "Brewsta!"

After the conductor would go into the next car I'd yell as loud as I could, "Baaroosta!"

Elliott got red; I was just a kid.

I had smoked cigarettes since I was about thirteen; I sort of wanted to quit but not enough to try. We were all up in Brewster for three days in the country, miles from town. Carl and his wife would not allow me to smoke in the house, and that first evening I ran out of cigarettes. No one would drive me to town to buy any. Horrors, I'd have to go three days without them. I struggled day by day and just craved the thought of getting back to New York City to consume pack after pack. I got back very late that night to Grand Central Station and just went home exhausted. The next morning when I woke, I thought, "Wow! I've gone four days without them. Maybe I can quit." I bought some of these little cherry flavored cigars and gnawed on them and bubble gum. I started exercising and got up at five o'clock in the morning to go to Central Park and jog a few laps around the lake. There were usually about nine or ten people doing this in Central Park at five-thirty in the morning. A month passed with no cigarettes, no cigars, and no gum, and my breathing got better, my voice became crisper, and my range increased. I quit; I did — I really quit this thing. Thanks to Carl! I never again had the desire to smoke cigarettes. Well, the group got better, extremely good, and I was in touch with Ron back home. He was out of the Marines, out of Vietnam, and interested in coming to New York to hear us and possibly become our sound man.

One evening at Carl's house I had a very big surprise. We were done practicing by the late afternoon and as was natural for most of these guys, they brought out dope, hash, alcohol, and just got ripped. Marijuana and Hashish never went well with me. I usually became introverted and frightened. I actually lost my senses. Well, they cranked up the stereo and played "Sprach Zarathrustra", the score by Wagner used for the movie *2001* A Space Odyssey and passed around the hash pipe. It was now dark outside, and I took two good hits of this stuff. I was gone. I kept spinning and feeling like I was floating to the ceiling; I needed to vomit but couldn't make it to the door outside. I crawled on the floor for fear that I would leave this dimension. I opened the door and hung onto to the grass outside. I heard a familiar chuckling voice that said, "Hi."

I looked up; it was Ron! Ron and his friend drove to New York City from Grafton, and Shelly told them where we were practicing. I couldn't speak, my mouth was dry, and my throat tight. I hung onto Ron, pleading and begging just to be straight again. I think I actually prayed to God. I apologized to Ron, "I smoked some powerful hash, excuse me."

Ron became very angry, shocked, and offended. He drove all this way just to hear this dynamite group I was bragging about, and all he saw was a drug party. Ron left immediately. There were no words for how lousy I felt. I guess I fell asleep outside, and somebody got me on the train back. Next thing I remember I was standing in the middle of the street on 42nd and Broadway not knowing how I got there.

Things were patched up with Ron and me, and he eventually came out to live with me along with all his musical equipment, lights, and PA system. We, Come As You Are, permanently rented a rehearsal studio near Elizabeth and Spring Street in the Soho District of Greenwich Village, just five blocks from my apartment. The name of the studio was called "Jude." Ron had an arrangement with the lady that owned this building; they'd let him stay there in exchange for his electrical and sound expertise.

Well, our search was on for a manager and record company and life in New York City was getting better. I taught guitar to earn living money and also worked as a 1970 census enumerator. I'd pick up a stack of long and short forms from my district manager. The government paid something like eighty-five cents for getting a short form filled out and about $1.50 for a long form. My area of coverage was mostly Puerto Rican, and many people wouldn't answer their door. You'd just see this big eye in a peek hole. I spent twelve hours a day going door to door, trying to fill out and complete forms. About two weeks later, I went to my district manager's place with a stack of completed forms. I was taken back as I saw him shooting something in his arms while sweating and grimacing in pain. I wondered, "How could this guy work for the government?" I was sent a check for almost $500.00 and a letter from the United States Census Bureau commending me on my diligent work as a census enumerator. There were many corrupt and dishonest things that I did there, everything from cheating the utility company to getting free food stamps. Cheating and scams were just made too easy there. It was very tempting. Some of these wrongdoings eventually caught up with me at awkward times.

Garbage pickup down here was different. Many people would just throw their garbage right out the window down onto the ten-foot wide concrete alleys in between the buildings. Once a month two men would come with a huge iron garbage can, hip boots, and shovel this juicy, rat infested stuff into the can, dumping it into the back of the garbage truck. It got to be two feet deep in my alley. Some folks bothered to bring it down to the street, but it was much more convenient to toss it five stories than to carry it down. This made for an interesting noise at two in the morning, along with the cat fights that became amplified between the buildings.

The summers got so stinky hot that on a clear day the sky was actually black from pollution with virtually no breeze. I spent many evenings with my feet in a pan of ice water sitting in front of an open refrigerator door. You had to make it through the heat and dead air somehow. The winters indoors were equally uncertain with old steam radiators banging and whistling.

I went to a local laundromat to wash my clothes, but many people had lines strung over to another building, and they just cranked their wash in and out to dry. Everybody knew what everybody else wore.

On my corner was a small park about fifty by two hundred feet. It was just a few trees with concrete, some benches, and a curling type court played with a broom. Many local bums would hang out here, drink garbage booze from a paper bag, sleep on the benches, and beg from sidewalk pedestrians. One bum became my friend; he was a sweet, humble man. It seemed he was always whistling and happy. On a boiling summer afternoon I saw him arguing with another bum. This other guy broke a bottle and slashed my friend's head open. I rushed over, but it was too late; he looked dead, covered in his own blood. The other guy started crying saying that he didn't mean to do it and just walked away. An ambulance came. Nobody cared; I conditioned myself to not care, either.

I seemed to be spending sixteen hours a day, every day, on this music group. One of the members of the band gave me these white cross pills for a mild stimulant so I could keep going. Well, they sure did stimulate me, but after using them every day for about ten days, it seemed that they just didn't have the kick anymore. Then he sold me (not free anymore) these potent black Cadillac pills. I'd take one at about ten o'clock in the morning. I couldn't eat; I just kept going until two o'clock in the morning the next day. I did this for three days, hardly eating anything. I had the shakes so badly, felt delirious, fearful, had no conception of time or days or people, and finally my body just gave out, and I collapsed in bed and slept for two days. That was the end of the speed for me.

I was quite productive with songwriting while living in New York, and finally a song that I began writing three years earlier was completed.* It was on one of those extremely hot and muggy August nights. I couldn't sleep and finally got up about two in the morning and wrote "Can't Sleep a Wink."

Can't sleep a wink, gotta hot room that's keepin' me up.
Sit up awhile try to think of something to do.
Dream I was swimmin' in a pond right outside my door.
My eyes are getting sleepy, think I'll dream just a
little bit more.

Other than "Mad Dog Fight," "Down and Out," and "Come as You Are," a burlesque theatre band theme song, I had numerous fragments of songs with titles such as:

Welcome to Story Day
Old English Prance
Save the World
Lazy River
Silver-Chested Boy
Country Raga in A
Classical Raga in G
Benny Boy
Mr. Man
Winter's Comin' On

What's a Fella to Do?
There's a Lot of Hard Times Comin' Now

Of all the time I spent in New York City, I hardly listened to any music but my own. I had a phobia about being influenced by other singers, groups, and songs, though I did continue to work at sounding like my favorite vocalists: Paul McCartney, Elvis Presley, P. J. Proby, Louis Armstrong, Esther Phillips, Robert Plant, Dean Martin, Stevie Wonder, Bob Dylan, Sioux Indian chanters, Cab Calloway, and several blues and gospel singers. There were many other vocalists that I admired, but their names escape me. My voice became a blend of all of these. My drive was to be the best and be unique. On occasion, when I had the money, I'd walk a few blocks to the Fillmore East or the Anderson Theater and hear the national acts: the groups that made it. Usually, I just would get depressed because I wanted to be there so badly. I got to the point where I convinced myself that I would become internationally known and even be instrumental in bringing peace to the world through my music. I was so bent on seeing myself as the greatest, wisest, most influential person alive that many people became mesmerized just listening to me talk. The more they listened, the more I got into it. I started to feel god-like with a world mission. This didn't subside when I left New York, either.

It's crazy when I think about how I had, within walking distance, access to hearing the finest musicians in the world. The small clubs and large halls were everywhere, but pride kept me out. Pride kept me (what I thought was) pure. Envy of those who knew fame became a deep-rooted bitterness. I realized that true artists will continue to do their art form regardless of whether they get paid or attain recognition. I was even asked by the owner of *Jude Studio* if I would like to sit in on a practice jam session with George Harrison of the *Beatles,* but my pride made me decline. About a year later I discovered to my dismay that this "session" was actually called "Apple Jam," the last side of George Harrison's triple album *All Things Must Pass*. This became regret number 3. I saw Paul McCartney several times at a rehearsal studio that we shared and didn't even bother to say, "Hi." I was no longer fascinated by stars.

A friend of mine worked for the Actor's Guild. He called me one morning and said that if I rushed up to Grand Central Station, I could be an extra in a Francis Ford Coppolla movie called *The French Connection*. It paid $32.50 every three hours. They needed a hippie type as an extra. I got up there fast. Sure enough, I looked like a hippie. Someone said, "Okay, sign here. Go in. They'll tell you what to do."

Well, there stood Francis Ford Coppolla and Gene Hackman. I didn't know who they were; I thought it was a B-grade French porn film. It wasn't until a year later while living in San Jose, California, that I saw in the newspaper that this movie had won an Academy Award.

One of my relatives called me on the telephone out of great concern. That day she saw on the national news that a five-story building on the corner of Houston* and Forsythe* was hit by a taxicab and had collapsed. I said, "No, I didn't hear about it," and I walked down to the street level, sure enough, just two buildings away, a building was completely destroyed. All five stories came down. I was amazed that I never even heard the crash. It took them forever to clean it up.

My dad and his lady friend drove out to visit me in June of 1971. What a surprise to see him at the door! I mean, he hardly ever left Ozaukee County in Wisconsin, and here he was one thousand miles away. He was shocked and showed disgust at seeing my long hair, beard, and filthy living conditions. Within two hours of being parked there, his car was broken into, a window was smashed, and a tire stolen. I really felt bad that he had to experience this. Automobiles with out-of-state plates were game for vandalism and theft. My dad became uneasy with me and my living conditions. He stayed less than eight hours and drove all the way back home.

I did greatly enjoy walking around the West Village. Many hours were spent strolling around in the shops, walking out on the pier and cobblestone streets, and looking at the grayish Hudson River and the Jersey shoreline. The Staten Island Ferry was mellow; Staten Island was quiet and cozy. Walking over the Manhattan Bridge to Brooklyn was inspiring. About fourteen bridges over the East River connect the Boroughs, and a lovely walk is guaranteed.

I bought tickets for a two-day rock concert at a stadium on Randall Island that is wedged between Manhattan, the Bronx, and Queens. Everybody was going to perform there from Howdy Doody to Led Zepplin. About two hours into this thing, rumors surfaced that most of the main acts had cancelled because there was no advance payment. Because of these cancellations, a mild riot started to occur among the thirty-some thousand concertgoers. I ran out immediately, got a quick bus over the Triboro Bridge, and felt safer back on Manhattan Island. I never looked back to see just how unruly the crowd became.

I remember going to the Anderson Theater just three blocks away from my building and seeing Marcelle Marceau, the great French mime, along with the Grateful Dead. The New York-based Hells Angels sponsored and chaperoned this event. They were very polite and called everybody "sir" and "ma'am." The Hell's Angels group home was about two blocks away from where I lived, and there was never any trouble that I could see.

Well, back to Come As You Are. We were in touch with a lady named Miriam who had her own talent agency. She was linked to the Sid Bernstein agency. His agency brought the Beatles to Shea Stadium. Miriam came down to Jude Studio on Elizabeth Street, to hear our group. She loved us and wanted to sign us to a contract. After a few weeks had passed, she presented us with a twelve-page indiscernible contract. As a provision in this managerial contract there would be thousands of dollars given us as spending money, a record contract, and an immediate tour of four countries upon release of a very rushed album. It was a six-year group and individual contract with their option of another six. Because the contract was so difficult to understand, we took it to an attorney for him to decipher. As it stated, they owned thirty-five percent of any monies we made as individuals relating to music, and they could shelve us in one year if we weren't successful. Well, as a seven-piece group and Ron, we had to make a decision. It was hard. We had spent nearly a year practicing, hoping, renting studios, and never performing. The night finally came for our decision. Miriam drove down to Jude Studio with another man; her hands were full of papers, eager to sign us. Ten of us were in a cramped studio, very quiet, no jokes, rather sober, with a cold tension prevailing. Not knowing for sure how everyone else felt, I spoke, "I'm not going to sign this."

Throughout the room, eyes grew large, throats gulped, and two other guys said sheepishly, "Me either."

Ron just watched. Miriam seemed to have a demonic grin. Her friend moved his shoulders and head but not his feet. Elliott and the trumpet player became enraged; they said a lot of loud words that I can't remember. I know that someone ripped at me, "I only stuck this out because it was a salable item; I could have made a lot of money fast."*

Miriam just chuckled and strutted out. People quickly left. Just Ron and I stood there with a cold and nervous demeanor. Finally I broke the tense silence and quietly said, "I feel relieved. Ron, I'm now free to leave New York. I'm going to San Francisco. Wanna come along?"

We instantly released a thousand cooped-up laughs. It was a celebration; I earned my right to leave New York City with honor, not defeat.

This probably sounds confusing. Why would I work so hard just to let it go? The people in this group never became close as friends; for many of them, it was just a business. I remembered my high school days and the Misery Sons; we had a common goal, and we had fun. We shared our sorrows and dreams with each other; we were one group. Fond memories of these guys came back, like when we would walk down the street singing, "Do wah diddy diddy dum diddy do," and just laugh. Or sitting in a booth at Jerry's Restaurant in Cedarburg and singing tight, loud harmonies on the *Beatles* song "Nowhere Man." We were best friends; we had real fun. The group in New York just wasn't like that. How could I take the chance of being bound for possibly twelve years by a contract and individuals who were just in it for the money? I'd rather have nothing and start over someplace else. I craved good, old friendships and honest people. I was weary of being a cream city brick in a concrete wall, but the challenge made me endure it all. Now the challenge met its fullness; I had new dreams, and I was free to pursue them.

Shelly was still around, though she had left several times to go back home to Grafton. Our relationship was on again, off again. We were like a convenience store with each other. You never do serious shopping at a convenience store; you buy just the immediate things you need, and you can expect to pay highly for it. She hated New York, and I know that she was thrilled at the prospect of getting out. We weren't certain if we'd go to California together or whether I would drop her off back in Grafton. I truly wanted Ron to come along, but he decided to stay on in New York and be the sound man for an all-girl rock band. It was sad. Well, I was sad. I wanted my best friend to be with me to experience all these new things together. He was quite content to be by himself and see where it would take him.

The following morning I bought the *San Francisco Chronicle* to see what life might be like on the bluer ocean. I talked with people who had lived there and studied maps of the San Francisco Bay area. I thought Haight Ashbury must be ready for me.

Oddly enough, many of the songs that were composed while cooped up in this two-room brownstone in New York were songs about nature and the openness of rural, rustic living, but none seemed more real and robust as "North American Bison" that I wrote just several weeks before leaving.

My imagination sailed as I envisioned all that my senses might take in while traveling west for the first time. This was definitely a creative fourteen months in New York City.

North American Bison

I've got things I want to say and things I want to do.
I got hot coffee boilin' and left-over chicken stew.
I gotta get me up some money 'cuz the rent is partially due.
I gotta find a way out of here 'cuz I got better things to do.
I wanna journey on this land, but I gotta buy myself an automobile.

I'm gonna travel in reverse so I don't miss any scenic views.
I'm gonna pick up all my friends while backtrackin' the A of SU.
I'm gonna see the glaciers freeze, watch the rivers turn from
brown to sky blue.
I see North American Bison, proud, brave, sturdy, and grand.
I'm gonna cry and fall upon my knees and
Promise God for this land I'll do all I can.

I searched the papers for a used van and finally found a 1963 Chevrolet Suburban. It was dark blue, $350.00, and came with a phony title, a Brooklyn special. I bought it, but waiting in line at the Motor Vehicle Department was very trying. They were located in the Transportation Department on Park Place and Broadway in the financial district, officially downtown. There were approximately fifteen windows for various things with each window having about twenty-five people waiting in line. You just didn't want to get in the wrong line; the Motor Vehicle Department is merciless. After about one hour and fifteen minutes, I finally made it to my window, never fully knowing if this was the right line. The marble floor was still wet with tears from the losers that had gone before me. I showed the counter-lady my receipt, where I had bought the car, and the title. She peered at me with squinted eyes and with a voice that could make sand paper curl, she growled, "This title's no good."

I acted out my ignorance as I replied, "Really? I bought it from a dealer."

She took my registration money and stamped a piece of paper. "Where da ya want da new title sent to?" she asked.

I gave her my dad's address. Boy, that was easy; it was nothing like the Motor Vehicle Department where I came from in Wisconsin. The workers would become flustered when more than three people came in to be waited on. They not only took care of your motor vehicle business, but they asked you everything from, "How's your brother doing on his new job?" to "Has your dad gotten over the gout yet?" You couldn't put anything over on these people. They even knew what I did on Friday nights and which side of my body the hernia scar was on. Nothing like the lady back in New York at the Motor Vehicle Department. She merely saw me as, Caucasian, number 373.

On my way back from the Motor Vehicle Department, I saw a guy slumped over on the sidewalk leaning against the Chase Manhattan Bank. He was pitifully out of it, incoherent. It was Bob, the guy that fourteen months ago had taken my $160.00 and fled. He looked pasty white and nearly dead. His clothes were ripped and filthy. Anger surged through me. I stooped down and with my left hand (my strong hand) and tightly gripped his shirt collar. I wanted to crush his head into the building. Looking into his sunken eyes with my teeth clenched and lips quivering, I screamed in his face, "Remember me?"

His head just bobbed around. I walked away feeling satisfied that he probably wouldn't live much longer. As the great evangelist, Billy

Graham said, "Know that your sin will find you out." Well, Bob's sin found him out.

For $80.00, a broker sold me an in-transit car insurance policy. I put an ad in the *Village Voice* to sell my apartment. A single lady bought it for $400.00. Packing day began. Feeling like we wouldn't be allowed to leave, Shelly and I decided to sneak out of the city at four o'clock in the morning. I felt like I was escaping. The van was packed full, very full. I almost had to break the ironing board in half to get it in. I had accumulated a lot of stuff, and I was determined to take it all. Well, we were packed up and gassed up. We said a quick good-bye to Ron and then we quietly purred out of the city, through the Lincoln Tunnel, and into New Jersey. It was hard to believe that I was leaving this city for good. I imagined being trapped there for years.

CHAPTER 10

DEFINITELY GOING WEST

About one hundred miles out of New York City near White Haven, Pennsylvania, I stopped to get gas and check the oil because this Chevy Suburban definitely used oil. A friendly guy came out with a sparky voice and asked, "Fill her up?"

I angrily snapped at him and said, "Yeah!"

It was then that I realized just how cold and suspecting I had become, thinking that everyone had a personal motive if they appeared friendly.

Arriving back in Grafton, I hung around for at least one week. The lure of seeing all my friends and being treated like a small-time star tempted me to stay. Word spread quickly among the circle of musicians and friends, "Hey, did you hear? Ray Last is back."

Lazy July days, soft lawns, and blue skies had a warm, soothing effect on my weary, rusted city bones. A local music group asked me to arrange songs for them. Rather flattered, I helped them out with a couple of songs for an upcoming battle of the bands. They sounded good but had to settle for second place. No, Grafton was still my home, but the wanderlust was burning. If I could survive New York, then California should be a sweet dream. Lying on the hillside grass at Shelly's parents' house with the sun soaking my skin, daydreams flowed through my mind. A song came; I grabbed my guitar and sang. A life's worth of joy rippled out into the open air as I sang, "I'm above the clouds now, I feel aaahh."

This was a refreshing sound of freedom emanating from my voice.

My brother was around, and I asked him if he'd check my van out to see why I burned so much oil. Donald thought I was a freak, and I was. I must have looked like a disease with a ponytail, beard, and dirty, torn clothes. He grudgingly said, "Yeah, I'll have a look at it." In a gruff, abrupt tone he gave me his professional diagnosis—"I don't know what's wrong. Rings, maybe. Just keep dumping cheap oil in it."

I didn't want any more worries in my life; I wanted everything to go smoothly. This van was a cause for concern; I had to drive it two-thousand miles to San Francisco. I held on to the hope that when I got there, then maybe everything would work out. Optimism worked like a Band-Aid on my oil leak. Buy oil, buy oil. Well, okay I did, by the gallon jugs. Every eighty miles I'd pull over and put approximately a quart in. On about the eighth day of anxious boredom, Grafton said, "Move on!"

You know what was so weird? Shelly and I preferred to leave Grafton at night during a thunder-and-lightning storm. "Wow did you see that?" I asked as the whole sky lit up. "Good thing we're grounded," I assured Shelly.

Hours went by, sleep was creeping up. A somewhat hollow sadness was filling me. I was actually gone; we had really left. The hometown security was gnawing in my heart, screaming, "Come Home!"

I'm not sure why, but I just knew that I had to go to California. I had to experience more. Music was out there. Yeah, music and the unknown.

By the time we rolled into Des Moines, Iowa via Interstate 80, the sun had been up for two hours. Hunger and fatigue was consuming me. There it was, the "Golden Arches." The last time I dared eat at a McDonald's® was in 1961, shortly after the first one opened in Milwaukee. Aunt Delores took me. I remember the nineteen-cent hamburgers and ordering from an outside walkup window. Boy, I had reservations about eating there. I mean, it was so normal. The blue van drove in. All eyes were on the long-haired freak and his hippie girlfriend. People were always joking, "Which one's the boy, and which one's the girl? Can't tell them apart, ha-ha." I was so sick of hearing that demeaning joke. We bought something and ate it in the van.

Des Moines looked like a regular small city. I was anxious for the mystical "Wild West." Would there be Indians on the ridges in Nebraska and Wyoming? Covered wagons and tipis would surely dot the prairie. Cowboys loping on by would lead into the Rockies. I was ready for the 1850s; let's have it. Nebraska began to fulfill my vision. Whoa, big sky, clouds swooped over, miles and miles of them, just like my song "Opalescent Merry-Go-Round." Wow! This was fantastic.

With the van pulled over for its oil fix, I got out and walked around. The sound was the wind. The air was uniquely scented from prairie flowers, such as Indian paint brush, blazing star, lavender aster, and blue-stemmed grass. Nebraska stood exposed, inviting discovery and imagination. Black-tailed prairie dogs became statuesque, fearing our presence. Their shrill call pierced the summer air. A hawk circled, waiting to catch one of these dusty rodents off guard. Meadowlarks and Redwing blackbirds monopolized the songs. Coyotes crept along rocky knolls as jackrabbits hid in the shade of the sage. Wild inspiration was rushing at me. I wanted to eat it—gobble it up. What do you do with all of this at once? "God is alive," I thought, "He's here; I know it. I think I sense his presence." Creation had me under its control; if I could only weep for the thrill of it. Any imagination I previously mustered together fell short of the real thing. I wanted to see more. Well, more came. The West had just begun. Towns like North Platte, Lodgepole, Cheyenne, and Laramie just rang of gunslingers and Indians. I imagined Buffalo Bill, Kit Carson, Jesse James, Annie Oakley, Wild Bill Hickock, Doc Holiday, and Pawnees on palominos, Shoshone, Paiute, Cheyenne, and Sioux. I had imagined Red Cloud and Crazy Horse sitting motionless on Appaloosas. I could almost hear the lonesome tune of a distant harmonica and a gently strummed guitar around the cowboy's evening campfire. Perched on a wind-seared ridge, my vision squinted; was I really seeing a mile-long herd of buffalo leaving behind a rolling cloud of dust and a thunderous rumble as a trace echo? Really, I'm not kidding; a boy's imagination took over. I may as well have been on a wild mustang galloping across this vast, open prairie.

The ominous outlines of mountains came into view. Were those really mountains out there? Yep, the map said we're about eighty miles away. Mountains come up slowly; I never knew that. First, you sort of creep into the foothills, and then the long, steady climb begins. A forest emerges; it was nice to see trees again. Would there be a steep, thousand-foot drop-off? That was my fear. Oh, I knew I'd get sick. I thought maybe the van wouldn't make the climb. Mountains were exciting, really quite breathless, especially to a rolling flatlander. I loved it. The first pioneers probably were not taken in awe quite as pronounced as I was. The contrast from New York City to secluded range and mountains was extreme and sensational. Give me a cabin and a Bowie knife, a clear water stream and splitting wood. Let the smoke ease into my nostrils on a crisp October morning. These eyes could be satisfied. Something spiritual was twining, swirling, and pulling at my senses from inside and out. Could I experience God? Nature had a way of sifting through my thoughts and nervous system. The nervous, chaotic tension that used to clog me up started to leave from non-use. Words became less necessary. I could hear my conscience. I never heard me so clear and undisturbed.

Driving off the road onto a pine-lined, dirt fire trail, I pulled over, got out, sat on a boulder, and boldly strummed some simple open chords. The sound from my guitar consumed me. Every moment was a song. Should I stop the circle of vibration to write it down, or should I just savor the experience and let it gradually pass from memory? A songwriter captures inspiration and builds upon it, and so I usually did. I wrote it down and worked it out. The gift of melody, rhythm, and chords was mine to keep, to share, to comfort, and to encourage. How is it with music that you can take nothing and create a measurable something? Music—it's beyond explanation, yet it exists.

My first taste of mountains, the Laramie Range, led into the Medicine Bow. Elk Mountain peaked at eleven-thousand, one-hundred fifty-six feet. By the time we passed through Rawlins, Wyoming, in the Sierra Madre, I could no longer imagine life without mountains. The great Rockies would soon cause my knees to quiver. I knew that I'd be a mere speck of a shadow embodied by cold, cast-iron boulders. Spruces were slanting as they pleaded, "Please, no rock slides." Bighorn sheep stood majestic, using jutting rocks as springboards. The hoof knows its footing. What can I say? This was rugged and truly *awesome*. You can scan hundreds of pictures and read a thousand descriptive words, even view a full-length movie, but until you are placed right in the middle of the mountains, you'll never experience the full sensation of being there. All other types of exposure pale in comparison. It must be lived. The Western mountains will never lose their flavor. My trusty twelve-dollar Kodak was busy snapping pictures. I'd had this camera since 1961.

Mountain air got thinner and thinner; my lungs felt it, and so did the van as it sputtered up and up in first and second gear burdened down by a ton of household stuff. I had decided to stay on Interstate 80 that passed south of Yellowstone and the Grand Tetons, but to the north of Colorado. Salt Lake City seemed to be the goal. I'd be relieved if the van made it through the Rockies. Winding down, down the snowcapped Wasatch Range, my brakes reeked of burning steel. A five o'clock in the morning, fog had settled in the valley. There seemed to be a quaint dirt road edging along the canyon's Weber River. I ventured on it as I would venture on many others in the years of travel to come; an uncommon tourist was I. Coasting at about eight miles per hour, all was extremely still as dawn yearned to have some words. I exclaimed, "Wow, look at those old cabins and barns! Hey, wooden carriages!" This was a village. Who lived here? There was a flickering light in the window. I shut my headlights off in reverence for this era passed by. Was this weird! There were horses, chickens, but no people around or at least they weren't up yet. Was this a Quaker village? Perhaps Hutterite. I thought we better leave; maybe they'd shoot at us. I didn't know. The van eerily drifted out by the silhouette of early morning light.

Oh, no, it was snowing in July! Interstate 80 became treacherous with cars, vans, and semis sliding, stalling, and pulling over. What a mess, trying to get back up the mountain into Salt Lake City! We made it, but I was shaking with fright. What if I couldn't get up and was forced to back down during this freak summer blizzard?

Cities didn't interest me. We gassed up, got out, pulled over by the Great Salt Lake, and walked on its sand. Millions of little gnats fashioned themselves into a black swarm hovering several feet over the beach. "Yuk," I thought, "Let's get out of here. Who wants to swim in that? Got any in your teeth? Come on, do you really float in salt water?" I read that the Great Salt Lake is five times as salty as the ocean.

A tourist road sign tried to point us north towards the east coast of the seventy-mile-long Salt Lake to where the golden spike is displayed that finally connected the transcontinental railroad in 1869. Nah, I wasn't interested. Instead, I headed west into the desert—the salt flats. A weathered sign read, "Next gas station, one-hundred-ten miles." Was that water or a mirage? I couldn't tell. Signs were posted periodically warning motorists not to get out and walk off the road. High water tables were everywhere; it was like salty quicksand. Well, signs were meant for regular people. I got out and listened to this crusty white stuff subtly give way under my one hundred twenty-five pound body. What a bruiser I was! I cautiously moved around some silvery stunted sagebrush as a tumbleweed hurried by. The radio station I had on in the van gave the weather for the Great Salt Desert—one hundred twelve degrees, clear skies, and some kind of wind from the south. The air was so dry that I actually felt chilled with just a T-shirt on. At seven percent humidity, I was at a loss for dry jokes. Sweat had drenched my clothes and car seat while driving. Delirium was blazing in my eyes; my thoughts were fried. This sun was hot in the cab of a van. The dragster spirit came out in me. I got this loaded-down Chevy van up to eighty-two miles per hour on the Bonneville Salt Flats. Not bad. The appearance of a gas station or some type of oasis could not come soon enough. Finally, after one and one-half hours of baking in the world's largest salt box, a gas station suddenly stood there. The peeling, cracked sign read, "Windover, Utah." This was a town? For the first time I had something in common with other weary travelers. We all had heat exhaustion. People cheered when they saw the Coke® machine and cold water cooler. Engines moaned and radiators sizzled. Clothing stuck like cheesecloth. Nothing lived here; how could it? The Great Salt Lake Desert—how did the pioneers survive this oven? Nevada seemed to be just a few hundred feet away. This was an open door to the Great Basin filled with tame mountains and numerous peaks exceeding ten-thousand feet described as a region of sinks and ridges. Supposedly during the 1860s, camels were used to carry salt to the western part of the state. When is the last time that you saw a camel in Nevada?

By now mountains seemed commonplace, and I started to form a preference. Evenings with the Nevada mountain sky, like all mountain skies, were filled with stars and an incredible blackness. The air was like none I've ever tasted. My eyes bathed upon the crimson-colored rock at sunset. Hours were spent staring out of my sleeping bag. Where does it end? Where did it begin? These same thoughts had puzzled and amazed me as a boy back in Grafton as I peered out into the night sky. There had to be another realm way beyond this. Was it obtainable? The morning gradually rose like a stage curtain, inexpressible beauty. All of my senses filled with peaceful stimulation. There was no question as to why the Native Americans were so jealous for the West; they must have understood nature like no one else could. Did they really talk to the Great Spirit? Small towns, canyons and rivers passed by, mountain after mountain. Peculiar birds sang. We ventured north of the highway to Pyramid Lake in far western Nevada on the Pyramid Lake Indian Reservation. I found unbelievably clear water and gorgeous skies. Sculptured ridges and spires laced and complemented the neighborhood of this crystal lake. Am I really standing here? Time to go. In another hour we'd be in Reno. Big deal, slot machines and such.

I washed up and brushed my teeth at a Standard station. It was a very clean place. I'm sure that I was dirtier than the gas station. Our baths were usually an aftereffect from swimming somewhere. I'd suds my body down in a cold water stream.

Well, Reno and I remained foreigners. Little did I know that what was to come would far exceed what I had already seen. California, Lake Tahoe, and the Sierra Nevada Mountains were unparalleled. I may as well put words to rest here. Ben Cartwright had it made. No wonder his sons, Hoss, Little Joe, and Adam, didn't want to leave the Ponderosa Ranch in search of a wife! Walking among these ponderosa pines, being soothed by the scent and the whisper, I thought for sure I'd found home. A Native American melody came from my voice, words I had never heard. I sang and sang until I grew faint. Did I really want to go to San Francisco? There were two things that John Muir, founder of the Sierra Club, and I have in common. We were both from Wisconsin and both overcome by the beauty of the Sierra Mountains, he in 1868 and me in 1971. The Sierras, heavily blanketed with pine, lent themselves to a gentle, deeply ridged skyline. Several golden eagles jealously guarded their territory, circling the azure blue Lake Tahoe with its three-hundred square mile basin, the largest of the alpine lakes in the United States. After viewing the area where the television show *Bonanza* was filmed and picking up a couple foot-long pinecones, we headed down toward Sacramento. Sacramento was dry, parched, and flat; that's what I remember with mile-long irrigation pipes; that's what I remember.

CHAPTER 11

DETOUR SAN JOSE

We breezed through Oakland, crossing the San Francisco Bay, and arrived in San Francisco at about five-thirty in the morning, very weary and not quite with it. I guess that we'd been traveling eight or nine days since we left Grafton; we were real slowpokes. A side-street gas station near Third and Mission seemed like the best place to park and get a little sleep. Knock, knock—"Hey, you can't park here; get out."

"Sorry," I politely explained, "We must have fallen asleep." Ooh, what a grouch. I thought that I had woken up all over again in New York City, only the accent was different. Where were all the flower children, the love, and the peace?

We spent a few hours aimlessly driving around town. It was difficult adjusting to the pace of the city, especially cruising down Market Street during morning rush hour. There were cars, trucks, busses, stoplights, and streets going up, streets going down. Even cable cars looked hurried. Some guy in a rusted-out pickup truck pulled up alongside the van and yelled an exuberant "Right on! I'm from Wisconsin, too."

"Far out!" I smiled and nodded. Hmm, I was starting to feel a little better about San Francisco, especially after seeing some buffalo in Golden Gate Park. The male bull almost let me pet him. Boy, to think that just two months ago I had the great urge to move to San Francisco. Now here I was. I wondered, "What do I do now that I've reached my destination? I guess I should find a place to live." After being captivated by the mountains, I had no desire to be a city dweller again. Juggling the map around, I thought that possibly living a bit north of the city might be pleasant.

Over the arched Golden Gate Bridge we went, which isn't gold at all, but more of a reddish brown. There was quite a unique view in the morning from the bridge with the fog lifting. The traffic was too heavy, though; we crawled bumper to bumper. I wanted out of this city. Finally, we got over the bridge. Gee, it was really built up, with very expensive looking homes situated in these dried up hills. Sausalito, Mill Valley, San Rafael—forget it—I could never afford to live there. Maybe we could just drive around the countryside and get a feel for the area.

Swinging around the San Pablo Bay, I headed south on I-80 and onto Highway 17, bypassing the San Francisco Bay. Some five miles south of Fremont, a foul, burning stench seeped into the van. The high-pitched squeal of metal-on-metal could be heard. I pulled off this busy freeway underneath a bypass. Because the traffic was too crazy, I had to crawl out the passenger door window because I was pulled up against an iron guardrail. Oh, man, my right front tire just stunk, and the iron was hot. What would I do now? Driving about five miles an hour with flashers on, I took the next off-ramp at Highway 237 and drove seven miles to a town called Alviso. Coasting in on North First Street, Pegasus, the flying horse, became visible. Great, it was a Mobil® station. Man, this place was desolate, hot, desert-like, with just some weeds and pasty, yellow dirt. No wonder, we were right in the middle of the salt evaporators, four square-miles of it, east of the San Francisco Bay. I was starting to wonder if this place really existed. I mean, a gas station, three houses, a bar, and a dog. Actually, there were about five streets running approximately one-half mile. Bummed out, I walked in the station. A Mexican-American greeted me, and I told him all about my problem. He pulled the hubcap off and said, "Yep, we'll have to torch it off. The iron melted itself together."

It was about nine-thirty in the morning and already eighty-five degrees. His friend, the welder, couldn't get there for at least five hours. Baking in this heat, I found it hard to believe that this was going on. California had some welcome for me. I petted the dog, listened to the garage's Spanish radio, and looked forlorn. It got hotter and hotter. The thoughts of going broke trying to fix the van put me in a state of mental destitution. I finally asked this kind Mexican man just how much this would cost. Raising my eyebrows with a sunken stare, I offered a suggested retail price. "We don't have much money, maybe $30."

He gave me an uninterested look and said nothing. A truck drove up, a big Mexican man got out, jacked up my front end, and blow torched the wheel off the axle. I tried making small talk, but he didn't seem to be listening. These people must hate me, all this bother over a filthy hippie. Well, great, the tire was off, but now they had to get a part from an automotive supply house, which was twelve miles away and might close at four o'clock in the afternoon. It was already three-thirty on a Saturday afternoon. If they couldn't get there in time, I'd be camped out there until Monday morning. The mechanic got there in time and back with the part. It fit, it was done, and he would settle for thirty dollars, cash. You must know what it feels like to have your vehicle operating again. These men really helped me out; I thanked them over and over. They must have seen that I was genuinely grateful. Even the dog looked happier. The owner of the station made me aware that the man with the blowtorch only wanted five dollars and the part cost them twenty dollars.

While I was enduring this long wait, repeated phone calls were made to Jon Johnson's mother, who lived in Mountain View about eight miles due west of Alviso. Back in New York, Jon the trombonist, made sure that I had her phone number and address. Jon encouraged me, "Be sure to look her up when you get there; let her know I'm doing fine."

I made one more call before venturing off to nowhere. She answered, "Hello."

"Mrs. Johnson?" I asked.

"Yes," she answered.

"This is Ray Last and I was a friend of your son, Jon, in New York City."

"Goodness, really? How is he?" she asked.

"He's doing fine; he told me to call you when I got to the San Francisco area, but I had car trouble in Alviso. It's finally fixed, though."

Jon's mom empathized with me and quickly responded, "You must come and spend a few days here. You can have Jon's bedroom. I'm sure you'd like to bathe and have a good meal. Do you like strawberry shortcake for dessert?"

"Mrs. Johnson, that's so kind of you; we'll probably get there around five o'clock tonight."

Don't you just love sweet ladies like that? I really wasn't expecting her to be so open and generous. We coasted into a beautifully manicured subdivision. Fruit trees, tropical plants, flowers, and well-kept homes greeted us. Mrs. Johnson stood in the doorway, and it seemed I'd known her for years. We chatted about everything, took a real bath, ate a splendid meal, and sure enough, she brought out strawberry shortcake with gigantic, sweet California strawberries. Boy, from destitute to king in one hour. She offered a wise suggestion concerning my renting dilemma, "Why don't you live in San Jose? It's much cheaper than San Francisco and is within commuting distance."

It made sense to me. Any kind of sound advice was welcomed. Mrs. Johnson insisted that I stay for two or three days to guarantee that I felt refreshed. I couldn't impose on her like that. Admittedly, it was hard getting out of bed, but I had a full day cut out for me looking for a place to live.

Extending the forty miles from San Jose north to San Francisco, there are approximately twenty suburbs in a non-stop direct line. Do you know the way to San Jose? How can you avoid it? All roads lead there. We said a kind good-bye in the morning and headed into San Jose. It seemed odd that no one had basements in their homes; they didn't need 'em, I guess. Where do you store all the junk that no one should see? Where's the furnace? Hmm. Houses without basements; I couldn't get over it.

My first impression of San Jose was that of a flat, clean, spread out, never-ending city, like a little Chicago. I bought the local daily paper, got two dollars' worth of dimes, and started calling the rental ads. Shelly and I must have looked at fifteen places. One seemed extra right, a small portion of a lower flat with a kitchen, an all-purpose room, and a bath. Located on Almaden Avenue near downtown, it cost one hundred dollars per month and one hundred dollars security. A wealthy, older, slightly handicapped lady with a cane owned it. She drilled me with questions and boldly remarked, "I don't like hippies; they're dirty, but I'll rent it to you. If the rent's not paid by the first, you're out."

With a mixed blessing in hand, I said, "Thanks, we'll pay you by the first. We don't take drugs or drink alcohol or smoke cigarettes."

She squinted her eyes as if to study my character and sharply spoke, "What you do is your business; just make sure the rent is paid on time."

"Yes, ma'am," I replied.

I knew her heart could be softened if I was gentle and polite. Over the months it worked. She actually smiled when I'd bring her the rent check. I always paid in person. Even her yapping, runt of a dog settled down. As the weeks passed, San Jose looked more and more like nowhere. I managed to get six or seven guitar students through ads I placed, but my heart wasn't into it. Going to these nice suburban homes with my electric guitar, I marveled that respectable parents would accept my appearance. People actually liked me, but teaching unenthused children was more a burden than what it was worth.

While driving around Santa Clara just northwest of San Jose, I made a left turn on the boulevard. Oh, no!, my steering locked and the left front end sagged down. I maneuvered into a gas station just a half a block away. The mechanic knew right away. "Your U-bolt broke off; I can't get to it for a couple of hours."

"What'll it cost?" I queried. I hated automotive repairs.

"Probably $30," he replied.

Oh, great, this was a fine mess. Frustration burned through my brain. I only had ten dollars on me. I remembered Jon Johnson giving me the name of another friend of his in the suburb of Campbell, Dennis Collins. Address books are handy. Dennis answered the phone as I thought; here we go again with my pitiful story. "Dennis, I need $20 to help pay for my van being repaired. I really feel embarrassed calling and asking for money, but Jon said I should look you up, anyway."

"Ray, I'll be right over. Give me ten minutes."

"Aw, hey, thanks a lot."

Sure enough, he was there quickly. A husky, likable fellow with a beard. We became casual friends and shared an interest in North and South American Indians. People had really been helping me out.

I would scan the help-wanted section, pretty much talking myself out of applying for most jobs. The prospect of working a straight job gave me the shudders. I was a musician; why couldn't I make a living playing music? I also placed ads, seeking musicians in the San Jose area to hopefully re-form the band, Come As You Are, for the third time. I received almost no calls and finally put that idea aside. The desire to start yet another group was dying. A carefree attitude started to form; new things crept into my life, more than filling this creative void.

Shelly's mother sent us a box of *Prevention* magazines that she had already looked at. Glancing through the first magazine on the top of the pile, I quickly became absorbed with this radical information on the benefits of eating natural foods and vitamins. I was shocked to read that much of what I had been eating for twenty-one years was harmful, void of nutrition, and deadly poisonous. Immediately, before I even read through that magazine, the natural foods conversion hit me. That very day we had purchased three large grocery bags full of regular food from the *Safeway®* store. Standing firm and convinced, I proclaimed, "We're not going to eat this garbage anymore. Let's find a natural food store."

Shelly just nodded, "Okay."

Paging through the *Yellow Pages®*, I found a natural food store listed. A Good Earth natural food store in Los Gatos was just eighteen miles away on Highway 17 at the foothills of the Santa Cruz Mountains.

There's a great distinction between a natural food store and a health food store, I quickly realized. A natural food store actually sold food, usually in bulk. A health food store emphasized vitamins and get-healthy-quick potions. The very next morning we drove down to Los Gatos not knowing what to expect. There it was: Good Earth. It looked like a nice place. Casually walking in, I tried to appear cool, calm, collected, and together. A middle-aged, natural-looking lady fixed her gaze on me. She was wearing an apron; I figured she must work there. Shattering the air with customers present, she spoke audibly and directly at us, "Is this your first time here?"

Here goes that Charlie Brown® grin again that seemed to surface in obvious awkward situations. A mumbled "Yeah," dropped out of my mouth.

"Well, good," her eyes sparkled, "Let me show you the store."

I felt like I was being introduced to a new, adventurous lifestyle. "We keep our grains and flours over in this section where it's cool," she informed us. Brown rice, short grain, long grain, sweet, wild, and exotic. Raw, unfiltered honeys, orange blossom, alfalfa, clover and tupelo, several mixes of granola (barrelsful). Mung beans (they looked like rabbit pellets), wheat germ (whoa, who wants to eat germs?), millet (little tiny yellow balls). Brown, unhulled sesame seeds, lentils (like little green M&M's®), organic carrots and potatoes (organic? Whoa, it's alive.), carob pods (just like chocolate), chicory—a coffee substitute. Hundreds of herb teas with weird names like fo ti tieng, ginseng, yarrow, golden seal, star anise, gota kola, and yerba maté. Goat's milk, tofu, soy patties, alfalfa sprouts, loofa sponges, yogurt with acidophilus cultures. Unsprayed bananas from Mexico, avocados, mangos, Japanese persimmons, kiwi, papaya, dates, nuts, Indian raisins, uncolored Monterey Jack cheese, and fertile brown eggs. Gelatin soaps and fragrant oils. Stone-ground whole-wheat flour milled at the store. I was stunned; where should I start? She had raw unsalted peanut butter that you scooped yourself out of a ten-gallon barrel. There was keifer milk and a shelf full of books, many by Adele Davis and Leland Kordel. Cookbooks, self-sufficiency books, how to books on building a log cabin and windmills. She had a mystical book by Yogi somebody with explicit photos of physically impossible Yoga postures.

She used no fluorescent lights in the store and the toothpaste that she sold was made in India from bone meal and peppermint oil. Cold-pressed oils, olives, sesame seeds, sunflower and almonds were also available. It seemed that I bought one half-pound of everything. You were encouraged to bring your own bags and containers.

This was my kind of place. Some people like to ski, watch football, play tennis, or go swimming. Me, I grew fond of hanging out in natural food stores. Knowledge of the healthy abounded. After several hours of tasting, bagging, and browsing, we lined it up on the checkout counter. Whoa, it cost almost $90! Well, I guess it was worth it or so I tried to convince myself. This super-energetic lady assured me with a, "I know you'll notice a difference within a week. Try it for a month." She knew I was hooked, and she was the only connection around. Leaving the store, I glanced side-to-side feeling almost illegal. Well, the days to come would be a connoisseur's playground. Is rice supposed to be this hard? No, I guess it didn't simmer long enough.

After three days of a strict natural foods diet I had to be honest with myself; did I really feel better? No, not yet, I had to give it time. Reading, studying, experimenting became a full-time, daily activity. The lady was right; let's call her Gretchen. I really did feel much better after thirty days. Six years went by before I ever shopped at a normal grocery store again.

Many physical changes occurred over the next few years. My eyes cleared up and became bluer, my fingernails that had unsightly ripples grew in nicely and smooth, my hair thickened, my skin had a darker, more supple texture, my breathing got deeper, and my heart rate went down. I never seemed to feel sick or zapped of energy. It was a good change, a lasting one. My lips never even chapped or cracked again. Even my concentration became deeper.

Along with this tremendous change in eating went an inquisitive interest in a self-sufficient, alternate lifestyle. The *Mother Earth News* publication had just come out. The first issue was called "A New Beginning."

There were articles and stories on communal farm living, building a tipi, making yogurt and digger bread, freelance cartooning, bringing about peace in the world, and numerous testimonies from people making it and living off the land. I anxiously waited for the next issue to come out. It all sounded so juicy and inviting. Be natural; be at peace; everybody's equal. Ecology, communal living, joy, health—it was almost like Utopia. Other issues had things like building a log cabin, homesteading in Canada, organic gardening, geodesic domes, foraging wild foods, living in a sheepherder's wagon, and on and on. I bought at least the first seventeen issues and ate it up. I've managed to keep them in mint condition to this day. I followed these articles religiously. Natural foods and the thought of living a natural lifestyle were stimulating, but not so my new job.

I spent seven hours a day in a phone salesroom trying to sell blocks of circus tickets to corporations and businesses. Reading the same script thousands of times over and over, presuming to be a Lion's Club member, I hyped it to the fullest just to make a living. Unfortunately, I think many people thought I was actually a good-hearted volunteer for one of these local organizations just trying to help underprivileged children. The plea went out, "Won't you help us out again this year with a block of fifty tickets?" After several months of phoning deception, I was appalled to find out that the organization only received approximately ten percent of the proceeds. The remaining ninety percent was divided among the promoters and carnival owners. One of the last phone jobs I had was about eight miles north of San Jose in Milpitas. Both Shelly and I worked there during the remaining days that the salesroom operated. It was a Friday, late September, in 1971. Together we made over $80 in just seven hours of calling. This was big money to us. We really only needed two hundred fifty dollars a month to live on.

Driving home, the sun had long since set. Humming along through a yellow light in downtown San Jose—CRASH! The van spun around;

there was broken glass, noise. I had been rear-ended. I jumped out, and to my horror, a black man lay in the street in a pool of blood. The front end of his little Toyota® was crushed in. He ran a red light going at least forty miles an hour. People hurried over and collected, gawking, muttering, whispering, "Somebody help the man."

There were sirens, flashing lights, confusion. They took him away on a stretcher. He reeked of alcohol, and bottles were in his back seat. Police probed me. "We're okay. No, I don't have a regular towing service," I answered.

"Drive them to the hospital for a check-up just to be sure," the police ordered.

"Okay, we'll go."

My van was towed away, and the police drove us to the hospital. Word was buzzing, the guy's in bad shape; he was the star linebacker for San Jose State football team. I became gut sick. What was going on? The police handed me a citation for running a red light. "What? Are you kidding? *He* ran the red light. *He* hit me in the right side. *He* was drinking; did you smell his breath? Are you gonna give him a blood alcohol test?" I ranted.

No response was given.

"Need a ride home? We'll drive you," the police offered.

"Yeah, sure, okay. Thanks," I answered.

Dazed and back in our lower flat, we hashed the scene over again and again and couldn't sleep; we just felt sick. We had no vehicle; what's going to happen to me? Would I get sued for thousands of dollars or thrown in jail? On Saturday morning, the upstairs neighbors, who were a very kind, quiet Mexican family, took me to see my van. It was totaled, a real mess. The junkyard offered me one hundred dollars for it. I sold it to them. What kind of car could I buy for one hundred dollars? Well, there we went with the classified ads again. Hmm, '63 Rambler station wagon, high mileage, no rust, good runner, one hundred fifty dollars. Dad would be proud of me now, an American Motors® son, finally. The man selling the car was very friendly and seemed genuinely honest. He was a professional skier with one glass eye. He sympathized with my predicament and said, "Listen, I'll sell it to you for $100 to help you out."

"Really?" I nearly cried, "Man, that's nice of you."

Good news: the Rambler ran like a charm.

The uncertainty of my court date lingered. I never experienced such a gut feeling before. There was no relief, no peace; witnesses would not come forth. I asked the man at the adult bookstore if he saw the accident and whether he'd testify for me in court. He gruffly exclaimed, " Ya, I saw the accident, you didn't run the light but hey, I just got outta' San Quentin; I don't need no cops or judges"

"Thanks, I understand," I said.

Days were spent knocking on doors asking questions. Some poorer tenants asked me to please go away. The corner gas station attendant saw it, but said, "You don't have a chance. The guy's a football star; they need him on the team. He'd be kicked off for the season if he was accused of drinking."

A well-informed man made me aware that a reputable businessman was being paid to testify against me in court. My response was half serious, "Naw, come on, not really."

He also suggested that the guy who hit me would not appear in court. In his stead his brother would take the stand posing as him. He sternly continued, "This happens in San Jose; certain people are protected."

Immediately I called my insurance company. I hurriedly told them what I knew; they acted like they were expecting this.

Thoughts were dark and frightening; would they jail me for years and years? Six weeks had passed. Out of desperation I got on my knees and cried out to God for his mercy. I never prayed like this before. My insides were pleading, "Please, God, help me." A sensation occurred, a feeling that God heard me. I tried to strike a deal with him. "If you get me through this, I promise I'll search for you," I promised.

The feeling never left. I daily remembered that I had humbled myself to the Creator. In the courtroom, I looked neat and confident. God had heard me. He had to have; otherwise, why would I feel so bold and sure? They rolled the chalkboard over. I drew and described the scene. Very calm, relaxed, I communicated my defense.

"Are there any other witnesses?" the judge beckoned. A man in a three-piece suit came forward, swore on the Bible, and discounted my story. "The person driving the blue van ran a red light". Either the black man or his brother testified that he didn't recall the event because of his unconscious state after the accident. The judge found me guilty of running a red light and fined me sixty-seven dollars. I felt like a lamb among the lions. This was justice? My eyes screamed a piercing stare at all present in the courtroom. They knew what really happened. I despised the words San Jose, reminiscent of the *Three Stooges* hearing the words, "Niagara Falls."

During this time of crying out to God, I kept noticing articles in the newspaper about an upcoming Billy Graham Crusade in downtown San Jose, only about eight blocks from my house. However, I was a skeptic; my attitude towards him and organized religion was, "They're just in it for the money, ripping people off." My Mexican neighbors invited me to come. I inwardly thought that the whole event was a scam but that the real God was some place else. But I still thanked my kind neighbor friends anyway.

An old violinmaker lived a few blocks away; I thought perhaps I'd buy a used one from him and learn to master this darling, petite instrument. What a surprise; he was from Milwaukee, German accent and all! He needed the drier climate to work on his violins, and so he moved to San Jose. He kindly sold me a beauty for only fifty dollars. I took some lessons from a college girl but eventually put this squeaking, irritating thing in the closet. Patience was required. I knew what that meant after ten thousand hours with the guitar. Anyway, I needed something more bodily, like a cello. Maybe someday. There's always room for *cello*. I still had my amp, microphone, and tape recorder set up. I wrote at least three songs during my stay in San Jose, and they all had to do with natural, rustic living. The impression was deep.

On the next run to our natural food connection in Los Gatos, we thought it would be nice to see what the often-mentioned Santa Cruz Mountains were like. The mid-November sky was clear, something not seen too often in the smog-laden valley of San Jose. We started the climb up Highway 9 to the thirty-five hundred foot summit; it was just beautiful with thick, redwood forests. Why had we waited so long to come up here? Oh, what a pleasant relief from the mundane existence we were having in the All-American City, as San Jose was dubbed. These were really mountains with actual mountain towns. How quaint. Hmm, I thought I'd eat some sequoia bark. Shortly after the summit, we saw the panoramic view of the valley; it could have been breathtaking if it hadn't been for the hovering orange cloud blanketing the valley. Yuk, we'd been breathing that stuff? I gagged in horror. That was all orange pollution. Well, it was prettier than the black soot of New York.

Idling through Boulder Creek just thrust me into visions of an 1800s mining town; Gabby Hayes probably chewed tobacco here. There were craft shops, no sidewalks, and hippies abounded. Dogs ran loose, and hippies were all around. Old pick-up trucks, painted VW® vans, and hippies were everywhere. Wow, I belonged here in hippie haven! These were loose looking, easygoing naturalists. Boy, I just yearned to live up here with all these free spirits. Boulder's main street was about a quarter-mile long, wedged between redwoods on winding Highway 9.

The town of Ben Lomond was next up; shops and houses were dotted along a half-mile curve, just a large path cut through the forest. My eye caught a sign hanging from a cottage window, "For Rent." I said, "Let's stop in and see what it's all about."

There was a house in the back by the Lorenzo River. I anxiously knocked on the door, and a clean-looking guy answered. Bounding like a sheepdog, I asked, "Is that place still for rent?"

"Yes, I just put the sign up ten minutes ago. Do you want to look at it?"

"Well, sure, but how much is it?" I had to think in terms of cheap.

He bubbled out, "Eighty dollars a month, eighty dollar deposit."

"Yeah, let's see it."

Wow, this was great, there was a redwood tree growing right through the porch! This cottage, as he called it, had one bedroom, a bath, and a kitchen-living room combined. "We'll take it, I mean, if we can have it. Can we have it?" I was tripping over my own questions.

He told me his name was Bob and said, "Let me get some information on you first. Are you two married?"

"No, but we live together."

He frowned at that answer and asked, "Don't you love each other enough to get married?"

No one ever asked me that before. I tried to muster up a clever answer, but I was at a loss. Admittedly, no, we didn't love each other enough to commit ourselves to a marriage; we'd just be together until something else came along, so what's wrong with that? I thought. My mind raced with excuses that I'd thrashed over before. I gave him a limp answer, "We never really thought about getting married." This guy was good. I felt intimidated just by his presence. I knew that he had it together.

"Come on in, meet my wife, and I'll have you sign a paper." His wife was one of the sweetest, most talkative, understanding people

I'd ever met. We felt relaxed and at home. We were all formally introduced, and Bob made me aware that he was once a leader of over two hundred people in a spiritual cult in the northern part of the state. Then he said, "I accepted Jesus Christ as my Lord and Savior. I left that cult. I've cleaned up my act—no drugs or crazy lifestyle anymore." I really didn't care to hear about Jesus Christ anymore; I mean that's all I heard as a boy. I just listened to him talk; I had little to say. I knew that God existed, but there had to be more than just a cold, structured church.

His wife offered us a cookie and coffee. I stepped back as if being attacked and asked, "Does it have sugar in it?"

They laughed heartily, "What's wrong with a little sugar? You should be thankful for food."

My mind finally got them in a trap\. I thought, "How can they know God and still eat sugar? Hah, see, he's wrong." We declined the coffee and cookies, not wanting to poison our systems. There was only forty dollars in my wallet. "Can we come back tonight and pay the rest?" I asked.

Bob nodded, "Sure, I'll hold it for you."

We drove away beaming; we were actually going to live there. I couldn't believe it. Quick, fast and straight back to San Jose, we drove. The landlady was immediately notified that we would be vacating within a month, sooner if possible. She almost seemed saddened to hear the news. Even that runt of a dog appeared woeful. Dennis Collins was happy for us and amazed. He knew people that had waited several years for a place to open up in the Santa Cruz Mountains. Within two days we were packed up and ready to go. Three carloads did it. We seemed to glide over the mountain, and San Jose was left in the dust.

CHAPTER 12

BEN LOMOND AND THE SANTA CRUZ MOUNTAINS

I f home is where the heart is, then I was home. Days and evenings were cool by then; a bracing air swept through my nose. Hardwood smoke floated, forming a train-like cloud. The smell accented and even embellished the atmosphere. The mild winter air was very tolerable and invigorating. I began to run about a mile every night. My normal heart rate mellowed at fifty-eight beats per minute. Long distance runners strive for that. The book *Better Eyesight without Glasses* opened my understanding of what eyeglasses really did. They never correct your vision; I took my glasses off. Depth perception was strange at first. My feet went clop, clop ahead of me. But after a few weeks I hardly wore them again. With eye and sun exercises, my focal distance was stretched. I was old eagle eyes; this was great. Not since fourth grade had my eyes known such freedom.

Santa Cruz, an oceanfront town, was only ten miles south on Highway 9. I joined a natural foods co-op and began to acquaint myself with the people, area, and creative lifestyles. The locals lived in domes and tipis, cabins, shacks, tents, and regular houses. I desperately desired to fit in. The internal urge to be somebody unique and important drove me to expose myself to as much as possible. Spiritual jargon proceeded from a thousand mouths, words like yoga, Buddha, meditation, bhakti, energy force, power spots, Krishna Murti, mind expansion, divine, past lives, rebirth, natural highs, out of body, guru, master, Avatar, in-tune and spirit guides. Many evenings were spent quietly sitting in a time-honored wooden church, a fifteen-minute stroll from home. I'd meditate on something, listen for voices, seeking guidance; how could I break through the ethereal that was beyond this realm? Was there a way? Humming a straight tone for a length of time seemed to pacify this for a while, but that grew old.

The performer in me began to surface again. Perhaps "Come As You Are" could materialize here as a real mountain band. There would be no ads this time, just word of mouth. Musicians were plentiful, competent ones at that. Within a month of searching and snooping, I had gotten together a nucleus for the group—piano, bass, guitar, and sax. High up on Alba Road going towards the ocean, we practiced in a run-down, damp, moldy chalet. After repeated tries at disciplined practice schedules, I realized that these people couldn't be tamed. They just wanted to smoke dope and party. There was absolutely no serious commitment. For the fourth time, the realization of a performing Come As You Are group died.

But on a happy note, I became stimulated and inspired to go solo—just me. Yeah, just me and my songs, what a hit! I'm a workhorse; I would have a great act. Reworking, practicing, creating, writing, I was in a fervor to perform at area clubs, mountain clubs, among real, appreciative folks. My mind exploded into visions of fame. Yeah, I dreamed of fame within months. I built a lopsided practice booth out of boards that I hauled away from a deserted, dilapidated mushroom farm on the Pacific Ocean. With salt-eaten, finely weathered grain, each board was a piece of art. A somewhat eerie ambience was present as I listened to the throb of the Pacific while pulling rusty, stubborn nails out of the boards. Several station wagon loads were carried away. I even built a kitchen table out of this stuff. Slivers kept me from slumber as I rested and thought while leaning on my handiwork late into the night. The girl that I would never marry, left and went back home to Grafton for the third time in eight months since we came to California. I didn't care; there was too much stimulation here. I had to expand and express my true character. Some lady friends came into my life, but only briefly. Interest in music and the supernatural engulfed my days.

Approximately two hundred hours were given to rehearsing for what would be just a one-and-one-half hour show. Songs were perfected like never before. I worked meticulously on every guitar line, every strum and chord, mastering my voice, phrasing, and changing vibrato speed. Rhythm, melodies, dynamics flowed. I was often carried away by my own music. Alone I practiced, alone I sang, alone I thought, and alone I lived. Loneliness was my closest friend; I got along with myself. Relying on other people and their peculiar ways made me frustrated and weary. My aim was to produce, progress and achieve, grow, expand, and experience; it seemed limitless. I could chase the horizon; I'd have it on the run.

Santa Cruz had the White Buffalo, a restaurant coffeehouse. I'd been there several times listening to folk singers. The owner consented to giving me a Friday evening from eight o'clock to ten o'clock to perform my songs. They couldn't pay me, but I'd be asked back if the crowd approved. That Friday came, very near my birthday in April. I'd be twenty-two and seasoned. I was white with fear and anxiety, so different from being on stage with a bunch of jolly guys. There would be no consolation or encouragement. I swallowed about eight bone meal tablets; reportedly they calm the nerves. Not mine. I could smell adrenalin. Driving down Highway 9, I may as well have been going to my funeral. What if I bombed? I wished it were over; I thought that I might throw up. Did you ever see anybody perform by themselves with an electric guitar as opposed to an acoustic? These people obviously never did. Up on the stage I carried my Fender Vibrolux amp, put my Fender Jaguar on its guitar stand, placed my microphone and boom stand just right, and noticed three hundred eyes fixed on me. When I first walked in, there was a roar of conversation and laughter, now the room suddenly became hushed. I didn't even have a joke to tell. Swallowing was difficult, my hands were freezing and pale blue in color; my tongue clicked inside my mouth. It's called stage fright, but tonight was different; it would never ease up. "Good evening, I'm Ray Last; I'll be playing all original songs that I wrote."

People just stared. I remember the movie, *The White Buffalo*, I saw as a boy about the white buffalo, very mystical. Well, I just dug in and started to play. Applause was politely given, but I couldn't smile. Nobody booed, but I couldn't smile. Nobody smiled, and I wanted to cry. I thought I could stick it out until ten o'clock, and maybe I'd loosen up, but I didn't. The music was too strange. I liked to think it was unique and innovative. Why did I love my music so much, yet nobody else responded positively? Within twelve minutes after ten o'clock I was already pulling away from the famed *White Buffalo*, as empty as a man could be with no one to talk to. I wondered, "What's wrong with me?"

Buck, my friend who was a part-time disk jockey on an alternative radio station invited me to perform live in the studio on the following Wednesday night. "Sure, I'd love to; do you really think I'm that good?" I asked.

It didn't take much to bounce back; I just needed an encouraging word. I played three songs and gave a ten-minute interview. The phone line wasn't exactly jammed, but Buck liked me. To my pleasure, he announced that next Friday night I'd be performing at the Club Zayante, way out on Zayante Road near Loch Lomond; the area's blue lagoon reservoir.

The Club Zayante had a freer, wilder atmosphere; surely I'd go over there. I even prepared an encore for when they stood up and cheered. Now, at the Club Zayante, less nervous, I began to play. Hey, far out, not bad. People were still talking, I wished they'd quit talking and listen, though. After the fifth song, some guys came up and asked if I'd play a little quieter. "We can't hear ourselves talk," they explained.

I played one more song and got out. Nobody noticed. The drive home was more pleasant than the drive home from Santa Cruz. Winding down mile after mile into Ben Lomond, as the warm sun set, thoughts screamed at me. Home alone, I didn't take drugs, didn't drink alcohol, I just went to bed and tried to sleep. At least I sweated there at the Club Zayante. In spite of these letdowns, I still continued to write songs throughout the remaining months that I lived in Ben Lomond, but the idea of performing was completely dropped. Instead, I concentrated on the spiritual.

Some flower people that I bumped into at the co-op invited me to a dome nestled in the mountains outside of Felton, the next town south of Ben Lomond. These were big doings, yep a dance, a dome dance. Anything goes; nothing's too freaky. I couldn't wait to go. Cars, trucks, and horses were parked vicariously on the slope of a clearing. Shadowed bodies glided in from all directions centering toward the dome. It was a big dome, nicely constructed. Inside was one cylindrical room, forty feet in diameter. People freely chatted. I pried my way into conversation, hoping to make friends. Perceiving that others felt uncomfortable also, I sought them out. Why were they starting to take their clothes off? Now everybody was doing it. I did, too; it was their party. We held hands in a continuous circle and slowly began moving counterclockwise. Chanting and moaning began. The moon shone through the dormer windows. So what's supposed to happen! Would I get zapped? The chanting became louder; girls screamed, but not from pain. Men grunted. I mean, I love music, but this would never play at the *White Buffalo*. The circle quickened; we were almost running. Nothing was happening to me, but I grunted with the men anyway. Suddenly the air split; they stopped, sat down in a lotus position, bowed their heads, and apparently went into a trance-like meditation. Pretending was fun; I had all night. Slowly, one by one, they came out of it. With brief uninhibited gleams, they seemed to share blissful experiences. I said something stupid like, "I have never felt like this before."

Really, I wasn't lying. I never felt so out of it before, whatever "it" was that they were in. I didn't stick around for small talk but went back home again, alone. The spiritual quest continued.

A group from New York was living high above Highway 9 in tents. This was their home. I picked a guy up one day in June on the way back from Santa Cruz. He called himself Harley. Harley said, "Do you want to come up and meet my people?"

"Sure," I said.

"Conceal your car; we're illegal up there," he instructed.

I followed him up a rocky ledge. There towards the top on a partially leveled eighty-foot area deep within the trees were several tents, pots, pans, a fire smoldering, clothes draped over branches, sleeping bags, and blankets spread out. Among the six or seven people, there were several girls who couldn't have been more than fifteen or sixteen years old, huddled around the fire. Their hair was long, stringy, and matted. The clothes they had on were one step above discarded, filthy rags. A pasty white complexion, undernourished appearance, and frightened expression emanated from their faces. They were three thousand miles from their New York home. It was a pitiful sight. What were they hoping to find here on the West Coast? My ear was bent with compassion to a story of hunger and drifting, the modern day nomads. I had little money myself but was moved to give them ten dollars. The next day I hiked up there with a box of food. Genuine smiles lit up within this cool, damp, fifty-eight degree rainforest. Good feelings filled me knowing that I had reached out to others in need.

CHAPTER 13

TIPI MADNESS

H arley made me aware of a couple with children who permanently
lived in a tipi. I had to see this. His directions told me to go one
mile north of the slanted barn outside of Soquel and one quarter-mile
east along the south bank of the river. When I got to the meadow, I was
to look to the southwest and I'd see a pale yellow tipi, a horse, and a
goat. I was to call out two times, "I'm a friend; I'm a friend!" Jim and
Nancy would come to meet me. I was to bring a gift.

My memory was as good as gold. I left shortly to search them out.
The sun finally broke through, the air had a warm, thick clinginess, and
water squished around inside my ankle-high moccasins. I disliked the
feel of wet leather, but trampled on through the muck and heavy dew.
Harley was exacting in his directions. Cupping my hands, I yelled,
"I'm a friend; I'm a friend!" My echo repeated this claim. Three hundred feet away, the length of a football field, two figures appeared. One
came out of the hole in the tipi; the other turned from what he was
doing. They motioned their arms for me to come over. Surprised yet
friendly, they offered me some hot rice and goat's milk. I graciously
handed them my gift of dried bananas, pineapples, and one pound of
carob pods. Nancy seemed hesitant to show me inside the tipi, so I just
stood near the door chatting. She never came out, just peered through
a partially veiled opening. Jim sensed the difficulty of the situation.
"She's nursing the baby," he explained.

"Oh," was the only intelligent reply I came up with. They really
lived here with two children. "What do you do for money? " Seemed
like a reasonable question to ask them. He went inside and brought out
some samplings of macramé handbags and colorfully dipped candles.

"We sell these in Soquel, Santa Cruz, and Monterey. Some stores put them on consignment for us."

"Do you have a car?" I asked.

"Yeah, but we usually walk and thumb our way around; cars pollute."

"Yeah, really," I agreed.

Incorporated into his language were some common, crass, swear words. He had a harder, more radical attitude than I cared to be exposed to. I was anticipating this flowing couple telling me about the thrill of living in a tipi and how the Indians had it so right—at least some inspiration of sorts. But they seemed bitter and confused. I cut my inquiry short and left after a brief fifteen-minute visit. Talk about bad vibrations.

Three days later I drove up the mountain west of Boulder Creek to look at another tipi. These people had a nice house and even had an address. I asked if I could see the tipi. "Sure," he bolted out as his wife beamed, "The tipi's in the back." Many children came skipping along.

"Yeah, I just put it up for the kids to play in. We have a campfire inside now and then."

"How big around is it?" I asked.

It seemed monstrous inside but really dark. They painted it black with yellow stars.

"Oh, it's about eighteen or nineteen feet in diameter."

"Wow, it's really neat in here. Where'd you learn to make it?" I asked.

"There's a book out called *The Tipi Book*; you can get it in Santa Cruz." And so I did.

I'd never been in an occult book store before; shelves were lined with books on Buddhism, Krishna, Hinduism, centering, guru this and that, swami somebody, astrology, tarot cards, EST, mantras for everyday people, how-to books for self-survival; strange posters hung from the walls, and incense was burning. A sign over a door in the back read "Meditation Room, Please Be Quiet." People lulled around in a hush; their eyes were big and shiny. Nobody blinked. Blissful expressions permeated from glowing faces. Everybody looked stoned, but they weren't. They were just in tune to the universe, I guessed. There were more books, more titles, more things to try, such as dances of the whirling dervishes, Krishna Murti, Tai Chi, I Ching, astral projection, Edgar Cayce, Alice Baily, crystal pendants, and yoga classes, on Wednesday nights from seven o'clock to nine o'clock. There were thousands of books that all seemed to introduce you to the divine within and without. All I wanted was a book on tipis. I was starting to gag on the haze that the incense created. There it was: a whole section on Indians. *Bury My Heart at Wounded Knee, Black Elk Speaks, Indian Sign Language, Cheyenne Memoirs, Ancient Rites of the Incas, Sioux Rituals,* and books on the Hopi, Blackfeet, and Crow. Incredible, where do I start? I was overwhelmed. I started out by buying three books, *The Tipi Book* by the Laubins, a white family from Wyoming, *Black Elk Speaks* by an old Sioux holy man, and *Indian Sign Language,* as I desired to talk less and less. Me buy books. How much? For some odd reason using fewer words to communicate seemed to be a sign of spiritual development. I've noticed over the years that very few people on a spiritual quest had a sense of humor. The lady with the flowing dress and halo whispered, "$12.95. Would you care to buy some incense?"

"Yeah, are there any that smell like pine?" I inquired.

"Oh no," I shuddered, "I let my guard down. She knows that I don't really talk in chopped up sentences." I bought a pack of pine-scented incense sticks; she threw in a small cone-shaped one that smelled like oranges. I floated out of the store feeling that I had made a wise purchase.

Back on the street people hurried by; they seemed so tense and unhappy. It reminded me of the old Indian chief in the movie *Little Big Man.* This old chief felt certain that the enemy couldn't see him because he was blind. I felt like nobody knew I was on the sidewalk because my consciousness was in another realm.

Hitchhiking again, I went directly home, browsed through *The Tipi Book* but became absorbed and captivated with *Black Elk Speaks.* It took me only two hours to read it. I wanted to be a native, a first nation people. Yes, a Sioux Indian. The book just oozed with spiritual stuff and supernatural dimensions, fasting, sweat lodges, visions, more visions, and a oneness with nature. Yeah, that's what I would do; I would seek visions for guidance and perhaps a spiritual teacher. Yeah, that's what I needed, a spiritual master whose feet I could sit before, but I knew he had to be an old Indian Holy man.

Bob still mentioned some things now and then about Jesus Christ, but it just sounded so boring and middle class. He handed me a paperback copy of the New Testament. I glanced through the first three or four chapters of the Book of John as he suggested I should, but quickly lost interest. Anyway, I thought the New Testament was just a revised version of the Old Testament. Bob let a Christian youth group use the building in front of mine on Tuesday nights for a social time. The leader knocked at my door one evening and said, "We really enjoyed listening to your singing; would you like to join us?" I really didn't want to; I was actually scared. They were all so clean and proper; Pat Boone had to have been their father.

"Well, all right," I consented. Fifteen cute teenage boys and girls greeted me with Osmond smiles.

"Would you like some coffee, cookies, or soda?" he asked.

I was thinking, "You kids get sick regularly, I bet."

They were so darling that I couldn't turn them down. I took a cookie and ate it. Sugar rushed up my neck, which became red and sweaty along with my face, and my eyes watered. I made them aware that I hadn't eaten cane sugar for ten months. They sang some simple songs and asked if I'd care to play their guitar. I declined and politely thanked them for inviting me. Never again would I play my music on a Tuesday night. They could hear me; I was probably disturbing them. Tuesday nights found me elsewhere. Nice kids, but this Jesus stuff was not for me. I was onto something big.

Harley had given me two gelatin capsules filled with peyote powder, because I had shared with him my desire to have visions and spiritual direction. Storing them for weeks in a drawer, I needed to wait for the right time to use it. I had a fearful anticipation. What would this stuff do to me? Would I get so high that I would never fully come back to my senses? Peyote is a powerful drug, derived from a certain low-growing cacti peculiar to Arizona and New Mexico. I'd been reading in some of my new books that North American Indians used it to gain visions.

The late June weather was hot and dry, perfect for wandering the redwood forests in Henry Cowell State Park. I fasted for a day, then met with Harley at his new camp. His friends had moved on, but he had stayed. We gave each other a firm embrace and Indian handshake. "See ya in about two days," I said with energy and optimism. Off I ventured into the redwoods.

This particular mountain forest extended five square miles before being disturbed by any roads or houses. I would encounter no one, being completely alone and at peace. A sleeping bag and quart of water jiggled on my back. It was the right time to take the peyote, just one capsule, to see how it would go. Holding the dark brown capsule high into the air with my right hand, I sent up a prayer, a prayer to an unknown entity, hoping to have my wish for a vision and a spiritual teacher granted. With one bold sip from the quart milk bottle, I swallowed the capsule. Well, it was done, no turning back. I hiked on, looking for signs; a spider web in the dew-laced grass beckoned my attention. The spider, a small, black, busy little thing, was still finishing up. My knees were soaked from bending down to study his handiwork; I asked in a whisper, "Do you have anything to show me?" Minutes went by, nothing came. I moved on. I started to feel extremely lonely and caught myself crying. Why do I have to go through this? Lightness began propelling me, great energy rushed through my system, and a happy outlook took the place of sorrow. I knew that it was getting hot; it was probably ten o'clock in the morning by then.

"Funny," I thought, "I still have bondage to time." I chuckled. A clearing came up; it was a rolling, slanted meadow. Yellow, low-lying flowers graced the area, but I dared not pick any; the balance was perfect. With reverence, I asked the earth if I could lie down here. There was no negative sign, so I gently laid down. My face absorbed the sun. Gradually I took all my clothes off. Why not? It was just me and nature. With my clothes folded neatly, I rolled them up and placed them in the canvas knapsack. Still wandering this clearing, I saw an old oak tree. An hour at least was spent leaning against a boulder, studying the scheme of its branches. What would I learn from the progress of the oak? A squirrel caught my eye, and we exchanged an argument. "You're too busy; slow down, or you won't live long," I warned.

A snide witticism was his reply, "You're a loaf; you'll waste away."

I continued to wander. At the edge of the spacious terrain was a sheer drop off.

A pageant of color spread out before me to view. Deep blues and greens, tones of bronze and toast subtly covered the slope and valley below. A winding river soothed my soul. The south wind brought a voice, prompting me to run. With the swiftness of a white-tailed deer and force of the bison, I charged clockwise in an imaginary oval. My breathing was heavy, rage was in my veins, and my heart tore wildly to be free of my chest. At the zenith of the fourth circling, I came to a sudden abrupt halt, extending my arms; I projected a roaring scream with volume and depth that shook the heavens loose. A foreboding darkness manifested; cold gray thunderheads were swirling. Hurricane force winds lashed against my face. I stood silent, arms outstretched. My legs, like granite, were firmly planted, teeth clenched and jaws hardened; I would defy this adversary. In a rash of transformation, all was gone. Songbirds confirmed a victory. My being was chilled like winter steel. Exhausted, upright, and enduring, I searched the skyscape for a remnant of this storm. This really happened; but what did it mean? An evening sun was beckoning at the edge of the redwoods. I found myself at the five-foot base of a tree, not recalling having walked there.

Wearing clothes again felt uncomfortable but necessary for warmth. Sitting on an army green, down-filled sleeping bag, I merged with the setting sun. Darkness like a sojourner gradually arrived. There was no fear as I speculated there might be. My body swayed with the rhythm of the ocean, yet the Pacific was perhaps three miles away. Stars were not stars after all. Spellbound, gazing, I stretched my mind to answer. Why are they suspended in the heavenlies? Night slept. Waking, I immediately began to plan where I should go and what I should look for. An anxious busyness rushed through me; reminded of the squirrel, I caught hold of myself. I need not go anywhere, or I could go slow, fast, or stop. I had time. Relax; time was not to be entertained. Happily agreeing with myself, I casually strolled. Rarely had I any thought of my original intent to experience visions and direction. I would do what I pleased; there was a whole day ahead. My body had a gait like that of a cougar; I felt so light, not burdened by weight.

It was day three of the fast, and again energy abounded. There seemed to be an old horse barn beyond the grazing land. Very cautiously I walked closer. It was abandoned. A five-foot spider web with intricate tapestry met me behind the barn. I'd never seen such a web. It must have been very old, and it was still unharmed. This was a discovery that I would appreciate forever. Keeping my distance, I bid farewell and ventured off. Some scattered pine trees came in view. This was what I missed: pine. I braced my back against one, expecting to get recharged off its energy. That's what a book had claimed that I had recently read. Pine trees have the identical energy aura as humans. You can feed off them; it's okay because they replenish quickly. I can't say that I noticed any surge of power, but I did notice laying quite close to me some very hard, stone-gray pinecones. These were petrified. Amazing. I put two in my knapsack. Boredom was setting in.

A group of tipis then appeared. What beauty, what harmony. This must be a sign from God. They complemented the surrounding backdrop of warm air, clear azure sky, and towering redwoods. These bell-shaped, enchanting tipis were cozily nestled in a comforting meadow. I scurried over and noticed that they were roped off, which must have been a fence for horses. I yelled, "Hello, hello," but no one answered. While crouching down to crawl under the rope, the air was shattered with a, "Hey! Whatcha doin' there?"

Like a frightened animal, I snapped around, "Just wanted to look inside, I'm thinking of making one."

This nicely groomed young man spoke as if reprimanding a dangerous criminal. "You can't go in there; that's a project we're doing for our environment class at the university."

I shuffled away, hands in pockets. My first encounter with a human being in two days, aside from Harley, and he had to be hostile. Had I really rambled this close to the University of Santa Cruz campus?

Joy and enthusiasm were quickly leaving me. Despondently, I admitted that there were no significant visions. The high expectation that motivated me now had backfired. I was tired, weary, and defeated, but I still had to guide myself home. The mid-afternoon sun warned me that I'd better have my sights on finding Highway 9. Judging from the position of the sun, I needed to hike east-northeast. Several hours had passed. Well within the redwoods, an early darkness was unfolding, like layer on top of layer. There was little time to find Harley. My directions served me well; like a beacon in a thicket, there rested Harley's tent. "Harley."

He popped his head out, "Ray."

We hugged again, and he offered me some warm rice with raisins. Slowly I chewed, having had no food for three and one-half days. My water was gone; Harley shared his. My inner being was a glowing vibration. I hadn't realized how necessary and fulfilling it was to share experiences with a friend. He listened intently with a perpetual smile as I talked with excitement about what I saw. My sentences were broken but expressive, "Clouds come, winds strong; I fight, win." I motioned, "Go soon, dark." And I left.

Walking along Highway 9 at night was impossible. The night sky gets so black that you can't see your hand in front of your face, and the highway winds and swerves. I'd never be able to walk the eight miles home. I'd have to hitch a ride. Terror overcame me. Would I be able to cope with reality? I had not realized how high I was—what an altered state I was in. I couldn't function in that world; I was afraid of people and society. Walking along the railroad tracks, I knew just where to get off to come down near the wayside on Highway 9. In the distance, a whistle was heard, a diminished chord sounded in perfect fourths. A train was coming! To my left was a wall of dirt and shrubs, to my right a jagged twenty-foot drop. It's amazing how quickly I could still react. I worked my way down, sure-footing the rocks. The earth was shaking from the thunder of the train. A destitute-looking young tree was all I had to hang onto. There was the roar, the wind, and the flying dust and boulder chips; with head down, eyes closed, I gripped this tree and waited it out. Was Johnny Cash ever this close when he heard the *train a comin'*? Finally, down on Highway 9, I saw my first vehicle approaching. Hesitantly, I put my arm out. All right! It was a rusty Volkswagen van. Volkswagen vans always pick you up. This royal blue van pulled over; the door slid open. "Hi," I nodded, "Just going to Ben Lomand."

"No problem, wanna hit?"

"Nah, not right now, thanks."

I looked normal compared to these freewheeling burnouts. Surely I didn't need to smoke marijuana, either. "Thanks for the ride."

Boy, they were gone. I mean, "*gone*" as in out of it. Hope they made it to their Tupperware® party.

Walking toward my porch, I noticed a car parked with Wisconsin plates. What's going on? There stood Randy Liska and Mike Haupt. They weren't sure what they were seeing; I must have had the appearance of a wild mountain man. Surprised beyond my ability to act surprised, I hardly knew what to say. The first thing I told them was that they'd have to excuse me; I'd been on peyote. Now these were two very uncomfortable guys. On a whim they drove the two thousand plus miles from Grafton, bringing Shelly back with them. Here we were, the best of friends at one time, and now we WERE worlds apart with nothing to say to each other. They never loosened up around me and headed back in the morning. Shelly asked if she could stay for a couple of weeks. "Sure, that's okay," was my response. Tension cut through the air.

Before Randy and Mike left in the morning, I just had to show them my lush garden. Beaming with pride, I pointed to the carrots, peas, corn, radishes, lettuce, broccoli, cabbage, tomatoes, peppers, sunflowers, watermelon, and strawberry plants. All this was crammed into a fifteen by twelve-foot piece of dirt. How was I to know that this would become an unmanageable jungle? This was my first garden. I knew little about rows and spacing. It all looked so small when I first planted it. They were just tiny seeds. To top it off, there was an eighteen-foot apricot tree in full fruit right in the middle. The desire to garden came back in January when I bought J. I. Rodale's manifesto on organic gardening and got a hold of Gurney's new 1972 seed catalog. I wanted to grow everything. Well, at least the rose bush survived.

Some people at the food co-op were talking about free-for-the-hauling pears. A famous brand fruit processor was letting two hundred acres of pears fall and rot to bring up the market value. I found this hard to believe but drove out there anyway, bringing a stack of paper grocery bags with me. Sure enough, just as they said, thousands of trees had been left to rot. What a shame with so many hungry people around here! I jumped a wooden fence and hauled bag after bag of juicy, ripe Bartlett pears. They weren't even sprayed with pesticides. With two full bags in my arms waiting to be packed into the Rambler, a voice jolted me cold. "Drop the pears or I'll shoot! This is private property!" I turned to see a skuzzy looking hermit of a man in his late fifties with a shotgun pointing my way. I gently lowered the two bags onto the dirt road and scooted for my driver's door.

As I got in, I barked back with a deep anger, "You're a sick man! There are people who can use these pears!" The Rambler spurted out, kicking up dirt, creating a cloud of dust between him and me. He was so creepy that I thought he'd actually shoot. Well, I got away with four bags, not a complete loss. Hours were spent slicing and placing them on door screens to dry in the hot California sun. One year later I was still eating dried pears.

Once every two weeks I'd make the trek to a goat and turkey farm. I probably drank nearly a quart of raw goat's milk a day and hardboiled the turkey eggs. The checked eggs only cost fifty cents a dozen, the milk was one dollar a gallon, and I watched him milk the goat. Turkey eggs are approximately two and one-half times the size of a chicken's.

The little round pockets in the refrigerator door couldn't handle it, and special flats were provided to transport and store these beauties.

Coming back in early August with eighteen dirty turkey eggs balancing on the passenger seat, I had the rare opportunity of seeing a herd of whales in the Monterey Bay off scenic Highway 1 near Watsonville. It was worth every second to pull over, climb the cliff, sit in a cove on the beach, and watch twenty to thirty gray whales whoosh, arc, and burst out of the water. Hard to believe that, at thirty-five tons and forty-five feet long, they could swim about so gracefully with seemingly little effort. The gray whale has a four-thousand-mile migration route from the coast of Siberia to Baja, California. To think that I had been given the express opportunity to watch them pass by on their way to the Mexican shoreline. I climbed back up the rock-laden bluff dampened by ocean spray, glad that I had stayed to watch.

Parties never ended in the greater Santa Cruz area, and I attended many but none so liberated as the outdoor one in the hills of Aptos. I was asked to bring my guitar and jam with other musicians. Things were going quite well in this secluded farm setting with swimming pool, three-foot-long fruit salad, and beautiful people until the hostess insisted that everyone take their clothes off. At least I had my guitar to cover me, but it was quite cold and clammy on my skin. Many people left to save embarrassment. There were crazy people, crazy ideas, and all for the sake of being radical. They called it freedom.

Montgomery Ward®, or possibly it was Gimbels®, in Santa Cruz sold fourteen-ounce canvas, six feet wide and as long as you wanted. I was determined to make my own tipi, a mammoth project. I bought forty-five feet of six-foot-wide canvas and began cutting and sewing, using thick, waxed thread, a sailor's needle, and a couple of thimbles. With the *Tipi Book* at my side, I followed directions to the, you could say, "T." Shelly helped me sew. We hand sewed and sewed, making difficult shingled double hems so that the water could easily run off. An inside liner had to be made also. Hands aching and blistered for days, it took us approximately sixty hours, nearly two weeks. Now we had to set it up somewhere. The area where Harley was camped on seemed right. Seventeen young redwood trees had to be cut, trimmed, and completely stripped of all bark. The trees ideally needed to be four to five inches at the base, rising to at least twenty-five feet. This tipi was sixteen feet in diameter, a slightly smaller one. It was two weeks in the making, and we set it up. What a beauty, a snug tight fit. We dug a fire pit inside. By moving the two nine-foot flaps, I could control the ventilation of smoke. The tipi was standing for two weeks before we took it down. Lugging this eighty-five pound, folded canvas up and down the cliff was a challenge, and the poles had to be taken out at night just to be safe. I wasn't sure if it was illegal to cut trees where I was. A light blue latex paint was used to paint the outside canvas. Someone had suggested latex because it dries like rubber and acts as a waterproofing. It sounded good to me.

The wanderlust was tugging again. I guess that I had run my course in the Santa Cruz Mountains. Maybe I should go back home to Wisconsin. Old friends passed through my memory, and the desire to be accepted and important pulled at my emotions. I contacted my aunt and uncle to see if I could live in my tipi on the farm up north. My aunt wrote back a kind letter gently saying, "No, it doesn't seem right." Well, maybe somebody around Grafton would let me. I mean, wouldn't it be neat and unique living in a tipi in Ozaukee County, Wisconsin? Then I'd sure be esteemed highly among the hippie types.

Bob was given a two-week notice in mid-August that we'd be leaving. He didn't even ask me to take down the several hundred purple cardboard apple separators that I had so artistically stapled and taped to the walls and ceiling of my kitchen-living room. Interior decorators to this day marvel over my creative design. Even the refrigerator was spray-painted mauve pink. Many, many trips were made to the co-op and food stores to accumulate two hundred purple cardboard apple carton separators. Only purple was acceptable.

And guess what? My chipped front tooth grew back in from eating natural foods! Donald chipped it with the butt of a play gun when I was twelve years old. Every time I'd say an "s," I'd whistle. Before and after photographs will attest to this phenomena. Dentists pooh-pooh it, but I don't care. See, I can say the word "see" and not whistle.

We had a strange-items-only rummage sale. Are you kidding? No, I didn't sell my petrified pinecones. With the Rambler bursting full of household goods and tipi poles secured on top, we took off north to Wisconsin on an early September morning.

CHAPTER 14

HEADING BACK HOME

W e made a brief pass through San Francisco. Cities made me uneasy; there was too much activity. Highway 101 running north and south along the Redwood Empire Mountain range took us into Ukiah. This was wilderness, prospector's heaven, with gorgeous scene after scene all over again. Toward the end of day two and five hundred miles into the trip, we were well into northern California in the Klamath Mountains. We agreed to be regular tourists in none other than Redwood National Park. You really must go there some time; they boast of the world's tallest tree at three hundred sixty-seven and eight-tenths feet and also perhaps the oldest. Once it was just a tiny seed even before Christ appeared; also the park had the biggest tree in diameter. A sign said that sixteen adults could sleep in its hollowed-out base. Gilbert H. Grosvenor, the founding editor of *National Geographic* magazine first visited these mammoth sequoias in 1915. So moved by their towering size, he was led to initiate the creation of the first national park system that year. Being a normal tourist wasn't painful after all; it was quite impressive, and we hardly got any second glances except by a family from Dayton, Ohio. Hey, I've got relatives in Dayton; don't stare at me.

Heading due east, the famed snow-capped Mount Shasta in the Cascade Mountain range came into view, very majestic at fourteen thousand one hundred sixty-two feet. The warm earth tones of fall were beginning to emerge, and days were much cooler high above sea level. An interesting lady at a grocery store told me that the season was too short to grow tomatoes. What, no tomatoes? Living in the mountains has some setbacks.

We traveled at a steady pace. If this Rambler gave me another two thousand miles, I'd be happy. So far, it had complained very little, but the mountains can be beastly on a vehicle. Mountains merged with mountains, one range after another. Lava Bed National Monument near the border of Oregon was dry and lifeless; if you go, bring liquids. Stars like diamond crystals sparkled unrestrained in the night sky, piercing through the pure, invigorating evening wind. The heavens drifted into eternity; where does it begin? Where does it end? There had to be a creator. Who had all the answers? I wouldn't give up the search. Anyway, God was probably watching me admire his handiwork.

We took the northern Nevada route into southern Idaho, and the pace slowed with mostly secondary roads winding up and winding down. Mountain driving was tiring. Oddly enough, the flat, parched Idaho terrain seemed to be a relief, but it took on a painful expression. Heading north out of Pocatello, Idaho, on Interstate 15, we drove through miles of eerie, lifeless moonscape. I thought it would be a good idea to see Canada. Why not? It would just be two extra days traveling. I'd never been to Canada. Did they speak English? Would the roads be different? Maybe we needed a passport. Some guy in Havre, Montana, just sixty miles from the border, cautioned me, "They really frisk long-hairs at the major crossings. Got any dope?"

"No I'm clean, just some teas."

"They'll rip your car apart and harass you; they hate freaks coming into Canada." He was serious. He told me about a dirt road, "A rancher's trail. Nobody travels it; you can sneak in and pick up the main road at Highway 46." Well, I reasoned that his suggestion was best.

I thanked him for his warning and advice and putt-putted along on nothing more than a wide prairie cow path. Man, it was getting cold; it was freezing! All we had for warmth were long pants and a light shirt. Oh, no, it was snowing! I mean this was a real storm. Did we have food and enough gas? I didn't have snow tires. Where were we? Miles and miles of prairie were being blanketed in white. I kept driving, bucking the northwest wind and plowing through snowdrifts. We'd have to pull over and wait until it stopped. I was nearly yelling while talking to Shelly to compete with the howling wind against my car. I didn't even know if I was still on the road; maybe I was going the wrong way. Without the sun as a guide, my sense of direction could be easily spun around. Last gasp thoughts took over my mind; we'd die out here, and no one would find us for weeks. While we sat without words, wrapped in blankets, I ran the engine ten minutes with full heat on, and I shut it off for fifteen. For three hours I continued this on and off cycle. Finally, the snow let up. The sky was showing a tease of clearing to the southeast. Without announcement, a pick-up truck with a plow cruised past us, slowing a bit as it neared the white Rambler. A burly man glanced out but kept going. "All right! He's plowing this road open." We took off behind him, keeping about one hundred feet between us. My blood came back; good old cheer was active again.

After an hour's worth of driving, we met with a two-lane paved road. It hadn't even snowed there. I figured it must be Highway 46; that was all the map showed. I guessed that we were in Canada. Hmm, I didn't feel any different; I was still me, same thoughts, same face; I just had to look in the rearview mirror to make sure. Nothing really big happened; there was no white line or river or forest beginning, just very flat land and wheat on both sides of the road. I knew this must have been Saskatchewan. Where were the forests, lakes, and rugged mountains? We pulled over for gas at the first town we came to, Climax, Saskatchewan. This was the climax for going out of our way to be in Canada? The price of gas was outrageous, forty-eight cents a gallon. A man inside the station made me aware that in Canada the gallon is called the imperial gallon, equivalent to five quarts. That's too weird for me, a five-quart gallon. I suppose one foot was fifteen inches. Looking at the map, I saw that Highway 13 just a little north of here would take us all the way across Saskatchewan and Manitoba, where we could head down into Minnesota. We drove and drove; it was maddening, worse than northern Indiana and Ohio. There were five hundred miles of wheat fields and sunflowers. Grain elevators stood like tin monoliths. I was so impatiently bored that I started singing a facetious song about driving through Saskatchewan.

We came down Highway 59 into Minnesota and junctioned at Highway 2 going east towards Bemidji in north-central Minnesota. It had been quite a beautiful state so far, heavily forested, teeming with lakes. Entering Bemidji, which they claim is the home of Paul Bunyon and Babe, my eyes caught a bold sign with red letters—*Gas war, 27¢ a gallon.* "Hey, let's fill up there. Hope they don't put water in the gas." Squeezing the nozzle, feeling fortunate to have spotted the sign, listening to those gallons guzzle in, a guy asked me what those sticks were for on the top of my car. "I'm heading back home to Grafton, Wisconsin, near Milwaukee to put up my tipi and live in it."

"Far out," was his response.

I proceeded to tell him that I didn't know where yet, but I was sure I'd find a place.

He excitedly exclaimed, "I've got a farm north of the lake; you can put it up there."

"Really?" I was ecstatic.

"By the way, my name's Jim."

"I'm Ray, Ray Last."

I followed him out of town around the east side of Lake Bemidji. About eight miles out, we turned onto a dirt, tree-lined road. "Well, here's where I live." He seemed so happy and energetic. This was a dreamland to me, with seclusion, rolling hills, and forests. Autumn colors were in full swing; a cool, sixty-degree wind carried the scent. Walking together, we had a vibrant conversation. He even toyed with the bass guitar in a rock band. I chose a lovely clearing about two-tenths of a mile straight back from his house to put the tipi up. Birch, poplar, oak, sugar maple, ash, spruce, pine, and tamarack generously graced the area. Horses roamed about. I couldn't believe that this all came together so quickly. Surely, it was meant to be. Anxious and pressed for time, I quickly left, driving straight through the five hundred fifty odd miles to Grafton to drop off Shelly and unload belongings that I wouldn't need. I headed back to Bemidji immediately.

CHAPTER 15

BEMIDJI, MINNESOTA

Three days later I cruised into Bemidji and was greeted by the thirty-foot statue of Paul Bunyon and Babe, his blue ox. My number one priority was getting the tipi up. First, the larger tripod poles were tied and raised; then the others were placed. Finally, with the canvas cover tied securely to the back pole, I grunted while walking it up into its notch. One-half then the other was unwrapped until they met in front and were laced together with straight, shaven sticks through reinforced buttonholes. The two eighteen-foot flap poles found their pockets, and the inside liner was tied. It only took me three hours. I dug a fire pit and cut some wood with my shiny, stainless steel Swedish bow saw. There seemed to be plenty of deadwood from fallen trees, mostly birch, pine, and maple. Controlling the smoke presented a real problem. Much of the larger wood was just too wet to burn smoothly. It was getting cold; what was I going to do? It was mid-September, and there was already frost in the mornings.

One of Jim's friends had a steel, ten-gallon barrel. "Here, try making a stove out of it," Jim's friend said.

I looked a bit puzzled and uncertain but answered, "Well, okay, I'll give it a try."

I purchased three-inch black stovepipe and fashioned an eight-inch door in it. Rocks were laid around the barrel to secure it. I couldn't run the pipe all the way out the top as there was no opening, so I wired a fine mesh screen at the top of the pipe to prevent hot ashes from escaping. Straw was laid as bedding on the ground and carpet remnants were laid on top of that. The stove was a success, and even the surrounding rock stayed hot for hours, but I truly missed the mesmerizing effect of an open flame. I don't think it's necessary to go into detail here, but I did have an indoor toilet. I felt like I was really settling in for the winter.

Local people told me that it gets really cold early; Bemidji is known as the "Icebox of the Nation." I grinned and took it in stride, feeling quite confident. I bragged, "I'm sure I can handle it; I'm from Wisconsin."

A friendly bunch of fellows from about two miles down the road gave me a surprise visit. "We heard some nut was living in a tipi out here."

"Yep, I'm the nut."

Speaking of nuts, they mentioned that there was, "One of those natural food stores you've been talking about is in Bagley, twenty miles west on Highway 2." That was welcome news. The next day I drove to Bagley and located the store in an old, one-room schoolhouse. Two really friendly folks tended the store. Two hundred dollars would buy me nearly a winter's supply of staples such as brown rice, oats, peanut butter, bread, mixed dried fruits, and assorted raw nuts. I bought natural vitamins as I ran out. With bags and boxes full of food, the Rambler and I whistled our way back, certain that we would brave this winter.

One-quarter mile west of Jim's lived a family that let both Jim and I get water from their well. Jim would haul three milk cans home with his flatbed truck, but I had to drag mine with a rope. This was a five-gallon, modern, stainless steel milk can; the can was eighteen inches around and about nine inches high, able to hold five gallons. Water became precious. I learned instantly how to conserve and use it sparingly. The first overnight snow glistened a soft pastel pink in the early morning sun. After the first snow in late October, dragging this can became a breeze. Once every five days I visited the water source getting my refill.

Word traveled around town about a hippie living in a tipi. A few curiosity seekers managed to find me. Some were brave enough to stop in and say hi, but several just kept their distance and gawked. A farmer harvesting potatoes in a field nearby hollered out an obscenity about you "such and such hippie." I wished that he hadn't done that. Up until then, people were friendly, and I felt peaceful. I wanted everyone to like me. I went out of my way to be friendly and non-threatening.

The Red Lake Indian Reservation was only twenty-five miles straight north, bordering the Upper and Lower Red Lake. The urge came to venture up there, introduce myself, and hopefully visit with the Chippewa and Ojibwa Indians. Surely they would be excited and supportive of my chosen lifestyle. I held the Rambler to a crawl through the mud-trenched road around Red Lake. Not wanting to appear like a tourist, I only gave a quick glance at people wandering about. Conditions were poor—tarpaper shacks with broken window, doors hanging by a hinge, garbage strewn about, and dogs that looked like walking skeletons with their ribs protruding. This was not what I had imagined. The weather was threatening rain and sleet; dark, heavy clouds guarded the ever-present misery. Taking a deep breath with sharp jabs piercing my stomach, I got out and knocked on a door. "What do you want?" The man sounded mean and irritated. Awkward and stupid are two good words that might begin to describe my feelings. With my voice shaking, I tried to talk with some composure. "My name's Ray; I'm really into North American Indians; I'm living in a tipi just outside Bemidji. I just wanted to visit some Indians; I don't mean to bother you."

To my right a door opened; a weathered man stood there. His eyes were sunken, and he had a fixed frown that exposed years of hopelessness. He was a true Native, with bronze skin, a large, curved nose, squinty dark brown eyes, rounded cheeks, and black hair that was nervously brushed back. There was an illness in his tone as he spoke softly, almost in an aching whisper, "We don't have it so good; mostly we eat fish we catch. We drink alcohol, and then we die."

I kindly nodded. Biting my lips, lowering my eyes, I apologized, "Sorry, I didn't mean to bother you."

A black-and-white shorthaired dog leaned against my legs; his tail managed seven or eight thumps against the left side of my Levis®. Stooping over a bit, I gave him a few good solid pats on the rump. His body was soaked from the forty-degree drizzle. He twisted his head upward, and our eyes locked. There was compassion in the shadow of sadness. Looking toward the man, my left hand motioned good-bye. I got in the car slowly with poise and drove away slowly. The man may have continued blankly staring, or he may have closed the door. I spent weeks trying to forget or explain what I had seen. Were they pushed off the land; did their culture gradually die? Maybe they're just lazy.

I deeply wanted them to have their old ways back. The sorrow that I initially felt has never left.

Jim had a large St. Bernard; I suppose that it's redundant to say that a St. Bernard is large, but this dog was also demonstratively friendly. I avoided him, as he would inevitably knock me over while working up four or five good barks in my ear. This dog was notorious for running away time and time again, but eventually somebody would bring him back. Could you imagine riding around with that thing in the passenger seat? He had a name that I can't remember, but he was definitely a male, which was always verifiable whenever Jim's girlfriend came over. It took three guys to restrain the dog. Let's call him, "Brutus."

Jim also had two horses and asked if I'd like to ride. "Sure," I eagerly responded, "But I really haven't seriously ever ridden a horse."

"Well, let's go anyway."

Jim said, cheery as ever, "I ride bareback."

"Well, that's fine with me." I eventually got up there after three or four tries while this horse patiently rolled his eyes.

We trotted for miles down the dirt road through fields and then found a trail heading into the pines. Jim yelped, "Hah!" His horse reared and took off in a full gallop into the pines. Mine followed after; I became frantic, squeezing hard with my legs and yanking the reins, but this horse just shot out. It was a wild West chase! I let go of the reins and clasped my arms around its neck. We were now plowing through the trees, pine branches slashed at my body and face.

I was screaming, "Stop, stop; I can't hang on!" All I heard were unbroken hoof beats, panting, branches swishing, and Jim laughing hysterically. He pulled up to a quick halt; the horses stopped. Breathing was hard, steam shot from flared nostrils, and Jim's eyes were wet from laughing.

"My barrette! I lost my barrette," I yelled, horrified. I'd wore my hair in a ponytail ever since New York, and I had made this barrette in Ben Lomond out of thick, oiled leather and a perfectly slender, smooth piece of driftwood from the Pacific. I cherished it and wore it daily. "It's lost; we've got to find it. By the way, why did you take off like that?"

Jim slyly answered, "Oh, just wanted to see if you could hang on. You were great, a real cowboy."

I would have rather he had said Indian. It certainly was exhilarating; I'd do it again. We trotted back gingerly, or whatever horses do when they walk slowly, and scanned the area, but never found the barrette. Two days later in the early morning, Brutus was barking outside the tipi. I thought, "That's strange; he never wanders down here." Peering out my door, I came face to face with Brutus's slimy mouth. He had my barrette in his mouth. "Brutus, you found my barrette; you actually knew it was mine; what a great dog!" I washed the dog drool off and didn't even get upset over the teeth marks he made in the leather and wood. It was good to be wearing my barrette again. By the way, I still have it buried somewhere in a box at home.

I started writing letters on birch bark to friends back home. The post office wouldn't accept taped on acorns as a stamp, though.

I loved dogs, and the opportunity arose for me to have a ten-week-old collie/shepherd mix for free. The farmer where the puppies were lived a good ten miles away. They all looked so cute, cuddly, and chubby. Their mama did good. The rather callous-sounding farmer said, "Whatever is still here after next week gets shot. We don't need no more dogs."

I was shocked at the thought. "Really, you'd shoot them?"

His firm reply was, "You bet."

It was difficult, but I picked one out of the furry batch—the one that kept licking me. Turning the puppy over, I looked at the man and asked, "What is it?"

He felt around with expertise and stated, "You got a female there," sounding as if that was bad.

Snow flurries whisked about on the second day of November; the temperature read twenty-eight degrees on the rusted thermometer nailed to his barn that boasted of some long defunct soda pop company. "You sure you don't want nothing for her?", I asked.

"Naw, just glad to get rid of them."

Gently I laid her on the seat next to me; her eyes closed, contented to be in a warm car. Wow, my own dog! This was thrilling. Not since I had Lucky at twelve years of age had I had my own dog. She'd follow me everywhere and fetch sticks. I could wrestle with her, and she'd sit patiently on the sidewalk when I went in a store. We'd take long hikes together; she was my good friend. She slept all the way home as my hand stroked her fur. I carried her down to the tipi. Jim came over with some dog food. Tripping, while exploring the tall grass, she never ventured far. What should I call her? Maybe Licker because she licked me so much or Licky; that sounds close to Lucky. The name Lika came to me as clear as the November air. Yeah, Lika; it even sounded Indian.

I'd heard of some people near Cass Lake that had a goat farm, supposedly mellow people. The term hippie was losing its effectiveness in association. Hippie became a vague term. Freaks usually were drug addicts, and mellow people were into natural foods and spiritual things. I preferred having the status of a mellow person. I drove unannounced onto their farm. Chickens, dogs, cats, goats, and horses all had free run of the yard. The leaves of the tamarack had turned to golden brown. What a tremendous setting they had. The clouds were cold, gray, and heavy with snow. The area was extremely peaceful, rustic and secluded. They could do whatever they pleased. Nobody seemed to be around, but a pick-up truck stood nearby. It must have been driven recently judging from the tracks in the slushy snow cover. I spent perhaps twenty minutes walking around the house and barnyard; every animal followed me like a Pied Piper. A billy goat had different ideas; he reared his horns and charged; all the animals fled with a great commotion. I panicked and ran for the porch; just as he was about to connect and butt me, he stood up on his hind legs and baaed loudly. Then he chuckled and walked away. This was a game to him; he thought it was hilarious. There was an echoing call deep within the pasture. I waved with my left arm outstretched. A man came into view with a beard and wearing a pullover cap, mechanic's overalls, and boots that came to his knees. We smiled and shook a hippie hand shake. He invited me into his partially self-sufficient house. This was great, really natural. We spent a good half hour chatting, talking about ourselves.

I originally wanted to see if he'd sell me goat's milk; instead I was persuaded to buy a goat. His wife came home in a nice car; anything with some treads showing on the tires looked nice to me. It seemed strange to meet people like this who were actually married. Marriage just sounded so hokey. I was given a crash course on raising and milking goats. A brown-and-white Nubian was chosen for being gentle and cooperative; she'd been giving about one-half gallon a day. They threw together a week's worth of feed and wrote down some basic instructions. Eighty dollars was the asking price; I had about ninety-five in cash on me, so I bought her.

"How am I going to get her back?" seemed like a reasonable question.

The guy said quite simply, "Put her in the back seat; they love to ride in cars."

"Really?"

"Yep, really."

Well, in she went and just stood there. We didn't have much to say to each other on the way home; the twenty-three miles seemed very long. I told her that she could sit down, but apparently she preferred to stand. Arriving home I commanded her, "Here, you wait in the car; don't go pooh-pooh, either." She seemed to smile and nod okay.

"Jim, Jim, I've got a goat, where can I put her?"

Jim came out laughing, as usual. "Far out; let's make a place in the barn."

I don't think that I ever gave this goat a name. I built an eighteen-inch high milking stand out of three-quarter inch plywood and pine logs and nailed up a feeding dish. Goats like to eat while being milked. Sure enough, at five o'clock in the afternoon she jumped up on the stand and started eating. Stands are convenient; they enable you to milk at eye level while comfortably sitting. I shared this warm, raw goat's milk with Lika, and we finished it off that night.

Boy, I'm becoming quite the thing up here, I gleamed. Evenings were spent huddled around the stove in my long underwear, flannel shirt, and Hudson Bay blanket. I'd read my book on Indians and their spiritual rituals. I'd meditate for half an hour attempting to empty my mind, or maybe I would just talk out loud to God. Lika lay there, curled against my body. We enjoyed each other's warm company. The only loneliness I experienced was that of a female companion. I thought often, "If only I'd have a wilderness lady, then my life would be complete." I sang often, mostly flowing repetitious melodies using vowel sounds while creating words. I had no guitar up there. Before bedding down fully dressed, I laid hot rocks inside my sleeping bag, mostly down around by my feet. These rocks stayed warm for three to four hours. It helped, but by four o'clock in the morning, my water had already frozen. Mid-November could get down to ten degrees at night.

My morning fire was always prepared the night before, laying out just the right amount of soft kindling, then larger hardwood sticks, and finally quarter-split pieces. I often used birch bark to start the kindling as it contained highly flammable creosote. Only one kitchen match was ever used; nothing was wasted. A rectangular tin plate was secured to the top of the barrel stove that proved quite efficient for cooking on and heating water. I drank an awful lot of yerba matė tea, a stimulant tea containing five percent tannic acid but little caffeine. It's the national drink in Colombia, South America; they sip it from gourds using a silver straw. I'd have to get up at five o'clock in the morning and milk my new pet. That seemed easy enough before going to bed but not too inviting at five o'clock in the morning. But I moaned and shivered, got the fire going, washed my face, brushed my teeth, put on coat and boots, grabbed the milk pail, and trucked up to the barn. The goat was gone! I whistled and called and searched frantically. How could she have gotten out? The fence was four and one-half feet high. I felt sick. Where was she? Was she hurt? Was she running around carrying all that milk? I woke Jim up, "Jim, the goat's gone; can I use the phone to see if she somehow wandered back?" I called the people; they felt badly and told me that goats get lonely; they need other animals or people.

"We'll let you know if she makes it back here." We spent the day searching, asking farmers; even the local radio station aired it periodically if anybody had seen my goat.

Evening crept in, I was out eighty dollars, and this poor goat was probably dead or dying. I only had one hundred dollars left; eighty dollars was a large chunk. Around the fire I talked to God, "Please, let my goat be okay and come back." I doubted it would happen, though; this goat didn't know that I was her master. An uneasy, sparse sleep kept me troubled. Lika sensed my sorrow. I checked the wind-up clock that I kept under a thick blanket because I couldn't stand the ticking. The glare from the flashlight against the glass made my eyes squint. It was four thirty-five o'clock in the morning; I might as well get up. In the distance, I heard a faint baaing. No, it couldn't be; it was getting closer. I shot out of the tipi without shoes or coat and shouted, "Where are you?" The goat excitedly came running over. Thrill was in the air. "You're back; you found your way back." With my feet nearly frozen, I said, "Stay here, let me get my clothes on, and we'll milk you. Thank you, God; thank you, God," I kept mumbling. Lika barked so hard that her whole body left the ground. I called the goat people first thing in the morning with the good news. Sure, they were happy, but suggested that I get another goat for company.

"We've got two that you can have for nothing. A Billy and a young nanny." You guessed it, I took them; but this time they delivered the other two.

"And on his farm he had three goats, E-I-E-I-O."

This billy goat had obnoxious habits and stunk. Jim and I castrated it, possibly the most difficult thing I'd ever done. A week later he died from an apparent infection. The mountain man in me strung him up in the barn and cut his hide off. The other two goats started to have mixed feelings about me.

I learned to tan my first hide; it came out stiff and bumpy, but I saved it. One of Jim's ponies died, and we both worked laboriously on its hide. The tail was saved to be used later as a wind gauge hanging from the top of the main pole of my tipi, the lodge pole.

The late November sun was setting early. Jim, in a frantic, horrified voice, came screaming down towards the tipi. I was a short distance away cutting more wood. "Brutus killed your goat; I think it's dead! He ripped its neck open." We rushed to the barn. There lay the Nubian milk goat, groaning, kicking, blood oozing from its mouth and nose, eyes bulging; her neck was ripped open. Almost instantly Jim leaped the fence and shot her in the forehead with his rifle. She gave one quick jerk and died. I took my time digging a hole, dragged her over and pushed her in. Dirt hit her scarred, blood-soaked face as I solemnly covered her up. What a way to go. I didn't want any more goats and told Jim that if he wanted he could have the remaining young one. Two days later, he shot it to butcher her for meat.

I had much more important things to do than raise goats, such as cutting and splitting firewood. I spent a good three hours a day, hauling trees from the woods, trimming branches with my ax, and cutting dead, foot-long sections with the bow saw, later to be split in half and quarters. The woodpile was getting high, taking up the whole south area outside of the tipi. I had no idea as to just how much I'd need to get through the winter. I just kept cutting and stacking. Lika enjoyed climbing to the top of the pile and whined for me to get her down.

Nobody came to visit anymore; below zero temperatures made for a chilly morning greeting. I was starting to believe the sobering stories and warnings of temperatures plummeting in excess of forty-five degrees below zero come January. It was never this cold this early in southeastern Wisconsin. It was getting so cold that I could actually hear the trees pop. I had to toughen up. Shelly who had left nearly two months prior to this, called one early December evening. Jim hiked down to summon me to the phone.

"Hi, how are you?" was her cheerful greeting.

My response was, "Oh, I'm doing okay. It's getting cold, but I'll make it."

She quietly asked, "Can I come up for a few days and see the tipi and how you survive?"

With hesitation, I agreed. "Well, oh, I guess that would be all right."

"Could you meet me at the bus depot on December 15th?"

"Okay," I said, "Call here and leave a message letting me know what time you'll be in."

The following day Jim asked if I'd like to go to his mom's and take a bath. He went over once a week. "Gee, a bath," I hadn't really thought about it. "Well, okay." It sounded like a novel idea: a hot tub, soap, wash my hair, and bring out my other pair of long underwear. "Yeah, I'll go over with you." You've all heard the one-liner about taking a bath once a month whether you need it or not. For me, it had been three and one-half months since my body touched water. My turn came to step into the tub. How would my skin react? Was it possible I could wash off this tough layer that had been keeping me warm? Aah, the water was soothing; I just sat and soaked and even shampooed my hair. Hey, I was a blond again. It took refilling the tub three times before the water started to clear. His mother would go into shock when she saw the filthy ring that I left around the tub. Lying in this hot water looking at the beautiful tile and matching towels, having seen their nicely furnished home, made me wonder why I lived like I did. This was so warm and comfortable; I could get spoiled before I even dried off.

Going back to my lodge, as tipis were commonly referred to, was just not very inviting. I'd have to get rugged all over again. Somehow this lifestyle was losing its appeal, but I would make it through the winter because I had determined that I would. Determination was my driving force. By midmorning the next day, Jim came riding over on his horse; his face was glowing. "The Miller's beef cows got out; do you want to go on a round-up?" We rode our horses about a mile and one-half south through a trail into the woods to an open meadow. Other riders came, joining from the east, west, and south of us, about ten in all. Frank Miller led the group. Everybody had a rope. Seven beef cows had taken off to the west; we planned to keep about two hundred yards between us. A rope? The last thing I did with a rope was to tie tipi poles. Could you picture me trying to lasso a cow? I'd probably lasso my own leg. Hey, I was only coming along for the ride. We headed west at a good pace. They were spotted five miles northwest. All riders merged in a circle surrounding the cows. "Look out!" One charged my horse; the horse reared, but I hung on. Really, I had no idea that these reddish brown beef cows were so mean and aggressive. Man, they looked like raging buffalo. Two were lassoed; two more ropes went around their necks. They were quickly tied between trees. These animals weren't gentle dumb beasts with udders; you don't milk this kind of cow. They were vicious and steaming mad. A cattle truck backed in; one by one, the ropes were pulled through the twenty-six foot truck, and cattle were prodded in. Deadly dangerous. The man inside the truck was close to death numerous times as the cows kicked and butted. It was breathtaking to watch him maneuver the ropes off their necks. He was crazy; what guts! Nobody got hurt. I felt like I should have been back at the bunkhouse, sweeping the floor instead. I was useless, but the men treated me kindly. Jim and I rode back, dazed.

Early that afternoon I was going to make a run to the natural food store in Bagley. I hadn't noticed that Lika was following me up to my car. I was relieved when the Rambler started right off. Two to three days sitting out in the subzero cold can really freeze up an auto. Starting to back out, I heard a high-pitched yip. Dashing out of the car, I screamed, "Lika! Oh, my God, I ran you over." She was alive but not moving. I immediately drove her the fourteen miles to the vet. She just lay on the seat without a sound, looking pitiful. "God, please let her live. Please, God, please." Tears were restrained only from shock. "She's got to live, she's got to live." The vet was still open. He tended to her and gave me his diagnosis.

"She's got a dislocated pelvis and possible hernia on the abdomen. She'd have to stay here for at least three days."

"Do you think that she'll be able to walk okay?"

"Hard to say, depends on whether I can set the pelvis."

My money supply was dwindling. Very concerned I asked, "How much do you think it will cost? I'm just visiting a friend in Bemidji and don't really have a lot of money along." I know, I lied about just visiting, but with only around ninety dollars left, I felt it necessary to scheme.

This understanding man said, "Don't worry about it, I'll see when you pick your dog up."

I passed the natural food store in Bagley on the way home but didn't bother to stop in. A certain empty sorrow controlled me.

On December 14, the sun had already set, and the note that I found on the tipi door said Shelly's bus would get in at eleven o'clock in the morning. Yeah, that's right; she was coming tomorrow. I really wanted Shelly to see Lika; she would have liked her. I built a fire and noticed my mustache thawing but found it difficult to relax. Thoughts of Lika being in pain dominated my mind. Instead of trying to talk myself into an optimistic mood, I went out and sawed more wood. About a hundred feet away I caught a bright flash out of the corner of my right eye; it took several seconds before I realized that flames were shooting from the top of the tipi; bright golden orange embers were soaring straight up. I was so slow to react, as if paralyzed and unable to run. Time was lost for a moment, but there I was, attempting to get in the burning tipi to at least throw my belongings out and hopefully save the tipi. Within minutes, the entire canvas and poles were ablaze. The fourteen bales of hay that were stacked two high as a windbreak on the north side had already ignited. Racing around, I realized that nothing could be saved and instead concentrated on throwing the wood off the woodpile as far and as fast as I could fling it. Flames rose thirty feet, engulfing the brittle evening sky. "It's all gone! It's over; all this work is gone."

Jim's flatbed truck came into view. Several milk cans had bounced off the side. By the time he got there, he had lost all seven cans that he filled with water. Jim was out of breath. "I saw the flames and just threw these cans on the truck. Most of them were full of water."

Feeling that I should console him instead, I said, "That's all right, it was gone by the time you got here." We both stood in shock and amazement. Watching the tipi collapse, he helped me push the remaining charred bales in towards the middle. "Jim, it was the creosote from burning birch bark; it must have gummed up the inside of the stove pipe and finally ignited. I shouldn't have burned so much birch bark. I guess it's under control, and you can go if you want to." I tried to hide my grief.

Jim genuinely asked, "You gonna be all right?"

"Yeah, I'll just sit here and make sure that it's all out. Two months from now I'll be laughing about this."

Jim seemed relieved that I had some light humor left in me. He made a fairly certain suggestion, "I'll call Sylvia Johnson; she'll let you stay there tonight."

"Okay, thanks." Sylvia was a casual acquaintance of ours, a widow who lived about two miles northwest of Jim's with her oldest son and twelve-year-old daughter.

I found a comfortable spot on what was left of the woodpile and blankly stared into the dying embers. Just when it seemed like nothing was left to smolder, a flicker would appear; my eye caught it for its last seconds. Many thoughts floated in; they were so very clear, singular and pronounced, wouldn't it have been great if I could have harnessed all this heat? Maybe it was a good thing that I ran over Lika; she may have died in the fire. It really didn't feel like it was ten below zero; I was not cold at all. How would Shelly react? I had lost everything that I owned, two hundred dollars' worth of food, all my books and blankets, and one hundred photographs that I treasured, dating back from the recording studio in Chicago to the mountains and salt flats and all of California's experiences. My Kodak® camera was still in the car with a full roll of film used up in it. I had no clothes or tools; it was all gone. Several hours of thoughts guided me through this tragedy; tears trickled down my cheeks as I pondered my life, the sorrows and disappointments, and deep wounds began to well up again. I called to God out loud and sang a song, "What's so big about material things?" My soul wept as I sang this over and over. The weeping subsided and uncontrolled laughter beamed out, shattering the night sky. I kept singing, incorporating laughter with the song, louder and louder. A relief was surfacing. Screaming, I sang, "What's so big about material things?" Then silence, like a comforting arm, led me down the road, guided by the glare of the moonlight reflecting off the snow.

Three subtle knocks on the old wooden screen door was enough. Sylvia answered, "Shh, everyone's asleep. There's some doughnuts and bread on the table. You can sleep in the room upstairs to the left; there's a sleeping bag in the closet." She had a sympathetic, concerned look.

"Thanks a lot, I'm okay." Someone must have recently bumped the old round clock on the wall; you could see the circle where the paint hadn't faded. It was two o'clock in the morning. I ate a doughnut, sugar and all, and drank one-half cup of water. The stairs knew just when to creak. One seventy-five watt light bulb nearly blinded me as I found a blue sleeping bag in the closet. "This must be it," I whispered to myself. I had a north bedroom, which was extremely cold because of a window that was broken out. Last year's plastic had long since ripped and was still flapping vigorously against the window frame. I found a piece of cardboard and secured it over the window. The sleeping bag had a moldy odor, but the comfort of a bed overcame me.

Waking, I noticed that the sun had already risen. Last night's theater seemed like a dream, but I had to admit to myself that it wasn't. A very nice breakfast was prepared for all of us; I was the first one up after Sylvia, her daughter, and finally her son. The atmosphere was jovial, and I found myself joking about the tipi burning. It was best to make light of it; these people could never understand. Sylvia asked if I liked Kris Kristofferson or Kenny Rogers. I had no idea who they were. She was floored, "You don't know Kris Kristofferson or Kenny Rogers?"

"No, really, I don't." I had to stop smiling, or she wouldn't have taken me serious. I soon realized that we were in country-western territory, heard it on the radio all day, and it started to sound quite depressing, but I was just happy and grateful for being treated so kindly.

I called the vet, and he said that Lika was recovering just fine, and I could pick her up tomorrow. Aw, that was good news. Sylvia sternly said, "You've got a dog? He can't come in the house; no animals in the house."

"Well, okay," I agreed. Her son helped me make a doghouse out of a horse trough laid on its side. We dragged it near the back door and thickly lined it with straw. It was nearly ten-thirty in the morning. Ron and Sandy, the couple that lived across the road, drove me back to Jim's so I could get my car and pick Shelly up at the bus depot. Jim was laying a tray of hot coals under his car to warm up the oil pan.

"Got cold again last night," he said.

"Yeah, really," was all I had to say.

Bemidji's bus depot was like a social center. Old-timers stood around savoring the warmth, talking about the same things that they say every year at this time, "Yep, by next weekend, she'll be thirty-five below." I was hoping they were wrong. Lake Bemidji was already reviving the glacier age. Too antsy to sit down, I just paced in front of the window. People scurried in and out of cars and buildings. My hands comforted the anxiety pains that kept shooting through my stomach. At three minutes after eleven o'clock a Greyhound pulled up. There she was, the second one off. I quickly stepped outside. Shelly greeted me with a robust, cheery "Hi!" I told her straight out that the tipi burned down last night and that I lost everything. Her face dropped, white with questions. She knew that I wasn't kidding. I appeared strong-hearted as if I could shrug it off. My Jack Benny expressions became prevalent, hands up, lips tucked in, eyebrows raised and shoulders hunched. We had little to say. Then I went and told her about Lika. My attitude struggled, trying to surface with something positive.

As we drove out of town, the first thing we did was visit the charred remains where the tipi stood. I poked around with a long stick. The hatchet seemed salvageable. Pots, pans, and the five-gallon milk can were blackened beyond usefulness. Jim could probably use the firewood, though. I introduced her to Sylvia and her family and made some small, uninvolved talk. I told her I was thinking that with the money I had left I might just buy some more canvas to make another tipi and pay an upholsterer to sew the strips together. Sounded crazy, but I had a stubborn, proud determination to make it through the winter in a tipi.

Shelly took the bus back the next day, but before she left, we drove to the vet to pick up Lika. Lika was walking and wagging and all excited up and down, her tongue never ceased from licking us. I took out my wallet expecting him to want at least sixty dollars. Aw, just give me fourteen dollars; that'll cover it. "Really, fourteen dollars, that's all? Aw, thanks a lot." I shook his hand the conventional way and drove back much happier. Well, I had just about seventy dollars left, and new canvas cost forty dollars and the upholsterer said he'd sew the six-foot strips for fifteen dollars. With a shade of modesty, he bragged, "I've done a couple other tipis already."

"Really, somebody else has a tipi up here?" I was very surprised to hear that. There were others like me in Northern Minnesota.

I labored several days, cutting and trimming trees. This time the poles had to be a little thicker at the base and longer, twenty-eight to thirty feet. I tried to keep the tops on. The tipi would be nineteen feet in diameter. Jim helped me haul the poles out of a pine forest with his pick-up truck, and I began the tedious job of shaving the bark clean with a draw knife. A draw knife has a long, curved blade with wooden handles on both sides. Originally this tool was used to smooth out wooden wagon wheels. The poles had to be kept standing and turned frequently to prevent bowing. Quite a few onlookers collected in Sylvia's back farmyard. "What you doing there?"

"Oh, I'm shaving tipi poles."

"Tipi poles? You got a tipi?"

"Yeah, I'm gonna put it up here in a couple of days."

"You're nuts. Good luck, you'll freeze to death." Conversations went like that. My outside work had to be put on hold due to a developing mild blizzard. Sitting in this warm, cozy house caused me to seriously question whether I could get the tipi up in time; a real storm was whipping in. I stood by the window and just stared at the driving, blinding, white onslaught that was drifting, swirling, and howling. The pine forest just two hundred feet south of the house was no longer visible.

The phone rang and startled me back. Her daughter answered, "Ma, it's William." Sylvia talked quietly to someone for less than a minute and said good-bye. She griped at whoever would listen. "Bill's in town; he's coming out to visit. If he starts preaching again, I'll boot him out the door." This was none of my business, so I didn't ask questions. About forty-five minutes later, a car drove up into the driveway; they dropped Bill off. He came to the door. After being let in, the atmosphere had the sensation of a cease-fire, borderline cold war. Bill, who was Sylvia's brother, seemed like a very pleasant, gentle man. His leg was apparently broken or handicapped in some way. He leaned his crutches against the refrigerator. The evening meal was a help-yourself-to-leftovers style. Everybody noticed Bill praying silently before he ate, and he mumbled something about the Lord. Sylvia snapped at him with condemning profanities. She told him to knock off the religious stuff. "I told you that I don't want to hear any more talk about Jesus in this house." Bill never appeared to be riled. He kept right on talking with a calm, controlled voice. "Jesus came to seek the lost and the sinners; why can't you admit you're a sinner in need of the Savior? Jesus loves you, Sylvia."

She screamed awful things at him and physically pushed him out the door, throwing his coat and crutches into the snow. Slamming the door, she proclaimed, "I don't care if he dies out there!" No one had much to say, and I couldn't think about food. I was feeling so bad for this guy; he was so dejected looking. Where was he going to go? My eyes were fixed on his fading, dark figure limping through the two-foot drifts with the northwest wind beating at his side and back. He walked across the road to Ron and Sandy's. Kneeling on the couch with my hands cupped up against the front window, I followed his ghost of a shadow, feeling somewhat relieved that Ron and Sandy were home to let him in.

Needles from the four-foot Christmas tree pricked my left arm as I sat on the couch. "This was a pathetic, haphazard job of decorating," I thought. My mind drifted back to when I was a boy and how artistically I placed the lights, ornaments, and tinsel on the tree. It had been six or seven years since I had even involved myself at all with Christmas. There was still a part of me that cherished those peaceful, caring feelings that Christmas often brought. I didn't allow myself to entertain that melancholy state. I had changed. That family stuff wasn't for me.

Still burdened for Bill, I bundled up to walk over and visit with him, Ron, and Sandy. Probably a good idea to start the Rambler so that it didn't totally freeze up. On about the eighth try, it finally kept firing. Very rough, but she officially started. The iron on my car had expanded so much that the door wouldn't shut. There was nothing I could do about that, just let the snow blow in; I could always brush the seat off. I picked Lika up out of a cuddled position in the horse trough and wiped the snow off the thermometer. It read, just as I had feared, thirty-seven below zero. Hurdling the drifts seemed like exhilarating fun. Lika just clung to my chest. Ron greeted me warmly, "Well, hi, we didn't expect all this company on a night like this." Prepared to stay a while, I took my winter garments off, even my boots. Vying for a position in front of the wood burner, my feet nearly fried. The warmth began to penetrate deep into my bones. Sylvia's house wasn't insulated, and everybody usually walked around with a coat on and blankets wrapped around them, but now I couldn't have been cozier with these fine people and a wood burner. Lika made friends instantly with Ron's black Lab. Yipping, rolling on the floor, growling, and biting his ear, she had a great time. Sandy heated up some packaged ginseng tea and cut me a piece of apple pie. This was living. The four of us sat around and talked a lot about spiritual things. I told Bill that he could tell me about Jesus if I could tell him about the native people's beliefs. He warmly agreed, and so we went into deep discussions about our views. Ron and Sandy listened intently and gradually began sharing with us their interest in Eastern meditations. Nothing was settled, but we all remained friends. Three hours had passed quickly.

Bill got up abruptly and said, "I'll be going now; it was a pleasure meeting you."

"Yeah, you, too," I said, a bit startled that he'd be leaving.

Ron and Sandy insisted that he stay the evening, but he graciously refused. Concerned, Ron asked, "Well, what are you going to do?"

Bill, with the voice of a martyr replied, "I'll walk; that's no problem; the Lord will guide me and keep me safe."

I admired his guts, stamina and faith, but I couldn't help thinking that it was frosted with stubbornness and pride. Ron looked shocked and baffled as he felt the need to apologize.

"I'll be happy to drive you back to town, but there's no way that I'd even get my truck out to the road; the plows won't be through this way for two days."

Bill assured us all, "I'll be just fine."

"Well, I said, I'll be leaving too, then I guess." I was really hoping that Ron and Sandy would extend their invitation to sleepover to me instead. The thought of going back to that house, a freezing bedroom, and hatred in the air, wasn't very appealing. With scarves over our faces, all we could see were our eyes. Then Bill and I shook hands and hugged each other somewhere in the middle of what was the road. I stood there with the wind at my back and watched Bill hobble away up the road in this blinding subzero blizzard. He'd never make it the ten miles back to Bemidji; I couldn't help but think that. Everyone had already gone to bed by the time I came in. Curled up in my blue sleeping bag, fully dressed; I could only think about Bill trudging his way through the snow as he talked to the Lord. I never heard another word concerning him from that night on.

First thing when morning came I went out to feed Lika. Her eyes were frozen shut; she couldn't move. Someone had said that they thought that it reached fifty six below last night. I didn't care what Sylvia would say; I took Lika in and called the vet. All he had to say was, "See if she thaws out." "You think she'll be all right?"

"Yeah," he assured me, "dogs can take it." Her eyes began to open within three hours.

"Well, happily she was back to normal by noon, but then Sylvia sternly commanded, "Your dog's got to go outside now." Sylvia's daughter loved Lika and probably felt as bad as I did that she couldn't stay in.

I went out to see if the tipi poles were still standing and noticed that a full gallon of antifreeze had frozen solid and expanded, ripping the plastic container open. Really, I'm not kidding, it got that cold. The poles were still standing, but I couldn't imagine where I'd put it up here. The snow was now very deep. I almost thought about raising it up in Sylvia's aluminum barn that had a forty-foot ceiling.

Two days later when the plow came through, I fired up the Rambler and drove over to Jim's. For being a California vehicle, the Rambler did all right. I needed to call my dad and see if he'd send me fifty dollars. I only had three dollars left. What was I going to do? The last time that my dad had heard from me was eight months ago in Ben Lomond when I sent him a tape of some songs I had written. Should I try to find a job up here? How was I going to make it? I can't stay at Sylvia's much longer; it was becoming very hostile there. I wasn't even allowed to use her phone. The hospitality wore off; the warm welcome had seen its limit. Even her son's friend who also lived there, started to hate me with a vengeance, calling me an intruder. After repeated tries during the day, my dad finally answered in the evening. "Yeah, Dad, it's Ray; I'm in Northern Minnesota. Can you help me out with fifty dollars?"

"You're where?"

"I'm in Bemidji, Minnesota, the northern part of the state, staying with some friends."

He swore at me and slammed the phone down. I guess I didn't expect him to be happy to hear from me, but I thought for sure he'd send me some money. He meant it this time; he wanted nothing to do with me.

Back at Sylvia's I sat in my ten-by-six foot, unheated bedroom and quietly strummed an old Kay guitar that was lying around. It had the fifth string missing, and the rest of the strings were rusted, but it was comforting to hear open chords again. I hadn't realized until then just how much I missed having a guitar around. I hummed a simple melody while strumming some chords. Not since four months ago in Ben Lomond had I played music. The night was frigid again, and stars shown through my north window. Sitting at the end of the bed, holding a guitar, everything seemed to be hopeful. A subtle voice assured me that tomorrow would be a good day.

Sylvia let me use the phone to call the social services office. Ron said he heard that they gave vagrants money to help them get out of town along with forty dollars' worth of food stamps. The bargain that I made with Sylvia was this: "if you let me use the phone to call social services and see what their hours are, I'll give you all the food stamps I get." She couldn't refuse. At the social services office, I humbly stood in line with other poorly dressed, poverty-stricken folks. When it was my turn at the desk, I surrendered with my arms up and matter of factly stated that I needed gas money to get back to Grafton, Wisconsin. That's about five hundred fifty miles. The lady was pleasant; let's call her Carol. She asked for my driver's license, which gave the Ben Lomond, California address. I explained as briefly as I could about my circumstances. She rolled her eyes a bit and wrote me a government check for thirty dollars. She asked: "Will $30 be enough?"

"Yeah, sure, that should be plenty." She told me where to cash it and placed it in my hand along with a book of food stamps worth about forty dollars.

With a kind twinkle in her eyes, Carol sweetly said, "Now I want you to buy gas with that $30."

"Yes, ma'am, I will."

By one o'clock that afternoon I was pulling out of Sylvia's driveway with Lika bouncing all over the front seat. One last glance was given to those golden tipi poles standing firm, glistening in the winter sun. A brief stop was made at Ron and Sandy's. They weren't home, so I wrote a note thanking them for being my friends. I had to stop at Jim's and thank him also. His door was partially opened; he wasn't answering. I cautiously walked in. He was lying on his side in the living room, moaning and breathing deeply. I woke him with some Epson salt that was on the kitchen table. His face was gaunt, his eyes squinted and bloodshot, and his voice was very weak. He started confessing to me something about overdosing. He knew it would happen; he couldn't keep taking that stuff. His heart hurt. "Jim, are you okay to be left alone? I'm leaving now to go back home. Should I get your mom over here?" The thought of his mother seeing him like this was enough to cause him to sit up. He gave a nervous, affirmative, "I'll be okay," and fell asleep resting against the torn up, stained recliner.

Driving out of town on Highway 2, heading toward Duluth-Superior, Paul Bunyon and his blue ox, Babe, seemed to nod their farewell, "Thanks for coming; see you again."

"I don't think so," I replied in my mind. I was glad to be leaving.

CHAPTER 16

JOHN'S PLACE

O n or around December 28th, the Rambler and I putt, putt, putted into Grafton. I had no feelings of defeat. To the contrary, I felt like a rugged victor. I had truly given it my all just as I had in New York City. I had become callused from the city and toughened from the country. Mike Haupt or Randy Liska would be my best bet on finding a place to stay for a while. Within half an hour, I located the house in Grafton where they were living. This place was a hangout; it seemed that at least six guys actually lived there, and another six just hung out or crashed someplace. John was the fellow who owned the house. His appearance was neat, straight, and clean-cut. He had a full-time job and went part-time to vocational school. Seemed odd that he'd let such a nice house go to pot, but this suited him just fine. Friends and strangers greeted me warmly alike as if I had found my way out of the lost tribe. It was good to be home again with real friends, new friends— people that I trusted. That was my welcoming party. John offered me the couch in his basement to sleep on for as long as I needed. This was very generous of him to give yet another freeloader a place to stay. The basement was warm, and I had access to the kitchen and bathroom. Lika could even come in once in a while. I needed to hang loose for a while, to rest, dream, and scheme. John's was the place.

Everybody oohed and aahed at my natural foods and weird teas. Humor abounded; it was good fun. I was revered as a teacher of new ways; hundreds of questions were asked of me, running the gamut from, "What's the difference between brown rice and white rice?" to "Can you actually contact the spirit realm?" Many nights were spent with my friends in deep conversation well into the morning hours. A possible cult was forming with me as the guru. Drugs here were plentiful, and I partook of my share. The more marijuana that I smoked, the deeper the supernatural conversations became. An image of the Avatar, the enlightened one, filled me with beams of purpose. It became glorifying to my ego to experience people seated before me, listening intently with awakened eyes. But what would I do for money? I borrowed about fifty dollars from Mike and assured him that he'd get paid back as soon as I got a job. A job! Oh, horrors, did I really have to? It was the necessary evil, spiritual master or no spiritual master.

I gave a quick call up to Ron in Bemidji and asked him if he'd store my tipi poles for me. I would be up by the end of the month to get them. He said, "Sure, I'd be happy to." Great, I had that taken care of. I still had planned on setting that thing up somewhere but not until spring. I was becoming soft, just lying around, slowly burning out. Marijuana tried to convince me to relax, take it easy, what was the hurry? It wasn't in my blood though, at least not my Polish blood.

Ron called back the next evening. "Your poles aren't there; I think somebody cut them up for firewood."

"What?!" Anger surged through me. I knew who had done this. I reasoned to Ron, "Of what use is soft wood to anybody? It burns like paper. They all knew that I was coming back to get them." Every negative emotion was eating at me: rage, revenge, frustration, sorrow, and hurt. "Thanks anyway, Ron; you tried."

He simply said, "Sorry Ray; we'll see you. Bye."

Bemidji still wouldn't let go as two weeks later I received a sober apologetic letter from Jim. It basically read, "Ray, I've been such a jerk. I've partied until my life fell apart. My girlfriend left me. I'm going straight; I've joined the Navy." Well, I was glad to hear that he wanted to straighten up, but the Navy? It just seemed like such an extreme measure for him to take.

Lika was moving out of the puppy awkward stage into becoming a beautiful dog, mostly collie with gorgeous markings and a white shaggy mantle gracing her chest. She was a good dog, followed me everywhere, and stayed when I said, "Stay." Everybody liked her. She was my kind of dog.

There was a rock band called Bonniwell Road practicing in the basement next to my couch. Certainly I was asked to join. Jim Bohn, a guy to whom I gave guitar lessons back in high school, was heading it up. Dan Burgard (Bogey), who sat in on bass upstairs at my dad's in 1968, was also there. Mike Haupt played clarinet, and my good friend Randy Liska completed it on drums. "Maybe we can get something going here," I thought. We practiced diligently two nights a week and weekends in John's basement. We did some older songs and quite a few contemporary ones that I had never heard as I had been out of musical circulation since 1969. It was now mid-January, 1973. I figured out all instrumentation and harmonies for the song "Roundabout" by the group "Yes." People were impressed at how good it sounded, just like the record. It was encouraging to see that I still had it in me.

On the premier night of our first public appearance, we were squeezed onto a ten-by-five foot stage in back of the bar at the bowling alley in Grafton. We were so nervous, but who could tell over the noise of the drunk crowd and six lanes of bowling? In all honesty, we stunk. Mistake after mistake was made; I was extremely embarrassed, and the band folded that evening. My heart and direction was not into putting in thousands of hours of hard work just to haul equipment around and hope to financially break even. Anyway, the bar/dance hall atmosphere was no longer my world. I was Ray Last; I was onto something big; I was onto the spirit world.

Steve Tillman popped in quite often at John's house. Last time I recalled seeing Steve was when we played together as boys on 11th Avenue in Grafton. We lived just a half a block from each other. Now he had long, stringy blond hair and a blue headband. Steve was the only other person I knew around here who was into natural foods and had an inkling for the spiritual. We met in the middle from extremes. That is, I came out of the Bemidji icebox, and he just arrived from the Florida Gulf Coast. With our common interests, we hit it off immediately, and we stayed closely in touch for years to come.

Nearly a month had passed before I let my dad know that I was back in Grafton. When I finally called him, he just yawned on the telephone and called me a freak. John's house was only seven blocks from my dad's, but we didn't bump into each other for another eight months. During this period of my life, I wouldn't have gone to his funeral. Family and relatives were kept at a remote distance.

Mike said that he'd lend me more money if I could find a farmhouse to rent, so I put an ad in the Ozaukee County paper. It read: "Couple looking to rent farmhouse in rural area of Ozaukee County.

Responsible." A couple of what? A couple of hippies and their friends. The same day that the paper came out, I received a phone call; a farmer had an old house about twelve miles southwest of John's place. He wanted two hundred dollars a month. Everyone at John's house was so discouraging, saying, "He'll never rent it to you once he sees you."

I boldly retorted, "Maybe not, but I'm going out there anyway."

CHAPTER 17

WAUSAUKEE ROAD

A rnold Schoessow was a no-nonsense farmer, who had a lot of everything. He was hard-working, firm, kind, exacting, open, and generous, with still enough room left over for light humor. The house he was renting was one-half mile south of his own. It seemed that he farmed all this land. To the east across Wausaukee Road was a forest with no homes for two miles. To the west were rolling hills, meadows, farmlands, and woods extending for miles. There was just one neighbor to the north and south a quarter mile away. I loved the place—the seclusion, the rustic ambiance. Trying to impress upon Arnold that I was responsible in spite of my looks seemed like a hard-driven chore. He did kink his ear somewhat to my sincere expressions for a peaceful, quiet, country life with natural foods and gardening. He consented; the place was ours. Beaming with joy back at his house, I met his wife and son. There were nice people. Moving in required nothing. Between me, Mike Haupt, Randy Liska, and Shelly, we had virtually no furniture or kitchenware. We soon moved into this big, empty, old log-framed, brown-shingled farmhouse.

Within a week I had a full-time job three miles down the road at the Organic Compost Company. I paid Mike back within a month. I truly wanted to finally settle down for a while. Money was no longer a worry. Now what could be more natural than working with cow and sheep manure, acres of it, mound upon mound? Seagulls knew its value. They made the eight mile flight west from Lake Michigan just to rest on these steamy manure piles. The late February winter seemed mild compared to Bemidji, and I spent fifty hours a week heaving neatly packaged twenty-five and fifty pound bags of manure onto trucks for spring and early summer delivery. Bull work, but I could handle it.

There were occasions when my work partner Bob and I would load flatbed trucks out in the open methane air. The gas that was created from decomposing manure got to us many times. The symptoms were uncontrollable laughter. Everything was funny. Once because of laughing so hard, Bob became buried in an avalanche of fifty-pound bags that kept falling off the conveyor belt. These bags had glue spread on the top of them to prevent them from shifting on the flatbed trucks. They came off the movable conveyor belt quickly, one after another. We could not slip up while palletizing five-foot stacks. But on this warm April day, the gas overcame us. We had painful, unstoppable laughter. Bob fell to the bed of the truck and bags just kept rolling off the line. He became buried! I frantically tried pulling the bags off of him. It was futile as they adhered themselves to one another. Bob couldn't breathe. I couldn't see him; I couldn't hear him. I kicked the conveyor off the truck letting the bags drop to the ground. I tore bag after bag off of him with maddening force. Bob looked faint with the fear of death and was covered with slimy yellow glue. The big question was spoken from my mouth, "Are you okay?" He started laughing, I started laughing, but our boss left his humor elsewhere. It took a few hours to clean up the mess of broken bags, and we never could remember the original joke that touched it off.

It was during my stay at Organic Compost that I became exposed to and learned to appreciate Paul Harvey's syndicated radio show at noon during the lunch room break. Many of the guys would huddle around the radio while eating their lunch out of real lunch boxes. The only noise you'd hear from them while Paul Harvey did his routine was some grunting, munching, and occasional laughter. "Good day, Paul Harvey." It was easy to get hooked on his show.

By the end of April, everyone else had moved out of the house except for Shelly and me. The spring of '73 would be a big one for me. Out came Gurney's Seed Catalog. I choose a sunny spot for a large garden. It had never been tilled before; there were only tall grass and weeds. Turning the soil with a shovel was physically demanding, but after twenty hours of digging, I had a virgin area fifty by twenty feet, ready to plant. Not so dumb this time, I used companion planting and wide-aisled rows. Say, don't ever buy a praying mantis cocoon; these insect-eating stick creatures tend to wander off. You can't fence them in, either. I guess all you could do was buy an infestation of insects so that the praying mantis wouldn't look for greener pastures. I mean, maybe they don't really eat insects; maybe they just pray them away.

I joined a natural foods co-op in Milwaukee called Outpost Natural Foods. This was truly an alternative grocery store. After you did your odds-and-ends shopping, you could use the scales in the back to weigh out marijuana. Outpost has moved twice since those days and is now one of the largest natural food stores in Wisconsin.

I still was driving the Rambler around, and it never did die, but it was virtually given to my friend Bob. All it really needed was a gas tank. I was parked on a hill at Boelkhe's Hardware store in the small village of Freistadt and glanced out of the window to see my car rolling down. A school bus laid on the horn and swerved to miss it. Smack! The back end of the Rambler hit a low cement wall. Gee, I found myself in the weirdest situations. The gas tank was ripped off, and all ten gallons ran out down the road. I can't say I remember how I got the car back home, but my makeshift gas tank was interesting, just a five-gallon gas can in the back with a rubber hose coming out into the gas line. Dangerous you say? Only if it exploded. I sure did stop for gas a lot. At that time we could still use Organic Composts gas pumps at twenty-seven cents a gallon. Bob needed a car bad, as he was moving back up north. The Rambler was his for fifty dollars. He even installed a real gas tank on it.

The late spring lay-off came at Organic Compost. Great, now I had a lot of time to garden, meditate, and just hang out. Walking barefoot through the fields, I caught red clover between my toes. The itch came in a big way to put my tipi back up.

I spread the plain canvas out on the front lawn. It stretched thirty feet, end to end. Hours were spent slopping light blue latex paint on it with a three-inch brush. My hands cramped up, and my eyes saw everything in a blue tint after staring at this cover in the glaring sun. Very significant interpretive designs were painted on it in multi-colors. Black earth, green grass, blue skies, clouds rising, a circular design for the four winds and a red, twenty-foot abstract eagle hovering over. Wow, it had to be spiritual now.

My good friend, Joe Zingsheim, the music storeowner in Grafton, told me about Melvin Uhlig and that I could probably cut nice straight cedar trees off of his property. I phoned Melvin Uhlig, who lived in Waubeka. By the way, Waubeka, Wisconsin, is the home of Flag Day.

After a very brief phone call, I headed up to his farm. Melvin was the real thing: in his mid-60s, with a heavy German-English accent; he was a purebred farmer. Chickens ran all over the yard, an ax was leaning on the stump, and a shotgun was resting by the door. I was really nervous; would he be mean? At least we had a common friend in Joey Zingsheim. Really, consider this, if you were an old farmer around 1973 in a very rural area, miles from a town, what would you make of a short, long-haired hippie wanting to cut seventeen cedar trees off your land so he could put up his tipi? Melvin hit a time warp; maybe he'd never seen anything like me, just read about it in disbelief. Even his dog's hair stood up. Melvin commented, "She usually barks when strangers drive up, but she's just staring at you." I chanced it with my left hand and petted her. Hmm, I got same dog functions and responses: wagging tail, slobbering mouth, uncontrollable body. The dog accepted me. Melvin felt reassured after witnessing old Spot's approval. He confidently stated, "Seventy-five cents a tree; they're down in the swampy area by the curve." Several months would pass before I actually journeyed up to Uhlig's farm to cut the trees.

I kept thinking a lot about having to get another cheap job, and by the end of May, I was hired on at Brown Deer Tree Nursery just a few miles north down Wausaukee Road. This seemed ideal, two hundred acres, all outside work, not much thinking required, and all the foreman told me to do on my first day was to grab an idiot stick. Hmm, I didn't even know what an idiot stick was. The workers, mostly Mexicans, had a good laugh on me. He threw me a shovel and said, "Get on the wagon; they'll show you what to do." Hey, nine hours of this was ridiculous. My hands had blisters, my feet were ripped up as I thought it would be natural to go barefoot, and I'm sure that my shoulders were sunburned. Man, those Mexicans could work. I thought it strange that they all wore dark sweatshirts in eighty-degree weather.

An older man that I worked with commuted from Milwaukee just so he could be out in the fields, forest, air, and warm sun, away from it all. He seemed very mellow and durable. His skin had layers of a dark tan. I remember working alongside him, digging weeds around the arborvitae bushes as he expressed his love for this very natural setting of forest, rolling hills, warm sun, good air, and hard work. He just focused on me with a contented smile; hands clenched as if squeezing a rubber ball, and vibrantly stated, "It looks so good I could just eat it!" He certainly had a tremendous appreciation for creation. We shared our spiritual longings, and he suggested that I study the teachings of Gautama Buddha. He made it very clear to me and firmly said, "But only Gautama, as this is true Buddhism." Well, Buddha was too foreign for me. I didn't want to break the spiritual rhythm that I was pursuing with the North American Indians. I felt like I'd betray them if I sought some other way to God.

I worked ten weeks at Brown Deer Nursery and then was sort of fired. I had permission from my foreman to leave at two o'clock in the afternoon on a Thursday to take Shelly to the dentist. As I was driving through the open wire mesh gate, an old man yelled out, "Hey! Where you going?" I never saw this frail-looking man before.

I yelled back, "I have to take my girlfriend to the dentist."

He waved a cane at me and proclaimed, "Don't come back," and proceeded to creep back into this little white house. I backed my truck into the nursery yard and asked the foreman what this was all about. He had a grieved look and told me that that was the owner who was visiting from Pasadena. "He has just fired you." Hey, maybe this was okay, I could probably collect some unemployment and food stamps and spend a lot of time reading the many spiritual esoteric books I'd been buying. I could fast for days and wander the fields talking to God and finally get my tipi set up.

Right around early August '73, I ventured back to Melvin Uhlig's in my newly acquired 1964 Dodge Pickup. I made a shaky wooden rack on the bed of the truck to transport the poles. The mosquitoes were so thick in this semi-swampy area where the cedar trees were that I had to wear a mechanic's jumpsuit, rubber boots, pullover cap, and gloves, just to protect myself. It was an oppressive ninety-ninety day, that is, ninety degrees with ninety percent humidity. The selection of young white cedar trees was super. Each tree was swiftly felled, branches hacked off, and dragged to the truck. Working hard and being dressed for October had drained me in the heat, but I only received about ten mosquito bites on my face. It could have been thousands. Melvin took a count of the poles and like a financial wizard with certainty, he said, "You've got twelve dollars and sixty-five cents' worth."

My third set of poles, and the same process was started all over again—I stripped the bark with a spoke shave knife and stood them up to dry. A good thirty-five hours was spent from cutting to stripping. My spiritual senses advanced to being able to see a yellow, blue, and green aura emulating around the tipi poles. A cozy spot was found to put the tipi up; it was a power spot. In one of the books that I was reading, the writer went into detail on the importance of finding your spiritual power spot wherever you are, whether in a room or in a field. He used a lower life form example of dogs and how they circle and circle before they lie down. I actually bought this theory for a while. All I needed was yet another ritual to layer myself with. Hey, as months went on, it got worse. More rituals were added, and in less than one year's time, I would actually have advanced to using a pendulum and watching it swing to answer my questions. My own personal spirit guides were called on constantly to decide where I should go and which roads to take, what tea to drink, and who to talk to. It became obsessively absurd. But let me not drift too far into the spiritual pulp. Back to my more normal tipi days.

Raising the tipi was a great thrill, really quite picturesque. It was about one hundred fifty feet from Wausaukee Road, and passers-by nearly came to a halt to gawk. I had determined to succeed with using an open flame fire pit, and I did. I buried three-inch stovepipe from the pit to outside. Using two pipe elbows, I brought it above ground about two feet and had an adjustable end on it so I could turn it in the direction of the wind to draw air on the fire. It worked actually quite well.

Friends I hadn't seen for year's risked uncertainty to drive out and visit. I was usually amicable. I offered them my blends of teas, along with a smoke of Kinnikinnick herbal mixture from my goat hornpipe. Yep, I saved the horns from that disgusting billy up in Bemidji. They made rather caustic-smelling pipes, but that was the price of partaking in a good spiritual smoke. After the air cleared, I recognized who my visitors were. I didn't believe it; they were Ron and Tom Roy! Even Mike Sipin came along, the man who replaced me as guitarist in my old band, the Misery Sons.

There was thick tension in the air; my conversation was centered on the ethereal esoteric plane, and theirs was just plain. That is, until Tom and Ron gradually started talking about who Jesus Christ is. I felt cornered and became angrily defensive. Both Tom and Ron sensed this hostility and continued to talk with peace and calmness. I just couldn't handle hearing any more talk about being saved or going to hell. Being saved from what? As far as I was concerned, just having to function in a crazy world filled with greed, hatred, lies, and deception was hell in itself. I shut out all their conversation and kept barking about how that I was truly living a spiritual life. I continued to tell them about how I fasted, kept my body clean, prayed to spirit beings, and mediated. With my voice raised and blood vessels bulging, I nearly screamed, "So there! Don't talk to me about spiritual things; you're the people who are lost. Why, I even converse at night with the Archangel Michael. Anyway, the Bible is full of contradictions, and the original language has been lost. I don't need your stiff beliefs!" I fully believed what the books I had been reading exclaimed about the Bible though I never read it for myself.

Mike didn't take these remarks too kindly, but Tom and Ron just quickly got up and said, "We'll be praying for you. We didn't come over to offend you, just to have a friendly visit."

Boy, I was broken inside. These were two of my best friends, but the chasm between us was great. I thought about the simple fun I had with Tom as he followed the Misery Sons around and all the clowning he did with us and Ma Swatko. I reflected on my visiting him in Grafton, West Virginia, and staying overnight at his home in Indiana after leaving New York City. I really liked Tom and, of course, Ron also. But I couldn't let myself be pulled down by sentimental friend-ship. This spiritual thing was quickly uncovering itself, and I knew that I'd break through to God soon.

They left, but others came in a different fashion, like Jim Bohn. Often we sat in the tipi lodge savoring the flickering atmosphere of the fire. Jim just sat in awe as he listened intently to the wisdom and insight that poured from me concerning spiritual matters and life.

In the fall of 1973 I purchased a beautiful concert body, Guild acoustic guitar. It was an F50 R model with Rosewood sides and back. I spent considerable time music store-hopping, trying out numerous acoustic guitars until I found this one. The price of this guitar was $1,500.00. It was the most expensive guitar that I looked at. I traded the music store owner my Fender Vibrolux Reverb amp plus $900.00 and took the Guild home. The sound that this guitar produced filled the air with loud, full, rich tones. This Guild brought a similar sensation to me as that of my very first Red Harmony guitar. I played and sang and played and sang. I don't know all that was going through Jim Bohn's mind and being, but he sat mesmerized while listening to my songs. I relished his audience; I was hungry for people to hear me and give me praise. The power of commanding their attention drove me to continue playing music and searching out God.

Steve Tillmann became a regular visitor as we had the same mindset for natural foods, fasting, meditation, and spiritual *loopyness*. Tom Johnson, one of the lead singers from the Misery Sons also dropped in for a friendly visit.

After working August and September at Wetzel's apple orchard picking Courtland's, Delicious, and McIntosh apples, I not only toughened up but became proficient at picking. When the apple season came to an end, I applied and was hired on full-time at the Kasch Company, a large toy distributor. Money became plentiful.

I placed a weekly order to Yes Books out of Washington, DC. I went all out purchasing weird, pathfinder books. Here's a sampling of some titles: *Alchemy, Science of the Cosmos: Science of the Soul* by Titus Burckhardt; *Secret of the Andes* by Brother Phillip; *Astral Projection* by Dr. Carrington; *A Treatise on the 7 Rays; Esoteric Psychology, A Treatise of White Magic, Reappearance of the Christ* and *Discipleship in the New Age* by Alice Bailey; *The Massage Book* by George Downing; *Edgar Cayce on ESP; Chuang Tzu* by Burton Watson; *The Heart of Confucius* by Archie Bahm; *Genesis Revised; Lost Books Of The Bible; Colour Meditations with a Guide to Color Healing* by S. G. J. Ousley; *Color and Music in a New Age* by Corinne Heline; *The Wesak Festival* by Alice Bailey; *Kirlian Electrophotography Data Package* by Paul Sauvin; *Guru Nanak, Guru For The Aquarian Age* by Premka Kaur; *Spirit Guides, Access to Inner Worlds* by Mike Samuels and Hal Bennett; *In Quest of God* by Swami Randas; *Magic, Its Ritual Power and Purpose* by W.E. Butler; *The 6th And 7th Books of Moses* by Lewis DeClaremont; *Cosmos in Man* by H. Saraydarian; *Music and Healing* by Lionel Stebbing; *Music, Its Secret Influence throughout the Ages* by Cyril Scott; *Aquarian Disciples* by Simons Roof; *Tai Chi And the I Ching Centering* by Gia Fu Feng and Jerome Kirk.

And, of course, a full array of North American Indian writings such as: *The 7 Rites Of The Oglala Sioux and the Sacred Pipe* by Black Elk; *Hopi, A Message for all People* by Dan Katchongua; *Indian Sign Language* by William Tomkins; *The Great Law of Peace of the Long House People, Iroquois* published by the White Roots of Peace;

The Good Medicine Book by Adolf Hungry Wolf. Finally, a book that greatly inspired and moved me, '*Lame Deer, Seeker of Visions.*'

It became apparent that I had finally whittled this spiritual arsenal of books and ways down to the Oglala Sioux. Well, that was a relief, now at least I knew what to dive into and to immerse my concentration on. I imagined at that time that I was probably was a Sioux warrior in a past life. Well, maybe. I mean, why would I be so intensely drawn to the Sioux and their lifestyle?

On a mid-September day in 1973, I headed for Winner, South Dakota. I had planned to hitchhike all the way with the hope of meeting up with Lame Deer. I just felt deeply that this encounter would be heavenly ordained. Great meaning, purpose, and direction would come from it. It just had to. Everything was so quickly falling in place. It was seventy-two degrees when I left that morning. All that I wore was a short-sleeved shirt, and I brought along a heavy flannel one, just in case. The six hundred fifty miles could easily be done in two days, I imagined.

After about five rides, I finally crossed the Wisconsin-Minnesota border but became stranded for hours at a highway bridge. It was about six o'clock in the evening, and the temperature was dropping severely. My flannel shirt just didn't do it. It began snowing; I thought that this was crazy; it was only September 15. I climbed up the slanted abutment under the freeway and laid my sleeping bag down. There was only eighteen inches clearance from the cement ledge that I was laying on to the bottom of the highway bridge. It wasn't quite as nice as Best Western, but it was flat, without bumps. Yeah, flat, hard, and cold. I laid up there all night being lulled into a state of depression and homesickness by the constant rumble of cars and trucks. About six inches of snow fell that evening.

At daybreak, while it was still blowing and snowing, I climbed back down and started thumbing a ride at the on-ramp. The first car picked me up. It was a nice car; the man was definitely a wealthy businessman. I couldn't imagine why he'd pick up scuzz like me. He was kind, friendly, and seemed really wise. All I really remembered about our conversation was his telling me that he was a Christian, and he didn't need to go through what I was going through. He very wisely turned to me and said, "You don't have to do this to know God." His wealth started to look pretty good. Especially inviting was his warm, luxurious automobile. He took me as far as Austin, Minnesota.

The people that I rode with before him warned me not to get dropped off in Austin, Minnesota. "Nobody will pick you up," they said. Well, I was in no position to be choosy. Anyway, I was halfway there. I stood and stood at the on-ramp as hundreds of cars passed by. It was now getting to be late morning. This day was turning into a nice mild sunny day with no signs that it had ever snowed overnight. The warning about not getting a ride out of Austin, Minnesota, was being fulfilled.

After six hours of standing there hungry, thirsty, and desperate. I finally made the decision to hang it up and forget Lame Deer for now. I just wanted to get back home. I walked several miles to the Greyhound station and took the next bus back to Madison, Wisconsin. Shelly picked me up around midnight, and I drove her car the two and one-half hours back home, wiped out, to say the least. So, what's the spiritual message here? None that I could figure out.

My fervent desire to penetrate the spirit world continued to become more pronounced. In late September, while running clockwise in an open meadow under a moonlit sky, I heard an audible voice speak clearly with certain authority: Ayuta, you will write seven songs in seven months and then leave."

I asked, "Who are you?"

The voice softly cut through the crisp fall air, "I'm the Archangel Michael." Whoa, this was too much, I was being divinely appointed to write songs.

The full name that I had heard that evening was, Ayuta Rai. I was soon to discover that this was a Native American phrase meaning: "Looks to the energy of the Lord." Shelly and all new acquaintances only knew me now as Ayuta. I disowned my birth name for a meaningful name. Even at the Kasch Company among the one hundred twenty-five employees, I was only known as Ayuta. It just stung at my pride to see my real name typed on my punch card at work, Raymond A. Last. I usually hid my card behind other cards by the time clock. For the next year and a half all correspondence to my father and everyone else was signed from Ayuta Rai.

There was a large fallen tree near the tipi, and many of my meditative hours were spent kneeling before this old tree asking it questions and seeking its advice and guidance. Borderline insane? No, I believe that I actually stepped over the border. It became more and more difficult to have normal conversations with anybody. And was understandably so. I wasn't normal.

I subscribed to a home-study course on musical astrology. This chart placed my keynote chord as D flat. I hate D flat. I mean, I almost never played that chord on a guitar, but sure enough, I forced myself to write songs and sing mantras in D flat. Admittedly, I felt no supernatural uplifting. Actually, the opposite occurred. My music was dry and lifeless. I dropped the course and saved big money. In 1976, Stevie Wonder put out a nice album called "Songs in the Key of Life." Perhaps he had a better musical astrologer.

Ah, but one course I did take and manage to complete was through the Institute of Herbal Philosophy, a twelve-week course designed to make you a crack shot herbal doctor. I learned a lot and experimented on my best friends. Shortly after I passed this course, the California Department of Health and Medicine shut the place down. They were illegal. What, no degree? You mean I'm out ten bucks?

Well, here it was, late November and my seven songs in seven months were right on schedule. Two songs were written in two months, "October Skies," and one other. Seven songs were actually written in seven months. They were really good songs, too. And oddly enough, the reel-to-reel tape of those songs has been lost—the only recordings of mine that were ever lost or misplaced since I began my own recordings at nine years old. I can barely remember any of those, 'Lost Songs'.

CHAPTER 18

ALASKA ON MY MIND

Around this same time in early winter 1973, I began corresponding with numerous people from Canada and Alaska who had placed personal ads in the *Mother Earth News*. As weeks went on, my thoughts focused on buying land up there somewhere—homestead land or maybe under a land contract. Both the Canadian and Alaskan Government Land Bureaus were extremely helpful, and I received a wealth of information that always included beautifully prepared brochures on rivers, lakes, mountains, forests, and wildlife. I did not have the desire to go through the entanglement of paperwork to become a Canadian citizen, so I set my sights more and more on Alaska, south of the Alaskan range, in a climate similar to southern Wisconsin's. Ah, yes, pure crisp air, snowcapped mountains, eagles, crystal lakes, and virtually no people. I could be self-sufficient; eighty percent confidence was mine already. Listen, if the Russos from New York City could go to the Yukon, I could homestead in Alaska.

So I found myself being controlled by yet another craze: Ayuta of Alaska. I started browsing through the list of self-help nature books and began to order books such as the *Mother Earth News Almanac, How to Tan Hides,* and *Free for the Eating,* by Bradford Angier. I also read *The Weed Cookbook,* by Adrienne Crowhurst; *The Herbalist* by Joseph Meyer; *Camping and Woodcraft* by Horace Kemphart; *Indian Uses of Native Plants* by Edith Van Allen Murphey; *Outdoor Survival Skills* by Larry Dean Olsen; *American Indian Medicine* by Virgil Vogel; and *Log Cabin Living, How To Build A Hogan.*

Really, being quite naïve is best when it comes to some types of daring adventure. There are many things I never would have done if

I had hindsight. Most interesting experiences would have passed me by. There's usually a fair amount of fear, apprehension, and uncertainty in venturing out into unknown areas, but unique individuals have this drive in their blood. The excitement and anticipation of experiencing totally new things outweighs the odds. I needed to start saving money though.

While working on the third song, I began taking the seven songs/seven months vision more seriously. My mind was set on leaving for Alaska at the end of April; four and one-half months were left. Winter was just settling in, and spring seemed so distant.

I acquired, from an old retired fox farm, a nice big insulated house that became Lika's outside home. But on these colder days I let her come in more. She was so good, and I guess that I was just happy that she was alive. She was missing for three days in November, which was very unusual for her. I called around to local neighbors and also Walter Peuschel, a farmer who took stray animals in for the county. There had been no sign of Lika. The good cheer that I normally had left me. Gee, she had really been a part of my life for over a year. I doubt that I would have gotten another dog. Lika just turned out the way that I had envisioned my dog behaving. It seemed so empty coming home from work and not having Lika run down the driveway to greet me. I used to spend ten or fifteen minutes wrestling with her on the lawn. She'd make all these whining dog noises out of excitement and joy. The thought that she was lying dead somewhere began to consume my mind.

After the third day that she was missing, I received a call from a boy who said he thought he knew where my dog was. "She's in a field, hurt bad, but I'm not sure if she's alive." I took off in the truck and drove the four miles like a maniac. Running through some brush and wetlands, I spotted an animal lying in the field some two hundred feet away. It was Lika; she was all beaten up. She was barely breathing, and her eyes were closed. Part of her lip was ripped out, and she had deep cuts on her face. It looked like maybe a raccoon got her. Gently, I carried her to the truck, whispering comforting words.

After bringing her in the house, she still was unresponsive and wouldn't even drink water. She just lay there limp, breathing erratically in her pitiful state. I kept applying Vitamin E gel from capsules on her lip and cuts. For three days she remained this way with no signs of improvement. I probably should have gone to the vet with her, but a part of me felt that I could be an aide in the healing process. On the fourth day—glory hallelujah—she stood up and drank water and even ate a little. Ecstatic relief ballooned in me. It was incredible. By the fifth day, she was chasing around in the yard again.

Shortly after Lika's big encounter with what may have been a raccoon, she had a miscarriage. The local vet said that she might not be able to carry puppies because of the pelvic injury that occurred when I ran her over back in Bemidji.

January '74 came on big. There were numerous below-zero days and lots of snow. I pretty much closed the tipi up until spring. It just wasn't too cozy in there at ten degrees below zero with thirty mile-per-hour winds. I spent evenings reading mystical books and studying Alaskan maps. In mid-January, we were clobbered with a blizzard. There were high winds up to fifty miles-per-hour and eighteen inches of snow.

As I sat, bundled next to the oil space heater in this uninsulated log frame house, I had an uneasy fear that the tipi was no longer withstanding the storm. The uncertainty became too much, so I bundled up with all my winter gear and set out to inspect the tipi, if it was even still there. Though it was only one hundred fifty feet from the house, the severe winds, biting cold, lashing snow, and four-foot drifts made for a rugged trek. It was about eight o'clock at night, and I groped about in the backyard trying to get my direction right. Obviously, all I could see was a shaded white sheet of snow. After about five minutes of exhausting trudging through the drifts, I bumped into the immovable cone. There it stood, fully draped in white, not only holding its own to the wind but showing no ripples. It was drum tight. "Boy!," I thought, "the native people really came up with a fabulous design." The harsh wind could not hit the tipi broadside, it just 'whooshed' around it. Legend has it that the Great Spirit showed them this design.

Working at the Kasch Company as an order puller and general warehouser was grueling and physically taxing. There seemed to be endless lengths of conveyor belts hooking into twenty-four loading docks. It was a big place—the largest toys, games, and crafts distributor in the country. Operating an electric, high lift, fork truck was at first very scary but then became fun. Those trucks rose at least twenty feet; they got a little shaky with a pallet full of cartons. I knew that my forty-five hour work week at the Kasch Co. would soon end. There were just a few months to go.

There were some sad and confusing periods during the dead of winter as I reflected on the roller coaster years spent with Shelly. Our relationship had dwindled to nothing more than a workable brother-sister arrangement. The chasm of interests became greater. We decided that we'd finally split up for good. *The Mother Earth News* was again our source of connection to the outside world. Shelly corresponded with a man from New York State, and I began writing to a lady from Houston, Texas. This lady named Pam seemed to have a real interest in what I'd done and where I was heading. The search for a girlfriend that could share my interests seemed like an ongoing ordeal. Maybe this lady was the one. We kept writing each other and exchanged photos.

In February, I worked on and completed the fifth song. I was in winter's home stretch. I know that the fifth song mentioned the month of February and how I laid in the sun inside my wood pile that faced south. I got a simple February tan from my own natural tanning salon. As I drove to work before sunrise, often I'd see dark billowing clouds over Lake Michigan. These towering bold shapes reminded me of a mountain range. Mountain consciousness was getting the best of my eyes and heart. I thought that maybe on my way to Alaska, I'd stop in Banff, Alberta. In a book that I had read that early winter titled, *Secret of the Andes,* the author told of the Brotherhood of the Seven Rays having a spiritual community manifested in the Rockies near Banff. It was worth a visit.

Impatience was a hard thing to deal with having less than two months to go. Pam and I were writing to each other weekly, and it seemed a certain thing that she'd take a bus trip up to Wisconsin and venture off with me to Alaska. By April 1, the sixth song was finished, and the seventh was in the making. Steve Tillman helped me build a camper on the back of my truck, and I had saved nearly seventeen hundred dollars by this time.

The list of things to bring became a priority. One of the most difficult decisions that had to be made was whether to bring Lika or leave her with Shelly. Back and forth in my mind the yes and no's went. Maybe she'd just be too much of a responsibility. I mean, I had no idea where I'd be staying and the adventures I might take on. It was hard. There were times during any given day that I'd find myself crying, holding my stomach over my decision to venture far north. I thought that perhaps I was making a very foolish move by leaving. Maybe I should stay in my hometown area. There were days that I had great reservations about leaving for Alaska. Perhaps I'd gone mad and could no longer think clearly. I had it really nice where I was, a halfway tolerable job, a rustic, peaceful rural home, and friends if I wanted them, my dog, my garden, my tipi, and my music.

During the fourteen months that I'd been back, I met numerous people in Milwaukee and outlying areas that were into a similar lifestyle as mine. We had sort of a cosmic magnetism when we were together. Maybe I belonged here. It's just that a meaningful purpose for my existence hadn't materialized just yet. One thing was certain; along with the seventh and final song came a gut fear and uncertainty. Could I endure being a lonely outsider once again in a foreign part of the country?

One chilly early April evening, I hiked out to where I had spent many nights and days seeking visions and seeking God. I stood alone in the high meadow under the sky that was teeming with stars. I talked it out to an unknown God, hoping for a clear understanding—hoping to affirm my decision. I wept in loneliness. Gritting my teeth, I wept in fear and anger. Why was I so compelled to wander and experience? No consolation came that evening. There was no one to go to for help. I could have just laid down in the young alfalfa field and wished that my total being would burst. Peace was not in the air.

On April 15, I met Pam at the bus depot in Milwaukee. Bad news, she was stiff as a board, literally scared speechless. Extremely uncomfortable falls short of expressing the feeling. First off, I hated downtown Milwaukee and had never even been to the bus depot. I couldn't even figure out where to park. Waiting for Pam was like sitting at the dentist; you knew that soon you'd be next. Would it be unbearably painful or would it go smoothly? The pent-up anxiety and unfamiliar circumstances lent themselves naturally to a sporadic pacing. When her bus finally pulled up, we recognized each other. She had very dark skin, being Filipino, but her expression and personality became pale. I was expecting that we'd explode with joy and embrace each other intensely in front of everyone at the depot. To the contrary, our meeting was quite anticlimactic. We walked the two blocks to my truck. I helped carry her bags and tried a number of conversational topics, but she hardly conversed, barely even smiled. Within the twenty-five mile ride home, it became apparent that I had made a major mistake in inviting her to venture along with me. The only electricity in the air was found in my frizzy hair. The next two weeks before we left really didn't go well between us. She was definitely frightened, confused, sad, and angry. Well, what was I to do? Go through with it, I guess. We had virtually nothing in common, especially in the spiritual realm.

Spring made its mark on the world around. Snow turned into a fading memory. The warm air was filled with one thousand scents. Songbirds performed. The tipi was respectfully taken down and neatly packed and stored in the house for Shelly to safeguard. My dad stopped over to say goodbye. Steve Tillman glowed with friendship and excitement. He knew that we'd always be friends wherever we were. On April 28, the truck was neatly and meticulously packed with clothes, simple tools, natural foods, teas, vitamins, guitar, maps, addresses and a ten-gallon wood stove with pots and pans dangling. On the back outside door flap, I had inscribed on heavy, four-foot by three-foot canvas, the words to the "Great Invocation," a prayer that I had recited thousands of times in an attempt to further the New Age movement. I can't remember exactly what day of the week it was, but by midmorning that day in late April, it was a balmy seventy degrees. Shelly conveniently and understandably was not home to see us off.

As we pulled out of the driveway onto Wausaukee Road, I allowed myself another look at the house and its memories. Hardest of all was seeing Lika's bubbling face and tail wagging as she sat on the lawn watching me drive off. We shared one last deep glance, never to see each other again. Oh, Lika, how I loved her. The tears stream from my face as I write this. My lip is quivering. I was spared from seeing her grow old and die. Lika will always be young in my memory.

CHAPTER 19

FIRST STOP – LAME DEER

I still had a great desire to meet Lame Deer. Winner, South Dakota, would be on the way to Alaska. Pam loosened up a bit and even frequently chuckled. But overall, the ride through Wisconsin and Minnesota was uneventful — pretty — but uneventful. Bypassing Sioux Falls, South Dakota, we opted to take the secondary Highway 18 straight into Winner, right in the middle of southern South Dakota. South Dakota was flat and boring, but anxiety rose up inside of me as I anticipated meeting Lame Deer face to face.

Heightened expectancy consumed my soul. Would he be my spiritual master? Maybe destiny was finally on my side. Spiritual experiences were such an integral part of my life that I became addicted to them. The next one had to be greater than the last. I knew that I'd be out of control if I let fantasy feed me, but I didn't care; I loved it. There was a wild sensational spirit that seemed to be energy in itself.

The morning of April 30, we entered Winner, a non-descript, small, middle-class town seemingly lowered onto this barren plain. My eyes scanned the area for what was called Indian Town. I dared to ask at a gas station where Indian Town was. The man pointed and politely mumbled, "At the end of town." There was no question where this village stopped and Indian Town began. Suddenly, there was no more blacktop, just dirt roads, a lot of dust, no green grass, hundreds of weathered, unpainted shacks having a facsimile of a neighborhood, and native children running all around. There were few cars; there were few cars that is, that seemed operable. I asked a teenage boy who seemed to be leaning without purpose on a mostly broken picket fence that had long-dead tree branches protruding through it, "Do you know where Lame Deer lives?"

He curiously studied me and nodded towards the house next door. "Right there."

"Thanks," I politely replied.

That's where Lame Deer lives? It seemed nearly unlivable! Walking toward the house, I began talking myself out of doing this, but soon I found myself standing at the side door. I followed through with a couple of knocks on the door. A lady, possibly in her late fifties, answered the door. Explaining to her who I was and why I came, I sensed on her expression that she'd been through this before. Just another white, curiosity seeking, back-to-nature hippie. She kindly informed me that Lame Deer was in New York City meeting with a publisher. "He would be back in two days," she hesitantly informed me. I was invited to step in for a few minutes into their two-room home. She offered me a cup of coffee, which I noticed was simmering in a two-gallon, blue porcelain kettle on the stove. It looked like mud. They actually dump one whole pound of coffee into the pot and let it simmer for days. Strong? I guess so. She called it black medicine. I declined, as I really hadn't had coffee for several years.

Lame Deer's wife offered to let me park my truck in their dirt backyard if I wanted to wait until Lame Deer came home, so I did just that. I pulled it up alongside the outhouse. There I sat, biding my time for two days. I played my guitar, read some books, chanted the Great Invocation, slept a lot, and tried to think of a way to tell Pam that she probably should go back home to Houston. What a mismatch we were.

In the midmorning of the third day, a car pulled up. With heart pounding and nerves racing, I stood nearly motionless in the middle of the yard. A Native American man with long black hair got out. With brows lifted and his gaze fixed on me, he walked closer. Sheepishly I asked, "Lame Deer?" He gave me a large grin and briskly came toward me. I didn't understand; I perceived him as a much older man, judging from the photos in his book, *Lame Deer, Seeker of Visions*. I guess that I had pictured perhaps someone in his early eighties. He looked much younger in person. Chuckling, he acknowledged the puzzled look on my face. "They made me look older for the photos." Those New York people said that the book would sell much better if I looked really old. Guys like you find it appealing." He was right; much of his wise mystique was now missing. He seemed to infer that some of the book was fictional with added sensational experiences and visions. "The publishers eat it up," he quipped. I couldn't tell if he was joking with me or not. Sales of books about Native Americans were certainly brisk in the '70s. My countenance dropped drastically after he told me these things. Suddenly every old Indian was a holy man, medicine man, or great spiritual leader. I felt let down and deflated. Lame Deer assured me that any money that he made from the sales went back into his people on the reservation. His intentions were good; he was a very generous man. Lame Deer began to tell me about a follow-up book that he was working on about his experiences and visions of traveling into the cosmos.

Lame Deer, demanding my attention, finally spoke to me in a serious tone. "If you want to know how real Indians live, go to Crow Dog's camp on the White River; tell them I sent you." It would be a good fifty-mile drive deep into the Rosebud Reservation, and I hurriedly left.

CHAPTER 20

ON THE ROSEBUD – CROW DOG'S CAMP

On the way to the town of Rosebud, I just had to stop in Mission to explore a Sioux trading post. I guess it seemed odd that a white man owned it, but he was friendly and quite knowledgeable. My eyes studied all the beadwork and intricate bone choke collars, really, all very beautiful. The Lakota people knew their craft. I bought about twelve dollars' worth of materials to fashion my own bone collar and beaded pouch.

Approximately eight miles southwest of Mission was the run-down town of Rosebud, consisting of a gas station, a few taverns, a general store, and some streets going this way and that. I asked a passerby how to get to Crow Dog's camp, and they thought I was nuts. His response was, "Nobody white goes down there, not since Wounded Knee." The Wounded Knee uprising was still fresh in the air; you could sense the rebellion. Just eight months earlier, young Sioux rebels captivated the networks, holed up in a shack, heavily armed. Most of the nation seemed to be on their side, at least that was my perspective. I certainly was rooting for them and not the US Government. I didn't appreciate his warning until I started traveling the long dusty road to Crow Dog's camp. Silhouetted Indians perched on ridges with shotguns started to become common.

The terrain changed also; level barrenness gradually rose into rolling hills and scattered pine. I felt like I belonged. It was a tease for me to allow my imagination to visualize tribes and tipis, old ways, sacred times, Oglala and Lakota chiefs, and a meaningful identity. The

Native Americans despised the word *Sioux*—a French name meaning "Little Enemy." The man back in Rosebud said, "About ten miles in, you'll see all the tipis, tents, campers, and Crow Dog's log cabin scattered along the White River." Boy, what a pleasurable ride. A peaceful anticipation filled me. I'd be special to them; I'd be accepted because Lame Deer sent me.

Coming down a five-hundred-foot tree-lined ridge, I immediately spotted the camp. By now my light blue truck was a dingy brown from this dusty, pot-holed road. Very slowly I pulled up to a ranch-type gate. Three young men with rifles approached me. Speaking calmly with assurance, I proclaimed, "I've been staying with Lame Deer, and he sent me here." One man with a skeptical look questioned, "You know Lame Deer?"

"Yes," I nodded, "we're good friends."

He sternly demanded, "Open up the back; let's see if you got any weapons."

I chuckled, "Me? No, not at all, just some teas, natural foods, vitamins, just my belongings."

They pretty much ripped apart my truck confiscating all the teas, vitamins, hatchet, knife, and camera.

"We'll give it back when you leave," they sternly assured me.

I tried to convince them that the teas and vitamins were just that, not drugs at all. They didn't buy my story.

"You can go in."

I gave an affirmative wave and thought to myself, "I'm on their side. Can't they tell?"

I noticed a handful of poorly constructed tipis and couldn't wait to show them photos of mine. I mean mine looked proud, sturdy, and authentic. An awful lot of tents and camper trailers dotted the area.

It was quite a lovely setting that Crow Dog had along the White River. I found a nonthreatening spot and stopped the truck. Pam preferred to stay put while I anxiously wandered about, trying to strike up conversation. It didn't dawn on me at the time, but these young guys probably found Pam very attractive. She could have passed as a Navajo girl with her dark complexion. I was given enough hard hints from the people to realize that no one wanted to talk to me. With blond hair and blue eyes, I stuck out, way out.

After this cool reception, I felt that it was best to go back to the truck and maybe just leave. I would have liked to have met Crow Dog himself, but that might not happen. My dream of being a native Indian just wasn't turning out as I had imagined. Pam wanted to get out of there; that was certain.

No sooner did I get to the truck than an announcement was made over the loudspeaker system. The announcement that was made was heavy and factual. "Tonight we will have a peyote ceremony; all are invited. Do not eat or drink from this time on." My body froze. Peyote, that's scary stuff, inducing hallucinations, demons, and visions. Some people never return, at least not mentally. Should I, shouldn't I; should I, shouldn't I. Yes, no, maybe.

By now I surely knew how sensitive I was to drugs. It didn't take much recollection to remind myself of what had happened to me on peyote back in Ben Lomond, and that was a small dose. But, could I live with myself if I declined to partake in a sacred peyote ceremony? Would I regret having not done this, having been so close? From late morning when the announcement was made until dusk, I struggled with indecision and just safely stayed in the back of my truck.

The sun had finally set on this gorgeous, early May day. People began merging toward the big log cabin. They looked like slow-moving shadow figures coming from all directions. A still, eerie ambience thickened cool night air. I had to decide soon. Fear enslaved me. I quietly told Pam, "I'm going to go in" and steadily walked toward the cabin.

I was one of the last ones to enter. Through an open wooden porch, I felt like I was thrust in. I was in; I'm not going back. Many people, perhaps sixty to seventy, sat on the floor with their backs against the walls; they were all ages, from teen-agers to very weathered looking adults. I saw an open space toward the left side in the back, next to an older teenage girl. I gave her a nervous smile and sat down. People didn't talk or smile. There was a deafening stiffness. What would go on in here? Many people took an empty soup or coffee can that was conveniently supplied. I didn't take one; not knowing what it was for.

Within minutes, two young men came over, peered down at me and motioned with their thumbs. It was unmistakably the "get-out" sign. As I got up to leave, I felt anger and dismay that they would not allow me to take part in the ceremony. One of the men whispered, "Crow Dog wants to question you."

Outside, I stood face to face with Crow Dog himself. Only the left side of his face was visible, his right side being eclipsed from the dim light coming from the fire inside. He was gentle, to the point, and made a quick, accurate study of my character. He softly spoke, "Some of the men think you are bringing demons with you. Is this true?"

I began nervously laughing, "Demons? Me?" I just shook my head in amazement. "No, I look to the energy of the Lord. My name is Ayuta Rai. I read Black Elk's books and met with Lame Deer. I made and lived in two tipis. I want to be an Indian."

After a moment of silence without ever seeming to move, he placed his right hand on my left shoulder and moved his head up and down. "Go in." His peaceful smile could not be hidden. The lines on his aged face displayed years of knowledge and wisdom. I proudly walked in having received his blessing.

I sat back down next to the same teenage girl. Boy, she gave me a sour, disapproving look. Perhaps eight feet from me, a half-moon altar was fashioned on the floor from rare, white earth. Coals were carefully taken from the fire and placed on the altar. Dried cedar leaves were sprinkled over the coals. They crackled and sent sparks flying as an old man chanted something in the Lakota language. Soon a thin cloud of cedar incense hovered several feet above the floor. It had a sweet, distinct aroma.

Crow Dog spoke from the entranceway. "I called this special meeting so that the AIM (American Indian Movement) would be granted favor and power. My son Leonard and many other men have just returned from three days of fasting and seeking visions. You must excuse him; he has had a hard time staying awake." Most everyone began laughing. I guess it was a personal joke; possibly Leonard was known for snoozing through these meetings. Even Leonard found himself laughing. Crow Dog was overly respectful of my being there as he first spoke in English on my account, and then in Lakota.

Leonard told the people how they had seen a very large gathering of eagles that formed the letters A-I-M in the sky. This they received as a certain sign of power for their struggle. Here I sat in the thick of an AIM strategy meeting. It was either Russell Means or Dennis Banks who was present at this meeting. Both were leaders of this movement. These were the big guns who were being hunted by the FBI. In an interview that I had read several years later, the article quoted Russell

Means as saying, "AIM people are now integrated into every productive and responsible segment of Indian and non-Indian society. The American Indian Movement has accomplished the impossible. AIM has worked itself out of a job."

Someone spoke and said, "We saw FBI agents being dropped by helicopter. We shot at them to get them running." Several people chuckled. There was a bit more hard military talk, and then Crow Dog explained just how the ceremony would be conducted. "The peyote has been ground up with some water added. You'll be given one teaspoon at a time unless you want more. No one is allowed to leave once we begin. The staff will be passed around; sing your song while holding the staff."

I noticed two men coming out of a small back room with a bowl and a spoon. A unique percussion instrument began to sound. It was a water drum. I had never experienced anything like it. It was a stoneware drum shaped like half of a basketball, partially filled with water, with a leather skin covering the top. Held in between the legs, it was played with one thumb, and the player was able to change pitch by tipping the drum. The first man kept thumping a fast-paced rhythm. Gradually, I became a bit mesmerized by the shaking of the five-foot staff and the pulse of the water drum.

I was about twenty-fifth in line to receive peyote. It became apparent as to why the empty cans were there. Numerous people vomited into them after taking peyote. They just weren't accustomed to the bitter taste. I started to wonder whether I'd have a negative reaction myself. The man with the peyote was now just two people away. Surprisingly, I had no fear or apprehension of what I was about to do. Actually, I was eager to eat a spoonful. Gee, a spoonful. All I took in Ben Lomond was a large gelatin capsule, probably a quarter teaspoon.

Well, here goes. I followed closely the movement of his hand as he dipped the very shiny spoon into the bowl and came up with a big glob of dark brown mush. Our eyes met, he put it in my mouth. Sloshing it around a bit, I swallowed it. Many eyes were upon me to witness my reaction. All the while I knew, as it slid down, that bitter as it may be, this was not nearly as bad as some of the bitter herbs that I drank daily. With head held high, I bravely glanced around the room as an acknowledgment that I was more than ready. The teenage girl next to me politely threw up. The people who vomited were apparently purging their systems of toxic poisons. Well, I was on my way. Nothing was happening, but that rhythm kept going.

After the peyote went around once, they began singing, quite enchanting voices and melodies were heard. There was a deepening of rich, sincere tones in the room. And this room seemed to shrink. People who sat thirty feet across when I first came in seemed to be right in front of me. A type of harmony spun around us. Nothing had happened yet, but I was feeling very relaxed, really with it.

When it came my turn to hold the staff and sing, I let it pass by. I didn't know what to sing. Odd that a vocalist such as myself wouldn't know what to sing. I was the only one who didn't hold the staff and sing. They all sang in Lakota. After a while, the language seemed not to be a barrier to understanding.

I sat in joy, perceived many thoughts and feelings, and slowly began to hallucinate while all the time wondering why nothing was happening. Time no longer existed; the drum and staff had perpetual motion. People spoke; I intently listened studying their vocal inflections and facial movements. They definitely had some things to say. I saw the Statue of Liberty crumble to a rubble of ruins and the Badlands emerge from under the water in its place. To this point, I had never even seen the Badlands before. Other visions came and with them symbols. One of the symbols I've remembered through the years and still use to accent a thought in writing is a circle with an X through it. This bland log cabin became rich in color, sound, and warmth. The activity was immense. Still, oddly enough, I thought that nothing was happening.

A second spoon came around. I gladly took it. Gradually, an overall bodily sickness began to overcome me. It grew more pronounced. My bones and muscles felt brittle and ached. A cold sweat broke out; my body shook uncontrollably from feeling extremely cold. I started to entertain the fearful thought that I was dying. As this serious condition was overtaking me, an aged lady was kneeling over the altar, staring at me, and chanting. What's going on? I desperately wanted to get out but recalled the stern warning that no one was allowed to leave. With eyelids scratching and nearly closed, I kindly asked the girl next to me if she'd move forward so I could lie down. I was really sick. She looked at me with a grunted expression; arms folded, and vigorously shook her head, "no." The old lady at the altar got more intense. My clothes were drenched with cold sweat. Back and forth our eyes locked;, finally the chills broke as if a cymbal crashed.

My senses returned; I felt weightless, full of bliss, and alive. I was so relieved that I had finally come out of this that I felt like screaming. Wanting to let this lady know that I was okay, I quickly fixed my eyes over to the white earth altar. She was gone! She was somehow instantly sitting where she was sitting before. She didn't even acknowledge my intense glance toward her. Weird. The evening went on with visions, feelings, insights into life, and singing, while the drum and staff kept a steady driving rhythm.

It began to make sense to me now; I was Crazy Horse reincarnated, come back to unite the Sioux Nation in power and strength. Yes, that was it; that was why I was always so fascinated with Indians, particularly the Sioux. I was really Crazy Horse. I had read that Crazy Horse was physically unique, being short and having light hair and possibly bluish eyes. I'm short, light haired, and blue-eyed. Wow, this was incredible, I had come to lead the Sioux. This peyote realization was difficult to contain, but I kept it to myself. I was never able to determine whether what I had read about Crazy Horse's physical make up was true.

Birds sang, the night sky had gone, and dawn entered in through the windows. It was a beautiful morning. The drum had stopped; the unity was quickly leaving. Several men began to serve breakfast of canned corn, bread, and water. I ate slowly, expecting traditional native food instead of US Government surplus.

At midmorning, it was nonchalantly spoken that the meeting was over and as was customary, the last person in this sitting order, left first, shaking the hand of all the rest. I was somewhere in the middle. As some of the younger men got up to leave, they bitterly refused to shake my hand or even have eye contact. I was deeply hurt, wanting to love them all as brothers.

I found myself in a very unusual dilemma. While having total consciousness, I wasn't able to control my motor mechanisms. I couldn't move my body—arms, fingers, legs, anything. I was paralyzed. I imagine that this could happen after sitting in the same spot for over fifteen hours. Everyone except me was standing, waiting to say goodbye and leave, but I couldn't get up. Panic; yes, that's a good word for it. Panic set in. Above me was a window ledge. I maneuvered my arms up and latched on with my hands. After considerable straining, I pulled myself up to a standing position. "Whew, I'm still all here." Walking like a clumsy clown, concentrating on every step—left, right, left, right—I shook hands with the remaining people and floated out of the cabin. It was like just that, floating. I swear that my feet never touched the ground.

I sort of gracefully glided to the truck. What a sensation: weightless floating. A man, singing from a high western ledge, captured the air. Possibly the sweetest, smoothest sounding voice I'd ever heard. The words and flowing sounds that he made were as if from another realm. As I turned to look back, I was dismayed to see that he was gone. I noticed another man gliding above the Earth just as I appeared to. He blended right into a stand of bushes and disappeared. The surrounding hills vibrated in a blue and violet aura. Smoke seemed to rise from various points. This was fantastic, and all along I thought that nothing was happening.

Crawling into the back of the truck, I excitedly shared with sleepy Pam that I was actually Crazy Horse come to save the Sioux Nation. I nearly wept as I told her my revelation. Pam nervously humored me along. I knew this, but yakked my head off anyway.

My euphoric peace was suddenly shattered by a jarring abrupt sound. "Knock, knock, knock," "You in there?"

"Yeah, I'm in here; hang on, and I'll open the door."

Five young, very furious, young men demanded that I leave now. "Get out! Now."

"Whoa, I'm not sure I know what's going on." That's the only response I had.

"We know you brought demons to the meeting, get out, or we'll kill you!" They meant it.

I asked to have court with them. Drawing in the dirt with a stick, I showed them the symbols that came to me. They didn't care. I shared many of my visions, and my great revelation of Crazy Horse. They grew more angry. "Nobody here got any visions; why should you?"

I guess these guys acted out of malicious jealousy. "Okay, I'll leave. It'll take me a while; I can hardly walk, much less drive."

It took some time to find my truck keys. All I really wanted to do was lie out in a field and drift away. I just couldn't function well enough to drive the truck, and Pam didn't drive. We sat in the cab; I managed to get the keys in the ignition. Good. The truck actually started on the first try. I felt like I was piloting a jet liner. The rumble and vibration that I appeared to be hearing from an otherwise quiet engine seemed unbearable. Now I had to turn this truck around to get out. First gear was found with ease. We were moving; I was steering! Gee, this truck seemed to float, just like my sensation of walking. We cautiously floated towards the gate at about two miles an hour, too fast for me.

Very slowly driving through the gate, the same guys that confiscated my belongings gave them back. It seemed like I'd been there for weeks instead of twenty-four hours. An amazing relief transpired once I got back onto the dirt road. We were safe. We would travel a few miles down the road and hang out until I straightened up again.

Mom and dad on the farm. 'up north' 1945

On the farm 1954-55 I am second from the right.

My mom, early 1950's

My mom and me
on the farm 1950

My dad playing
clarinet, 1940's

My dad's first race car, late 1930's

My dad in one of his many bands, late 1940's
He is second from the left with sax.

My dad's race cars, mid 1940's

Pantomiming the Beatles at
Grafton Junior High. Feb. 1964
I am on the left.

Christmas Eve, 1964 with my new red double
cutaway electric Harmony guitar

The Ekkos fall 1965, I'm on the right.

Misery Sons performing the entire
Beatles Sgt. Peppers album,
late summer 1967

Misery Sons summer 1967

Misery Sons early 1968

Chicago recording studio
late 1969 with the
'Come As You Are' band.

My first 45 RPM, 'Opalescent Merry Go Round' late 1969

Come As You Are
(A Burlesque theatre Band)
Presents
RAY LAST

SS-17702-01A
JPL-RL1
Side 1

Time 3:05
45 RPM

Opalescent Merry-Go-Round
(Ray Last)
JPL RECORD CO.
DES PLAINES, ILL.

Me in my new 1969 azure blue Camaro
on Bonniwell Road. 1969

My apt. building in the
Lower East Greenwich
Village NYC
208 Forsythe St. apt. 9

A crazy hair day,
early 1970

Ben Lomond cottage
late 1971

Ben Lomond CA sign

Inside cottage, by my
pink refrigerator and
purple apple separators
glued to the walls.

Bemidji MN tipi, fall 1972

Me with Lika

Wasaukee Rd. tipi,
fall 1973.

Wasaukee Rd. house

Packed and ready to go,
late April 1974

On the road,
early May 1974

Ben, the Hopi Holy Man,
walking on the right.
(red shirt and bag)

Boulder Co. first annual Spiritual
festival on the meadows by the
Flat Irons, June 1974

Mountain goats on Mt. Washburn,
Yellowstone National Park,
July 1974

My prized photo of a
mountain goat that stopped to
pose for me as the clouds parted
and the blue sky shown through

Dragi's photo of me September 1974,
East Kelowna BC.

Footch Kapoot in lower
level of a dirt floor barn, early winter 1976

Me playing my leather frills
1965 Fender Jaguar guitar.

The outside of the barn.

Footch Kapoot live

Me on the left
playing guitar

Footch Kapoot 'Good Clean Fun' Album Cover.

Footch Kapoot 8 x 10 glossy for
'Good Clean Fun' promo

Barn and practice garage
on Cedarcreek Rd., Cedarburg WI

Inside view of
'the loft'

Emma the goose

Hank Aaron and myself having lunch at Arby's
as he looks at my Milwaukee Braves and
scarpbook collection. Oct 15, 1988

Junior league baseball champs, summer 1964
I am front row on the right

Ministering in southern India, March 2015

ON THE ROSEBUD – JESSE EAGLE ELK

I still perceived the hills as being augmented in blue and violet tones. Smoke appeared to rise from prairie craters, but I was gradually coming down from my peyote high. One way I knew that this was so was when I started thinking again of the future. Where do we go from here? Should Pam come along? The vision of Crazy Horse gnawed at me. I need to find someone who could tell me what significance all the visions and signs had. We pulled over about four miles north of Crow Dog's. I fell asleep for a long time, submersed in a very deep, settling, peaceful slumber. I had to have slept for at least twelve hours. Disorientation came as I awoke. Inside the camper, it was very dark. For a second I actually thought that I was in my bedroom back home in Grafton as a boy. Groping about, I realized that I was contained in a four-foot by six-foot camper. Peering out of my Plexiglas teardrop windows, a light hue broke into the lower eastern sky. Where was I? It seemed as if minutes passed before I pieced together reality. The Rosebud. Peyote. Drained with a nowhere existence trailing me, I climbed out of the back of my camper.

The silent air bit at me, startling and blunt. It was going to be a while before this peyote wore off. My past seemed vague as I stood on the hard, reddish dirt. The strong scent of pine brought the morning wind.

Pam and I gathered sticks for a fire. This little wood stove had served me well so far. I washed my face with hot water and made oatmeal and peppermint tea. Life within me began to stir. The sun had a silent rumble as it shattered the sky. Darkness dissipated. "Let's drive into Rosebud and get gas. I think I can handle it," I assured Pam.

After just a few miles of driving, a man waved from outside his small, white house. I naturally drove in. His teeth seemed to take up half of his face as he smiled. We shook hands. You guess which way we shook. "I'm Ayuta Rai; this is Pam."

He robustly answered, "Jesse Eagle Elk. Ayuta Rai, what's your real name?"

I didn't want to answer that. He seemed disturbed at my calling myself Ayuta Rai. Not wanting to acknowledge his question, I reiterated my introduction. "It's a name I was given, it means "Looks to the Energy of the Lord.""

He kept pressing me to tell him my real name. "What is the name your parents gave you?"

"Ray. Ray Last," I hesitantly answered.

"Then I'll call you your real name, *Raylast*." He said it like it was one word. No one had called me that for nearly a year. He made it sound so cold. In defense of myself, I argued, "A spirit gave me this name because Ray Last doesn't mean anything; it has no identity; it's just a couple of words."

"But that's your real name," he said with certainty.

"Okay, fine, whatever you want to call me."

He just laughed. "Come in; meet my family."

The creak of the screen door introduced us into his home. Stepping into a small eight by ten kitchen, we were immediately met by the glow on his wife's bronze face. I immediately sensed that he and his family were genuine and sincere people. Their home was neat, clean, and quite humble. His teenage son was still asleep in a trailer house behind theirs.

The eagerness to express my deep love for Indians seemed to impress them. Jesse and his wife listened intently as I conveyed my experience at Crow Dog's camp. Jesse had little to say in way of interpretation, but he did immediately recognize from my description, the old lady who knelt at the altar chanting. "She was praying for you—for your protection." He seemed to know this with certainty. Well, I didn't understand. Protection from what? But it was reassuring just to know that she was at least on my side, bless her soul.

Jesse eagerly asked, "Why don't you stay here with us for a while; there's a Mother's Day meeting in two weeks; you should sing a song there."

I hesitantly answered, "Yeah, sure, Mother's Day." Jesse's invitation was so warm and sincere, but what would I sing? I didn't know any Mother's Day songs. Maybe I could write one. They offered me some black medicine coffee. I drank just half a cup and had the shakes for hours. Killer bean, that stuff.

Jesse's wife was a schoolteacher and began to tutor me in Lakota language. She was so generous as to give me her thick, hardbound Sioux dictionary. It's a beautiful language, poetic and smooth like French and Spanish. I caught on quickly to phonetic sounds and practiced speaking the language with them throughout the day.

Jesse said that there was another white guy living in a hogan just one-half mile up the road. I set out the next day to visit with him. Upon meeting him, he graciously invited me in and began to point out all the unique particulars of his six-sided, round log cabin. Hogans seemed to have between five and eight sides. Living in something round such as a dome, hogan, or tipi, seemed so right, as nothing in nature is square. Think about it. I sure have. Nothing in nature is square. The hogan dweller and I parted company in short order after we quickly ran out of things to talk about. That is, things that we had in common. We had many differing opinions.

Several days before the Mother's Day peyote ceremony, Jesse, myself, and another man, drove miles back in the hills to shovel buckets of white earth for the half-moon altar. It was off the beaten trail, to say the least. There was no trail at all. We went over hills, rocks, prairie streams, and a sparse pine forest. This man knew exactly where the white earth was. Somebody's dog came along for the ride; he hung on with all fours. Boy, sure enough, there it was, white earth, not clay, but actual dirt, moist and crumbly. Jesse shoveled about three pails full, and we drove somewhere to where the cabin was that the meeting was to be held. I knew we were still in South Dakota; I guess it didn't seem to matter much. I was just happy to feel a part of something. Jesse and this man treated me with humor and respect, but he still kept saying *Raylast*. I thought that I even heard this dog start barking it, *Raylast*. It was nearly dark when we got back to Jesse's, and I felt like a man.

A late supper was prepared. I supplied all kinds of dried grains, brown rice, wheat berries, and lentils. You know, things that crunch if they're not cooked long enough. A humble peace rested upon that house. Sharing the basic necessities gave this simple existence a fullness of worth. These people were transparent before me, and I began to enjoy the freedom that comes with being vulnerable. They also shared a deep love for their Christian religion, something that struck me as odd considering the culture and heritage, especially their involvement with peyote.

Jesse's wife had a certain sweet spirit about her, and Jesse boasted of her being chosen for her beauty to pose for a life-size statue of a Sioux Indian maiden, which is on display at a museum or shopping center somewhere in South Dakota. They picked the right lady for a model.

Mother's Day, 1974, came, and I was still at a loss for a song. Jesse comforted me with these encouraging words, "You'll know what to sing when the time is right." I never just sang without being prepared beforehand. We set out for the meeting cabin by mid-afternoon. I was eager for this one but still unsettled at having no song.

Jesse, his son and I were the first ones there. The first thing was to get a good fire going. This cabin sat as the only obtrusion on an otherwise rolling, barren terrain. We brought our own firewood, as there wasn't even a stick to be found. It certainly couldn't be said that we were *out in the sticks*. The only chunk of wood other than the cabin was the two-seater outhouse.

On Jesse's prompting, I brought my guitar along. A more conservative crowd began to filter in. They were mostly people over thirty, friendly and warm. It had the appearance of a country church service. People came in old trucks and even on horseback.

Coals were placed on the half-moon altar and cedar needles sprinkled over them. The air was quickly permeated with this sweet aroma once again. This time, though, there was no hostility. These folks accepted me and even welcomed me as one of their own. I don't recall hearing the water drum and staff, but the spoon of peyote did come around. The anticipation of deep visions made for a childlike excitement. Hours seemed to go by and still no visions; mostly I was just a spectator. People talked, sharing very personal trials and joys of their lives. Many spontaneously talked about their mothers.

While listening intently to all the wonderful praise for motherhood, I reflected on my own mother. I sensed a bit of loss that she had died so young before I really knew her, but mostly I just listened to the others. Jesse began to open up about how much he loved and missed his mother. He broke into uncontrollable weeping. I found myself moving toward him to awkwardly give him comfort, but then someone spoke to me, "It is good that he is releasing his sorrow." I remained seated. Jesse eventually composed himself, and people continued to share and sing.

I had a disturbing urge to get my guitar out and play. Indecision knocked me back and forth. Scared, yet greatly compelled, I turned around and opened the case. What a beautiful guitar that Guild was. Slowly I lifted it out to proudly show its elegance. I dared to break with tradition and asked permission to go outside for a few minutes before I sang. Jesse nodded to me that it was alright to leave.

While walking out, I was greeted to a mauve-toned eastern sky. It was dawn on Mother's Day. Being somewhat overcome by the magnitude of the skyline, I began to talk to my mother, interchanging conversation with her and God. Some tears came, but mostly a calm assurance with a quiet approval to go back in and sing.

Entering in, many eyes were upon me and the Guild guitar. An older man held my guitar over the altar while another sprinkled cedar on the coals. He seemed to be blessing my guitar. He spoke softly in Lakota and reverently handed the guitar back to me. I began a steady rhythm strum on an open A chord, switching to A and D. A song came from my voice, no words, just vowel sounds. My singing became louder; melody emerged around a pronounced rhythm. I lost consciousness of playing or singing. When my awareness returned, I realized that the volume of my voice and intensity of my guitar strumming shook the foundation. Suddenly, as if the air exploded, I abruptly stopped while in full force. Looking about the room, I shyly said, "I guess I'm done now." Not a word was spoken, hardly an expression was shown, and the meeting continued.

Breakfast was served among happy chatter; I had had no visions or great dreams but felt that I was among friends. People came up afterwards and thanked me for my song. Several people described visions they had while I was singing. "Really? Visions while I was singing?" I puffed up inside. A man in his nineties was ecstatically happy and told me that my music had propelled him into the solar system, and while out there, he had a vision that he was to meet his grandchildren in Scotts Bluff, Nebraska—grandchildren that he hadn't seen for many years. He was genuinely happy because of my song. Hey, too bad I don't remember playing, except for the last abrupt chord. Jesse said it, "When the time is right, you'll know it." An older man felt moved to give me his prized Bald Eagle feather. It was the middle tail feather that came to a beautiful point. I soon began proudly wearing this feather in a braid in my hair. As the man handed it to me, He spoke a type of future spiritual blessing into my life, "You will be as a Holy Man."

On the way home we stopped to visit with the old Indian that was licensed by the state of South Dakota to cut peyote buttons. It's legal for Native Americans to use peyote for their American Indian church meetings, but only a select few are licensed to enter the highly guarded peyote gardens of the Southwest. He brought out for all to see, his most prized possession, once in a life time, extremely rare, star peyote plant. This plant was revered by him as sacred. I couldn't exactly appreciate his affinity with this star embossed plant, but thanked him anyway for allowing me the opportunity to see it.

The next few days were spent searching within myself as to my next move. Jesse gave me a tempting offer for me to stay on the Rosebud and be employed by the US Government. The state would pay me $4.50 per hour plus supply free housing and a telephone. The job description went like this: use your vehicle to deliver firewood and take old ladies to town shopping. Four dollars and fifty cents per hour and free board sounded like good, easy money. Half of me felt restless and anxious to keep moving on; the other half was drawn to a deep sense of family and belonging, even if they still refused to call me Ayuta Rai.

I spent several days alone in a rocky, pine-dotted area seeking an answer. No answer came, no closeness to God. I passed off the Crazy Horse thing and all the other visions as just hallucinations with no substance.

A bit forlorn, I made my way back to Jesse's. The smell of burning embers invaded the air. The trailer house behind Jesse's had burned to the ground. Running to the house, I frantically asked, "What happened!" Jesse was deeply troubled but seemed to be in control. He replied, "A fire started last night; we don't know how. There was no putting it out." His son lost his house and all his belongings. I certainly identified with him, having gone through my tipi burning. I offered to give him a considerable amount of my food and some money, but he kindly refused my help. He pointed to a small shed and said, "There's plenty of food in there; you can even help yourself."

Opening the rotted door of the shed, I saw piles of government surplus USDA food. Bags of rice, pinto beans, and oats and cans of unopened peanut butter, cooked chicken, and corn. There was a lot. They didn't know what to do with it all. So I helped myself. The peanut butter was great; all the oil was on top, so it had to be heartily mixed.

Still, I wondered, what will he do and where will he live? These people were so poor, and now they had less. They would never be able to rise above this deprived system. They were born into it. To many of them, death must look like freedom.

I guess maybe the answer to my dilemma to stay or leave was being shown by what hadn't happened here. I'm an optimistic guy, geared for a better tomorrow. There was too much depression on the Rosebud prison, and the God I so anxiously hoped for was not to be found here. They didn't seem to know what they believed. Pretty much anything went. Everyone's visions were truth, even if they contradicted the vision of the day before. I had to be honest with myself; there was no true Indian religion, not that they were aware of. There was barely a facsimile of a culture remaining. All their spiritual fancies , from Roman Catholicism to cosmic planetary travel, were mixed together in the soup, and it ended up tasting like mud. They really had nothing to hang onto, no foundation for their belief. Spirituality here seemed at best to be nothing more than desperate attempts to temporarily distract themselves from their depressed condition.

Was I so easily sidetracked from my Alaskan journey by the *feel good* sensation of being wanted? I guess so. I told Jesse that I had decided to move on instead of stay and live on the Rosebud. He had a distraught look and attempted to sway my thinking by saying, "You're making a big mistake, Raylast; you belong here." I struggled with my emotions, but kept firm my decision.

By nine o'clock in the morning, May 27, Pam and I were ready to take off. We spent nearly one month on the Rosebud; it was a very memorable month. As we were in the back of the camper tightly packing a few more things, Jesse closed the hinge on the outside door flap and snapped the padlock through it. "Jesse, what did you do? Did you lock us in? Open this thing up; we're leaving!"

He laughed, almost uncontrollably. "Raylast, you're staying here."

I barked back quite angrily, "No, I'm not. We're leaving, Jesse, and I don't care if I kick this thing open and wreck the door. We're taking off!"

After about fifteen minutes of his teasing, rebuttals, and shifty laughter, he opened the back up. I was mad. He kept smiling, and my anger subsided quickly. He meant no harm. He, his family and friends just had a genuine fondness for me. We shook hands and embraced. As I pulled out onto the road, he yelled, "See you again, Raylast." I just waved my arm out the window, never looking back.

CHAPTER 22

BADLANDS, BLACK HILLS AND BEYOND

There was no question that the mystical Badlands would be the next stop. Everybody has heard of the Badlands, but I was psyched up for something special. Possibly my vision would come to light. Maybe the significance of the Statue of Liberty crumbling and the Badlands rising would be shown to me there. The day was beautiful, and the drive was short. An hour and a half later, the flat, purple-colored mesas could be seen from miles off. The Badlands absorb you. Tourists stop and gawk at all the conveniently marked places, 'Scenic View #17, 2 mi. Ahead.' "What a joke," I thought, "You had to be told when there's a scenic view." The panorama increased like heavy, intense breathing.

Various mineral deposits created pastel layers in a carved moonscape. Purples came from oxidized manganese, volcanic ash lent a cream color, and iron oxide dappled orange and tan. We were greeted by the truly awesome spectacle of jagged ridges and looping peaks. The wind-chafed sediments would not tolerate prairie grass; they left it behind for the greater visual sensation. The French trappers deemed this area a *bad land* to cross, and the Lakota Natives named it "Maco Sica," land bad. It was understandably so. Highway 44 led us deep into the canyons and cliffs on the southeastern border. Established as a national monument in 1939, only one-tenth of the White River Badlands is actually set aside as a national park, the total area being over two million acres.

I pulled off the main park road and took the risk of driving several miles into the less-traveled outback near Sheep Mountain. The solitude was almost frightening. Prairie dogs, jackrabbits, and a golden eagle kept a cautious watch on me. One-half mile to the north I spotted a herd of thirty or so buffalo. As you know, it doesn't require much for me to lung into an imagination of the past. Thoughts of Crazy Horse, Sitting Bull, and Red Cloud appeared as visions of tipi villages sprang up. It may as well have been 1850. A prairie rattler startled us stiff as he quickly slithered under a shrub. You take the good with the bad. A turbulent thunderstorm swiftly moved in with the force of a freight train. Minutes later the rumble passed over, and a double rainbow appeared, arching the extremes of the Badlands together. These foreboding thunderheads were visible for miles as they rolled their way east-northeast.

This was where we would camp; perhaps I'd be lifted from this eerie realm into a limitless, Western sky. The sunset was nearly indescribable, burning scarlet and burgundy patterns into the mineral cliffs. Dense billows of cumulus clouds gently drifted, searching for a resting place. The color, yes, it was the color and the calm. The sunset shouted, yet only the wind was heard as it passed on its puzzling course. Coyotes discussed the day's events and evening's activities. The glimpse of a Bighorn seeking retirement put a cap on the spirit of the evening. Sleep came, but it prolonged its coming. Daybreak met us with no less splendor.

Breakfast was made, tea was drunk, a final song was sung, and I thanked the Great Spirit for being so gracious in displaying his handiwork expressly for me. Samples of multicolored rock were taken as warm reminders. Possibly the energy of the Badlands is capsulated in these humble stones, I fantasized. I do believe if humanly possible, I would have set-up house there forever.

No, I did not visit the highly commercialized and infamous *Wall Drug* of South Dakota, "Window to the West." Though the bumper stickers and billboards scream at you to visit it. My rugged pride would not lower itself to such belittlement. Many years later as a family man, I gave in and visited Wall Drug. Bad land, good vibrations.

Now, if you know anything about the Lakota Sioux, you know that the Black Hills, which they call Paha Sapa, are sacred ground.

Just twenty miles west of where we camped on Highway 40 and 36, we sort of accidentally stumbled onto the beautiful, spacious Custer State Park in the southeastern tip of the Black Hills. Until this time, I had perceived a state park as sort of a tame, family-type campground suitable for bottled gas hook-up and hot running water. The name Custer sounded like grit in my teeth, but, nonetheless, the rich beauty of the Black Hills surpassed that of the Badlands. Really, I had no idea that a state park could be so wild and vast in area, nearly ten miles long and five miles wide.

Again, I took the dependable Dodge truck and drove well off the park road, over hills, meadows, and along a deer-buffalo trail in the French Creek area. The remainder of the day was spent camping in a very secluded grassy meadow; the scent of dense Black Hills pine elevated my spirit. Intertwined among the pine were white spruce, oak, aspen, birch, cottonwood, and willow. An occasional deer, elk, or Bighorn was a treasure to behold.

The Guild guitar got a workout, as did my lungs. Singing the visionary seven songs brought back purpose to my existence. The Black Hills beckoned for more of my music; I gradually acknowledged it.

A small herd of buffalo slowly made their way toward our little camp, curiously drawn by the compelling music. Anyway, at least I would have liked to think that they were lulled by my music. I bravely walked over to them with my camera, talking and gently singing. They just stood firm and studied me. A hush came over the herd, as one bison seemed to speak, "What do you make of this guy?" None of the herd knew for sure, but I guaranteed them that I came in peace. The camera was clicked a few times, and then all at once as if a silent signal was given, they in one accord began lumbering toward me, snorting and looking quite disturbed. When the shuffle turned to swing, I left the dance floor and ran. I mean, I really ran! You could say I was hoofing it. The great furry beasts were right behind. I jumped on the hood and onto the roof of the camper. Pam was inside and frantically pulled the door closed. These guys encircled the truck, dust clouds rose from the force of their nostrils. Reasoning with them did no good. What happened to the deep unity I had with all animals? "Hey, I'm on your side; I like Indians. White man's guns are no good." They grew tired of my covered wagon sideshow and gradually meandered away. At least I secured a couple of good photos suitable for framing. Bison aren't very subtle after all.

Another evening under the stars and a lengthy series of one night sleepovers ensued. As was customary, the chatter of diverse bird life awakened me. The morning was cold and clammy as a thick gray fog had settled in the Hills.

Because Mount Rushmore was only ten miles north, I thought, "Why not? We're this close." So up the winding roller coaster trail of Highway 16 I drove. These seemed like real mountains more than hills, not exactly molehills. I mean Harney Peak visible to the west was seven thousand two hundred and forty-two feet high. Mount Rushmore itself must be nearly that high. Switchback curves and tunnels, granite spires, one thousand foot drop offs: all this being veiled yet accented by the gray moving mass I know as fog. A wayside boasted a spectacular view of Mount Rushmore. I pulled over, got out, and saw nothing but dense moisture. Well, there probably wasn't much to see anyway.

Driving on a bit north, we rolled into Keystone, a made-to-look-authentic Western main street. It was lined with tourist shops and a Black Hills travel agent, advertising: "Ride the helicopter or an 1880s train; take a stagecoach through town or have a photo of yourself sitting with a Sioux chief in full headdress." Sunlight began to wage war with the clouds. I felt a magnetic pull towards the decked-out Indian chief. I can't recall his name, but he made sure that his English was very broken. "How. Me no drink firewater." I mean, he actually used that movie phrase. Come on, this guy was raking in a couple hundred bucks a day off people who were sorely misled—duped into thinking that he was an old Sioux chief. I just had to share with him some of my recent experiences with Lame Deer and Crow Dog and how moved I was by Black Elk's books. It was apparent that he knew nothing about these people. He was just a B-grade actor, but I'm sure that the Keystone Chamber of Commerce saw him as a good draw for business.

The would-be Crazy Horse Mountain project was nearby and underway, but I chose to pass. Some Indians back on the Rosebud had hostile impressions of Korczak, the white man who was attempting to carve Crazy Horse Mountain. They were vehemently opposed to him scarring the Black Hills with what they perceived as yet another get-rich tourist trap. When completed, Crazy Horse Mountain is supposed to be five hundred sixty-three feet high, and six hundred forty-one feet long. It appears that this would be nearly five times the size of Mount Rushmore. Decades and decades later, this project is still in process of completion. A whole tourist site has been established, and there's an exorbitant parking fee just to admire an unfinished work up close that you can view just as well from the road. Korczak died in October of 1982, but supposedly his last words to his wife, Ruth, were, "You must work on the mountain, but go slowly so you'll do it right." It's now up to Korczak's five sons and five daughters to carry on. An entire complex on this site has been planned, including a medical center, museum, and university. He was a great sculptor with a larger-than-life endeavor.

The fog had completely lifted, the air was warming, and we decided to head up Highway 385 to the northern end of the Black Hills to visit the disreputable town of Deadwood. Deadwood reeked of saloons and gunslingers, trying its best to hang onto its rugged outlaw heritage. On the warped wooden boardwalk, I met up with a really old, old-timer. This grizzled man was probably in his nineties, and it seemed that his only mission was to dispel the legend of Calamity Jane. Pulling me aside, he angrily exclaimed, "I knew Calamity Jane when I was a boy. She was a drunkard and prostitute. Even the dogs didn't like her." Gee, that's not what the travel brochure said. He swayed my thinking for sure.

Isn't it odd how we tend to romanticize and even glorify degenerates? It seems strange how time dismisses their crimes and honors them as heroes. The old man went on to say, "Wild Bill Hickock didn't live here; he was just passing through and got shot." Yes, as the headline read on August 2, 1876, "In the #10 Saloon he was shot with his back to the door by Jack 'Broken Nose' McCall. James Butler Hickock of Abilene, Kansas was shot to death, slumped over, holding a dead man's hand, aces and eights."

This old man that I met up with obviously needed to burn off some more steam, so on and on he went about how the original town of Deadwood burned down and what you see is just a remake for tourism. Boy, he had a way of killing the Old West flavor, but I was sold on his stories. Admittedly, though, they did a nice job of recreating an old western mining town with gunslingers, storefronts, and hitching posts. You could tell by the bland expressions that the shopkeepers and trinket dealers were still astonished by the great numbers of gullible tourists.

The town of Lead was just a few miles to the south, still boasting of the largest gold strike claim in US history, the Homestake Mine, to this day the largest producer of gold in the western hemisphere. The Black Hills gold rush of 1876 ushered in by an earlier expedition of General George Custer changed the face and history of the Black Hills.

Lead became one of the first mile-high cities, and, yes, gold mine tours abound. Black Hills gold-fashioned jewelry was sold everywhere. "There's gold in them thar hills." As the slogan goes, "The coward never started, and the weak died on the way."

The newspaper headlines of the 1870s certainly reflected the times of the Wild West:

"TRAIN ROBBERS FLEE NORTH AFTER BREAKING JAIL WALL"
"SITTING BULL FALLS BEFORE BULLETS RESISTING ARREST"
"WILD BILL HICKOCK SHOT AT THE #10 BELLE UNION SALOON"
"PREACHER SMITH FOLLOWED COARSE MINERS TO CAMP, STUB-
BORNLY PREACHING GOSPEL"
"SIOUX INDIANS SIGN TREATY"
"THREE HORSE THIEVES SWING AS JUSTICE REIGNS AT RAPID CITY"
"CALAMITY JANE CAPTURES JACK MCCALL"
"GOLD DISCOVVERED IN THE BLACK HILLS"

After my brief exposure to the grandeur and commercialism of the Black Hills, I could better appreciate the Native American's sorrow and grief in surrendering this land to their conquerors.

CHAPTER 23

DRAWN TO BOULDER: A SPIRITUAL MELTING POT

I tripped over a rock and landed in Wyoming, just a stone's throw away from the Black Hills. Near Sundance, on Interstate 80, I picked up a hitchhiker. He was a rugged-looking sort of mountain guy in his early twenties. Hitchhikers proved to be a valuable asset, as they always seemed to know about unusual happenings and people to see. This long blond-haired, blue-eyed lively free fellow was no exception.

As Pam scooted over, he jumped in. I asked, "Where you heading?"

"Boulder. There's a big spiritual festival there the end of June. I spent a lot of time in Boulder; know a lot of people there. Good, mellow people."

"Boy," I thought, "That really sounds interesting. I guess I had plans to shoot north and see Devil's Tower, maybe go into Montana and visit Custer's battlefield, and then head down into Yellowstone, but, hey, I guess we can take you all the way to Boulder. I've never been there, but I've sure heard a lot about it."

Another sixty miles west, we came to Gillette and took Highway 59 south. He mentioned that his name was Jack and filled my ears and soul by exclaiming all the esoteric wonders that Boulder had to offer, such as the Sufi Center, TM Training, Aropa institutes, tarot reading, natural food stores, and several natural food restaurants, including one called the Carnival Café. It sounded like the sort of place a young seeker would feel at home in. I certainly was in no rush to get to Alaska, and I still had at least sixteen hundred dollars. I was flying high. Shortly after Thunder Basin natural grasslands, Jack parted company with us at Douglas, in the east central part of Wyoming, wishing to stay on Interstate 25 so he could make the three hundred miles to Boulder by the next day, June 1. We took the leisurely, little-traveled Highway 94 out of Douglas into the Medicine Bow National Forest. It was always good to be back in the forested hills.

Medicine Bow was much more undisturbed than the Black Hills. We camped on the Laramie River that night, admiring the sunset shooting off Laramie Peak. They were modest, wild mountains, suitable for the novice pioneer. While sitting crossways from each other between a quiescent campfire, the tranquil atmosphere offered me the courage to confront Pam. As a whisper drifts with only the gentle flow of the Laramie River and a bird or two yet unsettled, I calmly broke into the air with words. "Pam, I think we should split up in Boulder. I don't think we really have much in common after all. I'd be happy to help you out with fifty or a hundred dollars to take a bus back to Houston." Ah, I finally said it after six weeks of this eventual uneasy encounter haunting me.

The faint glow from the coals showed a relieving calm on Pam's soft, baby-like face. She felt the same way. Her dark brown eyes even seemed to shine with freedom. For the first time since we met, we actually experienced a comfortable, easy friendship.

We slept outside that evening, yet another star-studded sky, quite cool though. The morning found me with my teeth chattering while tucked inside my frost-covered sleeping bag. We made quick business of our breakfast and wash-up things, and shortly after sunrise, June 1, we headed south to Boulder. By nine o'clock in the morning we were in Laramie, and as usual, just the name thrust me into the westerns. But unlike the movies, we had to stop at a supermarket to pick up a few things.

Now, this wasn't the nicely tiled, made-to-look-generic supermarket that most of the country adapted to. Outside was an actual wooden sidewalk with post rails for horses and pick-ups parked everywhere. Inside we observed Mr. And Mrs. Cowboy Slim behind a shopping cart—hat, boots, tobaccy, and slang. The real thing, and all this on hardwood maple floors. Well, this little hippie was out of his element—he and his flowerchild. They nearly gagged and bound me, tying the rope to the saddle and slapping the horse's rump. "Yaah!" Now, that's a good time in Laramie, seeing one of them hippies being dragged down a gravel road.

After watching a six-foot, five-inch cowboy heave two, eighty-pound bags of grits on his shoulders while having casual conversation with the brawly dude from the stockyards, I suggested to Pam that maybe we should leave fast and hang on until we got to Boulder. It seemed that all these western folks within eyeshot just froze in the wake of our coming and going. I tipped the brim of my dingy, ten gallon hat and sprang into the saddle of the Dodge yelling out, "Don't worry, partner; we won't be back!" Now, there's a place where Nehru jackets and paisley prints didn't sell well. As we drove out down Highway 287 into Colorado, I thought I heard a rumble and saw faintly in the distance a dust cloud from a stagecoach. It was probably just my imagination.

By noon we pulled into Boulder, having straddled the eastern foothills of the great Rockies, and rocky they were. Easing into Boulder on Highway 36, I realized that this city was much bigger than the quaint mountain town I had pictured. It had the makings of a real city. Yuk! However, the street names reflected the geographic and historical nuances of the area: Baseline Road, Arapahoe Avenue, Foothills Parkway, Olde Stage Road, Sunshine Drive, Gold Run Road, Table Mesa Drive, and something really novel, 28th Street.

I found my way to the natural food store on the far west end of town. This area of town still retained an old-time flavor with western storefronts and older homes that were all being tickled by the Rockies.

Pam and I said our awkward, business-like good-byes. As I wandered into the store, I found a very relaxed, peaceful atmosphere. People like me just hung out and chatted. The excited talk of the big spiritual festival kept entering conversations. I easily mixed in. Quite a few people lingered on the outside porch. I thought to myself, "The guy that owns this place is doing all right." Hippie/flowerchild garb abounded—flowing colorful shirts, leather belts, bags, beadwork, and the standard tattered Levis®.

Posters and flyers were everywhere, on walls, windows, and bulletin boards, boasting of all the upcoming counterculture events. Get ready for this arsenal of spiritual activities: "Ram Dass at the University Auditorium," "Swami Satchadananda" appearing somewhere," "EST classes," "Arica, three-day seminars," Various encounter groups, "Sufi instruction," "Tai Chi exercises," "Inner awakening" of this and that, "Shakti yoga," and "Divine Light Mission Welcomes You."

How's this for a name of your spiritual master: Balyo Jeshwar Paramhans Sat Guru Dev Shri Sant Ji Maharaj? What ever happened to that kid, anyway? He was touted as the lord of the universe; possibly he's off overseeing a different section of the universe.

Many other ways were advertised, such as "Tarot card reading, five dollars"; "Divine healing, no charge, contribution suggested"; and "ESP workshop, Tuesdays and Thursdays, 10 a.m., 7:30 pm or thereabouts." The *East-West Journal* was openly displayed and sold. There were also ads for "Anada Marga Yoga Society"; "Chogyam Trungpa Rinpoche is coming'" "Zen Buddhism'" "Vegetarian lifestyle'" "Alan Watts will be speaking at the University on joyous cosmology"; "Join the Sufi choir."; "Understand Pir Vilayat Inayat Khan's writings"; "Meditate on Mandalas"; "3 HO organization, Happy, Holy, Healthy" "Kundalini yoga"; "Crystal powers taught"; and "Macrobiotics by Michio Kushi."

Yes Boulder was certainly exploding with spiritual vibrations. If you couldn't find a way of enlightenment suitable to your peculiar make-up here in Boulder, you probably weren't suited for enlightenment, or else you possibly couldn't handle the choices. It was easy to understand how someone could burn out trying to get lit. I was determined to try everything at least once.

I slept in the truck that night parked along Boulder Creek under cottonwood trees. I practiced my songs and called up my spirit guides. I was bracing myself for the big one when my spiritual purpose and destiny would be revealed, surely, here in Boulder. The morning was warm and bright; it was summer for sure. I easily saw why these trees were called cottonwood. Balls of cotton-like stuff were flying everywhere. I thought maybe there was a gang pillow fight overnight.

The Family Table Bookstore and Restaurant was close by, so I stopped in to just hang around, listen, and ask questions. I was complaining to an older lady about a stiff neck and loss of voice that I was experiencing. She secretly scooted me into a back room and laid her hands on me. Apparently, she thought that I was healed now. I thanked her for her time and offered her five dollars, but she refused to accept money because this was her gift to share. Well, as much as I tried to convince myself that the pain was gone, I could not. That afternoon after eating in the soup kitchen for fifty cents, I timidly went back to her, suggesting that the problem still existed. Her piercing olive eyes reacted in astonishment, but she gave me the name of a lady who did aura readings and healing. "Call her. Tell her I sent you, but tell no one."

"Thanks," I said. Gee, I get to have my aura read.

I gave the lady, whose first name was Joni, a call and set up an appointment for seven o'clock that evening. "How much is this going to cost?" I questioned.

Joni answered with surprise, "Whatever you can afford." She lived out in a lovely suburb southeast of Boulder, and I thought that maybe I had the wrong address. Going up to the door, her teenage daughter answered. Joni quickly came to the door and ushered me into a small back room, a sort of den.

With the door closed, she talked smoothly in calm tones asking me about myself. As we sat across from each other over a card table, she held my hands and cautioned me not to speak. "I'll be going into a trance, and when I come out, I won't remember what I said." Okay, I nodded, like a dumb puppy. Well, sure enough, she instantly started mumbling about my past lives.

"The reason that you wear nothing on your neck or wrist is that you were a sixteen-year-old slave boy working on the pyramids. Your job was to operate a lever that released boulders to be carved. You had chains on your wrist and a collar around your neck. You were miserable and depressed. Oh! You let go of the lever; the rocks crushed you to death."

"I see a boat, Norsemen. You are a Viking in charge of a twelve-man crew. The only reason you set sail is to admire the land from far off. You love the earth.

"Indians, I see Indians and tipis. You are among them, but you are not an Indian but a blood brother. Your days are peaceful with them before white man came."

Joni awakened, startled and pale, almost out of breath. She asked, "Did you find things out about yourself?" I nodded and eagerly discussed the things that she had told me. She was very agreeable. She interrupted and began telling me about the aura color she saw emanating from my body. I was assured that enlightenment would come soon and was advised that I should always carry a fire opal for protection and power. I gave her ten dollars and thanked her very much. I still never got over how straight she, her husband, her children, house, and neighborhood were. I thought it odd that this would go on in a typical, suburban community.

As days went on, I reviewed over and over these past lives and auric reading. She obviously knew that I didn't like jewelry around my wrists and neck because I wore none. She knew that I preferred land more than water because of where I chose to live. And, of course, she knew my deep fondness of Indians because I shared that with her before the reading. I started to wonder whether she wasn't a hoax. And my neck continued to hurt. What do you think?

At early afternoon the following day, I wandered into the Carnival Café, the only all-natural-foods restaurant that I was aware of. It had the appearance of a typical mid-priced restaurant. Businessmen were seated at tables, and other respectable looking people claimed a stool here and there. I can't begin to repeat the menu, but it was expensive, at least for 1974: Lentil soup, $1.25, and Goats milk cheese sandwich on whole wheat bread with alfalfa sprouts, $1.85. Wee doggy! No wonder the clientele looked so nice; common slum like me couldn't afford to eat here. A glass of carrot juice was at least a dollar. It turns your fingers orange; be careful.

I really saw no one similar to myself but chatted with the counter lady anyway. She seemed normal and real. I mentioned to her that I heard that the restaurant let musicians entertain on Friday nights. She confirmed that, "Yes, that's true." So I booked myself for one hour that Friday. I would get no pay, just exposure. Here was my chance to test my seven songs. Perhaps people would be moved to a state of ecstasy.

That day was Wednesday, so I practiced and practiced my songs in the park overlooking Boulder Creek. I drew the attention of a good many people, some with questioning eyes, some appreciative, and some like-minded musicians. Even children sat and listened. One of the ladies that enjoyed my music was named Barbara. She lived in an apartment on Walnut Street in Boulder, and we became friends. It was easy to talk deeply about spiritual inklings with her. We seemed to meet each other constantly at odd spiritual events. Many months later I met up with her again in another city.

Well, I promoted myself as best I could in two days, placing notices on the bulletin board at the natural food store, bookstore, college, and several restaurants. Friday night eventually came. My throat felt better, but that same nauseous feeling gripped at my insides. Fear, fright, the same crud that did me in in the Santa Cruz Mountains. Maybe I'm not cut out to do solo work. I wore the cleanest dirty clothes I had and drove to the Carnival Café. My spirit guides were summoned to my aid.

Casually walking in at six forty-five that evening, the café was half filled. I professionally set my guitar case down on the five-by-ten foot platform stage, picked up a stool, and assertively boasted of who I was and where I had been. People politely smiled. Well, that's nice; at least they heard me. I belted out the seven songs and at least five others with full force. I do believe that the candles blew out six tables away. Nobody ate; they just stared intently.

The owner came over after the third song and suggested that I get a little quieter. "No one's ordering any food." I was very offended. These people seemed to love me. They applauded loudly and shouted out positive comments. I mildly argued with the owner, "But they like me."

He flatly responded, "We let you play because we wanted background music, not a show."

The pride and anger within me did not yield. I played boldly and sang my guts out. That was the last time I stepped into the Carnival Café, choosing to forfeit my complimentary free meal.

I had heard about Stephan, the man who did sand readings. I gave him a call and made an appointment to see him in yet another plush suburban neighborhood northeast of Boulder. Stephan came to the door, casually dressed; with a black patch over one eye, a man in his mid-forties. He had a nervous yet gentle air about him embellished with light humor.

We went out on his back patio on this beautiful seventy-five degree mid-June day. There sat a six-sided sandbox approximately two and one-half feet in diameter. Stephan assured me that it was a good day to read sand and asked me to sit on the northeast side across from him. He told me the story about the vision that he had to make a six-sided box to read people's past, present, and future. I was to take my hand and draw designs in the sand. "Mess it up a bit." So, with my left hand (I'm left-handed, you know) I made some uncertain squigglies. Stephan must have gotten together with the lady who read my past lives and aura because he communicated the same procedures. "I'm going to look at the sand and go into a trance. Don't talk to me; I'll read the sand out loud."

Well, there he went into a trance. His mumblings were in English but almost incoherent. I couldn't seem to grasp a message other than something about a lion. My eyes started to cross attempting to make sense of his ramblings. He miraculously pulled out of the trance and said virtually nothing. Walking me to the door, he needed to make himself credible by telling me that a man flies in weekly from Chicago to have his business sand readings done.

I wasn't charged anything for this initial consultation and drove away feeling like I just ate "Skimpy" peanut butter, the brand that boasts of leaving you just short of flavor. Perhaps I didn't listen hard enough.

Every day in Boulder had its moments of experience with cults and spiritual ticklings like the East Indian group that I met with for one week at six o'clock in the morning. Everybody had to wear orange; they were some sort of sun worshipers. As many as forty groggy people would show up each weekday morning. The leader was consistently late.

We did exercises and then screamed as loud as we could. A few bold animal sounds were suggested. After ten minutes of ripping out our lungs, we ran sporadically in all directions; then we were told to collapse and lay quietly until a marvelous state of bliss filled us. The only state anybody ever made it to was foolishness. Finally, on the fifth day, the leader whom I called "Yogi Come Lately" never showed up. Probably too blissed out to make it. I think that the early orange gang disbanded after that. I never went back.

Boulder had some quaint and commercially attractive areas sprinkled with small shops and boutiques. Footwork was my fondness. I usually parked the truck and walked for miles. There was an overgrown plant store wedged in between Ashrams and meditation centers. I felt compelled to peek inside. The owner, a soft spoken, nervous sort of man in his late twenties quickly asked if he could help me. He said, "Can I help you?"

Good line, I thought. "No, I'm just looking at these lush plants." I felt like I was standing in the vision of a green sauna. An invisible vapor barrier locked in the one hundred percent-plus humidity. "Boy, these plants are doing well in here." He was easily flattered and smiled proudly at the acknowledgment.

Being from the spiritually assertive town that Boulder laid claim to, he remarked, "I sense a spiritual awareness in you, a longing for deeper things. Have you ever had your tarot cards read?"

"Ah, no, I haven't. I really don't know much about those cards."

He jumped at the chance and asked me, "Would you like to come upstairs? I'd be delighted to read your cards. It's free. I just think that the cards have something special for you today."

"Well, okay," I hesitantly answered. Now I was the one being puffed up. Gee, he can actually sense that I'm really spiritual.

We went upstairs to his living quarters and sat facing each other over a very small, dark walnut table. He brought the cards out, handling them with a sacred reverence while explaining to me the meaning of many of the pictures and scenes. Most of it passed over my head. So he proceeded with his card-shuffling act, and laying down card after card on the table, he began telling me everything I wanted to hear. So far all that these readers had told me was what I wanted to hear. This session lasted about half an hour when I abruptly said that I'd be leaving. The plant man looked disturbed about my leaving and impressed upon me that I'd need to return in two days for further revelation. "It's imperative."

Somewhat agreeing, I said, "Well, I suppose I can stop in." Most of this session was nothing more than general sugary observations and very vague future descriptions of my life and personality.

He seemed sincere, so two days later in the midmorning I stopped in. He glowed with enthrallment at seeing me. He whisked me back upstairs and hurriedly seated me at the table. The cards were alive and bustling with news. The plant man warned me that physical harm might come to me in the next week and that I should stay with him in his upper flat and not venture out.

I laughed a good one and assuredly stated, "Things don't harm me; I'm protected. I think I'm going to go now; thanks for your time." He was shaken and angered, attempting to convince me that I was making a grave mistake.

Well, the writer of this book had lived in New York City, and it became quite obvious to me that he was hustling and using whatever crafty ploy to get me to be his temporary lover. I fled instead. My New York experience sharpened my awareness of his gay advances. I was definitely a full-blooded heterosexual. I had my own scheming to take care of; unfortunately, I usually failed with the opposite sex.

A group of friends that I was drawn to was living in a ranch house on the north end of town. Many of the people there were involved in organizing this great three-day spiritual festival. They were gracious enough to let me stay in their house for a week and sleep on the floor.

Through them, I became actively involved in the upcoming festival. I practiced music with a large group that would be singing songs on the back of a flatbed truck during the kickoff parade. They rehearsed over and over again the gospel standard *May the Circle be Unbroken* and some other obscure favorites of theirs. It was good being accepted and needed musically.

An all-ladies dance troupe had invited me to coordinate guitar music and percussion rhythms to their dance program, which was to be performed the evening of the first day of this festival in an open meadow under the moon. We practiced several evenings in a small, second story auditorium/gymnasium in downtown Boulder. They wore white satin, full-length gowns and did many erotic movements while chanting in dark, mysterious, minor tones something about the crescent moon. It gave me the willies! I never did discover their exact identification, but there was much argumentative division among them. My involvement was limited to strumming a few chords and tapping some simple rhythms out on the bongos. I certainly wasn't with their program.

The Arica Institute was a few doors down from the plant shop, and for thirty dollars you could enroll in a four-hour intensive encounter group to expand your mind and to dispel inhibitions. For thirty dollars I just had to try it. A fairly large group entered that day, perhaps thirty-five enrollees. We took our shoes off and soft footed on the thick carpeting. The instructor gave the underlying premise for this technique and made us aware that the four hours was only a sampler of what the one-, three-, and seven-day intensives were like. They were virtually guaranteed to transform your character, mostly from passive to bold assertive. Being always in control was stressed as an outward objective.

We sat in a circle and individually shared with the group things that we didn't like about ourselves and fears that we had. The more you spewed your guts, the more success you had. Group reaction was vital. After this somewhat emotional session, we were all instructed to scream. Shades of the early orange gang flowed past my ears. Mind-over-matter techniques were disclosed in the vein of "I'm okay, you're okay" and "I can do anything I put my mind to." Four hours did not go fast enough for me.

This forty-year-old instructor maintained his state of confidence; reminding us numerous times that this was just a sample of what was to be at the one-, three- and seven-day intensives.

There were quite a few very straight-looking business types in this group, both men and women. I guess they needed a little loosening up. As for me, I may have been too loose. The only inhibitions that I was aware of were suggested to me by the instructor. He continued to reassure us and affirm the quality of the Arica Institute by saying things, such as "See how much freer we all feel." He felt richer, I felt dumber, and the rest of the crowd was divided.

I couldn't imagine what would have happened to me had I done the seven-day for four hundred and fifty dollars. I'd either come out qualifying as an instructor, or I'd be a neurotic wreck. Enough of group therapy.

Baba Ram Dass, born Richard Alpert, was riding high on the success of his esoteric transformation book entitled *Be Here Now*. I'm sure that he was in great demand for speaking engagements, and he was soon to conduct a two-nighter at the university.

I just had to go there. The place was packed; fifteen hundred hot and sweaty spiritual seekers crammed shoulder-to-shoulder to catch a whiff of Baba's wisdom. He proclaimed himself enlightened while in India. He must be the real thing.

He finally came up on the platform after a long delay, mostly fielding questions from the audience, and he fielded them poorly. The people attending were not as gullible as he had hoped. They had discerning minds. Rumor flowed through the hall that he was drunk, and many in the audience became rather obnoxious with the organizers. This was not his crowd. Some people verbally attacked him and sneering broke out.

I left, no less disillusioned than when I stepped in. At least it was free. Well, I had to admit, he was there now.

Many people were kind and generous to me in Boulder. Another fellow let me stay in his lower flat apartment for a week and allow myself some decent hygiene and hot meals. Nice guy.

So many thousands here in Boulder were searching for a deeper awakening with God, for a sense of supreme purpose for their existence. I talked in depth to as many as one hundred of these folks, and when I broke through the blissful smile and air of attainment, I saw that many were in the same position as myself—disturbed, confused and still searching. At least they were able to admit it. That's a good start.

It was around June 27, the big day was the next day: the start of the first annual eventually worldwide New Age festival. A parade route was finalized through downtown Boulder, and I was asked to drive the beginning truck. (Yes, it was a Mack truck and steered like one.) They insisted that I have my face painted and wear a clown costume. So with face painted and clown costume on, I hopped in the cab. The Circle Be Unbroken group was on the back of the truck, singing and chanting. I estimate that two to three hundred people, weird people at that, took part in the parade.

At ten o'clock in the morning sharp, I started the truck and glided a comfortable five miles an hour through Boulder. Not an awful lot of spectators came out, as the town council and police department shunned this particular activity, but it was legal. I made a grueling left turn off of Iris onto Broadway and noticed sirens and flashing lights. Driving on, I just thought that it was part of the parade. Finally, a policeman forced the truck to the side and waved the rest of the parade by.

He yelled to me, "Hey, buddy! Let me see your driver's license." He probably didn't think that the hippie dressed like "Bozo the Clown" had one. I showed him my Wisconsin license, and he directed me into a parking lot. By now, half the parade members had gathered around the truck. I couldn't imagine what was wrong. Maybe I ran over the mayor, or worse yet, his Pekinese dog.

"Officer, what did I do wrong?" I talked like I had such a reverence for the law.

"You made an illegal left turn onto Broadway."

"But that was the parade route. I was told to turn there."

"The police never okayed it. That's a fifty dollar fine. Get out; we're taking you to the station."

He was serious, and I had to ask, "Are you serious?"

At this point at least one hundred people had encircled us chanting "OM." The vibration was great. But he put me in the back of the squad car and drove slowly to the station. Now I really felt dumb. Passers-by stared at me. I thought, "Good lord, I look like a clown." Children yelled, "Look, Mom, they're taking a clown to jail."

Sure enough, they actually put me behind bars with a couple of derelicts that were caught urinating in the street. I didn't have much to say to my cellmates. Actually, they avoided me, mumbling, "This guy's dressed like a clown at ten-thirty o'clock in the morning. What did you do — steal candy? Ha, Ha." Oh, they had no compassion toward the hippie.

After about an hour I was let go and the guard said," Your hippie friends got up the fifty dollars. You can go."

In the lobby, at least ten of my friends greeted me like I was a martyr for the cause, making me aware that the town was against this festival and would still probably try to stop it.

I was driven by friends off to the festivals grounds. In the meadow, near the very unique Flatirons rock formation, I saw tipis, tables, and innumerable handcrafted items. People mingled and sang. A flower child atmosphere presided. I had my guitar along and attracted a small gathering of interested listeners. The seven songs were meeting their fruition.

A large, thirty-by-fifteen-foot platform was being erected. Volunteers eagerly lent a hand. I did what I could, trying to remember which side of the saw to use. A nail here, a nail there, and a rather bluish enlarged thumb are probably why they call it a thumbnail. The hammer connects more there than anywhere else.

The stage was set, and by late afternoon an MC began giving the schedule of events. About a thousand people had been attracted to the area by this time. Various nobodies came up and gave fifteen to twenty minute speeches on *Mother Earth and the New Age*. The crowd politely applauded.

Then, on this very mild late June day, to my surprise, Lame Deer was introduced. I couldn't believe it. They actually booked him to speak. Well, he was decked out in full regalia, floor length headdress and the works. He appeared very impressive in all his colorful native clothing. As he came up to the microphone, a very strong wind rose up from his backside. He couldn't hold down the headdress, and it eventually covered his face. It was a moment of intense embarrassment for him. His speech was cut abruptly short. He took the headdress off and sat on a chair on the platform looking a bit bewildered.

I came up to him later, but he didn't remember my recent visit with him in Winner, South Dakota. He kept talking in vague, impersonal terms about his people. Lame Deer passed away around 1985.

Ben, a Hopi holy man, spoke the following day. He had a very kind, humble spirit about him. Wearing well-worn Levis® and a plaid flannel shirt, he communicated in a whisper-like voice, sharing stories of the Hopi's plight and future hopes. I liked this guy and sought him out later, but he was nowhere to be found.

Being attracted to natural settings, I set out to climb the Flatirons. Probably less than a quarter mile away from the meadow, these smooth, diagonal stone ridges were surely unique, jutting upwards perhaps one hundred twenty-five feet. Coming in from the backside, I was met by several others who had the same idea, though they were professionally decked out with mountain climbing gear, ropes, and spiked boots. I managed to get three-quarters of the way to the top, though it was difficult without the proper equipment. The view overlooking the meadow made the fifteen hundred-plus gathering seem so miniscule. I managed to awkwardly take a few pictures and cautiously descended back down. Being on flat solid ground again felt reassuring.

That evening, under a clear sky and crescent moon, the ladies' dance troupe performed their eerie ritual that worshipped the moon goddess and the crescent moon. Somebody was gracious enough to provide a large twenty-by-thirty-foot area carpet for them to perform on. I did my guitar and bongo thing as most onlookers attempted to grasp the significance of this dance. There still was no sense of unity of spirit among them. They couldn't have asked for a better evening under the stars though.

My truck was parked along the paved roadway that ran parallel to the meadow. I slept there the three nights. The following morning, the beginning of the third day, I gradually involved myself with a group of about two hundred Whirling Dervishes. The Whirling Dervishes have their origin in Persia. This rather interesting and somewhat complicated group dance sought to propel the participant into a trance-like state of ecstasy. The approximately two hundred people formed a circle within a circle. While holding your two neighbors' hands, the two circles slowly moved in opposite directions, chanting a type of mantra over and over. I knew not what I was saying; it didn't really seem to matter.

People were a giddy sort of happy, like when you swing really high and come down or rotate quickly on a small merry-go-round, sort of like the tickle you get in your stomach while riding in a car going over a dip in the road. We were having a good time.

The circles accelerated, and the chanting got louder. There was no question that a sensational vibration was taking hold. I became increasingly dizzier and slightly faint. Most of these people obviously were experienced at this whirling movement. As if on cue, they collapsed to the ground, and each person moaned inside with their own personal experience. Basically, I just wanted to experience being regular again instead of a blissful state of vomiting.

Somebody yelled out with a broad rimmed smile, "Who wants to do it again?" I declined in the midst of moaning and groaning.

I made a nice handful of friends during this event. There was a fragile oneness of spirit in that we at least were heading in a direction away from greed and materialism. General spiritual talk was free for the hauling. Some good spiritual stuff could be found in the mostly deceptive trash pile if you took the time to sift through and didn't mind getting your hands soiled.

I think that the highlight of the festival, as far as main speakers were concerned, was the unexpected mid-afternoon arrival of Swami Satchadananda. He was a highly revered holy man from India. The day was overcast and slightly cool for late June. A white limousine pulled up near the stage. The crowd of people rushed the vehicle. They obviously knew who was inside, and their anticipation drove them into an ecstatic frenzy.

An older East Indian man with soft flowing gray hair and beard, wearing a white cotton gown, gracefully stepped out. His name spun through the crowd like a fired-up whisper. A rumor was realized. "Swami Satchadananda, Satchadananda, Satchadananda." I couldn't help but experience the excitement. I, too, had heard of this great sage from India. It seemed like an honor to have his presence in Boulder. He was definitely the boost that this bourgeois platform required.

A number of his lofty-eyed followers helped him to the platform. A hush blanketed the scene. Only irregular breathing and joyous guttural vocal emissions entered as sound. He had an unmistakably happy mellow, frosted expression embodying his face. As if miraculous, the clouds opened just above us. Deep blue shone through, and a thera-peutic warm sun softened our chilled bones. He captured the moment.

I was eager to follow up with this man, to seek him out, but as days and weeks went on, I came to find hopelessly closed doors. His spiritual teachings were treated as any other organized business. Those entrusted to Satchadananda's managerial positions were more interested in signing me up on an affordable payment plan than being genuine, loving representatives of what he supposedly stood for. Satchadananda grew dimmer as a beacon of enlightenment. There were others that I would surely pursue.

Shortly after Swami Satchadananda departed, an announcement was made to the effect of "that's all, folks." But for those seriously moved by all this, a sunrise service would be held in the morning.

I stuck around that evening but was told by the police that I couldn't park my truck there overnight. I found a quiet, dead-end dirt road about a mile away and slept there that evening. Several other vehicles filtered in after mine. Some came to seclusion circle to party, some to love, and some, like me, to camp out. The odd mix of people rapidly brought down my spiritual attitude.

Very early the next morning, about five o'clock, I groggily drove back to the meadow. As usual, I was early. Several others wandered over, and then, Ben, the Hopi leader, suddenly appeared. He was now wearing a thick, red headband. Facing the east, dawn gave impressions of a clear sky. Ben started to gather sticks for the fire; I and others eagerly helped out. He said few words; he was truly a quiet, humble man. He seemed not to accept questions; he was just very intent on the ritual and the fire.

As many as forty hardy people attended, seated on blankets cov-ering the heavily dew-filled grass. Hardly a whisper was heard among us as a contemplative reverence set the mood, complemented by the crackling fire and crisp morning air seasoned with smoke. As a gentle piercing, Ben sang in soft melodic tones, delicately releasing a melody and language of true soul. A scarlet beam shot in the heavens. The sun-rise service had begun. All eyes were fixed on the great cadmium ball, rising with a thunderous momentum so distant that it could not be heard.

I was compelled to stand up. My arms involuntarily began to rise and stretch forth. Singing proceeded outward from my deep interior. My voice was strong as it radiated vowels and melodies I had never known before. After about a minute's worth of my American Indian type chant, I became very self-conscious of my action. A mild embarrassment came over me as I thought that possibly I had disrupted the sacred moment for many of the gatherers. Looking about, it seemed that no one really paid much attention to me. To my relief, someone else started singing. I remained standing, inviting the energy of the sun to regenerate me.

Most people dispersed after twenty minutes, and I walked calmly over to Ben, who was tenderly quenching the fire. I asked him, "May I have the ashes from this fire when they've cooled?"

He seemed a bit unsettled and answered, "Yes, I'll put them in a bucket for you."

"Thanks."

I told him some kind things about him, hoping that possibly he would remark at how moved he was by my powerful Indian singing. He said nothing and just threw a modest smile my way. Saddened that he hadn't opened up to me, I shuffled back to the truck and fell into a good slumber.

About eleven o'clock in the morning I awoke from my dislocated nap and hurried back to where the fire was. Shocked and dismayed, I found nothing. The ashes were gone, and the pit was empty. A few people, left to linger, knew nothing about it. I felt so offended that Ben hadn't even found me worthy to care for the ashes. I must have made a fool of myself out there during his ceremony. I desired to have these ashes in my possession as something to hang onto, to empower me with blessings. Drifting slowly back to the truck in a nowhere state of mind, I nearly walked right on top of the smoldering pile near the passenger side of the truck. Ecstatic with tears of joy, I thanked him wherever he was. But, how did he know that this was my truck? Esteeming the ashes as sacred and in my trusted keeping, I gently scooped them into a pail. I had gained a new power and ritual. Wisdom and guidance would be beckoned as I would wisely use these ashes or give them away to worthy people.

A great party was planned that evening for all those involved with this festival. It was to be held in a mountain house that overlooked Boulder and Denver. The house was literally built into the jagged cliffs on the very eastern slope of the Rocky Mountains. Up the winding Boulder Canyon Drive, I found my way to Gus' house long before sunset. Quite a few others were there before me. Walking down a path towards his beautiful home, I had some apprehension. Most of the cars and trucks were fairly new, and I'd surely stick out among the wealthy. I was greeted warmly by people mingling on his outside porch, which jutted out over the cliff. Long way down? You bet—at least four thousand feet. It seemed sturdy enough, but who'd want to live like this?

Entering in, I noticed that most people were dressed nicely. There were a few odds and ends, hippies like myself, but mostly there seemed to be casually dressed business folk: *New Age* business folk. His kitchen table was filled with bottles of beer and hard alcohol. Cheese, crackers, and general finger foods were laid out, also. The place was starting to get loud and messy.

I strove to fit in, throwing in some well-thought-out humor. Some people gave me a little eye contact and chuckled, but mostly I just didn't gel.

Gus, the man who was throwing this party, opened his refrigerator and asked if anybody wanted some good psylosibin mushrooms? Psylosibin is a strong chemical derived from certain mushrooms. I never had psylosibin and was a bit reserved, but it had to be better than destroying my insides with alcohol. I gladly took a healthy teaspoonful. Others seemed eager to partake also.

This Gus sure did enjoy people. I'd hardly ever met anyone with such an all-around happy disposition. When I helped him build the platform down in the meadow, he got zonked on the head with a two by four and just laughed about it. He came out of the same mold as Wavy Gravy. It seemed that his greatest joy was seeing people having a great time. I tried to cozy up to some of the girls there who I was attracted to, but usually they just humored me along.

Gus asked everyone to take their shoes and socks off and sit on the living room floor in a large circle. He wanted to film the birth of a cat. Nobody knew what was going on, but as was customary, nothing was too weird for me. These stiff-laced business types were starting to get mighty loose by now. With all of our toes touching as the hub of a wheel, he placed a kitten in the middle and started his movie camera rolling. Now, Gus, as director, told us to slowly pull back our feet. Pop! The kitten's head peaked through, and then his front paws. This little movie star was desperate to get out of the foot womb. Finally, he struggled with a terror-stricken expression and freed himself from the bonds of the feet. He took off. Everybody clapped for him. The party was getting crazy.

I stepped outside to commune with God. The effects of the psylosibin were taking hold. I talked to the trees and answered the wind. The evening air in the mountains was a crisp fifty-two degrees. All the lights of Boulder and Denver could be easily seen from this height. City lights had their own beauty, but it was to me a sad beauty knowing that it was just a reflection of worldly people and their city nightlife.

A very pretty lady and I began to talk under a pine tree. I believe that her name was Kathy. I had entered into an esoteric language by now and began to cry, sharing with her my grief as to how people were unable to live in harmony with nature and one another. She was very compassionate and even concerned for my well-being as I became increasingly more distressed and sorrowful. It's hard to say just how long we talked as time wasn't a concern.

The next thing that I remember about that evening was myself sitting on a rocky ledge facing east, anticipating the dawn. I could see out as far as my eyes were capable of seeing. A guy perched about ten feet from me suggested that the human eye could see two hundred miles.

Dawn began opening in all its richness and pastel colors. I meditated and chanted quietly. Turning about, I was surprised to see twelve to fifteen others quietly sitting, patiently longing for the sunrise. People all smiled at each other as if we had a speechless unity of spirit. It was reassuring to know that of the fifty or sixty people that showed for this party, that I was akin to a remnant. The first points of light showered the sky from north to south. Again, I stood up, balancing on an angle and raising my arms, began to sing. How far could my voice carry? An indistinguishable language went forth carrying with it an enchantingly melodious song. When the song was finished and the sun was fully visible, I turned to walk away. We hugged each other and several people thanked me for my song. I felt like I had a meaningful part in history and that the little hippie known to them as Ayuta Rai made an impact.

I was weak and a bit sleepy, so I curled up in the back of my truck and crept into a peaceful slumber. Loud voices and car doors slamming woke me to a veiled state of consciousness. It was nearly one in the afternoon. I walked back to the house to thank Gus for his generosity. Some women were scurrying about, hastily cleaning. I knocked on the door as I entered, sensing an intruder's emotion. I asked with a loud nervousness, "Is Gus here?"

A lady barked back harshly, "No, he went to work, and we're stuck cleaning up this mess."

I was amazed that he would be able to function enough to go to work. The vibrations from these three or four women were very hostile. A lot of anger and foul words were shouted back and forth. I gracefully left and headed deep into the Rockies, having no further connection with Boulder from that day on.

CHAPTER 24

ROCKY MOUNTAIN FLING

As I leisurely crept up Highway 7 going toward Rocky Mountain National Park, I picked up a hitchhiker named David. He lived in a cabin near a summit high in the Rockies. David came down into Boulder twice a month to pick up general supplies. He wasn't very talkative and told me little about himself, but I offered to take him to his cabin nonetheless. He lived near a remote mountain town named Peaceful Valley, less than ten miles southeast of the park. David definitely preferred a secluded life. His nearest neighbor was probably five miles away.

The Rockies are tough mountains, heavily forested, and I guess you could say very rocky. Some of these rocks were the size of a two-story building.

David showed me the stream that was his sole source of water. When it froze over, he just chopped a hole through the ice with his ax. I somewhat envied his living quarters and lifestyle, but he avoided my question as to how he made his money. None of my business I guess.

After making him aware that I was a musician, he informed me, "Did you know that Chicago has a ranch up here that they practice and record at?"

"No, really?" I quickly responded. "Wow, that would be great to live up here and record."

David told me how to get to their ranch, and I headed off in that direction. Chicago was a very famous jazz-rock group, internationally known. I easily recalled in my memory seeing them perform at the Fillmore East in New York City. I even saw them at a small club in Milwaukee in the late 60s before they were known as Chicago or even as Chicago Transit Authority. I believe that they called themselves, The Big Thing. The drive to the ranch was light and easy as I traveled the crest of the summit. Not a bad ride, when you need to not burn your brakes out going down or fry your engine going up.

I stopped at the locked gates at the entrance of what was supposedly Chicago's "Caribou Ranch." There seemed to be no activity, so I ventured out one-half mile onto an open meadow and decided to camp out there for the night. Others had been here before me. A large fire pit with a stone wall had previously been built there. Taking advantage of the mild, summer-like weather at ten thousand or so feet, I lay back and got musically personal with my voice and Guild guitar. A chance thought entertained me on occasion: what if someone from the group Chicago heard me and wanted to record my songs?

I fashioned a little altar out of colorful rocks and interesting forest objects and offered up the sacred ashes as a sacrificial worship to God. My conversation to God lasted a good hour. Chanting and cries for enlightenment enveloped the air, but God did not answer me. Once again, an empty forlorn emotion gripped at me. I not only could not communicate with God, but loneliness started to toy with my spirit again. Here I sat surrounded by the grandeur and awesome beauty of the summer Rockies and still was not happy. The Alpine tundra and multi-colored wildflowers could not soothe my troubled soul. I wanted God to talk to me, not just some supernatural experience, but was God actually having a personal interaction with me? By seven o'clock in the evening, the mountain air was cooling. At sunset I wept because of loneliness. Why couldn't I share this scene with a lady? Black is blacker the closer you are to the evening heavens. I couldn't see my hand waving in front of my face. Stars that can't be numbered showered the sky like diamond dust catches the sunlight.

John Denver's song, "Rocky Mountain High," falls far short of describing the majesty of the Rockies.

As I awoke on the morning of July 2, a glance through the teardrop window told me that dawn had brought with it a bit of frost, soon to dissipate when the great ball of fire rose. Rocky Mountain National Park and Estes Park were still in my sights to visit if for nothing more than to say I was there.

The tourist and tourism-designed attractions polarized me, but I made the most of a day and night at Estes Park. Many mountain peaks exceeded thirteen thousand and even fourteen thousand feet, a climber's paradise. Speaking of climbers, I picked a couple of guys up on my way to the park. They had all the right gear for big league climbing, rope, boots, picks, and whatever. No thanks, I prefer level ground.

One thing struck me as odd; there was no firewood to be had at densely wooded Estes Park. Somebody came around in a rusted pick-up truck and sold small bundles of wood to the campers for a dollar a bundle. The bundle was no more than a ten-inch diameter log fifteen inches long, split up into eight pieces. He made out quite well, but he didn't get my dollar. No firewood in a national forest—that's weird.

CHAPTER 25

YELLOWSTONE IMPRESSIONS

There was no other direction for me to go than north to Yellowstone. I had to see if the Yogi Bear© cartoons accurately depicted this area. The road leading out of Rocky Mountain National Park had the contour of a bent Slinky®. You had to go south to go north and east to go west. Eventually I saw the sign saying Wyoming and figured that I did something right.

I was now flirting with the Sierra Madres mountain range that were snuggled in the Rockies. For a time, I had revisited the great Highway 80 through Rawlins and Rock Springs. From Rock Springs, I veered northward up Highway 191. After driving for days in a cycle of ascension and descension, you'd get the impression that the whole earth was a continuous mountain range.

The Wind River Indian Reservation in west central Wyoming caught my fancy for a brief pass through. The Wind River Range is probably the first introduction to the Rockies that sojourner pioneers coming through Nebraska were exposed to. The Shoshoni, Crow, and Absarokas (bird people) had once populated this area, and the gravesite of Sacajawea is located in the southern part of the reservation in the eastern foothills of the Wind River Mountain Range.

Jackson Hole, being the name of a lush valley bordering the southeastern side of Grand Teton National Park, boasted of the first white explorers John Colter and Kit Carson, who hunted and trapped in this region in the very early 1800s. Thanks to John D. Rockefeller, Jr., over thirty thousand acres was purchased and donated to be part of the national park in the 1920s and '30s. But, it was the Grand Tetons that drew tourists in.

Entering on the eastern shore of Jenny Lake at approximately eight o'clock in the morning, the jutting monolithic presence of the triple-crowned Grand Tetons struck me senseless. Jenny Lake lent itself as a mirrored image of the Tetons. My twelve-dollar Kodak® started to thaw out in my warmly excited hand. Time had no meaning as I ponderously wound my way through Teton National Park along the fifteen-mile extent of Jackson Lake and lingered with high altitude-dazed tourists at Lizard Creek.

An onslaught of old western buildings and tourist shops thrust me headlong into Yellowstone. It seemed like a four-lane highway as I entered. Not so sure that I wanted to be a part of this, my reservations diminished as the deep green warmth of the lodge pole pines shed a sense of peace over my attitude. Again I was met with the passionate song of welcome home. Yellowstone sang as a chorus of blended themes. Even parents with unruly children had an unconcerned, involuntary grin about them.

Have you ever been there? Yellowstone became the nation's first national park in 1872, partly due to the remarkable photography of William Henry Jackson. There was no question as to why he considered this God-blessed area his sacred home.

The Crow, Cheyenne, Dakota, Bannock, Sioux, Shoshoni, Blackfoot, and Mandan all appreciated and respected Yellowstone's beauty and wealth.

Bison, the monarchs of the west, roamed at liberty along the roadways. They were quite the celebrities and patiently posed for numerous photo sessions, including mine. Elk could be spotted from afar, dotting the grasslands, while waterfowl, bluebirds, and eagles hovered over them.

I collected some obsidian, a lava-like stone, as a keepsake of my visit and kept secured in my memory the peculiar experience of sitting in one hundred five degree sulfur hot springs and then diving into the mighty surge of the Yellowstone River. The contrasting water temperature from one hundred five degrees to a cool, snow-fed forty degrees caused a genuine blood rush. I was sternly forewarned by some nearby hippies to grab firmly onto the banks as the rapid current would instantly take me under or send me helplessly downstream.

Well, as I made my way out of the hot springs and walked with apprehension the thirty feet to the mighty Yellowstone River, I had mixed thoughts about doing this. But, with mindless guts in full swing, I plunged in. Whoa! No, make that two whoa's. Whoa for ice cold and whoa for I can't hang on. I tell you, half in shock I climbed out onto the grassy bank before my toenails were completely wet.

I asked these storytelling bystanders, "Whatever happened to the guy who lost his grip of the bank?"

One of the jovial hippies in the hot springs laughed and said, "We found him two miles downriver, exhausted and near dead."

I moved on to the Madison campground and actually took advantage of real running water from a spout. What a novelty!

Just north of Madison campground was Geyser Basin, where mud pots bubbled and lava-like pools oozed of sparkling reds, yellows, and blues. The signs along the wooden walkway warned, "Do not touch, extremely hot." You could get a feel for fire and brimstone here like nowhere else on earth, I'm sure.

No travelers, hippie or otherwise, could bypass Old Faithful. While waiting for the next eruption, which took place approximately every sixty-seven minutes, I ventured into the world's largest log hotel, the Old Faithful Inn. The smell of well-seasoned fir and lodge pole pine was embedded in the air. Looking upward at the ninety-foot ceiling in the lobby, I also thought that this log inn must have the world's largest stone fireplace.

Well, the crowd was starting to rustle, making its way towards the paved spectator area to view Old Faithful. There I stood along with hundreds of others, camera in hand, sensing the anxious excitement moments before this infamous geyser shot forth. "Thar she blows!" A fine white spray thrust itself a hundred feet into the air. Ohs, gasps, and ahs nearly drowned the mammoth fountain's noise that was set against cumulus clouds, azure blue skies, trumpeter swans, and lodge pole pine. Though Old Faithful is not the largest of the over two hundred geysers found in Yellowstone, it certainly is the most adored.

Well, off the main road once again just north of Yellowstone Lake, I drove several miles back on what appeared to be a dirt fire trail. About two-tenths of a mile to the east I noticed a small herd of elk in a grassy clearing. Exiting the truck, I gradually made my way towards them. All the females took off, but the silky antlered male firmly stood, defying me to come any closer. I talked softly and sang gentle melodies. He continued to stare as if molded in concrete. I had a bit of fear when I was finally eight feet from touching his dark, moist nose. I made sure that he was pre-warned not to get startled when I took his picture. The two or three photos that I possess attest to our encounter. I sort of suggested to him that he stay put when my back was to him as I meandered to the truck. This seven-foot elk was very obliging and watched intently as I made my way back. I understand that the elk population there now numbers between eight and ten thousand and that the great fire of 1988 actually increased their grassy area.

I had a similar experience with a bull moose not more than half a mile from that meadow. The moose seemed more gentle and tolerant than the elk. The photo of the moose came out dark because his head filled most of the frame.

Spending the night in that area along Nez Perce Creek, hidden deep within the lodge pole pine, I drew in the smells, sights, and sounds of a Yellowstone most visitors never know. Concern over the reportedly three hundred or so grizzly in the greater Yellowstone area kept me close to the truck at all times. As dusk settled in, my second night in Yellowstone was teeming with newness.

I had determined that the following morning, I would head up to Mount Washburn. A kind, well-informed ranger had told me that sightings of bighorn sheep were common near the snow line. Mount Washburn was twenty miles north of where I camped. As I wound my way there, I took in the spectacular vista that Yellowstone's Grand Canyon created. The upper ridge was a glistening pastel yellow as the pristine sun danced off it. Possibly that is why it is called *Yellowstone*.

The lower falls of the powerful, thunderous Yellowstone River descended over three hundred feet. I struggled with a chronic case of dizziness as I glanced down this rocky, thousand foot chasm. It must have been a good rain that dug this trench.

Having spotted Mount Washburn's snowcapped peak from afar, I stumbled onto an unpaved road that seemed to head upward. Approximately four miles in, the road ended. This was yet another gorgeous summer day in early July. It was the best July 4 celebration that I had ever experienced cruising the mountains of Yellowstone.

Looking up, I figured that I could hike to the top. My strong, healthy, agile frame would be able to easily stride ever upward. With only cut-off shorts and moccasins on, T-shirt and Kodak® in hand, I eagerly headed up with a great anticipation of seeing bighorn rams and mountain goats. For some bent reason, I still placed some significance to my sign being Aries, the ram. I thought that maybe if I saw a ram, I'd experience a greater awakening of my spiritual self.

After about an hour of direct ascension, exhaustion started to enter my legs and lungs. I had to do long, upward switchbacks if I was to make it to the top. Patches of snow became plentiful, and I ate many handfuls to quench my thirst. Here's a phenomena that I haven't answered yet, how could I be skimpily dressed and still feel comfortable walking on top of crusted snow, which was nearly three feet deep? Why didn't it all melt? I bet that I'd freeze once the sun went down.

Nearly an hour and a half into this trek, I caught sight of the top. A lookout tower seemed to be at the very peak. The temperature was no longer mild, and I had hiked well beyond the tree line. The wind pelted me with a venerable force so hard that I had to lean forward and trudge along with my head down. My body grew weary along with my spirit. I was two days into a fast and had surely burned up a lot of stored energy by now. Why did I do this—just to hopefully see some mountain goats? I must have been loopy! I had only a half-mile to go and was stubbornly determined to reach the tower. My body worked its way into one big goose bump, and my teeth sounded like musical spoons. I nearly crawled the last three hundred feet because of hurricane force wind.

Gripping the tower's bottom rung of the ladder, I gazed upward. I lost count of the steps that I had to climb. What if the tower's lookout room was locked— if I actually made it there? How did the rangers get up here, by helicopter? The tower swayed gracefully in about a ten-foot diameter circle unaffected by the intense volume of the surging wind. I noticed that I was audibly talking to myself, counseling myself to maintain courage and sanity. "You're not going to die; it will be okay." I must have clutched onto this bottom rung for ten minutes before making an active decision to climb step by guarded step. Many times my body was viciously slapped against the ladder by unpredictable wind gusts. I never looked down. I asked myself over and over, "Are you doing this just to say you could do it?" I really didn't know. Possibly the grief of failure would be too much to live with having been so close, just like my indecisive battle over Crow Dog's peyote ceremony.

Finally at the top, I gripped the door latch with both muscle-cramped hands. It opened! There I was, thousands of feet above everything else, standing in a round room swaying back and forth with full three-hundred-sixty-degree windows and a panoramic view like I'd never see.

I saw snowcaps from Saddle Mountain and Pilot Peak up into Granite peak, Montana, a good sixty miles away. The view was remarkable. I took some shaky pictures with the twelve-dollar Kodak®. No person with a real body could sit in this eighteen-foot diameter booth for very long without regurgitating or passing out.

I stayed less than three minutes and made quick business of getting down except for five or six frustrating attempts to get the door to stay closed. Planted on solid ground at an elevation of over three thousand feet from the summit road, I briskly retreated.

Small white dots came into focus on a level overhang at least three-quarters of a mile downhill. Nearly jogging with anticipation as I descended, it became more obvious that these dots were indeed mountain goats. Oh, I was thanking God and anything else that came to mind. Fasting combined with thin mountain air can bring moments of unspeakable elation. The goats probably saw me before I saw them, but I apparently wasn't a disturbing presence. From at least a hundred yards off I was compelled to sing soothing peaceful melodies and was moved to undo the sacred eagle feather from the braid in my hair. Clenching it in my left hand with arms extended, I glided towards the group. They knew that I wasn't a hunter but just what I was, was apparently worth them sticking around for.

At first they began to slowly rise with a cautious fear, that is, all except the one seasoned bighorn ram. Pleading with a tranquilizing song and comforting words, I convinced them to lie back down. Unriled but a bit leery, the thirteen nannies and the bighorn fixed their gaze on this compassionately demonstrative hippie. These park animals probably read about us in the *Yellowstone Gazette,* but it was nothing like seeing us face to face.

Now, only thirty feet away, I sat down and gently conversed with them asking the Great Spirit, whom I felt immensely moved by at the moment, to give me yet another song to share with them. A communication level between these animals and myself was unfolding when suddenly the bighorn became noticeably uneasy and mildly disturbed. Perhaps he was jealous for his harem. Standing proud and erect, he began pounding the earth with his hoof, snorting and bucking his head. These were definitely hostile actions. Would he actually try to ram me?

Feeling my oats from the fast and oxygen-thin air, I bravely stood up yelling with a bold, harsh force declaring to him, "How can you treat me like this? I came all the way up here just to be with you, and you treat me like an enemy!" I grunted and screamed deep-throated guttural sounds like that of a half human, half bear.

"Aaaaaaaaargh!" The primal sound echoed tenfold throughout the mountain corridors. Listening to the natural playback, I astonished myself. I did that? The bighorn yielded to my call and proceeded to lie down, kneeling with front legs first, then his hind legs. I guess that we had an understanding here that I came in peace and not as a threat. Less than ten minutes had lapsed when the entire group in one accord rose slowly, leaping from crag to crag. With a shared sense of purpose, they gently moved on.

I still wanted to get some more photos of them, so hurriedly I rushed under the rocky overhang and carefully crawled to get a sneak close-up. Saddened, I saw the herd moving along a path opposite my direction. I was too late.

Up to this point in the day, a thick gray cloud mass had blanketed the sky. Still looking upward, the clouds briefly parted directly above me. A soft blue shown through, and there in a mystical appearance stood, majestically posed with the grace of a queen, one female mountain goat. I snapped her picture, and then she instantly ran off to be with the herd. The enlarged print that I had made of this is probably my most prized photograph. "Blue skies, smiling at me. Nothing but blue skies, do I see."

Abundantly blessed by this experience, I rejoiced as I trotted the descent to my truck. The rich history and natural wonders of Yellowstone could easily make up a book by itself. Please visit Yellowstone sometime and see for yourself what God has created, while withholding virtually none of his handiwork, from volcanoes to glaciers. If I were Yogi Bear© I'd be on my best behavior.

CHAPTER 26

BANFF, ALBERTA –
A DISEMBODIED
ARCHANGEL MICHAEL

Declining to be enticed again by the magnetism of Yellowstone, I followed its namesake river north out of Wyoming by late afternoon on or around July 7. Still entertaining the story written in the book *Secret of the Andes*, the remote possibility of Archangel Michael's spiritual retreat actually existing drew me towards Banff, Alberta, Canada. The aesthetic value of being welcomed into the "Brotherhood of the Seven Rays" gave my northern wandering a call of utmost belonging. Interstate 90 wove swiftly northwest through Big Belt, Tobacco Root, Pioneer, and the Sapphire Mountain range. National forest land surrounded this asphalt trail.

Dick, from Moclips, Washington, who I picked up hitchhiking, was a temporary passenger who welcomed me to stay with him should I ever be passing through Washington State. He wrote in my little yellow notebook, "Ask most anyone you see where I live; you'll find it."

A gas station in a small Montana mountain town refused to serve me gas. When I questioned the attendant as to why the pump wouldn't go on, he matter of factly stated, "We don't sell gas to hippies. The station down the road does."

Missoula, Montana, was my next exit. From there I ventured north, hoping to stop in the town of Big Fork on the northeast tip of Flathead Lake. I had decided to visit a couple there whose name I was given by yet another hitchhiker. Of the over one hundred and fifty addresses that

I received from gracious hitchhikers, bulletin boards, or the *Mother Earth News*, this was one open invitation I didn't want to pass up. The drive through Flathead Indian Reservation was hot, dusty, and dry. Is this where the Flathead Indians were banished to? Their barren, parched foothills were barely table scraps compared to the main course land reserved for white settlers.

I did my laundry at a desolate laundromat outside of Polson at the southernmost end of Flathead Lake. The temperature soared into the high 90s, baking the red dirt until you could hear it crack. No one was around at this laundry oasis. A few yellow warblers managed to get an even-tempered trill, but the afternoon atmosphere quickly claimed it. I mostly sat in the shade, admiring my darkened skin as I remembered the unbearable sweltering heat at the Mobil® station back in Al Viso, California. Who would choose to live here? By one o'clock in the afternoon, my wash was done. Up the east side of the thirty-mile Flathead Lake, I casually drove to Big Fork.

Outside of the reservation, the land became more forested and active with plant life. I easily found my destination, a ranch-style home, a little off Highway 35. Paul and Christina, the owners, weren't home, but within an hour they pulled up. Introducing myself, we shared some kind thoughts about our mutual friend, Gary. They seemed elated to have me as a welcomed guest and visitor. Christina fed me plenty, and I was even served my sojourner special: strawberry shortcake. I still preferred to sleep the night in my truck, but as they left for work in the morning, they extended their hospitality by letting me take their rowboat out on Flathead Lake.

The next morning, I spent several hours floating aimlessly the expanse of blue-tinted Flathead Lake. Anxiousness to move on set in as I sang and meditated in a buoyant spirit, and so I did move on, north to Glacier National Park.

But, before leaving, I wrote Paul and Christina a nice, spiritually laden thank you note and threw some of my sacred ashes on their front lawn as a blessing.

After having spent six weeks combing the spine of the Rockies from Colorado to northern Wyoming, I felt akin to these mountains; that is, until I began the ten mile ascent up "Going to the Sun Road" in Glacier National Park toward the Continental Divide and Logan's Pass. The Dodge® truck never left first gear nor exceeded eight miles an hour. The climb was steep and treacherous and filled with rockslide surprises and quick, unexpected showers from glacier-fed waterfalls. Real fear gripped me as the possibility of having to back down entered my mind as the truck barely chugged along. The road was only wide enough for one and a half vehicles. You either butted it out or politely backed down to one of the many single car waysides provided for this purpose. Fortunately, I only met one vehicle going up and gladly yielded at a conveniently provided wayside just one hundred feet back. Faint-hearted motorists would gladly drive seventy-five miles out of the way to avoid the thrill ride of going to the Sun Road!

Spotting an occasional black bear, golden eagle, or mule deer silhouetted against the Douglas fir temporarily distracted my intense roadway concentration. Gazing down five to six thousand feet with no guardrail and only a few sandbags strewn here and there, I sensed that I was on a no-return adventure. My muscles were tense and resembled the stuff that these mountains were made of, and my nerves were on red alert. I couldn't go back down, and I wasn't sure I could reach the summit. The Dodge® was running out of its reserve power. A sign, as if sent by God, leaped out at me as I rounded my five hundredth curve, "Logan's Pass, one-quarter mile, wayside picnic area." I couldn't imagine anyone wanting to picnic up here.

My breath came back as the terrain finally leveled at nearly seven thousand feet. A very large paved parking lot greeted weary travelers. It seemed that there was still twelve feet of snow up there, even in mid-July. Wonderfully surprised, I encountered a jubilant group of at least fifty partying hippies. The rest of the day was spent sharing stories, food, and good times with like-minded people on Logan's Pass. The Continental Divide had no adverse effect on our good spirits. A mountain goat or two curiously observed our celebration from afar.

Long before sunset, I bravely decided to descend the northern half of Glacier National Park and coast into Alberta, Canada.

I wonder whether the Blackfoot Indians dared to roam these wild and impetuous mountains. Their territory was directly to the east in northern Wyoming and southern Alberta. I understand that they derived their name from the trappers who first observed them shortly after they trekked through a fire blackened forest bed and their feet were ebony from the charred remains. Thus the name "Blackfoot."

I reread the *Good Medicine Book* by Adolph Hungry Wolf. He, being a descendant of the Blackfoot tribe, went into detail in this book about their legends, crafts, and sacred ways. Much of what he wrote about took place in the surrounding area of Glacier National Park.

Evening came early on the lower northern side, but I drove with swiftness and mountain certainty, avoiding snowshoe rabbits as they darted across the road in their hurry to get nowhere. Within an hour, I was near the basin and found the shoulder of the road. This was a sufficient place to pull over and have some irregular sleep while reliving the drama of the day in my dreams, being serenaded by the deafening mountain silence.

High expectations for Banff surged through my members. Maybe the seven songs would come to full fruition there. I mean, it was the Archangel Michael that assigned me the command to write them. The morning broke radiant as I crossed the border into Canada.

Hitchhikers wiped the sleep from their eyes and lined up in the first-come, first-thumb order. I gladly picked a few up and listened to entrancing stories of Banff National Park and the ever-attractive Lake Louise while we motored along up Highway 93.

The hippie phrase "far out" was getting too much use by our kind, and I lamented at the thought of it passing on in cultural history—and then it did.

The Columbia River accompanied us most of the nearly two hundred picturesque miles to Banff. Other than my concern over the amount of oil that the truck was using, I was peaceful, resting in a state of traveler's bliss.

I dropped off one of my passengers near Windermere, a small town on the Columbia River. As a customary gesture of friendship, a smoke of marijuana was offered. Usually I declined, knowing full well that my senses would be dwindled to near zero as I attempted to maneuver a vehicle. Though the area lent itself to high, lazy, peaceful times, I preferred to stay straight and continue on to Banff. I'd probably be there by two o'clock in the afternoon.

Plenty of bikers on their ominous black Harleys zipped past me like bees on a mission. Everybody was friendly though, and, anyway, I lived two blocks from the Hell's Angels hangout in New York City, and my dad raced Harleys in the 1940s. A caravan of Winnebago® RVs added a contrasting complement to the array of vacationers.

Mount Assiniboine came into full view, peaking at eleven thousand, eight hundred seventy feet, unscathed by the Continental Divide splitting it in half. Extremes were prevalent, from the soft, low-lying flowers like moss, campion, golden daisies, and pale purple fireweed, to the quaking vibration of a snow avalanche able to topple acres of white spruce with its sudden, blinding force. The numerous aqua-colored lakes seemed suspended in mountain crevices. Am I allowed to suggest that the lower Canadian Rockies were even more abundantly beautiful than that of their southern counterpart stateside?

If it weren't for the stubborn persistence of the transcontinental railroaders wedging their rails, spikes, and ties into these mountains, the town of Banff and access to this first Canadian National Park would not have existed. The year was 1885, and people flocked to take in the unique sulfur hot springs. The eighty-seven square mile Columbian ice field seemed to feed all these trout-infested, clear-water rivers with its estimated two hundred inches of snowfall each year.

Abiding tranquilly in the bosom of Bow Valley, I was gently ushered into the tourist town of Banff. Tourism seemed to line the streets. Clever motel names and logos, souvenir shops, mountain climbing and ski outlets, restaurants, and, of course, cocktail lounges abounded. They all sang their inviting choruses of, "Come spend your money here." Very few of the four thousand residents were just regular folks. Mostly their vocations were in tourism and national park upkeep. But, I was really there—two thousand miles from Grafton and halfway to Alaska.

Bushed from the heat and the six-hour meandering drive, all the free-loading passengers were safely let off at their destinations. I made a casual left turn off the main thoroughfare. Within a half a block, a sign on the north side of the street caught my trained, health-conscious eyes: *Natural Health Food Restaurant.* "Hey," I thought, "I'll go in there and see if they know anything about the Archangel Michael."

As I entered into this tiny but clean, five-table eatery, a young man in his late teens glided gracefully towards me. From behind the swinging service doors, wearing a spotless white apron and having the exuberance of a Golden Retriever puppy, he asked, "Would you like to see a menu?" His behavior was so infectious I almost said yes, but instead I pointedly informed him that I didn't really come to eat, I came because the Archangel Michael had sent me. A pasty-white, shocked expression instantly stole his glow. Embracing me tightly with both arms and his head firmly against mine, he joyously cried, "Brother, you're home!"

The thrill of a visionary realization lifted me as I grappled for words. "Really? You know about Michael?"

This buoyant busboy excitedly said, "Wait here, I'll call Brother Jim."

Less than two minutes had passed as I stood weightlessly, examining this ten-by-fifteen-foot patronless restaurant. Nearly air bound, he rushed back with the phone in his hands, handing the receiver to me. I spoke briefly into it. "Hello?" Brother Jim never gave me a cordial response. He just proceeded to drill me with questions in a cold, suspecting fashion.

"What do you know about Archangel Michael?" he sternly asked.

I happily told him all about my vision and communications with Archangel Michael in the early fall of 1973 and that I read in a book that he was overseeing an Ashram of the "Brotherhood of the Seven Rays" here in Banff. My answers seemed to pacify his pelting questions, and he told me to have a free meal on the restaurant and meet him at his house at seven o'clock that evening. My initial enthusiasm quickly diminished because of our anticlimactic, businesslike phone conversation.

There were three very young people working at this restaurant. An auburn cutie, no more than sixteen years old, took my order and seemed to have difficulty talking through her giggles and glowing eyes.

That welcoming phrase kept dancing in my mind, "Brother, you're home." Really? Was this finally the end of my search?

As I sat at the table eating brown rice and a bowl of lentil soup, I scanned through my memory of the inquisitive longings and spiritual adventures that I had been on. "Brother, you're home."

Maybe I'd take a wife up here out of this spiritual community. Maybe I'd become a great, highly revered teacher under the watchful eye and tutorship of Archangel Michael. Maybe I'd become famous as the singer/songwriter from Banff. The maybes drifted on through the plate glass window to the busy people on the street scurrying from one attraction to another. It was best that I leave in search of a quiet, remote area to rest.

A cold war battle began to wage against my emotions as I played over and over Brother Jim's reluctance to accept my story. Was he just jealously cautious for his spiritual community? Maybe fraudulent others gave him the same line about Archangel Michael. This had to be more than coincidence.

I parked the truck about one-half mile out of town on a dead-end road, biding my time until my appointment with Brother Jim. At seven o'clock sharp I was at his door on a back street in Banff. It was an older, two-story, white, wood-sided house in need of paint and yard work. Some teenaged kids plagued with acne dressed in white yoga costumes hesitantly answered the door. I introduced myself, "Hi, I'm Ayuta Rai. Brother Jim asked me to be here at seven o'clock to talk to him." By now I had attracted the attention of seven or eight of his other devotees, all of them dressed in white and seeming to be younger than eighteen.

Brother Jim waved to me from several rooms down while holding a phone to his ear. I just stood in the hallway while the others scurried back into what appeared to be a large meditation worship room bedecked with candles, incense, and floor pillows. The kids looked uneasy, almost frightened. Brother Jim briskly walked towards me with a plastic smile. He wore casual clothes and looked to be only in his early twenties. Something was wrong here; it just didn't have good spiritual pizzazz.

Brother Jim took me aside and whispered, "Archangel Michael's community hasn't materialized yet; he's still in the ethereal realm. He's still waiting to manifest himself and his followers. It may take as long as five years."

I furled my brow and said, "Oh, really? Five years? That's a long time."

Brother Jim assured me that five years would go quickly, and I should use that time to prepare myself for his manifestation. Considerately, he suggested that I not tell the others about Archangel Michael as many of them may not have been chosen as I have been. Continuing on he asked, "Why don't you begin by spending the evening with us, listening to my teaching and meditate. I'll get you a white robe to wear. We all wear white when we meditate."

This seemed bizarre to me, but I went along with the act. Sitting in the midst of twelve or so programmed teenagers, I listened intently as Brother Jim talked in vague, sugary parables and esoteric allegories. After two hours of this, we broke up for the evening, and I was favorably welcomed back by Brother Jim and the group as a whole.

Summing up my first impression of this self-made guru and his followers, they were a hole, void of substance.

Fully exhausted from the long, diverse day, I sat behind the steering wheel of my truck and nearly fell asleep as I chronicled in my mind the past two and one-half months of traveling. It seemed sketchy and lacking in direction. I drove four blocks up to the end of the street and parked in a cul-de-sac. Sleep came easily, but turmoil dominated my dreams that evening of July 10. Yes, they were turmoil- and fear-laden. I was growing weary of being transient as loneliness played havoc with my emotional stability. I'm Ayuta Rai. So what?

The next morning as I worked my way out of the back of the camper, a guy standing near his front door yelled a cheerful "Hi!" Looking a bit startled, I responded, "Hi. I'm just parked here overnight. I'm on my way to Alaska."

He unreservedly invited me to come in and have breakfast. "My name's Skip; I rent this house with three other people, Shelly, Nick, and Sandra. Most of us are going to college here."

Surprised, I remarked, "Really? I didn't know that there was a college in Banff."

After using his facilities and filling up on their last night's fruit salad, I gladly drove him the mile and one-half or so to the university. I never was impressed with college life, but was impressed with these buildings and how they seemed to be carved into their natural surroundings. Campus life here seemed more real and less hype than others I'd seen, a much easier, relaxed pace.

Skip offered me his accommodations for as long as I remained in Banff, and I surely took him up on that.

After dropping Skip off and strolling around the university, I stopped at a service station to seek their advice on my truck's oil usage problem. A fairly young, strait-laced mechanic inspected my engine and suggested that I drop a tablespoon of Comet® cleanser down the carburetor to help free up the rings. This sounded very radical and I told him so, but he became indignant, cursing me a bit and facetiously remarking, "If you know how to fix it, why are you wasting my time?"

I put on that old standby Charlie Brown grin again and bought a can of Comet® at the grocery store. Reluctantly, I dropped a tablespoonful into the carburetor and headed out of town to take in the beauty of Bow Valley.

Heading north out of town for a casual drive through the mountains, an interesting rock formation caught my eye. Perhaps I could climb that and seek a vision.

Just shortly after turning back to return to Banff, a jet-black cloud billowed out of the exhaust pipe. I lost all oil compression. Other motorists quickly passed my truck while giving me a "look at that filthy hippie" stare. The blue Dodge® pick-up died on the shoulder of the road, somewhere north of Banff near the Bow River. I was truly bummed out. This truck was not only my transportation but my home. I took my guitar out, locked up the truck, and thumbed a ride back into Banff.

Skip and another friend of his were home when I got back to his house. They drove me the eight miles out of town to my truck. Skip's friend seemed to know a lot about engines and handed me the devastating news. "Your truck is shot; the rings are blown out." I told him that the guy at the gas station suggested that I put Comet® in the carburetor, so I did. Skip's friend just hung his head, shaking it back and forth, mumbling, "No way. The guy's a jerk; he hates long-hairs, and he told you this as a joke." They helped me bring my stuff into Skip's house.

The Canadian Motor Vehicle Department in Banff made me aware that no US vehicles over ten years old could be sold in Canada. The Dodge® pick-up was eleven years old. I packed up many things that I didn't absolutely need and mailed them to my dad's house in Grafton. Skip, Shelly, Nick, and Sandra bought most of my teas, natural foods, and books. Skip's friend bought the truck from me for one hundred dollars cash. He said he'd take the ID plate off my truck and get a different one from the junkyard so that the truck would be legal in Canada.

I confided in Skip about my strange experience with Brother Jim, and he just laughed in agreement. Seems that he knew all about Brother Jim's scam to lure in unsuspecting teenagers, many of them runaways, many illegal US aliens, all being harbored by him in exchange for labor at his restaurant and general housekeeping.

Brother Jim was out of town for three days, and I offered to do dishes at the restaurant in return for my supper. I drilled these young devotees of his with questions as to Brother Jim's legitimacy as a spiritual teacher. Some of them began to open up and admitted that they suspected him of being a fraud. Rumors of sexual favors surfaced also.

On my second night at the restaurant there was a raid on the place, authorities were searching for runaways and illegal aliens without work permits. Four of us took off out the back and fled in all directions. No one was caught.

That evening, Brother Jim came back from an undisclosed location. I met him at his home and boldly confronted him, accusing him of being a fraud and just blatantly using these kids for his own gain. His face burnt with anger, and his shouting exposed an obviously weak defense. He hustled me off the front porch and slammed the door. I can't imagine that this little deceptive operation continued on much longer. So, he actually knew nothing about the Archangel Michael. It was just a ploy of his to recruit another follower.

Skip and several others suggested that I go to the Army surplus store in Calgary in search of a good sleeping bag and backpack. This was to become a consolidated version of my traveling home.

Calgary was eighty miles due east on the great Trans-Canada Highway 1, the largest city within four hundred miles. I hated cities, but with limited finances, I had to go where the deals were. The morning was overcast as I hitchhiked, but thankfully I made it in two rides and less than three hours. The Army surplus store was not far off the freeway and within a reachable walking distance. I noticed that an awful lot of cowboys were walking the streets and tearing through town yelling and honking horns. "Crazy cow town," I thought. I quickly picked out a nice wooden-framed Swiss backpack and down-filled army sleeping bag. The total for these two was around sixty dollars. I knew that this would have cost me several hundred at a specialty outfitter.

As I walked casually on the sidewalk whistling and smiling, a rusted old pick-up pulled over to the curb. A concerned hippie asked me whether I knew what was going on this weekend in Calgary. I replied, "No, I don't; I'm not from around here."

He sternly warned, "You'd better get out of town fast, definitely by sundown. The Calgary Stampede is this weekend, and these red-necked cowboys make a game of beating up longhairs. You'd be mangled— left for dead in an alley. Even the police get in on it."

I took his warning seriously and got in line at the freeway entrance to thumb a ride out. I waited about an hour in a light drizzle and found a ride straight back to Banff. Skip and company reassured me that I got a good deal on my backpack and bag.

So, early the next morning, around July 16, I set out for that rocky peak to seek a vision and guidance from God. Some locals told me that this peak was called Indianhead Mountain because it resembled an Indian chief's face and headdress and, come to think of it, it did. My first ride out dropped me off to what they felt was the closest location to the mountain.

My hike began gingerly as I strolled through a field of large white- and yellow-cupped poppies. Indian paintbrush was scattered about along with a grouping of buttercups. White osprey soared overhead, answering the call of symphonic yellow warblers on their migration elsewhere. I hit an impasse, a swampy marsh. Mosquitoes darkened an already steel-gray sky. Logs floated helter-skelter, so I took a chance at sure-footing my way across the thick, chocolate-green muck. I jumped in with an intensely conscious one-two balanced jig. I hopped from log to log across this hundred-foot slime expanse in less than thirty seconds. I stood relieved on solid ground with no more than a pint of swamp juice in my moccasins and, I might add, only ten to fifteen mosquito bites. Regrettably, I broke up the conversation between a muskrat and a beaver. I was hoping that I could find a better route on my return trip.

Hiking on through low-lying brush and sparse softwood forests, I bumped into an eight-foot high steel mesh fence. What was a fence doing out here in the wild? I followed the manmade path along the fence extending one-half mile to where it angled off to the right or east, which brought me conveniently to the base of Indianhead Mountain. Glancing upward, I shuddered at the thought of a steep fifty-five degree climb; the first third of the way was mostly grassy, but the remainder was rock laden. All I had brought along was a small Boy Scout-type pack on my back, a change of clothes, and one-half gallon of water. A light mist made for sloppy climbing.

Reaching the small summit within an hour, I thought I heard a lion roar and something else like a bull moose's far-reaching bass siren. These wild sounds carried and swirled through the valley below. The attempted ascent up the sheer rock side of the Indian's face came to a sensible halt as the very real possibility of losing my grip or footing and plummeting a hundred feet to my death caused me to back down, sort of like a cat maneuvering in reverse down a tree.

So there I sat in the sixty-degree drizzle and made the best of it. I meditated, chanted, and sang for hours, but it was more out of obligation to myself than a productive joy.

Evening came though I really didn't notice as the dark cast of the day dampened my spirit. A couple of birds winged around me, jeering in my ear with hostile heckling. Throughout the night I was entertained in a spooky fashion by an opera of roars and high-pitched laughs. They sounded forth from all directions, deep within the valley's nocturnal floor. Sustained howls from two lone wolves formed a silver-gray arc of tone. I was in no position to defend myself from the jaws and claws of pre-historic, saber-toothed tigers but as I found with the bighorn ram, I could shout and sing. The *Banff Weekly Gazette* would read "Hippie, Dismembered by Unidentified Wild Beast." The cowboy ropers in Calgary would breathe easier knowing that there was one less of me. "Yep, pardner, nature took care of that long-haired freak."

Sleep came slow and soggy, but it came. Morning sort of happened as variant hues of sunlight peeked out from behind the curtain of low-hanging clouds, but they never made their way onstage. The rain subsided, but it didn't much matter anymore. I and all my belongings were drenched. Gloom, depression, and an overall negative mood blanketed me as I retreated and despondently made my way back down. I walked the fence line along the swampy flood plain, listening as each step suctioned up muck and wet leather squishing between my toes and heels.

What was behind this fence, anyway? I found a long bypass detour around the swamp, though by this time I could have forged through it without wincing. Why I started singing Davy Crockett's theme song I'm not sure, but it helped get me through the marsh. "Davy, Davy Crockett, king of the wild frontier." Pneumonia never set in; I was grateful for that.

Finally, back on the road, a man picked me up and gave me a ride back to Banff, informing me that I had ventured onto a fenced-in wildlife game preserve. What I heard was actually laughing hyenas, approximately thirty of them, and several caged tigers. The wolves roamed freely.

While my wash was hanging on the line to dry at Skip's, I consolidated even more of that which I would take with me on my backpacking excursion to Alaska. My old license plates were neatly concealed in the bottom of my backpack, to eventually be sent back to the Motor Vehicle Department in the States.

By now I had acquired more names and addresses of people to visit along the way. Many of them were centered in the Vancouver, British Columbia, area, so it seemed fitting to head west the four hundred miles to Vancouver.

My good-byes and thank you's were said in a short note I left on Skip, Shelly, Nick, and Sandra's kitchen table. A handful of sacred ashes were thrown into the mid-July breeze, falling where they willed, on their front lawn. It was the least that I could do for them.

All in all, Banff was not very good to me, and the Archangel Michael had not revealed himself. Kindness and mercy were shown to me, but the overall picture was not very good.

CHAPTER 27

HOPE, IDAHO
LAKE PEND OREILLE

It was July 18, in the midmorning, and I was still only about seventh in line for a ride on the Trans-Canadian Highway. The mile-high Lake Louise gained prominence on billboards and bumper stickers. I'd only come thirty-six miles in three hours since departing from Banff. There's no question that the mountain grandeur of the Lake Louise region was splendidly captivating, but my patience wore thin as I sat on my guitar case with my right thumb locked in an outward position. No one had gotten a ride yet except for two girls in back of me. A couple of guys came on to a real find there. Single girls had no problem getting rides.

Mount Victoria peered down at me from her eleven thousand three hundred sixty-five foot vantage point.

By mid-afternoon, most of the hitchhiking highway gang hadn't latched a ride. I gave up and took out the Guild to comfort my hitchhiker's blues. Five or six others shuffled over, some with guitars and harmonicas. We slaughtered some basic blues jamming, and I struggled to remember the chords to simple Beatle songs. After twenty minutes of butchered music, we hung it up and wandered into the Douglas fir to set up camp.

The campfire and company was uplifting, but it would have been best for me to pass up the marijuana as it came around time and time again. An introverted fear stiffened me from my pure enjoyment of life whenever I smoked that stuff. I always said no more weed until the next temptation met my face. Giving in is easy; getting straight takes time.

The morning offered yet another unique complexion of color, sound, smells, and sensations. I was one of the first in line for a ride. It was six-fifteen in the morning, and I was impatiently desperate. I'd been holed up there for twenty hours. For me this was a record for time spent in patient endurance. By seven o'clock in the morning I was fed up, even angry. A desperate man does crazy things, so when I saw the next vehicle approaching on the crest of the hill to the east; I knelt in the middle of the road with hands reverently folded. I figured if they didn't stop, they'd either have to swerve into the oncoming lane or run me over. Who'd want to clean up that messy road kill all over their hood and grill? "Praise God!" I yelled. "It's a Volkswagen bus." They pulled over.

"Where you going?" they loudly asked.

I quickly answered back, "I'm going all the way to Vancouver."

They slapped my back and said, "You got a ride to Vancouver."

"All right!" (Far out.) It was worth the wait. I just laid back in the bus and took in the scenery.

In Kooteney and Yoho National Park, entire hillsides laid disfigured from the charred remains of a great fire in 1968. A sensitive eye could capture moose, elk, and caribou as they peppered serene grasslands.

Somebody in the front of the van with an East Indian name was hoping to see Baba Ram Dass and Alan Watts at eight o'clock that evening in Vancouver. Alan Watts was a proponent of Zen Buddhism. I hated to disillusion him, but felt a sinister fulfillment in telling him what I thought of Baba Ram Dass.

At a wayside near Sicamous on Shuswap Lake in the Okanagan Valley of south-central British Columbia, I met up with an extremely friendly couple named Zach and Pat. We chatted for a good half hour. They were from Idaho, hoping to secure work in the Okanagan Valley during apple- and pear-picking season starting in late August. I got to thinking that maybe it would be a good idea to work for six weeks or so as I was down to about eleven hundred dollars. Zach, Pat, and I really hit it off well, and they invited me to ride along with them as they stopped to inquire at orchards about work. The Okanagan Valley is noted for its fruit orchards extending from southern British Columbia through Washington State.

Zach and Pat had heard about a four-hundred-acre orchard near Kelowna, British Columbia that supplied cabins and running water to its employees. A few miles east of Okanagan Lake, there was oddly enough, a mountain called Last Mountain. We found our way along a winding road to the first stop town of East Kelowna. The town consisted only of a general store, gas station, and the largest combination orchard and vineyard that I had ever seen. The owner hired us on, no questions asked. He reserved a cabin for Zach and Pat and one for me. Gee, this was exciting—my own cabin with a community waterspout. There was even a men's and lady's washroom with showers. I had a real job and a real place to live. It was my first job in four months.

Apple picking wouldn't start for another four weeks, so Zach and Pat invited me to come live with them at their temporary residence in Hope, Idaho. Hope was in the northern panhandle part of the state on the northeast end of Lake Pend Oreille, pronounced (pond o ray). The French and Spanish Basques had settled this territory many years ago, and the names reflected their culture. A five-hour drive partly along the Columbia Pend Oreille River which divides the Colville and Kaniksu National Forests took us along the northern fringe of Lake Pend Oreille in Hope. Hope was a one-stop town with a general store/Post Office. I had no idea that northern Idaho was so mountainous and heavily forested with Ponderosa pine. It was truly my kind of country. The residents here said that the winters were mild because of being located on the western slope of the Rockies. The warm Pacific air takes the biting chill out of winter.

The day was hot, so the first thing we did when we arrived at the house was to walk the three hundred feet to the sandy beach on Lake Pend Oreille. I noticed a good many hippies appearing here and there and felt at home. Many of them indiscreetly swam in the nude, so I followed suit, or *no* suit, as was the case.

Back at the house, I gradually met the other people who crashed there. A girl of about seventeen who called herself Bluebird seemed very disturbed when asked to do the dishes as part of her keep. She didn't care that my name was Ayuta Rai and made it plainly known that she was on a spiritual high much greater than anyone else in that house. I left her alone in her obvious bliss. There were three small, one-room cottages in the back. Zach and Pat shared one of them, and I slept under a large pine tree unless it was raining.

There wasn't much to do, and the seven or eight people living here had no sense of unity. So, I wandered by myself a lot and happened upon a couple that lived three miles north on Highway 200. It seemed that they eeked out a living making and selling crafts such as stained glass and macramé items. By the end of August, they were planning to leave for South America so that their baby would be born there. They had a vision that one hundred babies would be born in South America who would be destined to become spiritually enlightened leaders in the world. They were willing to forfeit the beautiful home they rented, sell their craft tools and supplies, pack up only necessary items, and hitchhike a ruthless, dangerous journey of over five thousand miles so that their baby could be born in South America. I know that I had done some strange things, but I thought that they were radically extreme. Even if they made it, how would they survive? Lake Titicaca in the Peruvian Andes still enticed my spirit, but I could never risk the peril of travel with an expectant lady.

There was a dirt fire trail behind the cottages which seemed to wind its way upward into the Cabinet Mountains. I inquired of the folks at the house as to just how far the road went. They told me that it supposedly made countless switchbacks for ten miles up to the summit and how far beyond that, they weren't sure. Because of my fondness for these pine-veiled mountains and an easy access road, I decided to fast and hike to the top to seek God. Zach and Pat and a few others (not Bluebird) cheered me on and said that they'd be thinking about me while I was up there.

So, the morning of July 22, I took off with a small backpack and just a quart of water. A happy-go-lucky black-and-white bulldog named Buddy started to follow me. He wouldn't leave when I tried to shoo him away. Reason meant nothing to him, even after I warned him that I'd be gone for at least two days with only a quart of water. He just hung his slobbering, hot, July tongue out and tagged along. Buddy was all right, and he kept up quite easily, but he looked like a wet blanket in need of a dryer.

I strolled ever upwards the entire ten miles without stopping. My joyous singing kept me from delirium. Buddy's panting rhythm and my braided eagle feather flapping on my head set the pace. A wall of thick pine lined this unchanging, ten-foot wide swatch as it ribboned its way towards the summit. Miles of red dusty dirt challenged my moccasined feet.

Finally, after two hours and fifty switchbacks, we approached the crown. A spectacular view greeted us. A luxuriant green vista flanked by pure blue skies and drifting clouds like cotton balls pulled at my vision as I fixed my eyes on the aqua elixir of Lake Pend Oreille. My lungs searched their depths for a musical sound that could express the sensation welling up inside of me. A fountain of life began shooting forth from my members. What a wealth of beauty that was set before me!

Buddy didn't say much; he seemed to be smiling though as he leaned against my right calf. With both hands cupped, I managed to maneuver the quart bottle and pour some water so that Buddy could quench his thirst. He caught on immediately and lapped up the very last drop. All that was left in the palm of my hands was some foamy dog slime. I didn't mind because Buddy and I were all right.

To the northwest stood a one-story mound of granite rock. This was the true top of the mountain, so we strolled over and climbed its stepping stones. Incredibly elated, I saw before me a six-foot long pit dug out of the rock. The native people must have been here. They probably dug this out several hundred years ago. My heart raced with anticipation as I thought of how the Flathead or maybe Nez Perce sat here to seek visions. This was it! This was meant for me to find. God was guiding me.

We anxiously climbed down into the pit and remained there throughout the duration of the quest. I was very impatient, wanting something significant to happen, so I sat in the lotus position attempting to empty my mind for meditation. Buddy's mind was already empty, so he immediately fell into a peaceful meditative state. I sat and fidgeted, knelt, sang, looked into the sun, spoke audibly, closed my eyes to envision God, chanted, prayed, and eventually after five hours of this, grew weary and frustrated. Committed to being enclosed in this crystalline shell of quartz, feldspar, and mica, I continually glanced upon the heavens, scanning the open sky for a sign. A dark speck rode the wind, miles above me. It could only have been a golden eagle soaring in a two-mile orb.

Hours slowly passed. Certainly, God would honor my diligence by showering me with a visionary revelation of Himself. What did I have to do to get a big spiritual experience? Buddy left the pit momentarily to relieve himself as I shouted my plea, "Please, Lord, show Yourself to me." The volume of my utterance fell on deaf mountains, returning with a pale void. It was a man's voice, pathetically desperate. I recognized it as mine. If it was feelings that God wanted, I could give Him no more. The sacred Hopi ashes were ritually scattered in the wind. My eagle feather was clenched in my left hand while the southwest breeze cooled my sweat-drenched palm. Had I called enough? Should I now just quietly listen? Listening I could do.

There was a bit of solace given to me, sprinkled in the scarlet sunset over Lake Pend Oreille. The lake appeared to burn as if having had swallowed a molten ball. I sensed that my efforts were in vain. One last drink was taken for Buddy and me before snuggling up inside the sleeping bag. Stars taunted, "Come cry for your God, see if He hears in the evening." He did not hear; He did not care. God had to extend His hand to me. I was powerless in my attempt to attain Him. I slept but woke up frequently forgetting where I was and dreading the difficulty of going back down ten miles. Stellar patterns seduced my gaze and the nobility of the galaxy made amusement of my semi-consciousness until I drifted back to sleep. And to my dismay, Buddy snored.

An uneventful flaxen sunrise brought little cheer. My weakened spirit toyed with leaving. A committed discipline urged me to stick it out. The Indians must have had success in communicating with the Great Spirit; otherwise they wouldn't have carved this vision pit. The eagle returned to its flight schedule, though a little lower than yesterday. Attentive ears could hear its faint shrill: a predator's war cry.

I sang a song about overlooking Lake Pend Oreille and penned the words and melody there in the granite pit. The lake emanated a blinding reflection, emitting a pool of sparks. The sun was well upon it. As I sang this enchanting song from a seven-thousand-foot elevation, the thirty-mile oblong lake took on the appearance of a stretched-out seahorse. Optimism crept into my spirit; my petition to God grew intense once again. Standing with arms outstretched towards the lake, I gracefully waved the eagle feather to stir the Lord's attention. There was no penetrating His ethereal shield. The weather was perfect for this side of heaven, but I continued to wonder, was there no one or no method that could take me to God? Buddy and I sat back down as I pondered this dilemma.

Midday had passed, and I became bored with studying my fingernails while consciously experiencing every inhalation and exhalation. A jet-like distant sound broke my concentration. Within seconds, a fury of turbulent wind surged over my head! My hair caught the thrust of the blow and lashed against my face. Buddy froze, paralyzed, incapable of reacting. My gaze was fixed upon the seven-foot wingspan of a Golden eagle as it rapidly disappeared, absorbed into a southern vanishing point. For over a day this eagle had circled devoutly, centering his attention on the two creatures stationed in their granite tomb. Less than three seconds had passed from when I first sensed this gale force rumble to when it soared over me, leaving just a twelve-inch clearance between its claws and my skull. I could have been mortally wounded; Buddy could have been swooped up into lands unknown.

Shocked and dumbfounded, I grappled for the deep spiritual meaning of this encounter. Was this the answer to my hard-sought vision? What does it mean? After careful scrutiny, I took it as a sign to leave. Perhaps God had sent this Golden eagle as an affirmation that my vision quest had ended, and I was duly excused. This interpretation seemed to temporarily appease and pacify my curious notions.

Buddy and I took one last gulp and slurp of water and headed on down. As I sang, "Overlooking Lake Pend Oreille," the song's rhythm was right on step. The revolving melody gave enthusiasm to my attitude. Oddly enough, my thighs began to ache from the constant downhill jar.

Finally back at the cottages and drained of energy, I bid farewell to Buddy as he scampered back to the neighbor's house, his rightful owner. Eager to share my experiences with Zach and Pat, I was disheartened to find out that they had left to go to Oregon for a week. With nobody much to talk to other than Bluebird and some guy who was into hunting coons and drinking Coors® beer, I got strong thoughts about going to Vancouver, British Columbia, until apple season started.

In my little yellow book, I had the name of Barnuka Smith, who lived on East 10th Avenue in Vancouver. He was a friend of Scottie and Pierre's. And where I bumped into those two, I can't recall. But, I noted in my book "Barnuka's was a good place to crash for a while."

CHAPTER 28

VANCOUVER, BRITISH COLUMBIA

Getting a ride out of Hope was easy, but the guy who picked me up had one condition. I would have to ride with him two hundred miles south-southwest out of my way to Walla Walla, Washington. I'd gladly do that for the promise of a ride close to the Canadian border near Northern Cascades National Park. Walla Walla in late July was a hot, dusty, barren incinerator. It seems that it had just one very long main street.

My ride had some undisclosed business with someone at a gas station there, so, to make best use of my time, I walked three blocks to a cultural museum. The flute-like trill of a Swainson thrush followed me through the shade trees that led to the museum. The museum offered to sell samples of precious gems found in the area. I asked the lady at the counter if they had a fire opal, still hoping to obtain an inexpensive one to carry with me for power and protection.

"No, I'm sorry," was her response as museum patrons cautiously studied me.

I overheard a lady whisper to her husband, "I bet he wants to steal one." He nodded with absolute certainty.

The hostility directed towards me at this little local museum was too much to bear, so I left and began to walk back to my friend's truck. A police car crept alongside me for two to three blocks as I walked and then abruptly stopped. Two policemen jumped out and harshly demanded to know what business I had in their respectable Walla Walla. I told them that I was waiting for my friend and that his truck was parked right up the street. They searched me, hoping to get me for theft, drugs, or vagrancy. When they saw that I had over a thousand dollars, mostly in traveler's checks, they probed even deeper.

"Where's a hippie like you get money like this?" I politely told them where I was from and that I had worked to save this money.

They got back in the car and made a quick check on me, confiscating my driver's license. A tense five minutes passed and then one of the officers told me to step over to the car. As I stood near the passenger's door, I was made aware that it was illegal to stand on public grass, and that was a thirty-dollar fine. But, they handed me a reprieve.

"We'll drop the fine if you're out of town by four o'clock. We don't want to see you here after four, and don't come back to visit."

"Yes, sir, I'll be gone; you can bet that I'll never come back."

It was a quarter to three as I sat in the cab of the truck and anxiously waited for my ride to come back. By three-thirty in the afternoon he returned, and we hightailed it out of Walla Walla. The police followed us closely at least ten miles out of town into the rolling, sun-baked dust bowl.

After driving through the sunken oven of the Okanagan Valley, we eased our way into the modest Okanagan Mountain Range. We parted company in Tonasket on Highway 97, twenty-five miles from the Canadian border.

I quickly got a ride. Lorne and his friends from Vancouver heeded the call of a lone hitchhiker and his guitar. We camped out in Manning Provincial Park near Gibson Pass. It was good to be back in the wilds again and spend a night in the open mountain air.

Crows and meadowlarks woke us with a sweet-sour chatter, and by nine-thirty in the morning we cruised into Vancouver. The Trans-Canada Highway ran into Broadway. Lorne dropped me off right at Barnuka's house on East 10th, just eight blocks from his own home on Victoria Drive near Fraser.

Vancouver appeared to be a friendly, clean city, and the people in Barnuka's house welcomed my visit, allowing me to prepare a place for myself in the basement.

As I asked questions concerning the spiritual climate of Vancouver, I was thrilled to hear that many events were planned within the next two to three weeks. One of the first that I attended was in Room 102 of the Buchanan Building on the UBC campus. Baba Hari Dass, Ram

Dass' teacher, was giving a lecture. The northwest portion of Vancouver bordering the university was the hub of counterculture activity as it was with most college cities.

Seated in the classroom well before eight o'clock in the evening, I observed a short, thin, dark-skinned East Indian man walking in wearing a filthy looking, off-white, gauze material gown. He carried with him a hand-held slate board and chalk. As he seated himself cross-legged on top of the front desk, a younger man introduced him. He informed us that, "Baba hasn't spoken for thirty years, he chooses to conserve his energy." I may have the exact number of years wrong, but it was plenty of speechless seasons. The man continued, "Baba will be happy to answer your questions through me, or by writing them on his slate board." The television comedy *Saturday Night Live* had not yet existed, but Baba Hari Dass would have made an ideal host.

Most everyone among the twenty-five or so seated in Room 102 had a question to ask. Baba Hari Dass wrote mostly simple yes or no answers then wiped the slate clean with his sleeve. This man had the appearance of an unkempt street bum, from his black stringy hair to his feet that had caked on dirt. He boasted of not taking a bath in years. That's an energy saver for sure. After an hour of listening to seemingly vague, useless rhetoric from Baba, I took the bus back to Barnuka's just five city miles away.

A lady at Barnuka's demonstrated some yoga exercises for me to keep my overall body agile. Here it is, many years later and I am still doing those exercises faithfully.

Being naturally attracted to occult bookstores, I became a frequent visitor to Life Stream Books on 4th and Barrard. Many names of natural food and bookstores crossed my mind, but I believe that this particular one was called Life Stream. They had the usual assortment of hodgepodge reading material, which by now I was well familiar with after my exposure to stores in Santa Cruz, Milwaukee, and Boulder. You'd think that the overbearing incense kick would have worn off by now in these stores, but it hadn't. A mystically scented cloud hung in the rafters.

I noticed a sign that read, "Meditation room upstairs." So I went up. The walls were rather bland, but nonetheless, I maneuvered into a lotus position and envisioned myself floating away. But, the only sensation that I had was that of the scratchy carpeting on my bare legs. There were two other people up there before I came, and I had assumed that their purpose was to meditate themselves into a blissful state, also. This meditation room concept seemed like a bad joke, as did my unintentionally invited spirit guides.

I still couldn't shake the idea that maybe they actually existed. If they did, I was the more confused and controlled because of it. At times I became obsessed with asking them to guide every decision in all areas of my life, even to the extreme of having them choose which orange or apple in the pile to purchase. And if they didn't satisfy my conscience, then I'd pull out my trusty pendulum that I had made back in Boulder. I made mine out of half an acorn tied to a string. While holding it in my left hand, I'd watch to see if it swung clockwise when asked a question while suspended over an object, which meant "yes." Swinging counter clockwise meant "no." If it just swung back and forth, that was usually taken as a neutral sign. Some strange looks were directed my way as I fervently swung it over the fruit section at the grocery stores. It supposedly told me which fruit was healthier for me. Less pesticides, more nutrition. Sounds crazy? It was crazy. Just to catch the pendulum off guard, I'd swing it over the piece of fruit several times. Often I received many conflicting answers. The pendulum thing grew old and distrustful.

But—those darn spirit guides—I couldn't shake 'em. I started to believe that I either latched onto a couple of pranksters or mentally deranged minds. Almost none of their guidance made sense. Still, I was foolish enough to follow them. I was told that these were the spirits of deceased people. I often wondered what qualified them to be "guides." If dying was the only prerequisite, then a good number of people conjuring up guides were in serious straits. I finally left my spirit guides floundering at a bus stop with no transfer ticket. Life went on without them. Many people have good reason to believe that these spirit guides are actually demons!

A meditation workshop was scheduled at 3711 Fraser, just twelve blocks from Barnuka's. While walking to the workshop on this very beautiful early August coastal morning, I reckoned that Vancouver was probably the cleanest, most peaceful city that I had ever tarried in. The twelve blocks seemed to effortlessly pass under my feet as I whistled and sang. Only a handful of seekers showed to hear a nondescript, somewhat lethargic, middle-aged man discuss the benefits of visualizing a blue light in the middle of your forehead. Bingo, right between the eyes. Well, I skipped right home and sat on the musty carpeting in the basement in front of the long-since-retired couch that was my bed. I earnestly attempted to channel in a blue light. Well, I'll be, as hogs are to grits. I saw an electric powder blue dot in the middle of my forehead, with eyes closed, of course. This was incredible; I must have been almost there, almost enlightened. How many other people would be able to pull in a blue light with such little practice? Being a bit discouraged that no great transformation occurred; I found no consolation when telling others that I could now see a blue light. No one seemed too impressed.

Plenty of sunbathing was achieved in Barnuka's overgrown, weed infested backyard. I cleared a small area for my sleeping bag to lay on and broasted into a pool of sweat. This was definitely the darkest tan that I ever employed through a summer.

While mentioning to someone at the meditation workshop that I was searching for a fire opal, they suggested I stop in and see Steve at Number 3 Jailers Muse in Blood Alley Square, downtown Vancouver. Downtown is actually the upper north side; eighty percent of it is surrounded by water, making it almost an island. This was the theater, arts, and crafts district, reminiscent of Olde Town Chicago and East Side Milwaukee. The red brick cobblestoned alleyways sent my thoughts back to West Greenwich Village, New York City. It was very quaint and conducive to tourism, a type of Soho.

Steve owned a gem shop and was quite amiable towards me, readily identifying with my need for a fire opal. He brought out a pickle jar full of uncut opals and placed it on the weathered wooden ledge of a swinging door. Steve gently dumped the jar out and separated the fire opals for me. My eyes grew entranced at the brilliant, almost activated colors of red, yellow, green, and blue. They appeared as a moving warm liquid mass, ever changing. He said, "Pick one out."

I hesitantly replied, almost with financial embarrassment, "But, I really can't pay a lot for one of these. How much do they cost?"

Smiling, Steve happily answered, "You can have one; I've got plenty of them. And, anyway, they're uncut."

"Wow, really?"

Humbly, I sifted through a dozen or so and chose one the size of a half-cut shooter marble. Opening my macramé jute pouch, I dropped it in along with my owl-eyed acorn pendulum and vial of ashes. There, sacred item number four, including my eagle feather. Thanking him to the point of nausea, I gleefully waited at the bus stop, gripping the opal in my palm, sensing its heat and power. So, Joni, the aura lady back in Boulder, probably knew that I was destined to carry a fire opal.

It was midmorning back at Barnuka's and very quiet. I had the house to myself, an unusual occurrence. Sorting through Barnuka's record albums and desiring to hear some music again, other than my own, I came upon several recordings of Richard Wagner's symphonies. I can't say that I was familiar with his music, so I put them on. The concealing melodies suddenly lured me in. Gradually lulled into a moment of musical ecstasy, I began to dance around the room. A creative freedom welled up inside and showed itself through this music. I felt that I understood Richard Wagner's mood and intention like no other classical work that I'd been exposed to. I entered into a setting all my own. The consequences of embarrassment if someone suddenly popped in caused me to regrettably stop. I mused, "Someday I'll have a place of my own, and I'll revisit Richard Wagner."

I had heard about a two-mile-long nude beach on the western shore near the university so I thought, "Why not?" I'd never been to a nude beach, and certainly was not bashfully inhibited. So, appropriately taking along a beach towel, I hopped a bus west to the beach. There was a very long, steep, dirt-trodden descent leading to the beach. Following others, I soon came to the white sands of Wreck Beach. Boomerang shaped, it extended to the north into Tower and Spanish Banks beaches. Well, it was a bit of a shock on the eyes, but sure enough, there scattered by the hundreds were people with no clothes on whatsoever. They congregated on blankets, swam in the water and tossed Frisbees. Frolicking dogs made nothing of it.

Still keeping my cut-off Levis® around my midsection, I sheepishly strolled along the beach. Some people felt extremely self-conscious, judging from their nervous glances, but, still, they remained naked. Others, mostly older men, came to observe. They even brought binoculars. Some came to be alone, off by themselves, to read or actually sunbathe. And, some came to hustle the opposite sex. And, some like myself came out of curiosity.

The moment came when I had to let go of my self-consciousness or forever stand out, so I dropped my cut-offs and wandered into the water. It was bone-chilling cold and laden with sharp rocks. No wonder few people were swimming. Did somebody yell shark?

Lying on the warm sand, absorbing sun, my eyes grew weary from bulging. Was I noticeably staring? Attracted to a blonde about ten feet away, I worked up some awkward nervous conversation. She gave me one or two polite glances and communicated a total of six words, picked up her bag and towel, and walked away. The Rodney Dangerfield in me began to surface. To my astonishment, her friend, whom I was not attracted to, began talking to me. We casually chatted, almost completely overlooking our nudity. We seemed to be akin to each other on a totally friendly basis. Her name was Wendy, and she unreservedly invited me to her apartment for supper, a natural food supper. She was a tender-footed, less than physical lady who seemed to need my help getting back up the cliff-like path.

Wendy made a great supper around a staple of brown rice. I felt relaxed enough to let down my guard and opened up to her in many of my personal areas, including my hidden absurd humor. We were very easy with each other, so much so that she invited me to live there for the duration of my stay in Vancouver. I gladly accepted.

Sweet, quick good-byes were said to Barnuka and the gang along with my traditional sprinkling of ashes on the front lawn.

That evening, I entertained Wendy with the Guild guitar, singing most of the songs that I had written that could be drawn up in memory. Her solo audience was overwhelmingly appreciative.

Wendy was on vacation for most of the summer because she was a schoolteacher. Having so much free time, she suggested that we camp out on Vancouver Island for a few days. We took her car and boarded the ferry at Horseshoe Bay, crossing the thirty-five mile Georgia Straight into a town called Nanaimo. I felt regal, as if vacationing on a cruise liner. The water sparkled aqua gestures as the three-hundred-mile expanse of Vancouver Island summoned us to come explore the lush mountain forests, valleys, and bays.

A salmon run was on and many ferry travelers excitedly peered over the deck, taking in the rare sight of thousands of hard-driven salmon bucking the waters heading toward the Pacific.

The weather was heavenly and our mood lofty. Wendy just had to give me a ten cent tour of Victoria, the capital of British Columbia. Victoria is forty miles to the south of Nanaimo on the very tip of

Vancouver Island. My lasting impression was that of a gala colored, royal Victorian city, and I didn't have to go to London to see red double-decked buses. Flowers lined the streets and roadways and smiling police kept the traffic in line. I really wasn't much attracted to buildings, but I was in awe at the dignified appearance of the Parliament Building.

Driving northward inland, a good deal of time was spent admiring nature along Cowachan Lake at a twelve-hundred-foot elevation. My quick eye caught a masked shrew darting between rocks. Snowshoe rabbits scampered in brown and white swirls, as a red squirrel was busy gathering pinecone scraps, hardly noticing us. Startled, he began chattering a string of scolding rebukes.

It was just past noon as we made our way north past Mount Gray along the Alberni inlet. Back on the east coast of Vancouver Island, Wendy wanted to stop at arts and crafts shops, so we made the rounds all the way up to the town of Campbell River.

While Wendy wandered the small shops, I was attracted to an occult bookstore. The people that worked there seemed generally friendly, eagerly making me aware that they were Baha'is. I knew little of the Baha'is and their beliefs other than hearing the name mentioned in spiritual circles. They were extremely gracious and outgoing towards me while freely sharing their faith.

One of the ladies, named Isabelle, was bubbling with eagerness to explain in depth their doctrine, history, and beliefs. She, in rapid succession, relayed to me how in the mid-1800s a Persian merchant named Mirza Ali Muhammed or "Bab," had a revelation of himself becoming one of the great divine religious leaders on par with Moses, Christ, and Muhammed. Only a few years after propagating his new system, he was murdered, and another of his followers, Baha u'llah, assumed the role of spiritual leader and went one step further by claiming that he was the chosen one of all the prophets. He claimed to be immortal. Oddly enough, he died in 1892 at seventy-five years old. There were many other contradictions and discrepancies concerning him which I discovered later on. Thus, the Baha'is were formed. Abdul Baha, his eldest son, succeeded him and was instrumental in bringing the organization to the United States. And, upon his death in 1921, the torch was handed over to Shogi Effendi. Isabelle gave me the impression that Baha'is were a blended potpourri of religious beliefs, acknowledging nine of the great revelators of deity, among them being Moses, Christ,

Buddha, Zoraster, Confucius, and Muhammed. Isabelle continued to inform me that each one of these religious leaders ministered in their own time and culture and, in her mind, Baha u'llah was the greatest, the fulfillment.

I couldn't help but to reason with myself that if well over a hundred years had passed since Baha u'llah's commission to Persia, would his teaching still be applicable to the culture of the 1970s in America? Maybe a new prophet would appear out of their ranks. Either way, love, peace, and tolerance of all peoples was stressed. It sounded warm and attractive. They believed that we are all inherently divine. That seemed to be the underlying theme to many of the spiritual ways that I was exposed to.

Isabelle's captivating charm was infectious. I was moved to stay on there in Campbell River and further investigate the warmth of the Baha'is. She and several others invited me to stay at their home, an upper flat only two blocks away from the store.

Upon telling Wendy, she seemed mildly shocked and confused, but accepting. And so, we agreed to dissolve our camping plans and go our own separate ways.

The evening was spent quietly with Isabelle, another lady, and a man my age. I couldn't tell if anyone was married there, but that didn't seem to matter. Peace and serenity are honorable, but it appeared that they were void of humor and the freedom of active physical emotion and craziness. Theirs was a very serious, sober faith with little or no room for jesting. In spite of this, I was still open to visiting Corlett, the older lady on Quadra Island who was their spiritual liaison.

After a hearty fruit breakfast, I boarded the four-car passenger barge to Quadra Island, a restful ten-minute ride. The day was overcast and drizzling, one of the first such days since I had arrived in Vancouver two weeks before. Quadra Island was teeming with plant life, thick brush, and flowering vines along the narrow roadside. The island was dense with plant growth.

Previous arrangements were made by phone to meet with her at ten o'clock in the morning. Feeling sympathetic that I was caught out in the rain, a generous, concerned resident of Quadra Island offered me a ride to Corlett's. I had supposed that everyone knew each other on the island. Moving toward Corlett's cottage, which was overgrown with brush, moss, and dew-laden leaves, a damp chill bore down on my anticipating spirit.

As she answered the door, I saw on her face that she hadn't smiled for years. Negative lines around her mouth, eyes, and forehead read like a dismal road map. The atmosphere in this musty, dark room was that of a dimly lit funeral home submerged in the dirge of an organ. Our conversation died before it got off the floor. Corlett didn't talk unless I asked questions. She had absolutely no interest in my spiritual hunger and offered only vague, obscure answers as to what the Baha'i faith had to offer. If this was Vancouver Island's representative of the peace loving Baha'is, then it was clearly apparent why Isabelle and her friends were foreigners to pure joy and humor. Our visit was stretched out for fifteen minutes when I volunteered to leave. Her identity seemed to be in line with the dreary weather outside. Moss grows where the sun doesn't shine.

As I stood on the barge, I envisioned an oppressive cloud of gloom and evil blanketing the atmosphere of Quadra Island.

When I got back to their bookstore, the fog had lifted somewhat and murky taints of sunlight struggled to break through. My clothes, bones, and moccasins needed to dry out, so I truly hoped for sunshine.

Isabelle was not around. I just left a written message with the worker there. It read, "Thanks for your kindness. Corlett seemed depressed and unhappy. May the Great Spirit give you joy. Ayuta Rai."

My anxious desire to get back to Vancouver and Wendy sent my feet a hopping. I was at her apartment door by three-thirty that afternoon. Chamomile and peppermint tea was lovingly prepared while she laughed over my humorous insight of Quadra Island.

The half-dollar-man was my next target for esoteric experience. His name was actually Sivananda, "The Living Master of Vibration." He was to be at the Yoga Vendanta Center located at 1840 West 1st Street on the English Bay at seven-thirty in the evening, August 8, cost, two dollars. With little coaxing, Wendy got in on the act, and we observed this together.

Here in an upper loft, sat a rather obese East Indian man with nothing more than a pair of boxer shorts on. He placed a half dollar on the top of his baldhead and proceeded to intensify guttural sounds and inhuman-like vibratory noises. Within five minutes, in full view of thirty or so spectators, he opened his mouth and took out the half dollar. Astonished, people gasped and said, "Wow!"

I mumbled to Wendy, "I hope he doesn't put that coin back in circulation." She couldn't refrain from smirking.

Well, okay, I was out two bucks, but at least we witnessed firsthand a living master of vibration. So he vibrated a half dollar through his skull into his mouth. I hadn't noticed if it landed up heads or tails. I'm sure that the Western debut of the half-dollar-man advanced itself to even bigger and better performances.

It was either the Dalai Lama or Chogyam Trungpa Rinpoche that was headlined to speak before a great assembly of his followers at a second-floor gymnasium on west 4th. I had heard considerable mention of his fame and grew quite interested in the possibility of seeing him in the flesh.

As is common in my nature, I was one of the first to arrive and fortunately was able to seat myself to the front right of his colorfully adorned, lavishly cushioned, platform. Considerable time lapsed, and a steady flow of his devotees ecstatically filtered in. By eight o'clock, an estimated fifteen hundred people sat on the hard maple floor, elbow-to-elbow and foot-to-foot. We patiently waited anticipating the entry of this famed guru. A locker room odor permeated the eighty-five degree oxygen-starved air. Several high-ranking disciples gave long-winded testimonies in an attempt to kill time and appease the masses while awaiting the word of his arriving limousine. Weary of waiting and a bit uncomfortable from needing to relieve myself, I toyed with the desire to leave but realized the near impossibility of straddling and crawling over hundreds of unsuspecting luster-faced followers. Finally, as I was entering into the painful stage of needing to relieve myself, he stepped in.

An immediate hush settled upon the bowing worshippers. An array of flowers were cast at his feet. Being aided by two prominent admirers, he reclined on a burgundy pillow cushion in his makeshift throne. Groaning noises and humming sounds were silently heard throughout the room. This man was undoubtedly in control. Ten minutes passed as he took pleasure in receiving their worship and praise. Then he spoke, having the soft, quiet voice of an aged man.

An interpreter relayed his vital message for the evening. The thrust of his message was this: "You must recite the mantra that I have given you ten thousand times a day until black ooze is expelled from your pores. Then you will know that you are being purified." I shook my head in unbelief. Was he serious about black ooze actually surfacing on your skin? In spite of this absurd command, his zealous followers nodded an affirmation of revelation.

Let me tell you, if you chanted anything ten thousand times in a row, something's going to happen to you. Let's try, for instance, saying, "Mrs. Brown's broken cow." You may easily say twelve of these a minute. Now, steadily pacing yourself, it should only require eight hundred and thirty-three minutes of your uninterrupted time, or approximately fourteen hours. We should all be able to set aside fourteen hours of spare mantra time a day. He also left me hanging as to just how you should dispose of this black ooze once it surfaces. I left, severely disenchanted and spiritually enervated, robbed of a taste of enlightenment.

Walking down Broadway, thankfully breathing the seventy-degree Pacific night air, I heard two guys arguing and swearing at each other from across the street. The peacemaker image that I held jealously onto surged through my veins. Jogging over with a dire sense of urgency, I pleaded with them to mellow down, calmly shouting, "Brothers, let's be at peace with one another." (Good flower child line.)

One of the guys, having a drunken rage on his face, grabbed the knapsack on my back and threw me face first onto the sidewalk. He sat on top of me and mercilessly pounded my head, back, and sides with his fists, shouting obscenities until my ears hurt. It happened so quickly I could not respond or defend myself. Suddenly I heard another voice shouting, and my attacker fled. A man came to my rescue, seemingly out of nowhere. Helping me up, I quickly turned to thank him, but to my great surprise, there was no one there! It was then that I believed in the reality of guardian angels. I took inventory of my bodily injuries. My nose, right cheek, and forehead were bruised and bleeding from the concrete impact, but I seemed to have nothing broken.

Noticeably shaken, I hobbled the remaining ten blocks to Wendy's. She was not home yet, so I let myself in and tended to my wounds. After that night, the peacemaker in me took a low-key approach to settling disputes.

Over the remaining five or six days of my stay in Vancouver, I took in several other basic mystical mind-expanding seminars, such as

Yogi Bhajan's 3 HO foundation and hand reading at the Hobbit house on Nelson Avenue. There were introductory yoga classes at Shyan Yogashram on East 6th. I attended an open house on dreams and ESP, which included a complimentary meditation assistance program. And of course I exhausted the search for natural food stores, co-ops, and book outlets with names like Nature's Path, Manna Natural Foods, Downtown Natural Food and Juice Bar, Oasis Sunshine Kitchen, and, can you believe, a place called simply The Natural Food Store. Three fun-packed weeks in Vancouver left me with little else to imagine, but apple picking was bidding me, "come."

Wendy and I had grown quite close and congenial. A bittersweet parting had to take place. I know that we both had difficulty holding back tears. She needed a friend who liked her just as she was, someone who realized and brought out her self-worth. I needed someone to share my deep feelings, sorrows, and joys with. A wanderer can get chronically lonely. She understood my cynical and sometimes silly humor. I was okay by her standards. We filled a void in each other, but it had to end. Our actual parting took place on a cloudy weekday morning. Our sadness was one and we pulled it out like taffy. I was deeply entrenched in emptiness as I took the final steps downstairs onto the corner of 12th and Birch.

Walking to the on-ramp of the Trans-Canada Highway, my wavering pace had a grief-like rhythm. I stood there with backpack and guitar, almost hoping that I wouldn't get a ride. I allowed myself to fantasize Wendy pulling up in her red car, pleading with me not to leave, "Find a job here; live here; you belong in Vancouver," she'd convincingly say. It didn't happen, and eventually I had to step off to the side of the road because of melancholic crying. I was experiencing yet another in a series of deeply sad impulses. Did I really have to pick apples over two hundred miles away in East Kelowna? I felt like a shell of tears. My ears were attuned to the soulful call of a mourning dove that seemed to drown out the hum of the traffic.

A car pulled over for me, and I got in.

CHAPTER 29

APPLE TIME

The weather seemed dreary, though it may not have been. Still, the trip to east Kelowna was like dragging baggage to nowhere. The man who picked me up in Vancouver was a lumberjack enroute to a logging camp near Emory Creek along the Fraser River. Because of the torrential rain that we ran into, he offered me his car as shelter for the remainder of the day. This was my overnight motel. Nothing like a wet, gloomy logging camp to snap you out of depression.

Loggers get up early I discovered: five-fifteen in the morning. Seemed unreasonable, but by sunrise I groggily stood on the Trans-Canada Highway, seeking a ride. Quite surprisingly, a vibrant lady veered over. Excitedly, I remarked, "Wow! I just got out here." Her energy level rubbed off on me, and my spirits rose.

The lady told me that she just got back from Lima, Peru, after taking an exhilarating train ride over a sixteen-thousand-foot ascent and hopping a barge at Iquitas, Peru, for an adventurous Amazon River journey. While in Peru, she had for food, a staple of snakes, parrots, monkey, and deep-fried spider delicacies. Indiana Jones would have gotten the willies. The name she wrote in my little yellow book was Penal McKay. She entreated me to go to Peru. "You haven't lived until you've experienced it." Her vivacious spirit almost ignited mine. I actually considered dumping my plans and heading for Peru.

She dropped me off in Salmon Arm on Shuswap Lake, and a ride was easily had south on Highway 97 to Kelowna. I gladly hiked the two miles to my new home on the orchard. Most of the workers hadn't arrived yet, though some seasoned pickers were finishing up cherries. I introduced myself to everyone that I met and discovered that a couple from Wisconsin lived there year 'round.

About sixteen cabins divided into two rows gave the appearance of an old West mining town. Mine was the sixth one on the east side. First thing I did was make some short-grain brown rice on my four-burner wood stove. This was living: my own home for at least six weeks with outside running water and a real hot shower.

While walking the expanse of the four hundred acres, powdered dirt rose like a mushroom cloud under my feet. The weather was dry. A song came, a happy melody called "The Bells of My Lord."

> The Bells of My Lord reflect the sound when I walk on the road of the light in the sun.

> The Bells of My Lord sound the aura of peace among children, among workers, among kings.

> I finally cry with love for the Bells of My Lord.

When I got back to the cabin I completed the lyrics and strummed it on the guitar. A different mood began to set in; optimism tugged at my sorrow until sorrow gave way to hope and hope to desire. It seemed like months since I'd heard myself whistle. But, here I was, deep within the ripening McIntoshes, whistling. White-crowned sparrows harmonized with their happy trills. "Zippety-do-da, zippety-a, my, oh, my, what a wonderful day."

I wrote my dad a letter now that I had an address for a while, signing it Ayuta Rai. He had no idea where I was on this planet Earth. The last he had heard of me was the day before I left Wausaukee Road in April. It was now mid-August, and the valley sun meant business.

I was drawn to a stand of pine trees. I came back the next day with shopping bags to scoop up the fallen needles to use as carpeting on my floor. It was a strange idea, but it beat pine-scented aerosol cans. Nobody dared comment on my pine needle floor, partly because everybody else working there was weird in their own way.

Zach and Pat pulled up the following day, and we had a grand reunion. I took it easy on the drugs as we celebrated.

Word went out, "Courtland's start this Saturday, seven to noon. Bartlett pears by mid-week."

By the early part of the week, most everyone had arrived, an odd lot crew for sure. The people that I had meet that week were, Ann Marie and Christian, a young French couple from Quebec; Charles, a middle-aged science teacher; Kim, a run-of-the-mill, early-twenties white Canadian Hindu practitioner; Chad and Bruce, two burly white South African hitchhikers making their way across the continent; at least ten native Canadians, men and women; one guy named Red, who was a foul mouthed, woman-chasing drunkard; and Zach, Pat, myself and a notable crew of about fifteen others. We were definitely the dirty dozen by the end of an exhausting, solar-baked day.

You'd find out within the first two hours if you could cut this physically demanding labor. Between twenty to forty dollars a day was the expected earnings at approximately six dollars a bin. A bin is a four-foot-by-four-foot-by-three-foot deep wooden container. That's a lot of apples. Pears are considerably heavier, they're much denser. After the first day, I simply wanted to die and be with my maker. Nearly every bone, muscle, and joint ached, especially my shoulders from the weight of the buckets. I was astonished to see that several of the women did better than the men. The native people initially grunted and worked the hardest.

An apple a day may keep your doctor away, but six or seven keeps you on the toilet. I learned that painful lesson after day two of a severe bout with diarrhea. Grapes are worse; the grapes have wrath.

We were all expected to be on the hay wagon by seven o'clock in the morning to be transported into the orchard. If you missed the wagon three times, you no longer had a job. Ann Marie, Christian, and Kim relied upon my six o'clock in the morning wake-up service. As I knocked on their doors from the French quarters, I heard, "Salut Ayuta," and from Kim, "Yeah, I'm up." Sometimes it took three knocks to get a response.

I was making about one hundred forty dollars a week and was able to save virtually all of it. Being the frequent supper guest of Zach and Pat helped me to save money. Pat taught me how to use chopsticks, and by the fourth meal I nearly mastered this art.

The native people came back, season after season. They were quiet, hardworking, polite, and humble. That is, until the Friday night trip to

Kelowna. Every weekend brought them back obnoxiously drunk and physically brawling. Fights broke out, and windows were smashed. Usually by three in the morning, they'd had enough, and one by one they slowly passed out. All I could do to ward them off was to bolt and secure my door and chant some peace slogan. Alcohol can do ugly things to gentle people.

Red was left for dead in the dirt one Saturday night. He found that trying to hustle a native gal was a major mistake. Three husky, violently inebriated, native guys pulverized him within minutes. I felt bold just peering out the window. Red survived the beating but packed up and fled two days later. His cabin remained vacant.

Kim, whose cabin was next to mine, would often engaged with me in deep conversation about spiritual things. He was primarily engrossed in the Hindu god, Krishna. In his attempt to make converts, he gave me his copy of the *Bagavad Gita*. Kim impressed upon me that this book was saturated with spiritual principles. I politely took the book but doubted that I'd ever be able to finish reading this massive work.

Kim ran briefly through some basic beliefs, such as Jesus Himself was empowered by Krishna to do good things for earthlings. Krishna was supposedly the eighth incarnation of Vishu, one of the gods making up the Hindu trinity of Brahma, Siva, and Vishu. The founder of the Krishna society, S.C. Bhaktivedanta Prabhupada, was quoted in the book as saying, "There cannot be any happiness within this material world." He had a very low view of family and friends, leaving his own wife and five children to come to America to propagate Hinduism and write extensively. He called it, "retiring from marriage."

Well, I slowly began reading it, seven or eight pages in the evening, but found difficulty in maintaining interest. Somehow, Krishna who was supposedly a blue-skinned, multi-armed godlike humanoid was just too much of a stretch for me to believe, much less give my life to. I did however, make an earnest attempt to find information on just when, where, and how Hinduism was started. The information that I gathered was very vague, and the sources I found conflicted each other.

While gnawing on my first juicy, sweet, crisp McIntosh of the day, I caught a glimpse of a red fox darting through the ripening Delicious grove. The tractor driver did a little hunting on the side. Word would spread quickly through the fox dens to "stay low."

We freely helped ourselves to grapes by the bucketfuls. People were floating in grape juice, and I don't think that I could have drunk another ounce of the stuff, but by evening I was out there stealing expensive golden grapes, sweet as orange blossom honey, a coal blue grosbeak blended on a vine stimulating me to practice my own warbling whistle.

One very warm Saturday afternoon, while walking back from Kelowna, a man pulled over and asked if I would pose as an Indian for him in his photo studio. Me, an Indian? With my blonde hair, blue eyes, and Polish nose—I guess it was the eagle feather and braid that made the impression. "Sure, I'd be happy to pose for a photo session."

We drove to his studio on Crawford Road, and he busily set up the lighting. Having been given copies of the photos as payment, I'd say he did a decent job of disguising me as an Indian for what he had to work with. Stop in when you're in the area for a free five-by-seven from Dragi Photo Studio.

Chad and Bruce, the crazy South Africans, were constantly falling off ladders and left dangling on branches. If it weren't for their great sense of humor, they'd be dead or comatose. They were two of the most daring, careless apple pickers in the history of the profession. But, one day while Chad was twenty feet up in an ancient McIntosh straddling two branches, a branch gave way under his two hundred twenty pound frame. The crash was heard for acres around. Workers from all directions came running, gravely concerned. There was no boisterous laughing coming from the daredevil duo. Chad's ribs were bruised badly, and laughter wasn't the best medicine. He was lifted gently and placed onto the wagon and driven to town for X-rays. The two South Africans were severely warned by the owner that he would not tolerate any more crazy escapades, or they'd be out with no pay. Chad and Bruce's British accent no longer bellowed reckless and jovial, and Chad lost a week's worth of work while his ribs healed. I love the way that they pronounced South Africa, "Suid Afreak," rolling the "R." Part of their fun was the danger of risk, and that was denied them. They probably ventured north to take on black bear in the Yukon.

Ann Marie was the sweetest, most gentle thing since yellow butterflies in spring. She often made me baked goods, feeling sorry that I had no woman to care for me. Her generous offer of teaching me to speak French met its endurance point, as all I seemed to do was giggle.

Well, French is beautiful, but I just couldn't get into a serious frame of mind. The only two words that I managed to retain over the years are *merci* and *salut*.

In exchange for these French lessons, I taught them guitar. Ann Marie and Christian managed to pick up a few guitar chords, but we all struggled in our learning abilities. At least we struggled together.

Thoughts of Peru, Lake Titicaca, the golden sun disk, and the Brotherhood of the Seven Rays crept in steadily as September took hold. I had an overwhelming urge to hitchhike to Peru to see for myself if I was a "chosen one" for the Brotherhood of the Seven Rays. This prompted me to set up appointments at a doctor's office in Kelowna to receive the necessary series of shots in order to secure a passport to enter South America.

Cholera, yellow fever, malaria, and several other vaccines had to be administered. The shots did not cost as all medical attention in Canada was socialized, paid for by the government. I took advantage of the opportunity in spite of my weakening fear of a needle. At five years old, I passed out while holding my mother's hand, waiting to have my pre-kindergarten shot. From that day forward, I've always gotten weak at even the thought of a needle being jabbed in my body.

But, with courage and a no-choice option to aid in my follow through, I got all shot up. The shots were given over a period of three weeks. Supposedly, this is a type of homeopathic prevention. The disease is actually injected into your blood so that you become immune to it. People have told me that by eating poison ivy, you'd become immune to it. Never tried, never had to; I'm not allergic to poison ivy.

The worst shot of all was cholera. The doctor, in passing, mentioned that I might experience mild nausea later in the evening as a reaction. I was healthy and tough. I mean, if I could easily stomach raw peyote and other bitter herbs, I could certainly handle something that I didn't have to taste.

Around midnight that evening, I began to experience the cold shakes and sweating, accompanied by tenderly sore muscles and brittle bones. I tossed and moaned, being frightened that possibly I was having an unusually severe reaction. Death began to play a role in my every thought. After several hours of growing agony, delirium set in. I was only conscious of feeling bitterly cold and shaking uncontrollably as I lay on my sweat-saturated mattress. What if I mistakenly was given the wrong shot? This was undoubtedly the worst pain and sickness that I've ever experienced, even to this day. I knew that I was helplessly dying. Eventually, my system gave out, and I went into an unconscious state. At five o'clock in the morning I awoke, drenched in my own sweat. But the disease had passed. Bodily warmth enclosed me, and I felt light and alive.

Bouncing out of bed, I dressed myself and cheerfully thanked the Lord for delivering me. At lunchtime I called the doctor to voice my concern over the shot and reaction. He admitted that mine was a rare occurrence, but it made me aware that what I experienced was just a small dose of what it would be like if I had actually contracted the disease. Most people die. That was a sobering thought. Well, okay, now I can withstand a cholera invasion.

I was required to have just one more shot, which was an inoculation against yellow fever. They only scheduled yellow fever shots in Kelowna once a month, but the nurse told me that I could get it any day in Vancouver. With two weeks left of apple picking, I had no choice but to wait and return to Vancouver. I had to go to the Embassy building there anyway to receive a passport. I'd use Dragi's photo for my passport snapshot.

Of the few books that I carried with me, *Secret of the Andes* was one. I read through it many times to enhance and confirm my desire to venture the Andes and go to Peru. I reread Emory Hachem's letter, the man from Maryland that searched for the abbey near Lake Titicaca. I preferred to believe that it did exist, and he just wasn't chosen rather than to suppose that this whole thing was a hoax.

While often pondering just which one of the seven rays I possessed, I also envisioned a close, harmonious community comprised of the spiritually elect. Surely, I would have a major role with my musical gift. I tended more towards the rich blue tone, that was probably my color of acceptance, or maybe a rich, yellowish orange, a cross between a dandelion and a tiger lily.

One Wednesday around six o'clock in the evening after another fatiguing nine-hour day of apple picking, a knock came on my door, probably one of the guys wanting to jam again on guitar and harmonica. Extremely surprised beyond mustering up intelligible words, I stood overjoyed. "Wendy!" I screamed. Just what my wandering soul needed! She was on her way to Osoyoos to visit relatives and took a chance on finding me still here, picking apples. We had a great time talking, and I couldn't stop feeling silly. Wendy sort of rolled her eyes when she heard of my plans to go to Peru, but she understood well my wandering spirit. We were friends forever.

Evenings were getting cool, dropping into the low fifties. Word shot through the cabin complex that the Aurora Borealis was on. I ran out with the excitement and curiosity of a child. All the orchard workers came out, laying their blankets on a grassy area. A reverent silence rested in the late September air. This was an amazing display of colorama. Luminous propellants whooshing, darting, scanning the heavens. A full spectrum of red, yellow, blue, and green arced their way from west to east in the northern sky.

A bucket of popcorn came around. This was better than an outdoor theater. Most of us sat there until nearly midnight draped in blankets and sleeping bags as our eyes absorbed the explosion of color filling sixty percent of the sky. As I understand it, the Aurora Borealis is not to be confused with the northern lights. The northern lights are primarily a steady white glow, not the shooting effect in multicolors of the Aurora Borealis.

Tim, who sat near me throughout this light show, told me of a guy he knew who was driving through Alberta, Canada, high on LSD when the Aurora Borealis hit. This guy flipped out, thinking that the world was ending, lost control of his car, and overturned it in a ditch. The guy died, but his passenger lived to tell the frightening story.

I counted myself fortunate and blessed to have witnessed such a beautiful natural phenomena. The summer of '74 had come to a memorable end, in spite of my efforts to clench tightly to the last remnants of a seventy-degree afternoon. Enter fall, the introspective season. Pat gave me her parent's address in Portland, Oregon, should I be passing through some day or wished to write her and Zach.

Bringing my Guild guitar with me the four thousand miles through the U.S., Mexico, Central America, and halfway down the west coast of South America seemed very foolish and impractical. The problem was conveniently relieved when the lady from Wisconsin said that she'd be happy to drop it off at my dad's when she visited her Wisconsin family in late October. I trusted her. What else could I do? Excess baggage had to go.

Reading through the *Bhagavad Gita* was a labor of guilt, but I finished it two days prior to leaving. This ranked among the most boring of spiritual philosophical writing that I had ever read, but I promised Kim that I'd read through it with an open mind.

Krishna is reputed to be the supreme personality of the godhead according to A.C. Bhakti Vedanta's comments and translations, he, himself, being the last representative in line in a series of many since Krishna himself. Dates were vague or purposely omitted as to when or if Krishna ever appeared on earth.

Hinduism is steeped in reincarnation, which I know to be in conflict with the teaching of Jesus Christ. How could they be the same person in a different body giving contrary messages? It just didn't gel. The setting for the *Bagavad Gita* was a battlefield called Kuruksetra. Krishna, while standing in a chariot, instructs his friend and devotee, Arjuna, in the way of enlightenment as a great battle is about to ensue. The thrust of the message throughout the book was that the material world is useless and should be discarded. Detachment from sex, friends, material possession, and even the joy of beautiful, natural scenery, is demanded in order to attain to enlightenment, Krishna consciousness. Hindu's claim that until a person willfully does this, they keep coming back, placed in a different body until they get it right. Well, I truly loved God's creation and simple means of enjoyment. To deny the beauty of creation seemed absurd.

It was about this time that I began to get fed up with every egocentric claiming that they were the great divine one. All others were lesser, little gods. From Baha u'llah to Krishna to Brother Jim in Banff, from Buddha to Christ to Sun Young Moon, they couldn't all be the Supreme Being. My search hit a bitter, angry frustration. There were probably ten thousand frauds living in the world claiming to be the messiah, the chosen one, the avatar, and the all-in-all holy one.

I thought about those poor Hare Krishna people dancing around chanting, eating sugared dough balls to stay high, sacrificing to demigods in hope of getting rewards. Their mind was stripped from their spirit, and they just jumped up and down, forcing a blissful smile until their cheeks ached. How long could they hang onto the façade of happiness? How long would it be until they experienced a total breakdown? One month? Two years? Then what? My searching was still on but with a sharp, discerning mind, determined to know the true God.

Well, allow me to settle down into more pleasant thoughts. Ann Marie and Christian likewise gave me their address in Quebec. I believe I wrote them a small encouraging note some six months later and had good intentions to write periodically over the years but never followed through.

I was able to save approximately eight hundred dollars over the six weeks at the orchard in East Kelowna and felt financially quite secure. That kind of money would go a long way in Peru. Six weeks in the Okanagan Valley and one human being among billions making an impression and being given impressions was something money could not buy, and nothing could take it away.

Zach and Pat graciously offered to give me a ride to Vancouver, and from there they'd head south to Portland. I had six more traveling hours with my good friends.

CHAPTER 30

A CHANGE OF PLANS

C ontact was already made via the telephone with Eric and Julia, two friends that I had met on my first visit to Vancouver. They happily offered to let me stay in their nicely furnished apartment for two weeks while I waited to get my yellow fever shot and passport application processed.

Being so pumped up about venturing to Peru, I bought two record albums of Peruvian flute music, one title being *Flute Indienne* by Los Talchacos, with songs like "Canto Del Cuculi," "La Llamada, and "El Indio Del Altiplano. While listening to the simple melodic music on stereo headphones at Eric and Julia's, I was pleasantly launched into peaceful imaginations of mountain villages etched into the Andes and humble, gracious Aymara Indians dressed in bright array. The villagers peacefully sat around an open fire as we sang together, playing stringed instruments and wooden flutes. They would welcome my own creative interpretation of their music. By the end of side one, I was reclining on the golden banks of sun-drenched Lake Titicaca, fourteen thousand feet above and thousands of miles removed from maddening civilization. These would be my people of the region, and I would bring them truth and joy. I was certain of a destined rendezvous with my guide who would take me over the snow-capped Andes to the paradise valley of the Brotherhood of the Seven Rays. There, pure bliss and immorality would give life to leisure, where there would be no more worries, fear, or distrust. The anxiety of a chaotic society would fade from memory.

Eric came walking in, and I was sharply thrust back to reality. "Yellow fever shots are given every Tuesday," he informed me. "You'll have to wait another week."

"Well, I'm sure that I can find things to do; I really appreciate you letting me stay here," I calmly answered.

"Sure, no problem at all," he assured me.

While coming back from the British Embassy on Concelor Street the next day, a bright orange poster screamed at me from the window of a natural food store. A noted Sufi leader from Iran was going to present himself before his followers at the Sufi center on Kings Road. My brief exposure with the Whirling Dervishes in Boulder left me with a teasing for more. What were these people like?

It was early Friday morning, the first week of October, as I stood in front of the Royal Bank Building waiting to board the bus over Lions Gate Bridge, crossing the first narrows into North Vancouver. A fifty-eight degree fog had settled upon this downtown arm of the city. The dampness worked its way into my bones. After asking for a green bus transfer, I sat on the cushioned seat, bouncing like a Muppet, glancing at city streets. Fortunately, the transfer bus brought me to within one-quarter mile of the Sufi center. Surprised to find such a pleasant semi-rural area this close to the city, I strolled a dirt road lined with sycamore and eucalyptus trees. It was cozy. People were busying themselves with last-minute details awaiting his divine arrival, so much so that no one seemed to be interested in talking to me. Shuffling my feet in the dirt under the all-natural canopy of a sycamore grove, I observed the rookie Sufis vying for the master's approval when he heard of their good deeds.

Well, the great moment shortly took place. A white Audi slowly cruised the lane as hundreds of followers ran to greet him, lining the drive shouting praises and throwing flowers. I stood there in the distance, removed from the hoopla in body and spirit. This was not my spiritual master.

How I yearned for the excitement of welcoming my own Lord with all my fellow brothers and sisters! I deeply envied their sense of community, being devoted to a leader and worshipping at the feet of the master. All the thrill, the noise, laughter, and joy were not mine to share. I listened from afar as he spoke through a PA system. It was the same generic stuff: all is love, all is joy, and realize the divine within yourself. I thirsted for something more than Sufi slogans. Where's the meat, the bite, to his message? I boarded the bus back to the city while he was still yakking away at his spellbound admirers.

The weekend found me anxiously biding my time, enduring the days until Tuesday, the yellow fever shot day. Then, on to Peru.

Monday morning, almost out of habit, I was back at the occult bookstore that I had frequented, scanning titles and stretching my ears to take in the hush-hush conversation about somebody's blissful experience. I'd seen these book jackets hundreds of times before. The sincere seeker can be inundated with hundreds of paths and ways to spiritual enlightenment. Who do you choose? What else could any method promise? Every system had their own peculiar twist, but they all rubbed elbows in passing. Their mantras included buzz words, such as chant, deny desires, eat vegetables only, focus, exercise, breathe, drift, realization, macro, micro, alkaline, fruits only, visions, out of body, crystals, mantras, practice, attain, colors, auras, energy, life force, passive, assertive, do, don't do, yin, yang, mandala, magic, Bhakti, Shakti, Chakra, and karma.

I now had familiarity with fifty to sixty authors, but still I glanced through the shelves and flipped randomly through pages. There, on a bottom shelf at ankle level, sat two books by Franklin Jones titled *The Knee of Listening* and *Method of the Siddhas*. Curiously studying the preface, my attention was welded by the beginning pages. His approach stressed humor, and he gave concrete answers to suffering and searching. His lengthy description of an almost step-by-step method to realizing enlightenment caused a screaming inside of me. This was him; this was the guy! My expectations of who my spiritual master would be were being realized in front of my eyes.

I purchased both books and sat up in the meditation loft absorbing myself in his teaching. He called himself Bubba Free John, Bubba being his boyhood nickname and Free John being the English interpretation of Franklin Jones, a freed man. God is gracious.

A constant theme of his was that we continually avoid relating freely to others, ourselves, and the world around us. He strongly suggested that our prior condition at birth is freedom, but as months and years go on, we yield to desires, pressures, and acceptable behavior. I couldn't get enough. His followers were called the Dawn Horse Communion, and they centered themselves in San Francisco.

Within a half hour of first opening the book, I unreservedly with immense enthusiasm decided to head for San Francisco and join the Dawn Horse Communion. Peru and Lake Titicaca would be set aside indefinitely. My spiritual master was probably awaiting my arrival already. And to add frosting to the cake, I could cancel my yellow fever shot scheduled for the next day.

A small thank you note was left for Eric and Julia, and by noon I stood at the on-ramp to Highway 99 south. Like a beaver watching a fifty-foot birch crash, tumble, and roll into the river, I felt that my gnawing search was over. Now I would finally relish the greeting, "Brother, you're home."

An extremely happy guy named Ben picked me up. He had a soup can sitting alongside him with the label taken off. Holding it with his right hand, he cheerfully said, "Here, have some."

"What is it?" I questioned.

"It's psylosibin, I just picked 'em north of Vancouver."

I hesitantly picked out two gushy, quickly browning mushrooms and ate them raw. I never did care for raw mushrooms. As they slid down my throat, I wondered whether this was a wise thing to do, considering the effect they had on me at the party in Boulder.

The ride lasted less than forty-five minutes to the US border near Blaine, Washington, where highway 99 turns into US 5. It was right around October 8, and the weather was unexpectedly beautiful.

I noticed that I was feeling mighty light and giddy. Ben just bounced with laughter and belted out, "Boy, they're hittin' you good!" I knew what he meant, the psylosibin mushrooms were starting to have a noticeable effect.

He dropped me off at the border. "The customs crossing is just a mile up, you'll probably do best to walk it."

"Okay," I sort of answered him in a floating tone. "See you, Ben." We left each other laughing about just simply being alive.

The line of traffic was backed up for at least half a mile. As I swiftly cruised past all the dragged-out vacationers in their vehicles, I became very conscious of an uncontrollable smile and a terrifying thought shot through my system. What if the custom officials search my backpack and find my license plates? I kept them with me all this time so that I could send them back to the Motor Vehicle Department in Wisconsin with a US postmark. What if they discover from their records that I'd been in Canada since mid-August on a three-week visa and worked here without a work permit? I schemed as to how I might bypass this major border crossing, but there was no way out. My smiling had now become painful. How would I attempt to explain to these officials that I'm really not that happy and I just smile a lot?

I questioned whether I'd be able to sensibly converse when pelted with questions from hard-nosed custom officials. The psylosibin alienated my basic functions of speech, thought, and movement. As I hesitantly approached the crossing, the guard motioned for me to go inside. "Oh, no!" They're going to interrogate me. Standing at the white Formica® counter, I apparently appeared relaxed and in control. The uniformed man at the desk was pleasant while he briefly picked through my belongings as I laid them on the counter. "Okay, you can put it all back. How long you been in Canada?"

I had to lie, "Oh, two to three weeks."

He nodded. "Wait here a minute; I'll be right back."

I was certain that he'd return with two armed guards and handcuffs. At least he avoided looking at the secret panel in the bottom of my pack. My license plates were cleverly concealed. I began to noticeably fidget. He's been gone more than a minute. Something was wrong. He popped out of the back with the same pleasant smile, stamped a piece of paper and cheerfully said, "Okay, buddy, you can go. Sorry about the delay."

My heartbeat and blood flow came back to a facsimile of normal, considering the ever-present mushroom effect.

There was a sense of urgency biting at me to get to San Francisco as soon as possible, so riding the bus seemed to be the most logical. I seemed to glide the two miles to the bus depot in Blaine. Blaine's bus depot doubled as a post office and gossip center. Quick business was made of purchasing a ticket. The ticket lady seemed to repeat over and over the simple instructions of transferring buses in Portland.

"Okay, okay," I kept saying, anxious to wait outside away from all these discerning, glaring eyes.

The bus did not arrive for at least another hour, so I reclined against the building, trying to decide whether I was sick, hungry, high, or even here. Boarding the bus was easy, and I headed straight to the back, wishing to remain quietly anonymous.

Within minutes I found myself voluntarily striking up conversation with anything that had eyes and ears. Few people cared to talk to me. Did I intimidate them with my cheek-to-cheek ecstatic happiness?

By the time we stopped in Tacoma, Washington, to pick up passengers, my jaws and cheeks chronically ached and became rock hard.

When was this stuff going to wear off? Concern gripped and controlled my thoughts. I no longer enjoyed this high or the bus ride.

As we pulled into Portland station around seven o'clock in the evening, I was experiencing nausea and weakness. I had to recline on one of the many wooden benches in this auditorium-sized depot. I forfeited my transfer to San Francisco, knowing that I never would have endured the bus ride. Several kind people asked if I was feeling okay. Not to alarm them, I answered, "I'm okay, just a little tired."

Out came my little yellow notebook. Now was the time to call Zach and Pat. If they were here in Portland, they would help me out. Pat answered the phone and nearly screamed to Zach, exclaiming that it was him, "Ayuta Rai!" Within twenty minutes they arrived at the bus depot. They were a balm for my wretched condition.

I was given a tour of a Saturday night in downtown Portland. Unimpressed by flashing neon's and sequined black leather-skirted harlots, I preferred to just literally crash on the thickly carpeted floor in Pat's parents' rather lavish living room. It amazed me that Pat seemed to come out of very humble surroundings, yet she was actually nurtured in wealth. I slept for twelve hours, ate a great breakfast and lunch, and generally came around—once the psylosibin left my bloodstream. I had a lovely afternoon with Zach and Pat.

While boarding the bus to San Francisco, we hugged each other intensely one last time. "Thanks for all your kindness to a wandering sojourner."

CHAPTER 31

SAN FRANCISCO –
THE DAWN HORSE COMMUNION

The six hundred mile bus ride to San Francisco had graciously given me much time for reflection and meditation on Bubba's books, while anticipating the joyous union I'd experience upon initially encountering devotees of the "Dawn Horse Communion." Yes, they surely would exclaim, "Brother, you're home."

Four-thirty in the morning at the Greyhound station in San Francisco appeals to the lonely, destitute, transient drifter. Locker rental was only fifty cents, so I entrusted my backpack to their steel-gray chambers. I opened it cautiously, expecting, perhaps, a body to fall out, but I was relieved to find no guns, drugs, or secret code notes, just an empty locker.

The San Francisco morning was cool, but it seemed apparent that clear skies were overhead. The fifteen-block stroll from the depot at 7th and Market to the Dawn Horse center on Polk and California was tranquil. A few cars kicked up yesterday's dust as they worked their way uphill in second gear. Electric buses snuck up from behind with a scant crew of passengers having expressions like that of sheep to the slaughter.

The area of Polk and California was lined with small shops, boutiques, florists, and short-order restaurants. A cable car pranced, nervously awaiting the onslaught of tourists and commuters. The address of 1443 Polk was what I had written down. I noticed that the eight-foot wooden, glass-enclosed door only led to an upstairs. The door was locked, and a doorbell couldn't be found.

I knocked and knocked till the skin gave way to the bone on my knuckles. No one came down to greet me; nobody peered out the window. "Ah-hah, I know; it's a joke. They're purposely not answering. I bet Bubba's up there laughing profusely with all the others." I stood out on the street and boldly yelled out, "Okay, I get the joke. I finally made it. I'm here. Anybody up there? What, are you all still sleeping?"

Several pigeons were startled from their roost at five-fifty in the morning. Maybe I shouldn't have been yelling that early; what if they really were sleeping? That was not very tactful of me. So, I sat on the concrete sidewalk with my back against the door, sensing the gradual increase in city life—rumblings and horns, a distant siren, radios blare escaping through car windows, and shopkeepers groping for their keys. The sun peeked over the buildings and shone on my face.

A rather effeminate man with hurried, uneasy motions fidgeted with his ring of keys in an attempt to save valuable seconds opening up the flower shop next door. Calmly walking towards him, I happily said, "Hello."

Startled to the point of collapse, he just gave me a quick half glance as his right foot finally entered the fortified confines of his shop. I followed him in, pointedly asking if he knew anything about the people upstairs. His sharp remark was, "I'm not open yet. You'll have to leave."

His hand shook from an apparent nervous disorder. I repeated the question, assuring him that I wasn't interested in purchasing flowers, I just needed to know if anybody lived up there. "Do you know about the 'Dawn Horse Communion'?"

While squinting his eyes, he seemed to form a question mark from the top of his eyebrows around the eyes and down the sides of his nose. Looking impatiently exhausted from my presence, he quickly remarked, "All I know is there's a bookstore up there. Now, you'll have to leave; I don't open until seven."

"Thanks." I joyfully smiled as he scooted me out. Heck, just a bookstore.

Two doors down was a nicely decorated, atmosphere-laden pseudo natural foods restaurant and deli. The man at the deli, also very effeminate, was cheerful and eager to talk. "The bookstore opens at ten. No one lives there."

"Okay, appreciate your information," I cheerfully answered.

He nodded a polite, cordial California "Sure, anytime" gesture as I walked back out through the stained glass doors onto Polk and California.

The cable car's bell needed tuning, but I jumped on anyway. For twenty-five cents, I could at least say that I rode a cable car. The conductor and passengers seemed to have nothing better to do as they chatted their ever-genial small talk. "Nice way to go to work," I thought.

I utilized my dead time by wandering Fisherman's Wharf and Ghirardelli Square, shuffling curiously through the open markets of Chinatown. As I passed all the beautifully decorated, multicolored gables of the Victorian homes, I started to become impressed with San Francisco.

The uphill-downhill meandering had no effect on my physical endurance, and to my surprise, I conveniently found my way back to Polk and California, commonly known as Polk Gulch. At ten fifteen in the morning, the door to the bookstore was finally open. I nearly ran up the twenty-odd steps and burst into the store, catching a young man off guard in his vain attempt at meditation behind the desk.

Bolting out with enthusiasm like that of a Rocky Mountain sunrise in the spring, I joyously proclaimed, "I'm here, I want to join! I read Bubba's books up in Vancouver, British Columbia, and dumped my plans of going to Peru. I was here at six o'clock this morning thinking that everybody lived here, even yelled up from the street. Man, this is great!"

Extending my right hand for a good old firm hippie handshake, I warmly said, "I'm Ayuta Rai."

He sort of backed off and matter of factly told me his name, "Michael."

"Mike," I said, seeing immediately that he was subtly annoyed and did not take kindly to being called Mike, "What do I have to do next?"

He took out from a drawer what appeared to be a two-page application questionnaire. "Fill this out and read Bubba's books."

I boastfully made him aware that I've already read Bubba's books. "I even bought them; they're in my locker at the Greyhound station."

Michael seemed mildly impressed. "Good, then you have a basic understanding of his teaching."

"Sure do," I blurted out like a schoolboy who's finally completed his homework.

I cringed as I entered my real name on the form, placing in parenthesis my spiritual name, Ayuta Rai. There were basic questions about date of birth, home address, medical record, job, no job, employment experience, height, color of eyes, but virtually nothing as to why I wanted to join.

Michael did not seem interested in telling me much more. He didn't even seem interested in minding the store. I had to pry information out of him and was left with nothing more than, "Read as many of these books on Bubba's suggested list as you can. Most of them are available here at the store. Some of Bubba's tapes are available, also. Let us know where you're staying and a phone number where you can be reached. Someone will contact you for an interview and from there we will try to place you in a home. I can tell you right now that you need to get a job as soon as you can."

Michael's response hit me like a sudden cold high tide on the beach. He offered no jubilant welcome, no ushering me in the back room and showering me with belonging—just the facts, please. In an attempt to contain my dejection, I glanced at the books; surprised to notice many titles and authors I had never heard of.

Actually, I was angrily burning inside, mostly at the lifeless specimen up here supposedly representing the "Dawn Horse Communion." I felt like lashing out some hard comments at him, but instead casually walked out retaining an actor's superficial smile, never wanting to appear flustered and disappointed. It's all part of a spiritually together appearance. He was a jerk in my mind. Surely, he was just a beginner.

First things first, a place to stay. Walking back towards the bus depot, I remembered seeing a cheap-looking five-story hotel reminiscent of the St. Marks in East Greenwich Village, New York. A pleasant East Indian man greeted me at the counter. "Seven dollars and fifty cents a night, twenty-eight dollars a week."

I took a room just for the night, being optimistic of placement in a home by tomorrow. My scheme was to go back to the bookstore that afternoon and talk with someone else—hopefully somebody a bit more warm and informative.

Relieved that my backpack was still in the locker, I immediately went back to the hotel room and savored the southern exposure from the fourth floor. No view, just old buildings and an alley, but this nine-by-twelve foot cubicle was home for the day.

While meditating on Bubba with an intent desire to telepathically communicate with him, I had moments of a blissful high. I almost certainly knew that I had found my teacher. God answered my long sought-after quest, now more than three years in the making.

At midafternoon, I snuck back up to the second-story bookstore. Good, someone else was working. A lady in her late twenties was much more cooperative in offering detailed answers to my barrage of questions.

Well, here's the scoop as I received it on the conditions of studying under the teaching of Bubba Free John and entering as a disciple in the "Dawn Horse Communion."

> 1. I had to be interviewed in depth by one of his appointed devotees;2. I had to have at least a thirty-hour a week job;3. If found acceptable, I'd be placed on a waiting list for housing. These group homes consisted of between eight to twelve committed followers;4. That even prior to residing in a house, I must adhere closely to the practices and conditions outlined in two very wordy seventy-page manuals on conditions for practical and spiritual life;5. Bubba did not live in San Francisco, but at the forty-seven acre ashram in Middleton, California, called Persimmons, a two-hour drive north of San Francisco. I would be allowed to have weekend stays there on occasion at my cost and hopefully sit in the presence of Bubba for "satsang." Satsang is an East Indian term for meditating on your guru; and6. As I developed in my spiritual understanding of his radical teaching, I would be moved up to higher areas of responsibility, possibly being so blessed as to live at Persimmons with him.

Well, that definitely answered my questions. I was as eager as a colt's first day out of the barn in mid-April, bounding with life and enthusiasm.

The bookstore worker unmistakably sensed this and because of my persistence was able to speed up the process. An interview was set up for two days from then. She did make one suggestion that didn't sit well with me. She said, "I can tell you right now that you'll have to get your hair cut and shave the beard. Bubba demands a straight appearance."

A gut-level anguish spread through me. I hadn't had a haircut for almost seven years. These beautiful wavy golden locks hung halfway down my back, and my beard, goodness no! Not my beard! I started growing that five and one-half years ago at Power Products.

Knowing that my every move was being monitored, I painstakingly showed no visible signs of alarm or surprise. I even asked her for a referral of haircutters. The following morning, I squirmed and fussed as I sat in a plush salon in the lower downtown district. An undeniably gay man had a pleasurable field day on my head. By now I was getting the impression that San Francisco harbored a large homosexual population. I declined to look in the mirror and somberly walked the distance to my hotel, which I now rented by the week at twenty-eight dollars. Back at the hotel, I regrettably cut and shaved my beard, leaving only a lumberjack's mustache, which eventually was trimmed back.

Up to this point, my first day as a disciple of Bubba Free John's was nothing more than a set of rules and restrictions. I was so self-conscious of my new, clean San Francisco look that I imagined everybody was staring at me.

The "Help Wanted" section of the *San Francisco Chronicle* made my head spin. What was I qualified to do? What would I tolerate? Chuck's Burgers in the outer Mission District of southern San Francisco needed general help.

So, the next morning at eight o'clock sharp, Raymond A. Last met Big Chuck and applied for the job. Chuck was too busy readying the one-stop burger shop for the day's customers to pay much attention to me. After filling out a wrinkled application stained with cooking grease, I walked out unannounced. I was nearly forty feet away onto the sidewalk when Chuck barked out of the service window, "Hey! Where ya goin'?"

Half of San Francisco turned around, and I yelled back, "I filled out the application; didn't wanna bother you."

Chuck's volume lowered, "Come on in, sorry I'm so rude. That's how I am."

"At least he's honest," I thought. He took less than thirty seconds to review the application and then gave me an in-depth interview. Then in a somewhat commanding tone he asked, "When can you start? It's three dollars an hour."

I was slightly dumbfounded; I didn't even know if I wanted to work for him. With almost no thought, I blurted out, "Monday morning."

"Okay," he smiled. "Hey! See you at seven."

"All right," I agreed.

Well, being that it was Friday, at least I had the weekend to psych myself up for the reality of working a steady job. I knew it was my clean appearance that landed me this job at Chuck's Burger place.

Riding the M.U.N.I. bus the thirty-five minutes back to the hotel, I had a better attitude about my new straight look. I was actually acceptable by most people's standards, the first time that I felt this way since 1964, my freshman year in high school.

At three o'clock Saturday afternoon, I anxiously waited in a back room at the bookstore. My interviewer was late. Was this all part of dealing with my reactions? A young guy not more than eighteen years old walked in, looking a bit rushed and uncertain of what he was to do.

"I'm Ray Last; are you here to interview me?"

"Yeah, I'm Christopher." He earnestly held onto a makeshift smile and made a haphazard attempt at appearing in control.

It didn't take long for me to realize that maybe the table was turned here. I should be drilling him. His questions, which seemed programmed, fell short of senseless. The more we talked, the more I felt that he was assigned this duty because he lacked confidence in the area of assertive confrontation, part of what Bubba wrote about as avoidance of relationship. Oddly enough, he asked why I never swore. My only answer was, "I don't like to; it's crude." Then he insisted that I swear in front of him. I asked him why.

Christopher remarked, "Do you have a contraction about swearing? Do you see it still as something bad? It's not; now say a swear word for me, such as _____hole!" An embarrassing anger welled up inside as I quietly repeated the words, "_____hole!" He seemed happy that I finally swore and encouraged me to do more of it.

The interview was over. My head hung low. My gait dragged as I walked back to the hotel. What was going on here; were these people confused and disturbed? When did the real juice of the teaching begin? Did Bubba even know that I was here and being put through this ridiculous treatment?

I went to bed distraught, depressed, and disturbed. I constantly fought off the question of why I was there. My mind grew weary in battle. I had never encountered such pronounced indecision during my pursuit of God. Bubba Free John seemed to be more of a well-guarded secret than an open invitation. Most of Sunday was spent being pensive, even as I strolled miles of city blocks perceiving the uniqueness of San Francisco.

While lying on my bed, hours were given to paging through and scanning the manuals of conditions for living in the Dawn Horse Communion. Many East Indian spiritual terms were commonly used, so I studied them intently to familiarize myself with words and meanings such as:

> Amrita Nadi: The intuitive structure of manifest existence, which is the very structure of consciousness. The transcendent form intuited as divine reality rising out of the heart or very self into the bright or light of God.

> Sadhana: Appropriate action and spiritual life generated where truth is already the case, not where it is sought.

> Maya: Illusion, also the creative power of God where by the worlds are manifested.

> Kriyas: Spontaneous self-purifying physical movements usually of the spine and neck that arise when internal spiritual force is activated.

> Siddha-Guru: A completed one who lives in and as the very divine. One in whom radical understanding is perfect and who communicates that to others.

> Sahaja Samadhi: Natural complete spontaneous samadhi. The eternal and conscious state of truth lived in the midst of all activity and rest by the one who truly understands.

> Bhakta: One who follows the devotional path.

Satsang: Divine communion in the company of the divine person. The relationship between the siddha-guru and his devotee.

These are the terms and definitions as given in the *Dawn Horse Magazine,* Volume II, No. 2.

Sunday night's sleep was restless as I tossed in my mind what might lay ahead at Chuck's daily grind.

Monday morning, at six-fifteen in the morning around October 15, I joined the commuter work force, riding the bus. In the palm of my hand I held the picture of Bubba that I cut out from his magazine, the latest *Dawn Horse Magazine.* I knew where I was going but kept falling out of reality and snapping myself back: Chuck's Burgers, Chuck's Burgers. At twelve minutes to seven, Chuck was just opening the paint-chipped, hand-soiled, white side door. With a cheerful, "Hi," I greeted him. At first he seemed to not know me, but a quick reminder brought him assurance.

First things first. I was to sweep the parking lot, then slice lettuce, peel potatoes, dice onions, slap hamburgers into patties, and cut potatoes for french fries. Then I was to sweep the parking lot, slice lettuce, peel potatoes, dice onions, slap hamburgers into patties, cut potatoes, eat lunch, and do it again until three-thirty in the afternoon.

After a Monday through Friday of this slice-and-dice drama, Chuck saw that there might be real potential here, so he primed me with the possibility of being moved up from back-room servant to short-order cook. Well, I don't know, the thought of a career at Chuck's Burgers didn't exactly send me air bound. Even my smile had a twitch. Chuck needed more than a reliable secondhand man. He needed a help-me-cope-relaxer pill. A very irritable man was he.

On Friday, at four o'clock in the afternoon, there was no word at the hotel desk about a phone call from

Dawn Horse Books. So I called them again. "There is still no opening in a home for you. Sorry. Be patient; Bubba stresses patience." The lady's consolation was like a gift-wrapped box with nothing in it. So there was another week, another twenty-eight bucks, at the no-name hotel.

While simply hanging out at the bookstore on Saturday afternoon, I had easy conversation with James, a guy my age from England who was also somewhat new to the Dawn Horse Communion. James was lively and determined to sound like he was from the West Coast. "For sure, hey man, let's groove." His English pipe dream of being a hippie in Haight-Ashbury was being fulfilled. It all came together for him with an American girlfriend, an American guru, an early placement in a Dawn Horse group home, and a real job at the shoe store across the street. No wonder he was so happy.

James persuaded me to apply for a job there at Root's Natural Footwear, 1428 Polk Street, just across from the Dawn Horse Bookstore. Two days later I bought a pair of Roots shoes. They were similar to the negative heeled Earth® Shoes but not as radical and seemingly having better craftsmanship. I loved the shoes; I was sold. My genuine enthusiasm over the comfort of these shoes convinced Peter, the owner, to give me a part-time job on a trial basis.

I gave big Chuck a week's notice, and he nearly broke down. He handled almost nothing very well. His promising apprentice fled to sell shoes. How belittling.

James was encouraging while making me aware that soon there would be an opening in the home he lived in up in prestigious Pacific Heights. I clung tightly to his speculation and made sure that everyone who was anybody in the Dawn Horse Communion unmistakably knew that I wanted that room when it was vacated. But until then, I'd spend another twenty eight dollars for my third-floor container asylum. The kind East Indian offered me the room for ninety dollars a month. "Ah, no thanks, I don't think I'll be here that long." It was bad enough that I had already come to know many of the other guests by their first names. I definitely had been there too long.

My first day as a trainee at Root's Natural Footwear went quite well. The employees at Root's were all very friendly—Buck, Rob, Nancy, Barb, and James. It had the makings of a good, fun job.

Many hours were spent talking with James about Bubba's teaching and training. He invited me as his supper guest to my soon-to-be home. Guests were really frowned upon as this lifestyle wasn't open for public inspection, but James did some fast-talk convincing, and I was allowed to eat with them. Most of the other people in that home were cold or at best discerningly tepid. As the ten of us sat on the cool, damp hardwood floor, eating a very natural food supper, someone was selected from the group, and each person had to tell something that they didn't like about that person. People eagerly took pleasure in ripping that person apart. You weren't really allowed to defend yourself but instead were expected to welcome the criticism. The conversation stayed hot long after the food cooled down. Not a single person took an interest in my past experiences or how I felt about Bubba and Dawn Horse Communion. That evening, my hotel room felt like a shelter from the storm.

A movie about Bubba entitled *A Difficult Man* had been recently released and was being shown in a back room at the bookstore. I was so anxious to see and hear Bubba, even if it was only on film. Much of the movie centered around all the supernatural phenomena and his intensified teaching that took place that summer up at Persimmon. Excerpts of this group teaching were shown, along with his devotees being thrust into ecstatic bliss while seated in his presence. After viewing this film with thirty or so others, I wanted so badly to see him, to experience these emotional, uncontrollable states of joy. Surely he would single me out as extra special. Johann Pachelbel's classic "Canon in D Major" was used as background music to the film. Every time I hear that piece, I think of that film.

I was very surprised to see Barbara seated at this movie. Barbara was the friend I had met back in Boulder. She appeared very depressed and confused and unable to even muster up a smile. Her complexion was peakish as if she hadn't been in the sun all summer. I thought for sure we'd spend hours together sharing all the events of our summer. But, to the contrary, Barbara just mumbled, "Hi," and didn't want to talk. She lived in one of the group homes somewhere here in San Francisco but would not tell me which one. I felt genuinely sad for her. She obviously wasn't happy here; she was certainly not the same colorful person that I knew back in Boulder. I never saw her again but thought of her often.

Gradual separation from the things of this world was noticeable daily. I began analyzing my every thought and reaction. I needed to yield my mind over to Bubba. He should be my source of joy and entertainment. I reflected on his statement that Jesus represented the path of sacrifice of self; Krishna, mind merging with God; and Buddha, the release from desire. These were the three conditions of suffering, ego, mind, and desire. People were locked into a constant dilemma because they hung onto these three areas. Bubba's work was to undermine them in the disciple as Christ, Krishna, and Buddha had attempted to do, but failed as their teachings were limited. Bubba's was complete, so he told us. I drenched my mind with his teachings, reading the books over and over, listening to his tapes and scanning the *Dawn Horse* magazines. In theory it made so much sense. It sounded right. Until then I had never had such deep, concentrated thinking, training my mind to grasp these spiritual concepts.

Gradually, I began to enjoy the simple things of life less and less. I started to lose interest in beautiful things such as the ocean, songbirds, Pacific air, quaint buildings, music, sunshine, humor, and general attractions. Instead I found myself questioning whether I really enjoyed these at all, or was I just acting out an illusion that I had created through the years to give myself some temporary joy? Maybe I didn't really enjoy these things at all; maybe there was nothing that I really enjoyed. It was Bubba and Bubba alone that should be my pleasure: his presence, his work, and his communication of the divine. When someday I would finally realize that I was already free, already in the divine, then everything would be joy. As Bubba said, "The world will conspire to make you happy." He kept talking about his work and the individual as being "The Great Process." Perhaps this process had already begun in me. Possibly this is why I'd been stepping away from myself to study whether this was who I really was, or was I just living an illusion?

Terms were stacked upon terms, key words such as relationship, contraction, Siddha, Dharma, true self, conditions, the heart, way of understanding, the search, and Satsang kept falling over themselves as I attempted to decipher all the implications of a spiritual life. Every movement and peculiar nuance was consciously scrutinized. I was obviously obsessed with observing my every thought and behavior. Now, if I could just live among his devotees in a real house.

Word finally came through James that I could, "Move in tonight." "Tonight? So sudden!" I still had three days left on my room. After five and one-half weeks at the hotel, well into mid-November, I gladly forfeited a few days' rent. The address of this house was 3040 Jackson Street, and I'd be rooming with Bob, bunk beds if you please. Bob was from New York City, and we came close to being friends. Pacific Heights was a wealthy part of town on the elevated west side, overlooking the Presidio US Military reservation with a view of the Golden Gate Bridge. Rent was over five hundred dollars a month for this huge lower flat. The rent was split at least ten ways. Five hundred dollars in 1974 seemed outrageous.

The thrill of finally living in a group house, a micro-community within the whole of the Dawn Horse, made me bubble over with joy, enthusiasm, and openly sharing about how I sensed that Bubba's teaching had been working in me. Most people listened intently, some humored me along, and some just drilled me with the conditions that I was expected to keep. A civilian military atmosphere lunged at me from every corner.

My second day there, I picked up a dust-laden acoustic guitar leaning against the wall in a catchall area of the living room. While strumming a few chords, I shared with Jeff, another housemate, that I had music groups in the past and would sure like to write some music for Bubba and the Dawn Horse. Days later, a visitor at the house questioned me about my desire for music and suggested that it was best that I not play the guitar or sing, as I was just too attached to it and, "It would probably hamper *The Work*. Maybe later when you're not so desirous of it, then you can play and sing a little." His remark cut deep. I caught my response and timidly agreed with him. The guitar found its niche back against the wall, and music was officially out of my life.

Basic disciplines and conditions were tough. We were up at five-thirty in the morning, meditated for twenty minutes on Bubba's picture that was placed on a type of altar in a small meditation room, offered fruit or flowers there before him as a form of appreciative sacrifice, took an alternate hot/cold shower, at least three hot, three cold, did a numbered series of exercises, mostly calisthenics with yogic overtones, ate a yogurt breakfast mixed with fruit and nuts, and then took off for work. A regiment of devotees were we.

I was given full-time hours at Root's because of my ability to sell shoes. A split personality began to form: one, as a happy, fun-loving, good-humored coworker at Root's and the other as a sober-minded disciple in the presence of others of the Dawn Horse. The captivating quaintness of San Francisco slowly faded just as a billowing early morning fog blocks out the brightness of a sunrise.

Around three o'clock in the afternoon on a routine workday at Root's, a "crier" came in to Root's Shoe Store beaming with the hurried news that Bubba was coming to the city and all the devotees were to be there at six o'clock that evening. "Be there" meant in the large back room behind the bookstore. James and I were too excited to concentrate on selling shoes, but we only had an hour to go. Now, I'd finally see my spiritual master in the flesh. It was my turn to herald in my teacher along with his community of followers.

The news spread quickly through a well-organized telephone chain, and by five forty-five in the evening, nearly two hundred fifty people had merged to 1443 Polk Street. Many waited in the street, and some like myself stood anxiously peering down from the second-floor windows. The vibratory energy was like a glowing electric current among us. "Why the special sudden visit?" we wondered. At five fifty-four that evening, a white Mercedes pulled up. People rushed the vehicle. I only caught a glimpse of the top of his head. We were immediately ushered into a room to be seated before he entered. Memorable reflections saturated my brain as I easily recalled the large group sittings that I encountered with somebody else's guru in Vancouver and Boulder. Now, nervously sitting, intoxicated with anticipations of ecstasy, I nearly cried with an expectant joy.

Bubba walked in, unannounced. Sighs and groans filtered through the room. Several bodies quivered uncontrollably, but I just sat there eyeing up this bigger-than-life man. As an offering, I laid before Bubba's feet my precious eagle feather, my macramé bag with my fire opal, some ashes, and my owl-faced acorn. I gave him all that I had held dear to me. These anticipated feelings never materialized, as he matter of factly began to conduct a general business meeting. There was a lot of talk about finances and building projects. Forty minutes of facts and figures with only a shade of light humor was all I experienced. It was then, shortly after this session broke up, that I began to entertain serious doubts about whether I was meant to be there.

Two days later, at my group home, a three-and-one-half-year old girl was taken from her mother by two Dawn Horse devoted followers. The scene in our group home was tense and grievous. There we stood in the early evening as these people came and forcibly yanked this tear-stricken little girl away from her mother. Her mother could do little more than watch with deep anguish. The mother/daughter bond was too strong. It was a threat to *"The Work"*! One of the women sternly said to Kathy, the mother, "Observe your reaction, it's bull_____!" The atmosphere in the house that evening was dismal. I kept thinking to myself, listening to my heart, "This can't be right; this can't be right."

I cared little for children at that time and certainly had not the desire to be a parent myself, but a sickness, a gnawing sorrow weighed heavy on my spirit.

At three o'clock in the morning, I was awakened by a soft knock on the front door. Being an extremely light sleeper, I was first to answer the door. There stood two policemen with the little girl. "We found this girl about twelve blocks from here wandering the streets. She gave us this address. Does she live here?" Risking a possible harsh discipline by one of the leaders, I quickly answered, "Yes," and gave a sloppy makeshift explanation of how she wandered away. The police turned to walk away, and I held the girl's hand. I had never held a child's hand with such love and compassion till then. Her little soft fingers squeezed tightly around my first and second fingers as I walked her down the long hall to her mother's room. Just then her mother came out from her bedroom in a sleep-like state, still modestly draped. Mother and daughter's eyes locked; then they cried and hugged. Others were awakened, and while we all observed the reunion, there hung an unspeakable comfort in that dimly lit long narrow hallway. We were happy for them, but for safety's sake, we never verbally communicated that.

Two married couples that I was acquainted with were asked to separate because the husband/wife bond of unity was too strong. This seemed unreasonable. Getting into early December, many people's thought turned to their immediate family, close friends, and relatives. Though contact with people outside of the community was shunned, we were permitted a brief two-minute phone call to our parents or concerned parties at Christmastime. I called my dad just to let him know that I was fine. I ran out of things to say before the two minutes was up. Our group leader seemed pleased at that—no close ties there. If nothing more from this phone call, at least I was assured that the people from East Kelowna's orchard dropped my guitar off in early November. It was worth trusting them.

There was a park nearby, about a quarter of a city block in size. I quietly snuck out several times at night and strolled the calm serenity that this special place afforded. Being high up in Pacific Heights, much of the city was visible. The multicolored night lights reflected off slowly drifting clouds being nudged in from the Pacific. Though I fought it, I often allowed myself to drift in the peaceful moods of tranquility while seated on a park bench, staring out over the city into eternity. Reality here in the Dawn Horse Communion under Bubba Free John took on the image of a cold confusion. And confusing it was; the struggle left me mentally bruised and battered some evenings. Was I just not ready for spiritual life? Did I think too highly of myself and now had to be knocked down a few notches? Was all this stuff maybe not meant for me? The damp salt-water air, chilled by late December, bit at my nostrils as I walked back to the semblance of a halfway house.

As an odd assignment with the intent of observing our thoughts in public, four or five of us took off to see the movie *Lenny,* based on the life of Lenny Bruce, the New York comedian, played by Dustin Hoffman. While standing in line on the corner of Van Ness and Austin on this very cool forty-four degree early January evening, we actually had some good-spirited conversation, light humor, and awkward poking fun of each other. My roommates Bob and James were with us. We sensed ourselves having the potential of being close friends. But that was all part of the assignment; observe thoughts and emotions, so we intuitively backed off. My own thoughts and perceptions ran the gamut from feeling sorrow for and almost superior to the other regular people in line, to envying their freedom to pursue and enjoy simple pleasures and desires. I was virtually two people at the same time.

Seated in the theater, I recalled the last movie that I had seen, *Little Big Man,* again with Dustin Hoffman. It was three and one-half years earlier, just fifty miles south in San Jose. I caught my mind toying with peaceful thoughts of the past, some of the rare good times in San Jose, and surely the explosive opening of my life in the Santa Cruz Mountains.

Then, *The Work,* Bubba's writing and messages, like a cold steel bar smacked the side of my head. Observe and separate yourself. Identify mind, ego, and desire, the three principal areas of suffering. Fleeting joy yielded to humorlessness. Pretentious humor was plentiful, and it wore the tag of nervous uncertainty. To add thickness to dismay, the movie was in black and white and paved the road to an inevitable, futile, suicidal end. Lenny Bruce killed himself. The comedian was dead. A good bummer to view for a quick put-me-down.

Before we made it home in a borrowed vehicle, I realized that it had become impossible for me to enjoy anything. I did not enjoy Bubba, and after nearly four months he still had no contact with me. Several leaders made a passing mention that I was, "Really progressing in '*The Work,*'" and that they had relayed that to Bubba.

"Big deal, I thought, I don't want to be a leader here anyway." All anybody ever seemed to give themselves to was dealing with people's garbage. Even the people and the atmosphere at Root's was no longer comforting. I had never experienced myself being so void of hope. At least during the numerous tough times in my life, I still had music or friends or dreams to pursue. But, here, I laid it all on the altar of despair. Bubba's method of teaching was scented with the odor of a glorified mind science. It was like being wired for robotics.

My disgruntled attitude eventually sifted out among other Dawn Horsers. Around January 7, a phone call came to the house for me. A person high up in the echelon personally invited me to come up to Persimmon that weekend and stay for a few days (At my cost, of course). "Sit with Bubba; maybe you'll see things differently up here." This consoling voice had the stench of flattering concern. It was not concern for me, but concern that I was perhaps questioning too deeply, probing into sacred ground. "Possibly this will pacify him," they thought.

That Friday afternoon, I left in a van with four others for the two-hour ride north to Persimmon, near Middleton, California. A sense of patronizing on their part and subtle interrogation prevented me from freely opening up to these people, and cautiously so. I could trust no one, maybe not even James. I perceived most everyone as a potential informer crouching behind trees, rocks, and bushes, ready to run with dire urgency to the captain in waiting. My words, actions, and inklings of intention were under surveillance. Although it was counter to my character, I had to act coy for fear of them discovering my dissidence.

The van ride was a surface one. We pulled up to the gates well past dark. A sentinel of sorts checked us out and gave us the big, "Okay," to enter. How cheerful, like being back at Crow Dog's camp. The first evening at Persimmon, from my memory, I only recall being escorted through the chilled evening air to a hardwood floor, and there I lay me down to sleep. "Make me a pallet on the floor," as the old blues song goes.

The morning broke bright, a good sign if there was any. A number of others were snoozing on the floor, scattered pell-mell like a refugee barrack. Being the first to rise, I stumbled outside and was pleasantly met by a beautiful vista. We were in the mountains! A dusting of frost and a multitude of songbirds aided me. A goat bayed; a llama took no notice. The dogs scavenged for leftovers. Someone stood statuesque, leaning against a wooden railed porch. Very slowly, with polite reverence, I made my way over, walking in a great half circle so that my presence was apparent but subtle. This fair-skinned lady was staring blankly, perhaps in deep meditation. Her eye contact acknowledged my presence.

I spoke, "My name's Ray. I came up last night. First time up here. Do you know where I can wash up?" Wasting no unnecessary energy on me, she pointed with a tolerating, annoyed glance at a building to her right just one hundred feet away.

I responded, "It's in that building?"

She nodded a disdained affirmative.

"Thanks. Didn't mean to disturb you."

Walking through a creaking door with prudent discretion, the rusted coil spring yielded its resistance to my effortless push. This place had all the signs of a washroom with toilet, sink, faucets, urinal, shower-heads, and even a real glass mirror. Still keeping with the stringent conditions, I took a hot/cold shower, did my exercises, and meditated on Bubba's picture, which I carried in my wallet. This was no furlough, just a different camp.

By this time, many others were groping about with varying degrees of aim. I struck up casual conversation. Most everybody there answered in vague remarks. Information was not freely given.

While standing in line for breakfast in a large dining area, I sensed a bit of warmth as the evening chill was finally vacating my skin and bones. My exuberant smile did not connect with most people. The overtone was subdued and serious, even on the grub line. The day was spent taking in various classes, mostly question-and-answer sessions conducted by respected designated leaders.

A general session was called without Bubba present. It was revealed that overnight one of the devotees left (I call it "escaped") after breaking into the safe and stealing back the deed to multiple oil wells that he owned in Texas. These wells were valued at over one million dollars. After donating this property to Bubba's Dawn Horse Community, he, for some reason, had a drastic change of heart and fled.

Secretly I rooted for him, inwardly cheering him on. A million dollars almost thrown away. Wow!

I aimlessly wandered the grounds, biding my time, being sensitive to any spiritual signs, if just one, perhaps something to confirm my belonging here with Bubba and his devotees. It didn't happen. An almost pure, finely filtered boredom encased me, save for the affectionate dog and nanny goat. The llama was oblivious of my presence or else was too arrogant to stoop to my level of communication.

The tension displayed here permeated this winter air. Did no one know who they really were or did I fail to see that we were actually nobodies? If this was freedom from self, then my sense of freedom was veiled, tarnished, and soiled. Was I going mad or was true spiritual life nothing like I had imagined? Why wasn't Bubba around, mingling with his worshipers? Was he so private, not wanting to be bothered by general conversation?

Bubba's teaching continued to echo over my own personal thoughts. His sayings, such as, "Giving birth is no more miraculous than excreting solid waste." And that, "There is a new condition beyond this world," though he never revealed just what that was. Another popular phrase of his was, "The man of understanding is an aggravation and offense." Another was, "Purification is a process till perfection is lived and enjoyed." There seemed to be no individual self-worth. He mentioned that he literally absorbed the karmic conditions of his devotees. Perhaps I felt so lifeless because I was being absorbed. A revelation of his was "What is required of an individual is to not become spiritual but to become human. Now the individual lives in a subhuman condition." He communicated that the guru should not be the object of worship. His mind science seemed riddled with irony and paradoxes, illusions of now you know, now you don't. Oddly enough, I never knew or heard of anyone there that ever experienced this sudden, usually uneventful, once and for always, transformation. Yet, they vigorously stuck it out buying Bubba's word as God's truth. He spoke of the divine as some impersonal force that already existed as your condition, your true nature. It sounded so good with virtually no loopholes except those uncovered by the intensely discerning. Still, Bubba, through fast and slick talking, managed to take a knife to the loopholes. He may not have always had a clean cut, but he usually tore deeply into the threads. I found loopholes but kept them to myself.

In mid-afternoon, an announcement went out that Bubba would conduct Satsang that evening. All were more than welcome to sit quietly in his presence. I wouldn't pass this up. This was what it was all about, sitting at the feet of the great teacher, the Great Siddha, just as the apostles did with Jesus. The noon and evening meals came off with the same restrained flare as breakfast. It didn't matter much; I began to feel that maybe I wasn't the problem. Tonight would be the turning point. Tonight I would experience his divinity. Oh, how I habitually psyched myself up for the big one. But I had never before gotten this involved or come so close. There had to be a major reason why I also had stuck it out this far.

At seven o'clock in the evening, forty to fifty of us quietly entered the Satsang hall, taking our shoes off, maybe grabbing a mat or meditation pillow. We all in absolute silence sat before Bubba who was already present. The same things occurred as before from some devotees: moans and groans, sighs of ecstasy, bodies shaking, and even frenzied spasms.

But me? No go. I sat and stared at him while reading my own thoughts like a marquee. After thirty minutes, the void became greater. There was no electricity in the air, not even twenty-five watts, no communication whatsoever, not even at thirty feet. How much less when we were separated by a hundred miles or another continent? He held no pizzazz before me, spiritual or otherwise. Maybe I wouldn't even care for him as a friend. Satsang came and went. So did I.

Late Sunday evening back at the house, many, including James, were eager to hear stories of bliss and enchantment, miracles and revelation, but I had absolutely none to offer. They felt cheated. I now represented their house and came back clammy and bland. "Get a new representative," I said.

Bob and I got into a bad argument the next day over something trivial and dumb. We actually had a mild fistfight. We were two stubborn dudes, you see. I spewed my guts to James that day at Root's about my overall despondency and general weariness of being here. He was greatly relieved to hear that, as he had had similar feelings for months but was always afraid to make that known.

That day, we schemed as to how we would casually leave unnoticed and rent a place together. We felt like undercover agents with boyish grins. Freedom was just a day away, and Peter our boss was gracious, even happy to let us stay with him until we found a place.

I took pleasure in reviewing the contradictions of Bubba's teachings. These were my aces, saved for a time such as this. Hopefully, I could vacate without reservation or regret. Especially valuable was retaining a facsimile of self-esteem after seeing it erode to near zero. No longer would I be imprisoned under the confines of the invisible drill sergeant, being Bubba Free John and my mind. I questioned that if our nature is already divine, how did we come to acquire a karmic condition, this subhuman state? Bubba gave no explanation.

I recalled some of my Catholic upbringing and also a sizable amount of comments that Christian acquaintances shared, and it became evident that even though Bubba acknowledged Jesus Christ as a great teacher and real person in history, he actually seemed to know very little of his teaching or life. Bubba conveyed misinformation about Jesus. This somewhat troubled me, as did his allusion to the millennium, which is only disclosed in the Bible, yet he treated the Bible as unreliable fables. Another thing caught me as odd, that of the thousands of books on the shelf at Dawn Horse Books dealing with a myriad of spiritual topics, a Bible was not to be found. Bubba seemed to reject the reality of sin and Satan, yet in a tape entitled *Guru as Prophet* he stated, "It is not uncommon for yogis to become demonic." I reasoned, in order to be demonic, Satan had to exist.

Though the word love was used often, I rarely saw it displayed in his work. Compassion was a joke. His remark that the spiritual life is not something that descends or ascends but merely awakens in you, contradicted another statement of his from the tape *Guru as Prophet*.

I guess that the most troubling for me was his request for the dissolution of friends and family. I became more certain by the day that I was not present with the light, but with the darkness, as under a full moon as a little truth, a little sight, a slight recognition of God and the divine. He seemed to reflect the sliver of light but was distant from being the true light. Like a flashlight with weak batteries, if you smack it you might get some fleeting moments of brightness, but it quickly fades, or worse yet, goes out completely.

So, there were numerous reasons to be skeptical about the self-proclaimed man of understanding. And so, early on the Wednesday morning of the last week of January, 1975, at five-thirty in the morning, before anyone else was up, James and I clenched tightly our suitcases and quietly escaped. Once out the door, we'd be freedom-breathing fugitives from the Dawn Horse Communion.

CHAPTER 32

A TURNING FROM GOD

That very same day, Jerry, one of the top five in the Dawn Horse came into Roots Shoe Store inviting me to a quiet show down. He calmly demanded to know why we left, but I had little to say. As he walked out, he turned and warned, "You're making a big mistake. You just can't handle spiritual life." At this point in our escape, I cared less whether it was a mistake. I just existed on gut instinct. Get out; get out! That's all I knew. As weeks went by, Jerry and several others paid a few more visits on occasion, usually with stern overtones. One haunting remark was, "You can't run from Bubba; he always knows where you are. He's constantly in touch with you. You'll come back when you realize what you've done." That remark followed me for years. "You can't run from Bubba. You can't run from Bubba."

A friendly connection of ours stopped in at the store periodically to keep us abreast of news from the Dawn Horse. She exclaimed, "Bubba took off for Hawaii with a number of his women devotees." (The East Indian term for their kind is Gopis, google-eyed, blissed out female followers.) They were submissive, yielding, 'do with me anything you wish' type of people. James and I just chuckled over the questionable antics that Bubba pulled. Just good clean fun, I'm sure.

That evening we bedded down at Peter's quaint upper flat in the marina district in the far north tip of San Francisco just several blocks from the bay. My heart jumped as I gazed with awe at a wall full of record albums: blues, rock, and jazz. What a collection! And I was free to listen to music again, good old music. My spirit was quickly rejuvenated. The headphones became fixed to my ears for hours that evening. I was starved for music and was easily content with just listening.

Many peaceful hours were given to just walking the City of Seven Hills, especially the marina area. The ingrained character of the multicolored homes, shops, and streets lent itself to an easing of my soul.

Eight days later, James and I moved into a third-floor, one-bedroom apartment on Green Street, straddled between the marina and Pacific Heights. Things were taking shape again. I had an apartment, a job, a clean look, and nothing pending. I picked up a small used stereo in a pawnshop in the Fillmore district and gradually began purchasing albums, such as Led Zeppelin's album *Physical Graffiti* and Jeff Beck's *Blow By Blow*. I acquired several other recently released records by John McLaughlin and Paul McCartney's *Venus & Mars*. This music impressed and stimulated my desire to play again. By the third week of February, I had contacted my friend Ron who was now living back in Grafton. Arrangements were made to stay with him for a few days while I picked up some odds and ends and most importantly, my Guild guitar. Flying back into Milwaukee was pleasurable, and Ron and I had a lot to talk about, but my visit was short.

The first chords strummed from the Guild carried like a symphony in an amphitheater. Though it was only done in my small bedroom, that big bold sound shook the walls. I sheepishly sang when James would leave. Five months without singing or playing required hours of getting reacquainted with my voice and guitar. As the days went on, I became more bold with volume and eventually set up a sound booth. The sound booth was primitive, just a couple of used mattresses, but at least I wouldn't disturb the neighbors. A stream of creativeness endlessly flowed. I began taping this music with a small hand-held cassette player. This would be the beginning of one of the most musically explosive periods of my life: *The San Francisco Tapes*. An energy was released so powerful and saturated with emotion, that as I listen to them even today, many years later, I just shake my head and utter, "Phew!"

James and I gradually drifted apart. Our interests began to contrast. He still searched out spiritual things and had an innocent flower child air about him. My thoughts and desires had laid the search down. God knew that I had tried, and that was good enough for me. I never denied his existence; I just grew weary of searching. James and I did give it one last try as a goofy team of spiritual seekers by going over to Oakland to sit with Baba Muktananda, an East Indian guru, and one of Bubba's former teachers. He was world renowned, but after just a few short minutes of listening to him, we sarcastically snickered, "Same old bland stuff, find the divine within you, meditate, chant, and worship the guru." I no longer had an interest in discount spiritualism. Let the bland enjoy the bland.

In late February, Peter graciously treated all of his employees to a fine meal at an exquisite restaurant called The Greenhouse. Restaurant eating made me uncomfortable. I had awkward etiquette mixed with nervous uncertainty for fear of doing the wrong thing. Partly, I still carried with me a hippie image, at least in the perception of myself. Peter requested a bottle of very fine white wine. I took a few reserved sips out of courtesy.

Up to this point I had not even had alcohol since that near fatal party at my dad's when I was just seventeen. Unbeknownst to me, before the glass was empty, the beginning of a destitute journey in alcoholism began to propagate itself like a slow-spreading mold. An overripe bruised peach goes unnoticed as overnight a circular patch of fuzzy, grayish black mold infects the whole fruit and many others that come in contact with it. And so it was with me and alcohol.

At the restaurant, after downing one and one-half glasses of wine, I got loud and semi-obnoxious to the point where Buck, Peter, and Rob had to restrain me from causing further embarrassment at our table. I felt good, uninhibited, open, wild, high on humor, real sociable, and physically demonstrative. I expressed an unleashed raw energy. I could do anything and go anywhere; fear was instantly dispelled. In its place a new boldness, layered with an exaggerated self-esteem, thrust me into situations and relationships I would not have normally trodden.

The next day, yes! The very next day, I walked the threshold of a liquor store for the first time. Wine, wine, what kind should I get? I tried white Chablis, Burgundy, red Rosé, and even strawberry. It all got me there fast, but now I was becoming a poor man's connoisseur. Preferences were emerging. It was the Rosé that took the lead. I could hardly wait to get off of work so I could hurry home and get a satisfying buzz from my wine. It was now mine because I identified with and preferred brands and types. My claim was staked. This wine went well with me. It was my ally.

Though I wanted to deny it, wine induced sloppiness to my guitar playing and slurred diction in my singing. I usually felt extremely creative after the first glass, but I had the hardest time transferring that to the guitar and voice. A paradox had entered my blood, a paradoxical parasite. By open invitation, it set up house and began to master me, the owner of the house. I rejected the idea that perhaps I was being deceived. No, I convinced myself that I just needed to learn how to responsibly handle it. Yeah, right—responsible drinking. Just being content with waiting until I got home to drink didn't cut it anymore. I now became clever and crafty and undetected by putting wine in dark glass vitamin bottles and bringing it to work every day in my lunch bag. So wine began to have an integral role in my life. It vied for shelf space in the refrigerator, but I was very generous and was always happy to share my wine with visitors.

As a last-ditch spiritual effort, I grudgingly determined to finish reading Carlos Casteneda's third book *Journey to Ixtlan,* having read his other two: *The Teachings of Don Juan* and *A Separate Reality.* They probably have become classics in drug-oriented occultism, but many believe that his works were fictitious writings. Either way, Don Juan Matus and anthropologist Carlos Castenada would remain in my mind as a separate reality, a journey to nowhere.

James and I had a drugged-out friend named Phil who lived two doors down the hall. Phil loved my music and could often be found hanging out by our door as I sang my guts out. Occasionally he'd quietly rap on the door, and I'd ask him in so he could sit in his three-quarter spaced-out condition and groove on my music. Some audience. Phil was being paid as a guinea pig by the State of California to experiment with various drugs, under controlled observation, of course. Some days he barely found his way home.

Early in the morning, about three o'clock, sometime in the middle of March, as the apartment complex gently slept, I was awakened by the smell of smoke. I frantically searched our apartment first, and then ran out into the hall. Smoke was billowing from under Phil's apartment door. I screamed at James, who slept on the living room floor. "Get up, there's a fire!" He was still dreaming about daisies and long-haired girls, too much so to wake up. I shook him, "James, get up; there's a fire!" He clumsily slid into his pants and ran out the door, nearly falling the three flights down. My voice could certainly be heard throughout the building. "Fire; fire! Get out!" Just as I continued to scream, I heard the sirens from fire trucks.

Others were quickly filtering out. I ran back in to grab my Guild and precious personal belongings. Risking theft was less probable than having it all burn up in flames or becoming severely water damaged. At least three frenzied trips were made up and down until I managed to remove almost every article that I owned. There I sat on the sidewalk with clothes, guitar, stereo, records, books, pillow, and blankets. Call it overreacting, but Bemidji's embers were still warm in my nose. I was not going to lose all my stuff again to a fire.

Bright orange flames shot from Phil's outside window; his apartment was engulfed in flames. The tenants congregated around the fire trucks along with a barrage of instant onlookers. Everybody got out safely. James wrapped himself in one of my blankets to take the bite out of the snappy forty-eight degree air.

An ambulance arrived minutes after the fire trucks with noise, lights, confusion, and drill guard precision. There was a call for a stretcher. Five long minutes later in an uncertain hush, a body covered with a white sheet was rolled into the ambulance.

"Who is it; who was up there?"

The third shift policeman, calmly with professional tact said, "The guy was found leaning against the wall in his closet. He's dead."

James and I stood facing each other, dumbfounded. "Phil's dead." A smoke-charred fireman explained, "A gas burner was left on, which probably ignited grease from a nearby pan. Instead of containing the fire, your friend hid in the closet." Phil was too drugged out to cope with reality. He died from smoke asphyxiation. The excitement gradually subsided, and we were allowed to go back to our apartment.

Two days later, I had the grievous responsibility of waiting for Phil's girlfriend so that I could break the tragic, sorrowful news to her. She was soon to be returning from a three-day outing. Nervously, I waited at the inside entrance of our building with a quiver in my stomach. Cindy bounced in, cheery as ever.

"Hi, Ray!"

I pointedly blurted out, "Cindy, Phil died in a fire two nights ago. His apartment burned."

She grew weak and just clung to me, weeping in disbelief. I quietly whispered the particulars. Cindy leaned on the wooden stair railing in a type of shock. She had little to say other than that she regretted his being paid to take drugs.

Her only remark was, "I told him he was burning out; we didn't need the money. What am I going to do now?"

My consolation had little value. She'd have to be tough and continue on. I never saw her again.

CHAPTER 33

ON THE LOOSE IN SAN FRANCISCO

B y the end of March, James and I severed our roommate ties, and I rented an upper flat above a Chinese laundromat at 2669 Sutter Street in the Fillmore District. The area was a mix of ethnic groups, and I felt quite comfortable there. I was now officially on the loose in San Francisco. I had a good job, my own place, music, a new freedom in alcohol, and all kinds of schemes and avenues for finding a girlfriend.

The most logical destination would be the nightclubs, and San Francisco was dotted with them. Jazz, rock, blues, folk, they were everywhere. There was a remarkable jazz spot called Keystone Corner on Vallejo, off Broadway in the North Beach area. It was a very cozy place with the ambience of soulful music twining through the rafters. This club seated perhaps only sixty to seventy people, but these were very appreciative listeners, and the musicians savored the atmosphere. Over the months to come, I would stop in several times a week to hear jazz greats such as Cannonball Aderly, Yusef Lateef and his auto-physiopsychic music, Oscar Peterson, Bobby Hutcherson, and Alice Coltrane. She was performing publicly for the first time since her husband John's death in 1967. There were others of sizable stature that I saw there, and almost every artist left me feeling that the night was special.

I frequented Keystone Corner as if being personally invited as a preferred guest. Not an evening passed that I did not fancy some single lady seated at a table. I must have looked like I had just arrived from Latvia. Hippie turned swinger was an awkward transition for me. I never quite wiggled myself into that mold. I was just learning to be suave, hip to the singles customs, and would usually start my advance by asking the waitress to give them any drink they wanted. I spent more money on alcohol for women than I care to admit. Most of them took advantage of my generosity but never made it to my table. One of the songs I began writing above the Chinese laundromat was *Lose Money on Women, Buying Firewater Wine*.

Increasingly heavy wine consumption had not yet affected my ability to sell shoes, as repeatedly week after week I was deemed "Best Salesman." Some days, I sold over thirty pairs of shoes. I had fun with people, and I was very much sold on the shoes. They seemed to almost sell themselves. Various celebrities came in. It was my privilege to fit the political activist Angela Davis. (I never discussed politics.) The jazz keyboardist Herbie Hancock handed me a business type card with four unintelligible words on it. He proudly remarked to me, "Chant this every day, and you'll get anything you want." Well, I put the search aside and was really not at all interested in more chanting.

Leo Sayer, the then up-and-coming British pop rock singer, came in with a boyish excitement about being in the United States. He also shared with me his apprehension and uncertainty about being well received here in San Francisco, his first US concert date. He slipped me a couple passes to see his show at the Boarding House, a spacious nightclub on Bush near Leavenworth. I went to see him, mostly out of curiosity. Plus, he was actually shorter than me. He put on a tremendous high-energy show to a packed-out wild house. Leo went on to international fame throughout the '70s.

Many other notables, from politicians to sports figures, came into Root's. It almost became commonplace. I sold good shoes to interesting people.

I remember walking on Polk Street one morning and seeing on the front page of the *San Francisco Chronicle* that Jack Benny had died. This left me sad and a little emptier. He was a reminder of my boyhood years, watching him on television at my great-uncle Artie's. He was to me, a remnant of peaceful stability, and now he had passed on.

Because Polk Street was the hub of the homosexual community, nearly every week, one these men would wander into the store trying to sweetly romance me. I always acted kindly when rejecting their come-ons, but some of my pursuers must have been convinced that they could win me over and buy my favor. Bouquets of flowers and deli sandwiches were often left for me at the store with cute notes attached to them. One man insisted on cutting my hair at his apartment at no charge. I grew weary of being hustled by men. What I desired was the opposite sex.

I was obsessed with being part of the nightlife in San Francisco. A compulsion for not wanting to miss a show or event drove me to go out. The Boarding House night club became my place to hang out. I saw the outrageous and often disgusting local group The Tubes, there.

Other more civilized performers were more warmly appreciated, such as Stan Getz with Clarice Jones and Peter Spellman; they brought good jazz. Comedians Kinky Friedman and the promising new local boys, Steve Martin and Martin Mull, who always promised a memorable comedy act. Mel Ellis played at the Omnibus.

I frequented The Great American Music Hall on O'Farrell. It featured balcony seating, chandeliers, and padded chairs. I felt like I had to show my membership card to get in. The place was bursting with top national acts and superb locals like Van Morrison, Cajun fiddler Doug Kershaw, Taj Mahal, Freddie Hubbard, and the premier out-of-retirement mid-'60s California psychedelic group, the Beau Brummels. It was a thrill to see the Beau Brummels live after having performed several of their songs with the 4 Dimensions and Misery Sons in 1966–67. This local San Francisco group that once clung to national fame was noticeably nervous on stage. Would the papers give them a good review? I doubted it. I vicariously felt nervous and sorry for them. Trying to relive and capture the glory of the mid-60s just didn't happen for them. Also performing there was Les Paul, the great guitar and recording innovator of the '40s and '50s. When I yelled from the audience to Les that I was from Milwaukee, he asked me to come up on stage with him. My debut on stage with Les Paul lasted for only a few minutes. Les was actually from Waukesha, Wisconsin, just west of Milwaukee. I had a very nice conversation with him after the show.

A lot of money passed through my hands at the Great American Music Hall. It was not uncommon for me to blow forty to fifty dollars a night on drinks, trying to coerce women to sit with me. I often made a fool of myself but was usually too drunk to feel embarrassed. I was willing to be a fool in a stupor in exchange for the remote possibility of fostering a relationship.

Loneliness crept in like an overcast day. There was no rain, no thunder, just a gradually thickening cloud mass that blanketed my life, weighing heavily on those times when hope diminished. Loneliness gnaws and pokes at the heart. It lets up on occasion to ward off expiration so that it can prolong its sadistic agony. Like a cat that quickly maims its prey, but instead of eating it, maliciously plays with the wounded rodent, watching it squeal in a shrieking circle. Loneliness enters the bones as a dry cracking decay.

Truly, there was not a day that passed that I did not hash over the foreboding warning, "Bubba knows where you are; you can't run, and you can't hide from him." I couldn't distract myself from these seizing pronouncements. Maybe I really was not able or willing to handle spiritual life.

I lunged fervently into the world, dearly clasping to anything that afforded me some pleasure and joy. I don't know how many times I journeyed down to Cost Plus Imports on the Wharf and purchased senseless, nearly useless objects that caught my fancy—wooden candleholders, tie-dyed wall hangings, carved animals, straw placemats, and uniquely shaped chopsticks. I bought all this stuff because its possession gave me temporary joy. I began, for the first time, to envy the wealthy because they could purchase what they desired. I spent too much money on silly, fleeting, men's fashion clothing also. It wasn't me. What was me? Well, music was me.

So I engulfed myself in playing and singing in my upper flat. I had a south window and cherished that exposure. Enveloping myself around the Guild guitar with my back to the sun, I'd turn the cassette recorder on and allow myself the unrestrained freedom to pull out all my emotions in song. The five months spent in this flat produced some of the most phenomenal expressive music that ever flowed forth out of my deep person. Stimulating, explosive, subtle, and expressive music materialized through my voice and guitar, which thankfully is preserved on nearly eight hours of tape. Some musically emotional moods went on for hours nonstop. The Chinese launderers probably never heard me due to the rumble of their machines. In the midst of my suffering and penetrating loneliness, which I sang much about, I pulled from my conscience, happy songs about sunshine, friends, and clean air. Exhausted and drained of energy after one of these unplanned bursts of emotion through music, I slowly set the Guild down, gradually stood up, and sadly walked to the refrigerator to drink myself numb. "In my suffering, in my suffering," as one song I wrote painfully expressed . . .

I drifted in and out of other nightclubs and bars such as the El Matador in North Beach to catch Cal Tjader or Slat's on Fillmore to take in blues legend Charlie Musselwhite. Ivan Alexander's on Union had a great clientele basking in blues and basic rock. The reggae kick aroused my primal spirits as I managed to stomach a continuous menu of Bob Marley and the Wailers, Inner Circle, and Toots and the Maytals. Listening to three hours of live, next to monotonous reggae nearly sucked the life out of me. Not to discredit these artists, but you'd almost have to have been raised in Jamaica to fully appreciate the message and the music.

It wasn't just wine that romanced me, but drugs such as killer marijuana, Thai stick, hash, and cocaine were plentiful among the people I associated with. Though I stayed away from cocaine, I easily fell victim to the others and when blended with wine—good night! I was gone. Entire days were wasted in an attempt to function.

On July 15 and 16, the Rolling Stones did a concert at the Cow Palace in Daly City which borders San Francisco. This event was typical of the over-hyped, megastar performances. Thousands of us lined up in the parking lot ten to twenty-four hours early just to get good seats. The heat of the sun emanating off the blacktop was merciless as drugs and alcohol were freely passed along. At first you were concerned about what you ingested, but after a couple of hits and guzzles, not much mattered anymore. In fact, after a few hours of this, you almost had no recollection of why you were even there sitting on the burning blacktop. At least five thousand glassy-eyed concertgoers were herded ten deep to a row in a winding path set up with highway sawhorses for containment. The Cow Palace, a glorified livestock sales barn, now had a potential human stampede on its hands. When the fourteen-foot high double doors finally opened to usher in the human beef to slaughter, everyone started mooing. Yes, it was unreal! Five thousand moos in one accord. Some, now physically inept, stumbled and were nearly crushed under the unstoppable momentum of the crowd. This was maddening and humanly degrading. But it was only rock and roll, so what was to be expected? There were no deaths or even rumors of critically injured reported, as we dumbly filed in. Just keep moving; that's what mattered. We came prepared, vomit and all, to worship this demonic, blatantly immoral band, to lay our eighteen-dollar tickets on their entertainment altar. I was seated somewhere to the left of the stage where the volume of excitement was deafening. This was before the music even started.

Some mediocre local group came on and bored people, while at the same time a gallon jug of some orange stuff came around, so I gladly took a few good chugs. Less than five minutes later I became very dizzy and nauseous. Making my way as quickly and best as I was able to, out into the cement hallway, I immediately vomited all over the wall. Ah, that felt much better. Passers-by acted like this was nothing out of the ordinary. Even the stadium police ignored me. I found my seat, which was a near miracle for two reasons. One, that my sense of direction was still somewhat intact and, two, that no one stole it.

The MC announced Mick Jagger and the Rolling Stones, and the crowd became even more activated. Mick came out riding an inflated phallic symbol, par with his personality. The band got off to a shaky start, but that mattered little to me.

I was sick, deathly sick. Others who drank this stuff were having severe reactions also. Less than halfway through the show I had to leave. Maybe fresh air would help. Now, I prayed, once again, if I could only be straight. I groggily boarded a bus on Geneva Avenue outside of the Cow Palace and headed back to the city but was so sick that I had to get off in the outer Mission District, just a mile away in South San Francisco. As soon as I hastily jumped off the bus, I threw up. Weak and gaunt, I dragged myself into a side street and climbed into a portable toilet placed there for nearby construction workers' use. I regurgitated some more and fell asleep, leaning over the toilet. So, were we having fun yet? A knock, hours later, startled me awake. Now, to get my bearings. Where was I, and how did I get in here?

A hung-over bum politely yelled, "You okay in there? I gotta go!"

"Yeah, I'm okay; just got sick. Hang on." As I opened the door, daybreak greeted me as a reminder that life goes on with or without my participation.

Several bus transfers delivered me close to my door. The responsible morning bus crowd avoided contact. As I swung open the eight-by-ten foot enclosed wooden gate that led to my outside stairs, I sensed a glimmer of deliverance from this pathetic condition. While crashing on the living room floor, literally, a deep slumber took me in. I came around about ten hours later, feeling like I was sifting through a fog. It had to be poison. Yeah, somebody put poison in that raunchy jug of alcohol. An insatiable desire to eat an orange, drove me to get up and wander the streets for a store that might be open at eight o'clock on a Sunday night. About fifteen blocks away, up on Divisadero, I found a corner store open and there sat as a balm to my aching body, a crate full of oranges. I bought two, peeled and ate them as I walked home, feeling rejuvenated. What was so medicinal about oranges? I laid off of the alcohol for at least two days. I wasn't exactly on the wagon, but at least I saw it from a distance. It's sort of like the guy that returned his Root's boots because the leather turned into a slimy brown Jell-O like substance. He rubbed a whole tin of mink oil on them and stuck them in the oven at two hundred-fifty degrees for thirty minutes. The boots died, but they didn't dry out. No, I didn't give him his money back; he'd just have to flop around until the soles wore out. Too much of a good thing can turn you into mush.

By late July, I began having serious doubts about whether I should continue to exist here in San Francisco. Good thoughts of my hometown, Grafton, began entering my heart. Again, I yearned for my old close friends. I was no longer an outcast spiritual freak; I wanted to party and play music. Intimate friends were hard to come by here. As with myself, many people were transient, just passing through. My loneliness bit deeper than just the desire for a girlfriend. I needed people to relate to and to trust and enjoy. So again, as a form of consolation, I turned to the guitar and began singing songs about going back to Wisconsin.

The human quest to know the future still lurked within. I sought out several astrologers and card readers. I had a troubling decision to make and needed definite signs to confirm my inner yearning. If third-rate fortunetellers could add weight to my inklings, then I'd go with it. I came upon the name of Ger, an architect that did astrology charts on the side. During our initial phone conversation, I gave him the particular time, date, and place of birth. Three days later, I boarded B.A.R.T., the underground, underwater transit system to Oakland and met with jovial, witty, Ger. He had drawn up a very impressive, colorful astrology chart. I tape recorded the session with him so that I wouldn't miss all the qualities of my character that he conveyed. I truly wanted to believe that the chart was accurate because it looked so pretty. But when he suggested that I favor the antics of Mick Jagger, I had to halt the reading and question. Mick and I seemed worlds removed. Ger reduced his simile and qualified it to my humor resembling that of Jagger's. Well, I had no pending questions answered, but we did enjoy each other's company.

A week later I answered Rose's ad in the newspaper. She read cards, palms, and burned candles for only five dollars. What a deal! Rose was the genuine gypsy article with a dark, drab apartment and spooks everywhere. She asked what type of candles I'd like her to burn. I thought a second and replied, "How about some cheery Christmas candles?" Rose was humorless. Seems she mumbled something about poltergeists thrusting me to the floor. I halted the reading and questioned her interpretation. It was as ridiculous as her accent and gypsy babushka wrapped around her head. With the shades still down and curtains drawn shut, I slipped her five dollars. This was better than seeing Steve Martin. All I was looking for was someone to guide me in my decision to stay or leave. I didn't need a voodoo spell.

Parties were still high up on my list of things to do, and the owner of the Root's store in Berkley threw an all-out bash in a downtown warehouse, complete with hours of taped music, wine, beer, hard alcohol, elaborate fruit salad, finger food, and a belly dancer, who was hired to entertain the guests. I was so loopy from alcohol that by the time she finally came out, I got up and danced quite creatively with her on the dance floor. Three guys dragged me off the floor and threw me out the door. I couldn't come back in. I had committed a social no-no. I got too loose on wine and had too much fun.

Bill Graham, the renowned rock promoter, converted a huge indoor ice skating rink into a rock concert hall. He continued to call it Winterland. I took advantage of its close proximity to my place, just four blocks away. I watched several top bands perform there. One of the most memorable shows that I ever saw on the same bill was rock legend Jeff Beck and guitarist superb, John McLaughlin, with his unique East Indian influence. I managed to work my way backstage, undetected to just hang out with the musicians and roadies. Bill Graham wielded an iron hand when he wanted things done his way just as he had back in New York City at the infamous Fillmore East. He would shout and command, "Get those balloons out there!" in order to pacify the audience as they anxiously waited for the show to begin. Bill Graham died in a helicopter crash in October of 1991 at age sixty.

Others that I had seen at Winterland were locals Robin Trower and Journey, who both went on to national fame.

My eye caught an ad in the classified section of a local paper, "Musical astrology charts done. J. Rosenthal." I was nearly positive that this was the same person that I contacted in 1973 while living on Wausaukee Road. At that time she sent back my chart as having D flat for a keynote. Here we were, living in the same city less than one and one-half miles from each other. I had to contact her, but in writing. I kindly mentioned that songs in D flat just did nothing for me. Perhaps the chart was drawn up inaccurately. She immediately responded with a pleasant letter and a newly revised chart showing my keynote as B flat and its ascendant as D. She now placed me in a mystic relationship of the tri tone, a rare find. Her intentions were good as she took the time to write a detailed letter of explanation. She observed that I was either a very old soul or a new soul in my karmic past lives. A thirty-page complex handout followed, explaining the signs, tones, and vibrations of a given note, and contained words and phrases such as hidden keys, ruling planet, solar note, Dorian mode, harmonious unities, transcendental essence, regal identity, and past life recall that made my eyes cross and my mind ache. This was just too much, too late. She strongly indicated that I had great mystical ability and should pursue that area. Well, Joyce, I did, and quite frankly I became a mystical glutton. I appreciated her sincere help and concern, but I surely needed none of this scientific harmonious astrology to decipher when I was musically on or off. The blues was always evident, and the joys were undeniable. She seemed like such a sweet lady. I would have liked to have meet her.

The swaying decision to leave San Francisco was secured when Buck, my good friend and coworker made me aware that a Root's Natural Footwear had recently opened in Milwaukee. Perhaps I could get a job there. My experience at fitting and selling these shoes was invaluable. The owner's name in Milwaukee was Howard Silberman. I gave him a call from the store on Polk Street. We had a pleasant talk, and he, unreservedly, promised me a job over the phone if I did indeed move back to Grafton. Thrill shot sporadically throughout my system. The decision was set. I was going to leave. Buck and Rob were happy for me but sad to see me go. Peter was very understanding and wished me the best.

That day my plans were solidified. By the first week of September, I'd depart for Grafton. But how? I had no vehicle and had accumulated a wealth of borderline junk. The rock station KSAN had as a public service for those such as me, a ride switchboard. I called in my request, and they announced it daily. The third day, a lady named Gail answered my plea. She was leaving for the East Coast around September 5 and would be willing to have company. She wanted a paying customer though, not just a freeloader. Pay? I was very willing to do so. I consolidated my belongings and disclosed to her exactly what I had intended to bring along. Gail seemed certain that it would all fit in her car.

Nearly every day until departure, I played and sang upbeat, happy, and hopeful songs. See, Joyce was right; I really was a mystic, an *optimistic*. I sang with a force of jubilance that caused the Chinese below me to finally stop screaming at each other and silently listen. My variation of a theme around Chopsticks was their favorite. (I'm kidding.) But, I must emphasize, they were hard working people, and respected my peculiar lifestyle. We hardly said a word in English to each other, but just as the Puerto Rican family next door to me in New York City, so I was with the laundromat people, a friend in spite of the language barrier.

The most sorrowful of good-byes was said to Lydia, a good friend and frequent visitor of all who worked at Root's. She wrote me numerous cute letters while I was living in San Francisco. Her letters, which were usually filled with comical drawings, were always an encouragement. I sensed that she was extremely lonely also, but she never openly let that be known. My hope is that her life responded to fulfillment.

The chain that still subtly bound me to Bubba Free John would finally have some weak links, as I would distance myself by over two thousand miles.

I still managed to squeeze in a concert by Dizzy Gillespie at the Civic Auditorium. It's a wonder that his cheeks never exploded. They puffed out like softballs when he blew his horn.

The Krishna people came out in full force shortly before I left, with an open free breakfast for fifty thousand people in Golden Gate Park. And to highlight the day's gleeful activities would be the actual presence of his Divine Grace, A.C. Bhaktivendanta Prabhu Pada. They boasted of this event in a full-page ad in *City Magazine*, the weekly magazine about San Francisco, owned and operated by Francis Ford Coppola. Well, I had to admit; Krishna devotees were sincere but probably sincerely wrong.

My hard to come by, much prized ticket, to see Led Zeppelin, the internationally famed rock group, was never redeemed. Bill Graham promoted a series of "A Day on the Green" at Oakland Coliseum. Robert Plant, the lead singer, whom I always admired as a vocalist, was injured in an auto accident in Europe. Hence, the show was canceled. Though this was a great disappointment, it was probably best. Six hours of non-stop rock bands enclosed in an outdoor arena with drugs and alcohol more plentiful than air, may have left me for dead in the turf.

Christo Javacheffs, the New York based artist, was putting finishing touches on his plan to hang a twenty-four mile long, white nylon mesh fence, running across fifty-nine farmers' and landowners' properties in Northwest Marin County just north of San Francisco. The forty-year-old man had already made quite a name for himself worldwide with his wrap art, from wrapping the Vittorio Emanuele monument in Milan, Italy, to wrapping one million square feet of Australian coastline, to the much celebrated Valley Curtain in Rifle, Colorado. He started out small in the early '60s, wrapping little things like motorcycles and autos. I'd be left hanging in suspense, as my plans did not include prolonging my San Francisco stay to witness his project completed. Christo, as he preferred to be addressed, was a true *wrap* artist.

So I finally said my touching good-byes to James, Buck, Rob, Peter, Lydia, and seven or eight others. The full scope of my experiences here in San Francisco (and please don't call it, Frisco) would never be realized until years later. This would certainly be recorded as one of the fullest twelve months of my life. Other than material belongings, I would bring with me a wealth of stories and unique exposures, including unfortunately, a dependence on my sidekick, rosé wine.

This particular September 5 morning was memorable and picturesque as ever, as I waited curbside for Gail, whom I never met, and her mid-sized white auto. She could have left me stranded shoulder deep in personal stuff. The frightening thought did occur. But, she didn't. She pulled up at eight o'clock sharp in the morning. She was a bit taken back by all the stuff that I was certain I could cram in her car. We stuffed it in without having to break anything in half and motored out of the Bay area, two very excited people with nothing but a lust for life and a future to satisfy.

CHAPTER 34

HOMEWARD BOUND

G ail and I got along just fine, that is, until one evening about one hundred miles outside of Yellowstone National Park. She began pressuring me to sleep with her in her tent. Gail was adamant about this and firmly tried to assure me, "We'll enjoy free pleasurable sex together." Gail was in no way physically becoming to me. In fact, she had sort of a tough, masculine nature about her. I grew embarrassed and bashful when tactfully turning down her offer. She became ugly with rage and furious at the thought of rejection. Our travelers' honeymoon ended at that moment. She, with no prior thought or consideration, coldly told me, "When we get to Yellowstone, you'll have to find another ride. I can't travel with a man who won't make love to me. We've been together for over two days, and you've just led me on," she said.

This was news to me. After all my futile flirtations with women in San Francisco, and now, here I am, totally uninterested. Life can take a weird spin at times. That evening under the open sky and Ponderosa pine, a gray squirrel sat at my feet, reminding me that I still had friends. I had forgotten how crisp a September mountain morning could be. Gail's sunrise greeting was just as crisp, but unrelenting. I staged a well-rehearsed explanation, almost a confessional excuse of sorts as to why sexual love meant more to me than just bedding down with a stranger. Gail fully intended to follow through with her bitter threat. She quickly drove the, "misery one hundred" miles straight to Yellowstone. She at least gave me a choice as to where I wanted to be *dumped* off as soon as we entered the park.

I chose the Madison campground, which was, of course, hippie haven. Picture this, me sitting on a blacktop parking lot, nestled amid a guitar, stereo, speakers, boxes of clothes, kitchenware, blankets, records, toiletries, and at least a half-gallon of wine. Who'd give me a lift the twelve-hundred-plus miles to Wisconsin? Would you? I felt doomed to perish in the very park that first brought me such joy. I couldn't even leave to get something to eat for fear that thieves would clean me out. But God, my old buddy in perilous times such as these, would show mercy and bail me out. Rick and Matthew, two freewheeling spirits, were parked just yards away. They had an empty pick-up truck and responded positively to my *big* question. "Sure, we're going east; we'd be glad to take ya." These were two very generous, good-humored guys. My down time lasted less than twenty minutes from Gail's guile to on the road again. You know, I hardly minded having to ride in the back on the open bed of their red pick-up. My hands and cheeks got a bit cool, but their dog Benny made for warm company.

On our second night of camping out somewhere in Northern Montana, two very scuzzy greaser types wandered over to the truck, startling us as we quietly conversed around the campfire. At knifepoint they demanded any cash and anything else they could use. As pacifists, we obliged them. Fortunately, my wallet was concealed in a box of clothing. They hurriedly grabbed some money from Rick and Matthew and threw out a crass, bandido comment, "Thanks for your generosity; see ya." Then they fled. In sympathy, I gladly gave Rick and Matthew fifty dollars.

It took a long time to get to Wisconsin from Yellowstone—over five days. Those guys had a gracious heart for hitchhikers. They'd drive a couple hundred miles out of the way to take somebody to their destination. Benny and I shared the pick-up with a good many people.

We made our way up into Manitoba, Canada, and by September 11, the weather was getting brisk. I was to start my job at Root's Natural Footwear on or around September 15. On the morning of September 14, we pulled into my dad's driveway. They dutifully took me right to his door. Rick, Matthew, and I vigorously shook hands as we parted. I thankfully handed them some more cash. Off they ventured to the east coast. My guess was that they got there by late October.

It took nine days to get from San Francisco to Grafton, but none of that mattered. I was home. I wasn't sure just how well received I would be by my dad but had speculated that due to my much cleaner appearance, his slant would be in my favor. *My favor* meant that he was at best neutral, and he was.

Ron and I visited briefly, and he invited me to come hear his newly formed rock band practice out in the little unincorporated town of Lakefield. Music tugged and pushed and often used delicate persuasiveness as a lure to activate my interest. The urge to be involved in a band again grew stronger every day. This was still the focus of who I was. If I couldn't give the gift and talent back to people, then surely my life would ferment. Of course, I enjoyed the self-centered praise, but a greater portion of the joy was knowing that all this sacrifice and diligence for music wasn't wasted, left to rot unnoticed.

Steve Tillmann and I, within days of my being back, renewed our relationship. Of all the people that I had known here, this reunion was by far the warmest. Steve, who was then working as an autobody repairman for a used car lot, offered me a white, 1965 Rambler for my very own vehicle. I gave him one hundred dollars, and the deal was set. We took a pleasant, leisurely ride in my spiffy Rambler out to the beautifully wooded hill country of the Kettle Moraine area.

The Kettle Moraine is known for its winding, humble mountain terrain, rolling farmland, and forest, with gorgeous vistas carved along an old glacier route. Fall was just beginning to reveal itself; the emergence of a special season was beginning. What is it about early fall in Wisconsin that seems so magical? Certainly it is the smells of harvested wheat and alfalfa. Also the sight of ripening McIntosh apples, corn and pumpkins and the wind that waved the weeds, such as goldenrod, Queen Anne's lace, chicory, red clover and purple thistle in an array of colors. Red sumac display their royal crimson leaves as brilliant orange marigolds wage battle with an early frost. Sunflowers stand as monarchs of the field. Hollyhocks toss their pleated skirts as cattails get all puffed up. Birch and sugar maples emanated a skyline of flaxen and reds accented against the deep green of pine, cedar, and spruce. The contrasting colors enhanced each other. Geese, crows, blackbirds, and sparrows hustle in excited congregation. Guernsey's stand on an early morning frost, back dropped by an autumn curtain. Cumulous clouds playfully exchange shapes as they effortlessly drift without will wherever the wind takes them. Ten thousand crickets lulled us into a trance with their shrill tangled rhythm. You could see and smell the summer rain as it ascended back to heaven.

The sun showered its welcomed warmth into sixty-three-degree atmosphere, reminding the screen door that it was seeing its last week of use. Its partner, the car window, dared only be rolled down one inch. There was even something more than just the physical senses, though these alone warranted deep appreciation and invited calmness of mind. There is a mystical air that can never be grasped. It beckons and teases but does not makes itself known. It was fall in Wisconsin. I remembered what I had missed as my lungs joyfully expanded with the freshness of cool, clean air. There was no better friend to share this with than with Steve Tillmann.

On our casual, often detoured ride back, Steve and I once again got looped on a liter of cheap wine and whatever other mind-altering substance we could scrape up. We got the cork wet and couldn't get it in the bottle again. So we used that as an excuse to finish the bottle. At least there's something to be said about screw-on caps. The beauty of the Kettles became vague and obscured under the stupor of drugs.

The pace at Root's Natural Footwear on Downer Avenue in Milwaukee was a lot slower than in San Francisco. I found myself leaning behind the counter for up to one-half hour before anyone even ventured in. We may have been under great pressure to keep functioning at the San Francisco store, but here I experienced an opposite effect— sheer boredom. Howard and I and the other two employees were amiable with each other, but the reason that I came to work was to work, not bide my time. On occasion while biding my time, I'd still pick up the *East West* or *New Age Journal* with a chance sediment of hope that maybe there would be something spiritual that could still attract me.

On the inside front cover of an *East West Journal,* was an application in the form of a questionnaire published by the International Community of Christ. I answered the fifty-odd questions as a lark and sent it in. They were to evaluate my esoteric answers and send back an analysis of my spiritual readiness. The International Community of Christ had some bizarre claims that when properly worded were quite convincing. According to their teaching, Jamil, the Christ child, appeared in the Peruvian Andes from 1959–62 and taught their founder, Gene Savoy. He claimed that Jamil came to Earth for a short period to re-establish true Christianity. The guarded secrets of the energies of nature were revealed to him. Many other claims were given such as: we too could experience our own light body, and we could survive solar and cosmic radiation. They taught that Christ should be experienced, not worshipped as a person. Gene Savoy's decoded New Testament was to clearly show how, through control techniques over mind, body, emotion, and spirit, we could evolve into immortality. This supposedly was an ancient system of Cosmology. An expensive book with cassette tapes costing one hundred thirty-five dollars for the package deal (what price secrets) was made readily available.

So, okay, I took the spiritual awareness aptitude test, as they called it, and anxiously checked the mailbox for my results. This was high anticipation, almost as intense as waiting for your Kool-aid® club membership to arrive in the mail. There was reason for skepticism being that they were headquartered in Arlington Towers, Reno, Nevada. If God wanted me, he was going to have to try harder.

Several weeks passed, and I had completely forgotten about The International Community of Christ. There it sat, in my dad's mailbox, the long-awaited letter. The envelope vibrated with positive results, even the mail man got a buzz. The letter addressed to me immediately got to the point. I scored very high. The rave report glowed with encouragement and exhortation. It read something like this, "Ray, you are on a high spiritual plane. Act soon; do not hesitate in ordering the books and tapes. It's vital for you to begin soon." It sounded rather flattering, but a week's paycheck was too great a sacrifice. I held off and pondered the significances and consequences of following up or dropping it. A month later I received more information from them along with a limited opportunity to order other newly published works by Gene Savoy in beautifully hardbound covers with gold lining. I had to pass. Nearly every other month I received more letters and flyers from the ICC. They made it sound like the door was soon to close for the chosen few. What if I missed the call? This all seemed rather juicy: immortality, light body, energy experiences, tapping into the universal force, power, and pure joy.

The pull of music in my life was stronger than the persistent enticement of Gene Savoy and his IC of C. But, still, the curiosity in me crept up, and I gave it one last shot. I called their office in Reno, expecting to interact with spirit-filled holy ones. Instead, a cold, rather abrasive lady answered and said, "We don't take phone calls. You're welcome to correspond."

"Thanks," I quipped, and hung up. I'd come a long way towards discernment in my great search. They didn't get my money.

CHAPTER 35

FOOTCH KAPOOT

M usic was the thing for me, and of course, a girl friend if at all possible. One night flings via the single bars came my way on occasion, but mostly they were regrettable and no relationship took form. I pried my way into Ron's band. I wasn't really asked, but they found it difficult to tell me no. The band needed help, or so I thought, and I was that much-needed help, or so I thought. Mike Haupt was in it and several other musicians that I had met and played with in the past. There was no bass player yet to be found, so I convinced my new friend, Frank Tarentino, whom I met at a local bar, that he should take up the bass. I encouraged him, "You'd be really good. You've got the potential." He gave in to my coaxing, bought a bass, and was welcomed into the band with mixed reactions. With a little tutoring, he progressed nicely. We practiced diligently in Kenny Burhop's basement. Kenny was the drummer.

Early winter, 1975, had set in for good, and this group began to shape up. We had to have a name. The phrase, "Footch Kapoot" was used jokingly in our community circle. It was an old German saying, meaning "broken down but repairable" and pronounced *Futch* as in Butch and Kaput. We adopted that name as the name for our group: Footch Kapoot. I tried my hand as an artist and painted Footch Kapoot's name and symbol on a four-foot by five-foot plywood board. The painting was that of an evening scene looking through a knothole into a dimly candlelit room observing a tired, rejected man in a nightshirt and cap having one last drink of wine out of desperation. He was truly broken down but repairable.

Grumbling and dissension were always prevalent in the band. I suspected that it was because of my barging in and somewhat taking over. These guys were quite content with just being a basement band, getting together for fun.

We actually played out four nights: real bookings with real pay. But, friction was always in the air. Our old buddy, Tom Roy, sat in one evening at a high school dance and acted as MC/disk jockey. I usually had fun. I usually got drunk. Some people complained in secret that my drinking was getting out of hand. I tried to suppress and deny those whispery accusations.

Finally, towards the middle of March, after driving home from a high school prom-type job, I decided to leave this group and start my own. The evening was March 14, 1976, and it was the night of the worst ice storm that Southeastern Wisconsin ever experienced. We all made it back safely through treacherous driving conditions, but the band could not exist on that unity alone. When I announced that I would be leaving, I was ecstatic to find that Frank and Mike wanted to come with me also, to start a new group, still under the title Footch Kapoot.

While seeing the jazz rock violinist John LuPonty perform at the Oriental Theater in Milwaukee in February of that year, I made the acquaintance of a long-haired, droopy mustached person named Mark. We were quite surprised to find that we hailed from basically the same area. At the time of our initial meeting, he made me aware that he played the electric guitar, so I kept that filed in my memory should I ever seriously start my own group. And so, in March of 1976, I looked Mark up and auditioned him. He was good, very bluesy and better than I would have expected. We asked him to join, and so he did. Now we were four. Randy Liska was drifting about and was relatively enthused about joining this band as drummer. My heart was set on having a pianist, not just a generic keyboardist, but a good pianist. Ads went out and feelers were followed up on, but competent, available pianists were hard to discover. Footch Kapoot continued on without one.

Rehearsing in garages had its limits and setbacks, and by early summer we rented the lower level, dirt floor of an old barn. Old carpets were collected and served as flooring. Carpets were also hung on the whitewashed, three-foot thick fieldstone walls. The place started to evoke a cozy atmosphere for good times and music as long as summer was still with us.

Having one eye open for any spiritual break, I still picked up the *East West Journal* when the whim struck; I was easily coerced into buying the July 1976 issue, as they ran a featured story on Bubba Free John and the Dawn Horse Communion. I had to know what he was up to. Still, one and one-half years later, a day did not pass when I would find myself entertaining thoughts of returning. According to the article, Bubba had quite an extended vacation in Hawaii that lasted well over a year. Upon his return to his ashram at Persimmons, which was now enlarged to over five hundred acres, he broke the shocking news to his followers that he was retiring. Retiring? Do gurus retire? He was only thirty-eight years old. The Dawn Horse Community was thrust into a quandary. Somewhat bewildered myself, I released a puzzled chuckle. I assured myself that it was best that I not be mixed up in the middle of all that. Judging from the collection of books on the bookstore shelves written by Bubba after 1976, I'd say that he retracted his retirement plans. He now was going under the title "Da Free John." Obviously, an even higher status.

Footch Kapoot continued to work out songs throughout the summer days without a pianist—songs, such as *Moondance* by Van Morrison, *Born to Run* by Bruce Springsteen, *Cocaine Blues, Big Time Woman,* and *Money* by Pink Floyd, *Mother Earth Blues* by Eric Burden and the Animals, *Can't Always Get What You Want* by the Rolling Stones, *Feeling Alright* by Joe Cocker, and *Jessica* by the Allman Brothers, plus five or six originals that I wrote.

A young college girl gave me a call from an ad that I had placed in Milwaukee's counterculture, the almost underground newspaper *The Bugle American.* She answered the ad on a dare from a girlfriend. Her name was Sue, and her enthusiasm over the phone bought her an audition. As I drove down to Marquette University in downtown Milwaukee, I wondered as to whether this would be worth my while. She had no previous experience with a music group and wasn't a serious pianist. As we met in the student union where the grand piano was, I immediately sensed a lively humility that posed no threat. We both felt quite at ease with each other. She ran through a sampling gamut of her repertoire on the piano and displayed a rich, full sounding voice. There was nothing uniquely stunning about her ability, but I sensed real potential there. We bid each other farewell, and as I cruised down Highway 43, I seemed more and more convinced that she was right for Footch Kapoot. Now, to persuade the other guys.

September had come again and the bottom of this barn was getting mighty chilly. I got a hold of an oil-burning space heater like the type I used in the house on Wausaukee Road. It only had a three-gallon tank, so replenishing it with fuel oil was an ongoing chore, but once this thing got rumbling, we started getting mighty warm.

Because of the stimulus of having a working group, there was a creative surge in my songwriting. I worked on and completed several songs at a time. I spent many hours alone in this musty, dirt-floored barn singing, writing, and practicing on my Fender Jaguar guitar. I had not played this guitar since I lived in Ben Lomond. I wrote fivesongs during the time spent in this old dirt floored barn, "Das Is Wonderful," "The Andes Tune," "Sleepy Time Day," "Versality," and "Times Comin' Round."

We borrowed a portable electric keyboard (yuk!) so that Sue could audition with the whole group. It was unanimous between Mark, Paul, Mike, Dave, and myself: Sue was in. That is, if she wanted to join. This was shocking news to her. She was supposed to be going to college for business administration, not rock and roll. This decision was traumatic for her, but she agreed to give it a try. So now Footch Kapoot was complete and moving right along. The making of a group was being realized. We all, except for Sue, held down full-time jobs, so getting together evenings and weekends was to many of us, a real sacrifice. The few weeks prior to Sue's joining, Paul, another old friend from Grafton, and Dave, a new acquaintance from Milwaukee, replaced Randy and Frank as drummer and bassist. Dave also doubled on bass saxophone, adding a unique dimension to our music. Sue's weighty decision in favor of joining, propelled us to practice more diligently. The partying cooled down, and I was less prone to being nearly inebriated during rehearsals.

The experimentation with biorhythm charts seemed to be an up and coming counterculture fad. I was given a book on Biorhythms to look at. I anxiously began charting my days and weeks. It was easy to become absorbed and even addicted to religiously following the layout of the sine wave chart. Acute conscious attention was given to observing my power days, down days, and periods where creativity was more active. One of the claims of the book was that, the decision-making process would be more keen at certain intervals, so then it would be best to hold off until that time came to make pertinent decisions. Throughout October and November, I charted my course in a pocket notebook so that I could readily have at my disposal this vital resource. Aside from a temporary self-induced psychological uplifting, I had to once again be honest with myself. Does this really work? Do I really have on/off periods as this biorhythm science suggests? No, this was nothing more than another familiar side path leading into uncharted, overgrown brush. I smartly turned around and walked back. At least the beaten trail was more predictable.

Now that we had finally found a pianist, we needed a piano. Good old Joey Zingsheim, the music store owner, gave us a deal on a small Kohler and Campbell spinet piano. He also threw in for me some basic tuning tools and a crash course in tuning. This poor piano didn't take kindly to the conditions of the barn and the inevitable constant moves. I found myself giving it a facsimile of a tuning twice a week.

More and more songs were worked out. Our instrumentation and vocals were becoming quite polished.

But, the temperature of early December, oh, it was getting quite cold. We seemed to pull in closer toward that space heater. One evening after practice as we huddled closely around the oil burner, it exploded. The door blew off with a booming impact, and the nine-inch stove-pipe flew apart. Bright orange flames shot out from every crevice and opening. Barns start on fire easily, so we urgently did what we could to subdue the flames. No one was hurt, and we all somehow saw it as humorous, as the reel-to-reel tape recorder kept running and recorded the excitement. This was all the catalyst that Footch Kapoot needed to make an immediate, unanimous decision to move out and find a heated place to practice.

Again, an ad was placed in the local paper, "Rock jazz group needs a place to rehearse. Responsible." I liked the part about being responsible. My experience has been that the nature of jazz-rock is far from synonymous with responsibility. But, nonetheless, a man named Gary answered the ad shortly after it ran. He had a small barn with an attached heated three-car garage northwest of Cedarburg, eight miles northwest of Grafton. The building was previously used for light industry. It was two days before Christmas when we went out there to look at it. The barn and garage were filled with odd junk and bales of bamboo shoots. It seems that this was a bong factory. Bongs are water pipes made from bamboo for the express purpose of smoking hash and marijuana. Gary was the new owner of this property along with a fieldstone house, about two hundred feet up a hill. He knew nothing about bongs and drugs. He agreed to rent it to us for one hundred dollars a month. Can you believe it?, not only was there an oil burning furnace and cement floor, but it actually had a real flush toilet! This was luxury living compared to what we came out of. Gary and Footch Kapoot had a deal, and on January 1st 1977 we moved in and celebrated big. We salvaged our old rugs and carpets and hung them up for insulation. We just couldn't part with those musty things.

That evening, New Year's Eve, was our first official job at the Random Lake Auditorium, a New Year's Eve bash. We already started repeating our songs by the second set, but it was doubtful that anyone noticed. The whole evening turned into a sloppy, boisterous drunken episode with me in it neck deep. We managed to remain standing and actually played our instruments until shortly after midnight. Nobody in the band seemed to be too with it. The weather was cold that night, fifteen degrees below zero.

Being the new proud owner of a big, brown, twelve-foot Chevy step-van that Steve Tillmann sold me, I had the responsibility of hauling around the equipment. At two-thirty in the morning the van started, and I somehow found my way back to our new place in Cedarburg. The furnace was cooking there and unfortunately, the heat had no problem escaping through the cement block walls.

More bookings were gradually lined up, mostly small clubs and bars. The group kept getting tighter, and we felt the necessity to record a demonstration tape of our songs along with having pictures taken and posters made. The rustic farm setting around the barn lent itself nicely to some photogenic sessions. Goofy times were plentiful. Saint Studio outside of West Bend, almost fifteen miles northwest, was booked for two days. The six of us managed to tightly squeeze into a kitchen-sized studio. We recorded at least ten songs to have transferred to cassette. As always, a half-gallon of wine was kept by my amplifier in a brown paper bag. Others in the band had their own peculiar conscious-altering devices ranging from whiskey to marijuana. Footch Kapoot got loud and crazy. The owner of the studio, Lee St. Louis, being big on country-western music himself, wasn't quite prepared for this. He composed himself remarkably well, though, and actually seemed to enjoy us and our gamut of songs. So, we recorded a real mix of blues, basic rock, and jazz to be used as a sampling.

A few weeks after this demo session, Dave was replaced on bass by Rob Abel, a superb bassist and easygoing guy. Rob added a new rejuvenated pulse to the group, and he sang. Having four strong vocalists, Sue, Mark, Rob, and me, certainly made available a variety of solo voices and incredible harmonies.

By March and April 1977, we seemed to be playing out four and five nights a month. One club on the north side of Milwaukee, called, Shelter From The Storm, took us on as a house band of sorts. The evenings that we were booked to play there were packed to maximum. The clientele at Shelter From The Storm responded to us in a resounding fashion. Applause, cheers, screaming, foot stomping, and contained chaos often broke out—exactly what every rock band strives for, a vivacious, healthy reaction from an audience. I knew that it was mostly drug- and alcohol-induced, but it seemed honestly justified.

We worked day jobs that were hardly bearable. We all had problems, disappointments, tensions, and even tragedies. It seemed good for the band and the audience to be able to shove all this aside for an evening, forget about it, allow ourselves to be distracted, and let the music, people, and good times console us. This was all we had. We got wild and crazy and so did the audience. Throbbing heads and hangovers came and went, but maybe it was worth it if we could just hang onto the memory of those uninhibited nights. The insatiable thirst and craving for the next one, the anticipation of another wild, unreal evening helped to get us through our oppressive week. This was the cycle for the common lower-class person, especially the single and lonely.

My job at Root's Natural Footware fit hopelessly snug in this defeatist, dead-end category. I had the added responsibility of being the assistant manager without the salary. This job became insanely boring, flavored with tension. In March of 1977, I contacted the Kasch Company, where I had worked in '72 and '73, to see if there was a warehouse position open. There was, and many people there were happy to see me back. I eagerly forsook the shoe business and Milwaukee's stylish east side for a good old physical, low-profile punch-clock job. It would be physically taxing, but my mind would be free to concentrate on the promising future of Footch Kapoot. Plus, there were other benefits to be had there. It was a third the travel distance from where I lived. I'd be working with a number of like-minded, singles bar-crowd types, and I'd make more money. There was no more city driving to deal with, just twelve miles of pleasant country roads from the south-west end of Mequon to my new home in the barn where we practiced.

April's spring was a gladly welcomed thing. There was a three-roomed loft in the barn that had been used in the past as office space. With a little work and ingenuity, Steve Tillmann and I converted this loft into living quarters for ourselves. Steve adhered himself nicely to Footch Kapoot as roadie and handyman. He was just always there at our disposal, and he was greatly appreciated. With his help, we made this loft into a uniquely shabby upper flat furnished with a refriger-ator, telephone, gas space heater, carpeting, chairs, table, lamps, stereo system, abundant plant life, and even a kitchen counter and sink with real hot and cold running water. What more could a past hippie, soon to be rock star, want? It was our own place in the country, living where our band practiced and no concerns about finances! Now, I still had that void that a girlfriend could fill, but I was working on that.

The Rambler American had to move over when a used 1972 lime green Ford® Pinto took its place as my main vehicle. This painted piece of tin seemed to be designed to produce anguish for its owner. The green Pinto was a bad bean.

Living on this long-since-retired farm allowed me to get back into the nature swing again. I took a stab at planting a garden. The earth on the north end of the barn was black and moist. Years of cows and horses trotting about made for rich fertilizer. Peas, radishes, carrots, tomatoes, corn, sunflowers, and cabbage screamed with life as they grew and thrived in this potent soil. The barn was located on Cedar Creek Road. This was about as picturesque a setting as rural Wisconsin offers. Many long, peaceful, meditative walks were taken. . Maples, Oak, Evergreen, and Cedar trees lined the banks of the winding creek. Young alfalfa, wheat, and corn arced their way along the rolling hills. A new season, optimism for life abounded. April and May invited me to stretch out and expand.

My songwriting, likewise, was not contained. Vague references to the Lord and spiritual niceties filtered into my thoughts and songs. The International Community of Christ still hawked their goods through the mail, and the same troublesome visions of Bubba Free John and the Dawn Horse Communion tugged at my spirit. The seeker doesn't know when to quit. And for the faint remote possibility of having the future foretold, especially in mind that of a woman in my life, I drove down to the south side of Milwaukee and had yet one more astrological chart drawn up by a lady named Miriam. My money and time was again wasted, but we all tend to grapple for a glimmer of hope. She was so off base in her reading that she never really made it to the ballpark. Parts is parts; charts is charts. Even a child in their fantasizing can be more accurate on occasion. The deep longing for an emotional spiritual experience was instead channeled into music. That was all that was real to me.

By early summer, we were performing steadily at clubs such as The Brass Lantern, The Poor House, The Fox, Shelter From The Storm, Sugar Mountain, Sundance, Buffalo Joe's, The Living Room, The Beach Bar, and various college gatherings. The name Footch Kapoot spread quickly throughout southeastern Wisconsin, and the decision was made to purchase a renovated school bus to travel in and accommodate us for overnighters.

The blue bus was not without its problems though, such as having bad brakes. On a late Saturday afternoon in mid-July 1977, while humming along down Highway 43 heading into downtown Milwaukee on the way to Sugar Mountain, the brakes gave out. Hundreds of cars were crawling along in a three-lane traffic tie-up, most of them enroute to the Milwaukee Brewers game. As I laid my foot on the brakes, the pedal just hit the floor. Steve Tillman was standing up font with me and I shouted, "Steve, there's no brakes!" Steve acted quickly and threw a V-shaped block of wood that we used as a back-up emergency brake under the right front tire. But the bus just effortlessly hopped over it. If our bus hit this stalled traffic at forty-five miles-per-hour, the riveting effect of bumper-to-bumper collisions would be incredible. The far left lane of this four-lane interchange seemed to have much less traffic. Immediately I pulled into that lane, willing to face the consequences of sideswiping a few cars over colliding with several hundred. The bus moved into the left lane without incident, and I just kept ramming a cement retainer wall with the front left tire until we came to a stop. With hearts leaping out of our chests, Steve, Mike Haupt, and I stepped out of the bus and began to collect ourselves. There was no damage—none whatsoever—not even to our fender! My legs felt like Jell-O®, and my arms quivered like a vibrator. We were actually safe!

No collision, no injuries. Unbelievable! Steve crawled under the bus as the traffic lulled past. He yelled up, "Our brake line's broke!" So he pinched off that line, dumped a pint of brake fluid in, and on our merry way to Sugar Mountain we proceeded.

Sugar Mountain was a second-story, bar/dance hall on Milwaukee's south side. We quietly sat in the bus in front of Sugar Mountain waiting for the others to arrive. We had one regrettable treat waiting for us. Our spinet piano had to be heaved up twenty one steps to the second floor. This was pure bull work. We must have sounded like a chain gang as the seven of us shouted in unison the numbered step we made it to. "One!, two!, three!, and finally, twenty one!!". This was enough physical labor to nearly wipe most of us out, but the work had just begun. At least seven trips up and down had to be made by each person before all the equipment was in. Amplifiers, guitars, a ten-piece drum set, a nine-by-twelve foot rug, two four-foot speaker cabinets, a saxophone , microphone stands, a trunk filled with costume and stage paraphernalia, hats, a bell tree, lamps, and even my precious stuffed porcupine. We transformed a bland, barren stage into a strange and cozy living room. People were as entertained watching us set up all this stuff as they were with hearing our music.

Aside from developing a possible hernia through hauling equipment, there was still another risk involved with performing at Sugar Mountain. We took the door, that is, they charged one dollar for customers to get in, and that was our pay for the night. The more that came, the merrier we were. One evening after four hours of grueling work and throwing around equipment, we only took twelve dollars at the door. Not much of an incentive to keep playing, but we did. We loved the music and a chance to play. Other nights at Sugar Mountain were more profitable for us as sometimes up to three hundred paying people came to hear us. Carrying all our things back down the twenty-one steps seemed easier and more jovial on the return trip. We were easy on the brakes on the way home. We would get them fixed the next week, I was sure.

The following week we played an outdoor concert at Vollrath Bowl in Sheboygan. Sheboygan is fifty miles north of Milwaukee on Lake Michigan, famous for its bratwurst festival and the vaudeville song named after it, "Mention My Name in Sheboygan," "the greatest little town in the world," as the song goes. Even the Everly Brothers recorded that one. Vollrath Bowl resembled a natural amphitheater, that of a sunken, oval, earthen coliseum. Mark was driving the bus on this particular day and exercised his bravery by taking this blue chunk of steel down the grassy one-hundred-foot embankment to the stage area. The brakes held their grip somewhat, and we began unloading without mishap.

Spirits were high; we were pumped up for a good time. By this period in Footch Kapoot's life, we reached a low-level stardom status and had the luxury of having a backup band perform before us.

The masses were filtering down into Vollrath Bowl. A good number of people were spread out on the grassy basin, but foreboding thunderheads loomed overhead. We cut the backup band short so that we'd be assured of getting some music in before the rains came. Well, halfway through our second song, which was "Money" by Pink Floyd, the rains started coming. Footch Kapoot, the budding new band, quickly became a scrambling rose. The fifteen hundred or so people making up the audience fled to their vehicles as we recruited a handful of volunteers to help us get all this stuff in the bus for fear of any water damage. The loading of the school bus was completed in record time: fifteen minutes. We were all drenched, and the packing of the bus was never done so sloppily before, but we lived up to the name Footch Kapoot—broken down but repairable.

Oddly enough, we managed to be very good humored through this downpour. It was the ordeal of trying to get the bus back up the hill that silenced our laughter. Saturated grass and soft earth made for near-zero friction. At least fifteen people pushed and grunted to help get the bus back up this thirty-five-degree incline. The tires spit up a mud storm as they carved six-inch ruts that buried our feet in muck. When the bus finally hit the zenith and balanced once again on level ground, exhaustion limited our victory cheer.

Other things were not quite right with this tubular mobile home; the carburetor had a habit of starting on fire. That was all right in the winter when the added heat was welcomed, but usually this was cause for grave concern. A good explosion would bring us into the presence of our maker.

We tolerated its idiosyncrasies, knowing that the ownership of this bus was but yet another small step to stardom. Robin Leach, of *Lifestyles of the Rich and Famous,* had not yet made contact with us at this point. We were still savoring the lifestyle of the poor but fearless. "Hang in there," we kept telling ourselves. "Persevere just a little bit longer. The big break is soon to come." When you're this good, it's just a short matter of time until you're discovered. The uncovering of Footch Kapoot was an anxiously awaited certainty. Who wouldn't want to cash in on a band of this caliber? Sure enough, by midsummer, *who* gave us a call? *Who* went by several names: one was Contemporary Talent Associates and the other was Rainbow Production.

Paul's last job with us as drummer was at Shelter from the Storm on May 28, 1977. He decided to leave when the realization came that this group may very possibly become full-time with extensive long-range plans. We had to be free to uproot and travel. Paul had a very secure job, and Footch Kapoot was anything but secure, so the search went out for a drummer. An odd lot bunch we were . Rainbow Productions recorded a twenty-minute video of us in their studio and booked us for a six-nighter in East Dubuque, Iowa. We had to work in a new drummer—any drummer—. Our songs had complex rhythms with distinctive beginnings and endings. Because of the urgency, *good enough* would have to be good enough. We all managed to take a vacation from our regular jobs and now the blue bus would be put to the ultimate test. Could we travel three hundred miles one way without breaking down? The bus did it as we rolled into the low-income factory town of East Dubuque, Iowa.

Doubts began to stir about whether we should have taken this six-nighter at all. As we drove around while listening to the local rock station searching for the club, an advertisement for us came on the radio. "Milwaukee's own, Footch Kapoot will be at the Dive all week playing your favorite rock oldies from the '50s." "Rock oldies from the '50s?" We stared at each other, astonished. They've got to be mistaken. We were years and styles removed from basic '50s rock. Did the guy at Rainbow Productions lie just to get us booked here? He did. The posters about town exclaimed us as '50s rock, golden oldies.

The club owner was crude, hard, and insensitive. Here it was, a late Tuesday afternoon, as we meticulously set up our equipment. A biker gang walked in, the real thing—black leather jackets, skull and crossbones, greasy hair, unshaven, and generally disgusting. They plopped themselves down at the tables closest to the stage. The atmosphere was tense. We didn't look like a '50s rock band. The leader, who bluntly introduced himself as *Gunner,* slowly walked towards us. His scuzzy mouth opened and out spewed this warning, "You guys better be good." He then sat back down with the rest of his crew. This was obviously their club, and they had claim to those tables. We felt a slight sickness warring in our members and fretted at the thought of what the consequence might be when they found out that we are primarily a contemporary jazz-rock group that performed numerous originals. Would they knife us in the back of the building after the show? Would they drag us by our hair while cruising their Harley's down Main Street? Possibly they'd show mercy and just slash the tires on the bus and bust a couple of windows. Gunner was not a pleasure to behold, but the show must go on. Irving Berlin would surely have reworded some of the lines to his song, "No Business like Show Business" if he had experienced this. Bless Irving's heart; he lived to be one hundred one years old. He probably never had the express opportunity of performing before the likes of Gunner and company. Sylvester Stallone was in town filming the movie *Fist*, and many of the people involved in that movie began to make themselves known towards the back of the room. This was the hottest Tuesday night going.

Well, at eight o'clock in the evening sharp, we began to crank out the harder, rockier songs that we knew, such as "Can't Always Get What You Want by the Rolling Stones," "Feelin' All Right" by Joe Cocker, "Born to Run" by Bruce Springsteen, "Money" by Pink Floyd, "Lady Madonna" by the Beatles, and eventually we eased into our other, more diverse songs, like my song "The Andes Tune" and "Gringo in Mexico" by Maria Mulduar and "One Day at a Time," a song that Sue wrote. The crowd went absolutely crazy shortly into the first set and to our great relief, even Gunner stood up and started stomping his feet, yelling and applauding. We were in with the bikers! Footch Kapoot cruised through its trial run.

Unfortunately, our drummer, Mike, the novice member, tripped over half the songs, occasionally messing the whole group up. He was a very friendly guy, but belonged more with Gunner's group than our own. He had an obscene, foul mouth and filthy habits, but we were stuck with him for six nights. He never came around rhythmically and continued to destroy song after song. The music was too much for his basic rock background. I would be the one that would have to confront him when this six-nighter was over; he just didn't cut it. This would not be easy for him to swallow, as he liked us and our music.

After the first night, we asked the owner for a one-hundred-dollar advance. We were broke and had virtually no gas or food money. We all slept in the bus at a distant campground outside of town to save money. We were seven people with less than forty dollars between them. That's sad. The owner flatly refused us any advance and even went so far as to suggest that we may not get paid at all if the crowds don't come back. "I wanted '50s rock and look what I get: *youse!*"

We did not receive this news well, and immediately I called the owner of Rainbow Productions to get some things straight. His only consolation was a slight chuckle, remarking, "I thought for sure he'd like you once he heard you guys."

We somehow secured a fifty-dollar advance, either through him or the club owner, but six days in East Dubuque was too much to bear. Time dragged aimlessly on as boredom drained our spirits during the day while biding our time at a run-down campground. Evenings were spent pumping out the music, hoping the numbers would show up. On Friday morning as we grappled about waking up feeling miserable, I quipped, "I'm so darn swell happy I could puke." The seven of us broke into an uncontrollable laughter that lasted a good half hour. Somehow, there was a certain release when we finally saw the humor in our predicament. We were stuck here for six days, wishing it were over and hoping we'd get paid. On Sunday evening, the last night, the last set finally ended. Our agony was soon over, but the owner was coy. He actually tried to avoid paying us at all. We being a very feisty Footch Kapoot group by now, aggressively confronted him. He compromised and said, "I'll pay you half".. We flipped out. I called Rainbow Productions and things were settled. We drove out of town at sunrise, never looking back, and never dealt with Rainbow Productions again.

When we arrived at the practice barn, my home, I immediately took Mike aside and told him that we liked him as a friend, but his drumming just didn't fit in. He looked shocked as his tough guy demeanor disintegrated. I perceived that he was crying. It's not easy being a leader and having to make difficult decisions and confront people openly. Everybody else in the band was glad that this burden fell on me.

Mike did line up for us a job though. He booked us to play play for a van convention on an open field at Great Lakes Dragway in southeastern Wisconsin during the drag races. Several hundred vans formed a circle, (Gee, just like a wagon train.) and we played in the middle of them. The roar of the dragsters hardly complemented our music. The evening, you could say, dragged on. We all got very stoned and drunk and by the fourth set could no longer function. It really mattered not as most of the van people had passed out by then anyway. So this is what they did at a van convention. Mark apparently drove the bus home; no one seemed to remember.

Still another drummer was lined up to audition. Paul Schneider was his name. Paul had a clean appearance and was very polite and courteous. We ran through samplings of seven or eight songs with him. Without openly acknowledging it, I knew that the five of us were very impressed by his drumming. We invited him upstairs to my loft. After some small talk, I confidently said, "Paul, we really like your style of drumming. Do you want to join?" He was taken back and surprised as all the others unanimously agreed. With a humble smile, he answered, "Sure." Footch Kapoot was complete.

Paul was extremely adept at latching onto the songs, and in short time he began adding his own dimension. Rob felt very comfortable exchanging bass lines with Paul's drum rifts. More songs were introduced to our list, such as "Old Judge Jones" by Les Dudek, "Reasons" by Minnie Ripperton, "Tall Tale" by Rob, "Cy the Depot Master" by me, and "Dreamburst" by Mark and Sue. Serious talk of recording an album was tossed about, and we found ourselves attempting to decide which songs would be best suited for an album.

As we moved into the fall of 1977, most of the kinks were corrected in our blast furnace heating system. We either froze because it wouldn't kick in or sweltered when it came on with a gust of hot wind. We tolerated its inconsistencies but cringed at the oil bill.

Footch Kapoot was definitely gaining increased attention, and our following grew larger. The bars evolved into auditoriums, and the money started becoming reasonable. We actually began to pay ourselves a modest wage instead of just paying off debts. The long-entrenched dream of never having to work a straight job again was visible, out in the reachable horizon. We all would have gladly quit our jobs on a second's notice to pursue a creative future with Footch Kapoot.

Working at the Kasch Company, stacking cartons upon cartons of toys had long since become nearly mindless drudgery. If it weren't for all the female coworkers who loved to flirt and tease, I would have sought a less physical job elsewhere. Many hours were spent fostering intimate relationships that never made it past the loading docks of the Kasch Company. Mostly I was used as a sounding board as these ladies shared deep, personal stories of their boyfriends and potential lovers.

People almost always found me interesting, but then after allowing me the stage in our conversations, they'd move onto their friends, those people they enjoyed being around. The freedom to be off by myself to think and create, to piece together the overall busyness of the world was invaluable, and truly I desired and cherished those times, but when I sought companionship and close ties, I could only at best wedge myself into a wheel that was already turning. The loner personality that was nurtured over my then twenty-seven years, traveled with me. In one moment I perceived myself as an exploding genius with an insatiable burst of ideas and art, then when the dreamer's frustration surfaced, I fell into feelings of rejection and worthlessness. The live performances with Footch Kapoot and alcohol eased the struggle.

On stage I was not only allowed to be at the center but was expected to self-indulge, to seek and crave self-glorification. But, when the show ended, those who were my worshipers only minutes before, treated me as an equal and to my crushing dismay, even lesser. More and more people seemed to shed pity upon me. What else could they do? Only a rare person could identify with the struggle of never having arrived, always traveling, dreaming, hoping, and striving to pursue but never being able to get off at that destination. The train rarely stops to accommodate the desires of one passenger. My years of pleading with the conductor, who had yet to show his face, were still lived in vain from what I did not receive from the world in admiration and respect, I deceivingly bestowed upon myself. It wasn't the stardom that I sought and certainly not the wealth. It was the fulfilling assurance that I could see my creative endeavors realized shortly after they sprang forth and developed. You never really bury ideas and dreams; you just keep shuffling and pacing the grounds of the potential gravesite.

In 1969, just days before leaving for New York City, during one of his angry drunken stupors, my dad spoke these harsh almost prophetic words to me. "Ray, you're so self-centered. All you think of is yourself.

No one likes you!" I peered down at him from my upstairs bedroom. Without saying a word back to him, our eyes connected for a moment as I thought, "This is my dad, a pathetic defeated drunken man."

Of the few things I recall my dad saying, I remembered this the most. Was it true? Was that my enslavement—self-centeredness—that brought both extreme ecstasy and near suicidal destruction? Maybe this was why I couldn't cut it with Bubba Free John—because I wanted to have the position of guru, to call the shots, and design the program. I had difficulty following directions, taking orders. I desired to bask in admiration. I was *so* special, *so* gifted, *so* unique, truly an innovator and revelator. Self-centeredness was essential to accomplish my goals.

We reserved two days in December at Saint Studios to begin to record our first album. The songs were all original, and I was the writer of most of them. "Das Is Wonderful" had a waltz beat laden with intricate instrumental arrangements and showered with vocal harmonies.

"The Andes Tune" was my crescendo ballad of a man trekking over the snowcapped Andes of Peru driven by a real-as-life dream that he would meet his woman waiting for him at the bottom of the mountain. The song was a masterpiece in drama and production.

"Sleepytime Day" was conceived and written in the dirt-floor barn in November of 1976. It started out with a slow, hard-step rhythm and worked into a peppy Dixieland swing.

> Everybody's sleepin,' nobody wanna get up,
> Ya, it's a sleepytime day but it won't take long to come around.
> Everybody's lookin,' cold gray cloud hangin' low.
> No, it won't be long, old man winter come around.

"Versality" was a hard-driven, nostril-flaring rock song about a stagecoach driver, Jack, and his son Pete, who were about to be held up by four bandits. But seven Indian braves came to their rescue and warded the desperadoes off.

> There's old Jack, he ain't comin' back, he'd been ridin' gun all day long.
> There's little Pete, sittin' in his seat, keep him company 'til sundown.

The horses ain't been fed, we been pushin' instead.
Plenty of time at the Nevada line.
An Indian scout tells them to look out, there's four guys
up the road.
He comforts Pete, sweatin' in his seat.
Let's see what we can hold.
They had on their side, seven braves with knives.
The four men rode away.
We been out all day, whatcha tryin' to say.
    Pa, I think I'm tired.

The song definitely had spark and a good guy ending.

Mark and I put together an instrumental entitled, "Theme from the Pet Dome." Steve Tillmann found a half-shell steel dome about one and one-half times the size of a basketball in the bottom of the barn where I lived. We had no idea where it came from and still don't. It resembles a round steel shell casing, and it had a hole drilled through the center of it. We strung a twine through it and called it our pet dome. As we played this song on stage, Steve would dance with it as it gleefully dangled by a rope. Later, we perfected the act by having it perform actual tricks, such as rolling over, playing dead, and staying when we told it to, "Stay." It's so absurd, that people just loved it. I've used the pet dome on numerous occasions for simple entertainment. I always wanted to market a brass desktop model. Nobody would finance the venture, though.

Another instrumental that we did on the album was a concerted effort called, "Don's Mom's Green Boiled Ham," a precision jazz-rock exercise of power and drive. When the song ended eight minutes later, we felt both invigorated and exhausted. The fictitious story that I contrived, which led to its title, was that of a hardware store owner named John, who sold his longtime customer, Don, a claw hammer with a defective handle. Don and his mom owned a meat market, so to get back at John for selling Don a broken hammer, Don's mom sold John a rancid, green boiled ham. Nothing like small-town revenge.

A few other songs decided upon for the album were: "One Day At A Time" by Sue that was a sweet, melodic pop-sounding song, and "Tall Tale" by Rob, a basic slow rock rhythm and melody.

With me utilizing my dad's alto sax, we created a small horn section compromised of Mike on clarinet and me. On stage we called ourselves "Slick and Sleazy Breeze." I was Slick and Mike was Sleazy. We'd introduce ourselves by saying, "I'm Slick, he's Sleazy; we're Slick and Sleazy Breeze, just flew in from the West Coast." I also played alto sax along with Mike on the clarinet on Mark and Sue's melancholic, ethereal piece called "Dreamburst. "

And so the nine songs were buffed and polished until the sheen could get no brighter. Nine songs extended themselves into fifty-five minutes of recorded music. That much time recorded on an album was unheard of and frowned upon by engineers and manufacturers. The sound quality would be reduced; we were informed that most albums run thirty to thirty-five minutes total. We held onto an artistic stubbornness in spite of the advice otherwise. I guess that we wanted the listeners to be exposed to as much a variety of what Footch Kapoot was capable of doing as possible on one LP record.

We titled the album, *Good Clean Fun.* And, to give a story to the title, we had a photo shoot of all six of us sudsing down on a warm day in a metal horse trough. We truly had good, clean fun on that August day when Gordy Simon, the man who first encouraged me to go to New York, came over to the barn to photograph the group for promotional purposes. Our horse trough bubble bath turned into a playful, childlike zaniness. We got so clean that our fingers squeaked on the guitars and piano. I didn't need a bath for pert' near two years afterward. Other opportune photo sessions were taken at a historical wooden covered bridge and a steel bridge with the ever-drifting Cedar Creek passing underneath.

We needed a name for our record label, so we called it Cornball Records. "Cornball" was a phrase used for silly, slapstick humor. We had what we advertised as "Cornball Night" and would often throw hundreds of cellophane wrapped cornballs into the audience. The album cover would be the same as the painting on our four-by-five foot display board.

With the members in the band at an unstoppable, enthusiastic high, I sat back on my couch in the loft and allowed myself the simple relaxing pleasure of reminiscing back through my musical past: the places, experiences, people, highs, lows, anticipations, and disappointments. Now, I traveled back in memory to that day in February of 1964 on stage at Grafton Elementary School, pantomiming to the Beatles' "I Want To Hold Your Hand" and "She Loves You." Even though we were only pretending, it was that profound experience of hearing girls scream while capturing the audience's rapt attention that propelled the release of creative juices with the desire to musically entertain. Something snapped that day—something finally broke. I realized early in life just what it was that I desired to do: to sing, play a guitar, and be an intimate part of a group. Now, almost fourteen years later, the reality of taking this the distance was in view. Footch Kapoot had all the necessary ingredients and more. What we lacked was outside help: financial support and promotion. We were a low budget ball of fire. Paying for studio time, artwork, and record pressing was a weighty financial burden. It was bitterly frustrating, but we were forced to keep it within our monetary reach. Lee St. Louis understood and was generous with his time and equipment.

Those early December days leveled out at about twenty degrees; heating the loft of the barn was difficult. There was no insulation, and all I had was a small gas space heater hooked up to LP gas. While my ceiling radiated a very warm eighty-five degrees, the floor swirled around a fifty-two degree draft. The bottom of the barn had no heat so I could forget about the coziness of a warm floor. As winter dug its way in, the conditions only grew worse, and the bathroom downstairs was just one step up from an outhouse. As the bathroom grabbed whatever heat it could from the practice room overflow, ice formed on the inside walls, and often I toyed with the temptation of just renting a regular confined apartment so at least I could be warm. But I cherished my rural privacy more than the comfort of heat. I stuck it out.

As we loaded our equipment that early Saturday morning in mid-December, I felt that we couldn't be any more ready to record than we were that day. Each song on an individual and group basis took thirty to forty hours to complete from inception to full arrangement. We performed these songs at least fifty times live. I believe that our greatest concern was whether we could capture the spirit and power of the songs on tape. Interest can wax low when the same part is played over and over until a satisfactory take is had. The mood at Saint Studios was big and a nervous anticipation prevailed. I started on my first glass of wine at nine-thirty in the morning. Others in the group welcomed a quick guzzle of hard alcohol and even a pinch of marijuana. We didn't have the rowdy evening inebriated crowd to cheer us on, to light our fire. So, that morning, an alcohol fix took its place as second best.

Shortly after setting up, it became apparent that we were just too much for Lee's cramped four-track studio, but we all cooperated one hundred percent and surprisingly recorded song after song. By early evening we shut it down, exhausted, drunk, partially stoned, and overall happy with the vocal and instrumental takes that we completed. On Sunday morning, we took off where we left off and by Sunday evening had accomplished more than we had hoped for. All nine songs were nearly completed except for some minor odds and ends. That following week I spent a number of hours with Lee and his son, Brian, mixing all these tracks together.

We were pleased with the overall project, considering the time, money, and equipment that we had to work with. Mark's guitar playing showed through as he bit into songs with his guitar, his "searing monkey wrench" as he called it. My voice held out remarkably well, and Paul's precise drumming was not hindered by his being confined to a sound booth, having only headphones on and a window to peek through for his cues and personal contact. The master tapes, along with all artwork, were sent down to Nashville to be pressed and manufactured. Now all Footch Kapoot had to do was keep on playing and wait.

As could be expected, delays came. I was to be sent an acetate pressing for approval but weeks went by before I finally received it. It was sent to the wrong address. When it finally came, I called everyone over to hear it for its virgin run. We quickly approved the test record and I gave Nashville Records the 'go ahead'. When the call came that they were ready for pickup, I drove the distance to Nashville and loaded the one thousand records into my lime green Pinto.

Upon my return to the barn that evening, we had a great celebration, playing the record until the needle almost ate through to the other side. Plans were excitedly concocted to promote this thing, and our hopes were running high. Posters were printed announcing the release of our first album—by Wisconsin's own Footch Kapoot. We made sure that the record stores were well stocked and pried our way into several FM rock stations to plead and pester them into giving us airplay. A great record release party was planned at the Poor House in Grafton, a club that we performed at frequently. Friends, talent agents, promoters and all the people closely involved with the group and this album were cordially invited. We did all that was humanly possible for what we had at our disposal to promote us and the album *Good Clean Fun*.

As weeks went on, some encouraging news began filtering in. A few copies were sold at the stores, some agents took notice, the *Milwaukee Journal* wrote a story on us in their weekly entertainment section, and we just waited, suspended in anticipation for the news of the *big break*. But, the big break held off, and all the initial self-induced hoopla quieted down. As months progressed well into spring of 1978, we seemed to have hit an impasse. Our wage for an evening increased and work seemed fairly steady, but we felt trapped, almost destined to be imprisoned within the borders of Southeastern Wisconsin. Sensational verbal promises dissipated to a stirring speculation. No agency or manager was willing to gamble money and time on our unique sound and crazy theatrical show, at least not in Milwaukee. Footch Kapoot was overripe and seemed doomed to fermentation. We did not have nearly enough bookings to permanently quit our jobs, and we weren't free to pack up and relocate elsewhere perhaps to a different section of the country where we'd be appreciated, such as San Francisco or possibly Los Angeles. Please, no, thank you, not New York.

Summer found us moping, dragging at low ebb. The enthusiasm for working out new material just wasn't there. Two of Footch Kapoot's members casually suggested that we gradually change our format, get more into contemporary songs and some occasional disco, something that would at least guarantee us acceptance and steady engagements. Just the word *disco* nearly made me vomit. Horrors, no! Not disco. I'd rather work at the Kasch Company and strum my guitar alone. The whole concept behind Footch Kapoot was the freedom to express, experiment, and create, to get loose or to get serious, to be unrestrained. I couldn't imagine any other option and sorely chuckled at the thought of being just a no-name, mediocre top-40 band. How could we discard our hard-sought identity? For weeks, ideas and suggestions surfaced with little or no serious discussion. I had one minor consolation. In spite of the group's grumbling and unstable unity. She came in the form of an admiring fan turned girlfriend. Jen found me attractive, humorous, and a creative wonder. I needed that, for I was potentially heading in a downward swing.

It seemed a mystery to a number of people and most of all to us who were members of Footch Kapoot, why crowds went wild over us, but the very people that could propel our careers kept their distance. The evening of June 3, 1978, would prove to be the pinnacle of our popularity. The stage was at the Poor House again. Closing time was one o'clock in the morning, but the still-packed house kept chanting and screaming. "Foooootch Kapoooooot!" "Foooootch Kapoooooot!" We were back in the off-stage dressing room, exhausted after four hours of pumping rock and roll. We didn't really take the reveling seriously until it hit chaotic proportions. No one was leaving. The owner came back frantic with concern. "Give them another song and tell them we have to close. They got to get out; the cops are already standing outside the door!"

With mixed feelings, we went back out there being greeted by an overwhelming reception and tore right into "Born to Run," Bruce Springsteen's pounding, driving rock classic. When the song ended, the screaming started all over again. But, after considerable pleading on our part and a show of force by the police, the crowd cooled to a grumble and dispersed. As we packed up equipment for probably the seventieth time on this mild early summer evening, our heads and spirits were still buzzing from the almost savage wildness of the audience. The reel-to-reel tape recorder captured yet another entertaining explosive show, encore and all. You must keep in mind that alcohol and other substances controlled the greater majority of these people, and it's very probable that the following day, once they straightened up, they'd have little or no recollection of what transpired the night before. They were an on again, off again, following—not much to rely on. And my desire to perform was often times on again, off again. So in spite of a growing following, we just couldn't break out of the small club circuit to the more serious concert halls.

I found myself beginning to drift further away from rock type music to a softer acoustic sound. A song that I wrote in August '78, called "Mud Turtle Creek," reaffirmed that I could sing and play just by myself. The inspiration for that song came from my many walks along Cedar Creek Road as I observed mud turtles perched on rocks, oblivious to stress, anxiety, or the burdens of life. My dad often drove slowly on Cedar Creek Road to take in the quiet splendor and meditate on peaceful thoughts. He too enjoyed seeing the mud turtles. The words to the song spoke to my hearts yearning for a quiet peaceful life......

Did you see down by the creek, older man, deathly deep;
He's only layin' sound asleep.
Bluejays playin' 'round Mud Turtle Creek.
Got lots a things on our heads,
Deep in debt over our heads,
But we eat good and smile.
We sleep on a bed.
We're swing and we're swayin'.
Ah, easily sustained,
When I'm here most every day, when you're here most
every day then we smile, oh how we smile.

The pressure of keeping Footch Kapoot together, working full-time, and drinking alcohol and doing occasional drugs, began to collapse my sides. I escaped temporarily by drifting away on my walks. I yearned for a simple life again. Too much noise, confusion, and newly introduced internal arguing among the group, was pulling me closer to that decision to get out and fold it up. I'd rather just hang out for a while and relax and try to enjoy life again.

A small-scale greenhouse was growing in the loft as I found comfort in caring for plants. The place took on the appearance of an enclosed, self-contained jungle. An eight-foot Swedish ivy hung lusciously from the ceiling along with numerous spider plants. The floor was dotted with yucca, dieffenbachia, schefflera (umbrella plant), mother-in-law's tongue, jade, cactus, and various succulents.

Enthusiasm for writing and arranging with Footch Kapoot grew more dim. Night after night, I drank alone, trying to ward off depression. I put on all my favorite records until I became numb to sound and just passed out. An occasional visit by Jen or Steve was usually uplifting, but my uncontrollable wine drinking eventually eased me into a worthless stupor. Jen left me some evenings just full of pity as I poured out to her over and over again, the despondent saga of my failed hopes and dreams. I must have appeared pathetically defeated. In early August, I followed through with the decision to leave Footch Kapoot. It was either that or experience a complete breakdown. The other members reacted in shock and disbelief that I would quit after two and one-half years of enduring such toil toward the goal. Becoming a top-40 disco band was not an option that I could live with. So, with truly heavy hearts, we decided to play out our last remaining engagements.

In the middle of August during an oppressively hot evening, I came to a casual conclusion that killing myself would be the best thing that I could do. My simple plan was to take a knife, walk down to a secluded area of the creek, stab myself in the heart, fall face first in the muck and quietly die. No one would find me for months. I couldn't go on another day, battling depression and living with unrealized dreams. Though I never did find God, I was convinced that He knew that I had earnestly tried and that would have to be good enough. I wrote my suicide note on a pink three-by-five inch note card (which I still have). It reads: "The night that Ray Last killed himself, it was hot and muggy and a few things didn't go right." I drank one last generous glass of wine while seated at my round wooden table. I never remembered finishing the glass as I woke up four or five hours later in a daze with the knife still clenched in my left hand. Passing out prevented me from taking my life. I stumbled over to the couch and slept off a 'bad' night.

We played out our last job on August 26 at the Beach Bar in Belgium, Wisconsin, which was about thirty-five miles north of Milwaukee on the Lake Michigan shoreline. The occasion was something like the Seventh Annual Manure Fest. The year previously, we played at Manure Fest, having a hay wagon as a stage, planted right in the middle of a barnyard. The cows made little of it. This year's Manure Fest was less jubilant, being that it was contained in a dance hall and not out in the dung-filled air, and, of course, it was Footch Kapoot's last fling.

As people filtered out after our last song, I was left standing, feeling a bit empty and out of sorts. Jen and Steve supported me during this awkward demise as the other members of Footh Kapoot suddenly departed after helping to load the bus. There was little to say but plenty of sadness. The Footch Kapoot era ended, but we exited at our best. There was no organized effort by fans of ours to persuade us to stay together, and there was no attempt by any other members to prompt me to reconsider my decision. I suspect that secretly they all shared a bit of relief in that the long, unreachable pursuit was over, and we dissolved with honor.

CHAPTER 36

A LIFE ON HOLD

The following morning broke bright and beautiful. As I calmly sat on the cement loading dock that was attached to the barn, I heard a horrible wailing noise. Emma the goose, and Brandy the dog, hurried over to get in on the action. There was a sound of something dying. Rushing over to the fence, I saw Nester, the Nubian goat, laying on his side, shrieking in agony. Lucky the horse was standing on Nester's tail! Lucky seemed oblivious to the crisis as he calmly chewed on fresh alfalfa. I quickly leaped the fence and lifted Lucky's hoof off of Nester's tail. Nester darted away from me as if I was the culprit causing this.

That story is always good for a laugh, as is the one about my cat named Clare. She was very sweet and usually quite bright except for the morning when she decided to sit on the top of the stove while coffee was brewing. I started to smell a very foul burning odor. As I turned, looking towards the stove, I saw smoke rising from the burner. I screamed, "Clare"! She immediately leaped nearly ten feet into the air in absolute terror. Her tail had caught on fire but there was no damage to her skin. With the same mindset as Nester, Clare thought that I had caused this and avoided me for days.

Emma the goose was a real gem, also. Every time that she was frightened, she'd stick her head in the middle of the tire swing. Emma and I never became friends, and she did many things to spite me, like pecking hundreds of dents in the sides of my green Pinto, or standing firm in the center of my gravel driveway daring me to run her over. What a defiant goose!

Even though it was late August, early September, Steve still came over to take his outdoor solar showers. He had painted a two-hundred-gallon horse trough black, which was situated twelve feet up on the flat portion of the horse barn. A rubber hose ran out of it with a shut-off valve leading to a showerhead. Steve's ingenious shower setup was suitable only to the very rugged and hardy. I tried it twice, but only on very hot days.

Often while driving around the rural area where I lived, especially in early fall, I would hear in my mind entire, angelic sounding symphonies. Each instrument and vocal was as clear as if it were performed live in front of me. I attempted to convey to Jen just how captured and moved I had become by these recurring musical visions. She could only hear my futile explanations, adding polite niceties as her comments.

Relating musical experiences and sensations proved difficult for me as the majority of people that

I encountered were not able to appreciate the vision and work behind a song. There are a myriad of artistic and highly skilled people who seem to go unnoticed. Many people as if with blinders on, can even walk or drive past God's creation without hardly being aware that it is all around them. So, here I sat, a life on hold. I felt like I was placed on the back shelf for a later day. I had no direction, no goals. A nagging lackluster smothered my enthusiasm and dreams like an asbestos blanket over a flame. Held there long enough, the flame would be extinguished.

I continued to write songs, maybe more than ever. Those songs were blunt and truthful as I tapped into my life, what I'd done, where I'd been, and where I was then. Was I at the end of the line, having missed my destination? I couldn't go back. What would I go back to? If there was no future stirring in my members, then why was I alive? Music and God were the front-runners along with a solid mate, but the embers barely had a flicker left. The drive for music had left me drained and frail; the pursuit of God left me more puzzled and perplexed than when I first anxiously began. And, Jen, though we hit it off sometimes, we were finding that our worlds often clashed. I had only one or two friends left, and Steve, being the sure friend, began losing his sanity, his grip on reality.

As I laid on my uncle Artie's blue flower patterned couch, one of the few things that I inherited after his death, I easily thrust myself into despondency. I began to drink and smoke dope more than ever. Even those little white pills that were sure to give me a buzz began to scream at me daily, "Take me, take me!" The most-simple mundane activities now seemed to be a chore. Apathy and deep depression was showing on my other-wise glowing face.

As a glimmer of hope and purpose, I got in touch with my old musician friend, Ray Freese. Ray and I had somewhat competing music groups back in the 1960s while still in high school. He was a good guitarist with his own unique vocal style. I thought that maybe Ray would like to get together with me, and we could start some kind of a simple acoustic-sounding group. After contacting him, he showed some reserved enthusiasm and was open to getting together a few times to see what kind of songs we'd work up. Big plans started to untangle themselves in my mind, and I already came up with a name for the group. I'd call it the "Northern Melody Band." Beautiful harmonies, recognizable tunes, and primarily less involved acoustic instruments: guitars, bass, fiddle, cello, violin, sax, flute, harmonica, bells, percussion instruments, and probably piano. Well, Ray Freese made it known to me that he was not too interested in committing to a project, and after just two sessions up in my loft, we forgot about it. We disbanded before we even banded.

I began working on songs by myself, songs like "Ghost Riders in the Sky" made famous by Vaughn Monroe, and Elvis Presley's "All Shook Up, " Fats Domino's "I'm Walkin'," the old 1940's standard, "Pennies from Heaven, " plus more of my originals. And, of course, four or five select Beatle songs. But, soon, that interest drifted away, and I simply reserved myself to listening to records at an intense volume just too artificially stimulate me. I sang and danced around the room pretending that I was on stage performing before mesmerized crowds. I had inherited Footch Kapoot's PA system in exchange for making the remaining payments. With two, four-foot high by two feet deep Peavey speaker cabinets and a six-channel control board, my fantasy concert performances almost took on real proportions. I had the volume up unbearably loud and thrust myself live on stage with the Beatles, ELO, Elvis, and a host of others. The phantom performances ceased when I'd come to a near collapse almost every evening, drunk, stoned, and exhausted. At least I slept well.

And then it happened. On a late Saturday morning in mid-April 1979, I experienced an apparent heart attack! The pain in my chest and intense thumping of my heart, thrust me into a panicked state. I died! Immense fear gripped me! Absolute panic and darkness was sucking me upward! My spirit/soul left my body. I was frantically reaching out towards the ceiling in an effort to stop myself passing through. I had a very strong sense that if I were to go through the ceiling, I would never be able to come back. Seconds later, a force thrust me back into my body. As I was experiencing unbearable pain in my chest and an overwhelming panic, I got up, off my bed, and began walking around in hopes of calming myself down. I quickly called the local hospital, the same hospital that I was born in. The receptionist, being very concerned for me, wanted to get an ambulance over. I told her "No, I'm pretty sure that I can drive myself."

The twenty mile drive to the hospital was one of the most intense rides of my life. After being rushed to emergency, I was thoroughly checked out. To my amazement, the doctors could find nothing wrong! They treated me like I was making it up. The pain subsided as I drove back to the barn with my brain in a foggy haze. For nearly two days afterwards, I let off on the drinking and went on long walks.

I lived with the fear that the physically demanding work at the Kasch Company would probably be the final blow. I expected to die there while heaving boxes and holding my heart. Chest pains began to come on frequently, and I experienced a noticeable shortness of breath. I knew that it was the alcohol causing this, but I didn't care. I couldn't quit; I was enslaved and began to accept the real possibility that death was eventual and near at hand. Daily I broke out in a nervous, fearful sweat thinking that this may be it. But, *it* never happened, and I'd fool myself into thinking that I had once again warded off death and that I was master over alcohol's sting. The phrase "responsible drinking" seemed like an oxymoron. It has about as much genuineness as plastic silverware, new antiques, or a sign I recently saw advertising "fresh gas." For me there was no such thing as responsible drinking. It was all or nothing. Reflecting on my life, as often I did, I perceived myself as more of an observer here—someone who sought new experiences just to say that they did this or that. Perhaps if I lived for five hundred years, I would have still lived mostly for experiences. I seemed to have come to my final impasse, where all that I had left and all my worth was being packaged in my memories. And to those I often gave a distorted view, weeding out the bad and accenting and even exaggerating the highlights.

Christmas came but mostly I sat up there in the loft alone, except for my occasional seek-and-conquer campaigns to Shelter from the Storm, the Poor House, or even all the way up to Buffalo Joe's in Sheboygan. My mission was to find a woman, if only for the night. Rarely did I have victory. Finding my way home afterward was a goal in itself. One early Saturday morning about 2 am, the police pulled me over just two miles from the barn. They said I was driving erratically and made me walk the white line. I told them that I was on my way home, and they quickly informed me, "You're going the opposite way. You're going to have to keep your car here. We'll drive you home."

Well, I couldn't tell them that I lived in the barn, so with rapid cunning, I said that I lived in, "That stone house, but please let me out at the bottom of the driveway because if the dog sees a car pull up, she'll start barking and wake everybody up." They believed my story and dropped me off by the road. I was very fortunate that evening for having not been given a ticket or questioned extensively. One lie leads to another.

I met a lady at Buffalo Joe's one evening while I was still performing with Footch Kapoot. We took a real interest in each other, and I was amazed to find out that we had both lived in Ben Lomond, California, at the same time, less than one-quarter mile from each other. I let my mind and heart race with the possibility that I had finally met my soul mate. She sang in a band, ate natural foods, and seemed to be linked up with my spiritual experiences and yearnings. So I braved it and called her one evening, probably in early May 1979. She happily agreed to get together with me at Buffalo Joe's, sort of as a date. I was very nervous and unsure of myself that Saturday evening as I drove the fifty-three mile trek to Sheboygan to meet her at Buffalo Joe's. My self-confidence was clinging to my feet when I opened the door to Buffalo Joe's. The band and the nightlife were already in full swing. Glancing throughout the room and peering along the bar, I finally spotted her comfortably wedged between two guys, guys much bigger than I. She was laughing and drinking when she made a flicker of eye contact with me. I just stood there on the dance floor feeling awkward and embarrassed and mildly stupid. What was I to do, barge in and take her away? A good fifteen minutes passed before she finally came over to chat. By now I had downed three glasses of wine and one shot of tequila to instill boldness. After less than one minute of choppy conversation, she walked away to dance and be entertained by a number of men whom she obviously knew very well. My ego was grieved. Why did I allow myself to get so pumped up out of proportion about our being perfectly matched? A bad evening was made worse by my continuous drinking.

Finally, this lady who I'll call Linda, smoothly walked over and subtly said, "Would you like to go to my place for the evening?"

Like a jerk with a collar around his neck, I sputtered, "Sure!"

She saw my condition and offered to drive. We sat in her car while she smoked a joint of marijuana making sure that she offered me plenty. Smoking marijuana for me at this time was like groping about in the dark with my feet cut off at the ankles. The next thing that I remembered was her coldly telling me to wake up and go home. "Listen," she said, "I brought you home thinking we'd have a good time in bed, and all you do is pass out. You'd better leave." I agreed, still in a stupor. She drove me to my car, which was still parked at Buffalo Joe's and spit up gravel from her car as she spun out of there. I was left fumbling for my keys.

The sun was just beginning to rise as I finally pulled up into my driveway. Two days later I penned a country-western song about my defeated, rejected evening with Linda called "Strange Times and Alcohol."

I recorded this song at Saint Studios, thinking maybe I'd have a country hit. It had all the ingredients, tenor voice, country drawl, and broken heart. I'm about the only one who has ever heard it. That February evening at Buffalo Joe's with Linda manufactured me into a double fool. I found out later from a friend that Linda was a prostitute, and I was just one of many that succumbed (almost) to her cozy seduction. If it weren't for my passing out, she would have had a successful evening.

The struggle for glimpses of happiness and self-worth became increasingly more difficult. Another song in my string of depressants was titled "Old Man". This song was about a lonely, bitter man who stabbed himself to death at the age of one hundred five, just to finally end his emotional suffering.

Old man he's layin' down,
Talkin' 'bout your life.
See a picture on the wall
Of a son and his wife.
Boy, you might have lived a lonely life,
But you're probably better off.
Seen men commit suicide
To feel freedom in their veins.

CHORUS

(Where's the Lord at a time like this?
Probably out doin' some gardening,
Pulling out the weeds, plantin' some seeds.
Spring don't wait for no man.
(Decisions, decisions)

Old man he long gone now, but he talked
about his life.
Hundred and five years with hardly a smile,
Killed himself with a knife.
Year after year he's still workin' hard,
All the things he loved, he lost.
Seen men commit suicide
To feel freedom in their veins.

My relationship with Jen had come to a virtual end except for some passing visits and aimless phone calls. I wrote a song about this broken relationship with reference to the four or five other intimate ones that I had over the past years. I called it, "Me and My Woman." Some of the lyrics are as follows:

Suck the well till it's dry,
Then you turn around and drill another.
A tear in your eyes,
But the world's heard you cry before.
You know that there's more,
You're at the end of the rope,

Wish it was longer.
But how you cry, cry, cry;
Aw cryin' all over your face.
Whoa babe you try, try, try,
To make sense of yourself
'cuz you got you here in the first place.
And it's the last place we wanna be in,
Arguing again, me and my woman.

At the end of March, 1979, I purchased my first 35mm camera. Through Gordy Simon's advice, I bought a Minolta® XG7 with an adaptable Vivitar® flash. I went berserk taking photos of wine glasses, fruit trees, plants, sunsets, sunrise, the creek, people who visited, and people at work. The bar, silo, horses, goats, dog, and the elusive, flighty, Emma the goose. One very upbeat song that I wrote in April, 1979, was about one of my spontaneous photo sessions around the farm-yard. Emma constantly tried to thwart my creativity. It's called "Emma the Goose."

Tryin' to take a picture in the noonday sun
Of Emma the goose and dog on the run.
Tryin' to get the dog to sit down by me,
But Emma the goose, she's peckin' at my knee.

CHORUS

(Peckin,' peckin,' peckin' at my knee;
Yer gettin' in the way of my photography
Honkin,' honkin,' honkin' out loud,
I'd crack ya in the neck but you
Won't bend down.)

The song goes on and on about my failed futile life but keeps coming back to the chorus.

The spring of 1979 was one of the first springs that gave me little or no rejuvenation. The warmer air, flowers, and birds hardly made an impact on my run-down spirit. As the song "Me and My Woman" stated, "I'm at the end of the rope, wish it was longer." Nothing brought my spirit up; nothing could give me hope or an incentive to keep on. Yet I wrote another song in early May called, "We Said Goodbye," a song about a desperate man fighting with mixed feelings of having to let go yet desiring to hang on. My total being was in conflict with itself. I wanted to die; yet I still wanted to live. The song summed it up with the last phrase, "I'm lonely, yes, I'm lonely, yes, I'm lonely right now." I was truly alone, surely I was not a pleasure to be around. People at work and old musician friends of mine noticeably avoided me. A negative atmosphere is not inviting to happy people. Even music as a last ditch resort, my music and all the others that I loved, could no longer muster up any enthusiasm in me to sing, play, or just listen. My stimulating resources finally ran out. "Suck the well till it's dry, then you turn around and drill another." There was no more *other* in my life, no more wells to drill. Even my first glass of wine for the day did nothing to uplift. Still, I drank out of habit and bodily addiction. With the summer coming on, I wrote a well-wishing, dream fantasy song about being in love in summer. Yet, as I sang this, actual tears ran from my cheeks, forming a clear shiny streak down the body of the Guild guitar. "Ah, you've never been in love like you're in love in summertime."

This Kind of Summertime

Things are gettin' lazy; things are gettin' slow
In the summertime when things let you go.
Love you in the night, love you in the day,
In the summertime when love gets its way.

And when I saw the buds breakin' out,
And birds were buildin' nests
And when I smell some warm clean air.
I know some people miss,
Prayin' so they can find,
This kind of summertime.

Things are gettin' lovely,
Things are feelin' fine,
Regardless of what, you're in this
Kind of summertime.

Love you in the night, love you in the day,
In the summertime when love gets its way.

Oh you've never been in love like
You're in love in summertime.

On Saturday June 2, Jen gave me a call out of concern for my well-being, I'm sure. She asked if I'd like to go with her to the Brady Street Festival the following day, Sunday. The Brady Street Festival was an annual event on Milwaukee's east side, a carry-over from the thriving late '60s hippie community. A three-block section was closed off to traffic, allowing people to sell their crafts and make merry music. Thousands would show up; the counterculture was still in full force and often in full regalia. Beads, headbands, patchwork Levi's®, and painted faces; this was their day to show strength in numbers. Marijuana smoke slowly merged to form a train-like cloud hovering protectively overhead. For a brief passing of time, you could allow yourself to experience the remnant of a living flashback, the thrill of a cultural revolution. Even though many of the participants were just actors, re-enacting a period, still it remained vitally fresh in most people's spirit. I didn't like large crowds, and the day was hot, near ninety degrees. Cut-offs and Root's sandals were all that I wore.

Near the corner of Astor and Brady, in the midst of the hot and sweaty thousands, Jen took my arm and nervously said that she needed to tell me something. I sat on the outside steps of a bar as Jen stood before me and began to pull a folded piece of paper out of her purse. She, with uncertain confidence, began to read me a poem. "God made the flowers and the trees, the birds and waters." The poem rambled on of niceties about God as I sat half listening, wondering, "What's the point?" When she finished her one-page oratory, she quickly glanced at me seeking my approval. Raising my right eyebrow, I mumbled, "That's nice." I obviously didn't get the subtle message that she was trying to convey, so with great boldness she blurted out, "Two months ago I gave my life to Jesus Christ!"

The first reactive thought that flashed in my mind was, "Good night, you bit the dust, you've lost it!" But nearly instantly upon hearing his name spoken, the name Jesus Christ, my entire body was covered with goose bumps and a sensation like that of a quickened transformation began to envelope me. The great sense that Jesus was calling and tugging at me caused me to break out in a mysterious joy. It was as if I was injected with a happy drug that had an immediate effect. Without thought, I unreservedly exclaimed to Jen, "I don't know what's happening to me; I feel like Jesus is calling me. I feel like I'm being transformed on the spot. This is the experience I've sought after—this spiritual enlightening!" As I stood to walk among the crowd, I still continued to sense a thrilling glow emanating around me, almost shielding me. Jen did not believe me and became a bit annoyed, thinking that I was mocking her conversion to Christ. I truly tried to convince her that I was experiencing something marvelous and supernatural, the unspeakable excitement of God touching me.

Suddenly, within minutes, I happened upon Tom Johnson, an old friend of mine from high school. He even had a short stint as lead singer in the Misery Sons in the early part of 1968 before the group disbanded. As we talked, I saw that he was drunk and stoned and had a very loose, filthy-looking woman hanging on his arm. A compassion welled up inside of me like none I'd ever experienced. I felt pity for his degenerate condition. He looked so pathetic and lost, so removed from reality. A paradox danced about me. Literally, less than five minutes before, I was like him; my lifestyle had linked up with his. Get drunk, get stoned, and grab a loose woman. Now, almost as if I could not even identify with his wretched condition, I hardly knew what to say. It's as if I didn't want to be stained by his drunken disease. We became quite uncomfortable with each other and this awkward situation in spite of not having seen each other for ten years. My vibrant countenance fell. The regeneration that I was enjoying momentarily ceased. God had instantly given me the ability to recognize sin. The stark awareness that I now had, caused me to see it as frightful and ugly.

CHAPTER 37

THE BATTLE IS ON, GOD PURSUES ME

I now had an overwhelming burden for Tom in his very lost condition. I wanted to free him from his devastating course. God, for that hour, gave me His eyes and His heart to see sin for what it is, yet to have a deep compassion for the person controlled by it. The joy of Jesus pulling at my spirit began to subside, and in its stead, a great turmoil having the volume of war, began to attack all that I had: my mind, emotions, and even my physical body. The battle was on.

As we drove back home, Jen's disgust for me turned into heated anger. She would not believe my story that, "Jesus is calling me." After dropping me off at my barn, she immediately left with a cold, spiteful, good-bye, leaving the dust from her car swirling behind.

I could not rid myself of this war. The ripping out of my person became painful. Pacing nervously about in the loft, I felt like a spectator thrust against his will into a vicious battle. The battle was to 'the death', and I didn't even know which side I was on. I tried to reason with myself, to get my mind back to who I was, thinking that maybe I was experiencing early stages of insanity. I fought to hold on to all that Ray Last identified with. I countered the attack at my identity by openly repeating those things that brought me joy, to build this wall of assurance that I still knew who I was. "You can't strip me of this! I love music, wine, dope, friends, girlfriends, rustic living, and the attainment of fame. That's who I am!"

My wall was made of sand as the voice of Jesus gently pleaded with me to let that go. The chasm was wide and deep, but if I jumped, would he catch me in the air and lift me to safety? "I can't jump," I snapped! "This is all I know; this is my security."

Jesus responded, "Your security has crumbled; it's a mirage; you have nothing left to lose."

I begged him in a rapidly weakening state, "Go away; I'm going insane. You can't be real; my mind is turning inside out." There was no one to talk to, nothing to console me. My allies had fled, and I was left to fend for myself. "If I could make it through the night, I'd be all right." I thought. This was a very thin, frail hope, but I needed to buy some time.

The evening spent on my couch was without rest. The urge to vomit was upon me, but that was false also. My body just didn't know how to react to this beating I *was* taking. My defense just filtered out into the night sky. I was not even certain who the enemy was; I was just caught in a crossfire on an open, exposed field. I was hit but did not die. Rolling, tossing in pain, there was no relief. I could find no aid. The battle was torturous, but who was doing the torturing? If I yielded to God, I could never have myself back again. An explosion would occur, and I would scatter to dust. Was 'His' constant calling real or imagined?

Remarkably, I was able to function that Monday morning at the Kasch Company, but the struggle was relentless. This insanity was like a tightly clenched claw with increased pressure upon my head. The pressure seemed to compress my brain; it would not release its merciless grip. "Jesus, Jesus, Jesus",: His name kept echoing through the hollow gunshots and the exploding shells.. In my war scenario, I ran frantically, clutching my stomach and dodging unseen artillery. While breathing spent gunpowder and billowing dust clouds under a war-blackened sky, I begged for relief. I could not take it anymore. What was happening to me?

After work let out at 3:30, while driving the country roads home, I was amazed that I made it through work. The general noise in my spirit quieted as the thought of Jim Bohn came to mind. I hadn't seen Jim for almost seven years. I knew through rumors that he had become a Christian. Old friends and musicians would mention this on occasion usually in a critical, mocking way. "That's it!, I'll call Jim; he'll tell me about Jesus. I've got to have answers." Immediately after getting home, I called information to get Jim's phone number. I didn't know where he lived or even if he was still in Wisconsin. "Sorry," the operator said, "no listing in Grafton or Cedarburg."

Finally, there was a listing for a 'Jim Bohn'. Excitedly, I called him. A lady answered and said, "Yes, he's right here. I'll get him." There was a pause with a noticeable hush and whispering.

Jim came to the phone. "Ray?" His voice seemed to have an unsure happy quiver.

I responded quickly, "Jim, I think Jesus Christ is calling me. I'd like to talk to you about Him."

Jim answered swiftly, almost without thought, "What time would you like me to come over?"

Relieved, I said, "Seven would be good."

The three-hour wait seemed to drag, but there was finally hope in the air. I wholeheartedly wanted Jim to confirm what was burning within me—that Jesus Christ was real and that I could know Him. This could very possibly be the revealing of the truth that I had so desperately searched for in the past, from my innocent talks with God as a boy to the intense meditation overlooking Lake Pond Oreille. From the misleading of astrology charts to the deceptive highs of peyote and mushrooms. The desire and richness of a deep spiritual longing was still very much alive in me. Unquestionably the greatest desire in the pursuit of my life was to experience and to know God.

At seven o'clock sharp, Jim drove up. He walked nervously towards the loading dock to greet me, heavily ladened with a stack of books in his arms. I was beaming with gladness as I attempted to put Jim at ease. He was overly excited to the point of stuttering. It was definitely good for us to see each other again, though now the table was turned. Instead of his sitting in my tipi, absolutely mesmerized while listening to the ramblings of my self-made wisdom, I was the eager inquirer in quest of spiritual knowledge. I poured a confidence-building glass of wine and politely asked Jim if he minded that I drink.

He hesitantly responded, "No, that's fine, do whatever you like."

I took a sip and set the glass on my table. Wine just didn't go right with the moment. As I communicated to Jim all about the turmoil that I was experiencing in my mind and spirit, I openly shared about my many beliefs. I pelted Jim with a myriad of questions.

"Jim, what about reincarnation? I believe that we keep coming back until we get it right."

Jim's calm response was taken directly from the Bible, as were most all of his answers and responses. "Ray, it says right here in the Book of Hebrews, Chapter 9, verses 27 and 28. 'And inasmuch as it is appointed for men to die once and after this comes judgment. So Christ, also, having been offered once to bear the sins of many, shall appear a second time for salvation without reference to sin to those who eagerly await Him.'"

Jim continued, "The Bible also tells the story of the rich man who kept his wealth to himself and despised the beggar named Lazarus. When Lazarus died he went to heaven, but when the rich man died, he went to Hades where he was in constant torment, and he begged that Lazarus would give him a drink of water. But, the answer received from Father Abraham was, 'Between us and you there is a great chasm fixed in order that those who wish to come over from here to you may not be able and that none may cross over from there to us.' The rich man asked that his five brothers be warned, but Abraham's response was that they have been warned by Moses and the prophets, and if they rejected Moses and the prophets, they would even reject someone risen from the dead.'"

I stood in awe at Jim's pointed answer. I couldn't recall ever having heard the Bible explained so clearly before. I always had hidden doubts about reincarnation. His response straight from the Bible seemed to confirm my doubts. Jim added, "Ray, I'm convinced from the Scriptures that you only live once. There is no reason to believe that reincarnation exists. Satan has the power to deceive people into thinking that they have past lives and can communicate with the dead."

And that was my next question: "You know, I never wanted to believe that sin or hell or Satan really existed. I still have a hard time believing that God would send someone to hell. Especially me. I mean, He knows full well that I really tried to know Him. I feel that I am better than some people that even go to church."

Jim quoted from Romans, Chapter 3, verse 23: "For all have sinned and fall short of the glory of God."

He talked in length, again from the Bible of how satan deceived Adam and Eve in the Garden of Eden. He began to rattle off things from the last book of the Bible, the Book of Revelation and all about the 'End Times'. "Ray" he pointedly said, "There's over 350 references to sin in the Bible".

"Jesus, the Son of God, the second person of the Holy Trinity, sacrificed His life so that your sins and my sins would be taken away so that we might be restored back to God. He made us sinless and blameless once again, just as Adam and Eve originally were before Satan lied to them." Jim had reasonable intelligent answers in abundance.

I saw my makeshift religion crumbling quickly. There was no foundation to it. But it was still difficult for me to accept that millions of people would be thrust into hell, some Godless, agonizing eternity, just because they didn't acknowledge Jesus Christ. I mean, there were a lot of really nice people around, people that do really good things for the world and others, people that are kind and humble and generous with their money and time. What would happen to them?

Jim spouted yet another verse from the Apostle Paul in the letter to the Ephesians: "For by grace you have been saved through faith and that not of yourselves, it is the gift of God, not as a result of works that no one should boast."

And from the Book of Romans, again, Chapter 1, verses 19 through 25: "Because that which is known about God is evident within them for God made it evident to them. For since the creation of the world His invisible attributes, His eternal power and divine nature have been clearly seen, being understood through what has been made so they are without excuse. For even though they knew God, they did not honor Him as God or give thanks, but they became futile in their speculations and their foolish heart was darkened. Professing to be wise, they became fools, for they exchanged the truth of God for a lie and worshipped and served the creature rather than the Creator, who is blessed forever. Amen." Jim told me that in the Book of James, it clearly says that all good things come directly from God. Whatever goodness people have is given to them from God.

I began to flash back to what Bob Carey had said to me back in Ben Lomand and also Sylvia's brother Bill in Bemidji. I vaguely recollected what Tom Roy had discussed when he visited me at my house on Wausaukee Road. I couldn't refute or find fault with them or what they were saying. I just didn't want to believe that knowing God could be so simplistic. I didn't want to admit or even view myself as a sinner. I had tried to work my way to God, and I failed. The verses that Jim had quoted made sense. It fit together; it was like reading a book with the lights on. I wanted to believe, but I was still hesitant and resistant.

Our visit lasted until eleven o'clock, and Jim left me with one more verse. John, Chapter 3, verse 16: "For God so loved the world that He gave His only begotten Son, that whoever believes in Him might not perish but have eternal life."

Jim suggested that I read the gospel according to John, and Paul's letter to the Romans. He gave me a Bible and said he'd really be praying for me along with others who knew that he was coming to visit me. I assured him. "I'll stick with it; I'll get the job done."

He said, "I'm sure you will."

As I peered out my north upstairs window, watching the last glimmer of taillights coming from his gray, '77 Chevy® Nova, I glanced into yet another star-emblazoned summer sky and calmly walked back to the couch. I knew that I had to deal with this now. Just Jesus and me. By now I would have been long asleep, passed out hours ago, but I was very awake and the straightest that I had been in years.

Laying on Uncle Artie's blue flower-patterned couch, with my head resting on a pillow, I began to quietly talk to Jesus. As I actually spoke His name, calling Him, it seemed like a comedy act. Me, talking to Jesus, talking out loud to someone that I couldn't see, someone who may not even hear me or even be real. But, I said, "I'd get the job done." So, I was doing it, talking out loud to Jesus. "Let's settle this thing once and for all. Are you real—do you hear me?" The air rested silent, almost in hiding. I heard no voice, but kept talking and talking. Hours went by, and I realized that I was reliving my entire life, relating my experiences, feelings, thoughts, desires, anxieties, and fears to someone who may not have even have been hearing. My voice grew louder, more intense and serious with the passing of time. I was finally seeing my life for what it was. It became apparent to me that I wasn't the good, clever, caring person that I perceived myself to be. This one-way conversation took on the form of a confessional. People who I had hurt flashed through my mind. Scenes of selfishness became almost unbearable. The sexual lust that often drove me was exposed as repulsive and disgusting. The great self-pride of needing to be right even when wrong, reared its piercing head, showing itself as intolerable. I nearly wept. Was I this bad? I truly pleaded to Jesus to show me the truth. "Please be real, please, would something be real, something I could trust?" Up until now, all was deception, all was for vainglory. "Jesus, are you real? I've got to know, now. I've got to know." I began to shout loudly and groan. A sickness like that of experiencing hell gnawed at my body. Screaming as loud as my lungs could endure, I yelled, "I hate myself! I can't stand who I am. I did everything the way I wanted to do it; my life's a mess; I hurt people; I'm sick of myself; I don't want to be in control of my life. Jesus, please, show yourself; Jesus, I want you to be Lord of my life!"

At that very instant when I called Him Lord, I actually felt Him enter my body. I simply had a 'knowing' that Jesus came into me. As I laid there perfectly still and calm, an incredible peace consumed me. I had never before even remotely experienced a peace like this before. The feeling of being perfectly clean and purified caused me to barely recollect ever being dirty or living in darkness. As if that ugly past was erased!

Hundreds of tiny electric sparks danced all over my body. The room began to vibrate with a very low sound like that of the bottom bass pedal on a church organ. My body vibrated in sync with the room. Another most unusual occurrence took hold, I had no thoughts, none what so ever! I was only conscious of the presence of Jesus. I believe that I was given a taste of what eternity will be like. We will not be riddled with thoughts of the past, present, or future, we will just only be aware of God and live as if in a quantum state. Time will not exist. Eternally present, now, in an always perfect state in Christ.

The room became dimly lit with a soft soothing light. This most incredible experience lasted perhaps five minutes though I wasn't conscious of time. I found myself face first on my carpeting in uncontrollable laughing and weeping. I was fully saturated in the love of Christ. It was His love that was calling me, and His love that overwhelmed my very being. Body, mind, soul, spirit was drenched, submerged in His love, the pure love of Jesus. I laid on the floor in that condition for at least half an hour. It seemed that I was releasing decades of pent up emotion and it manifested as intense laughing and crying for joy.

The only word I was able to speak was His name, which I repeated over and over. This was raw, pure, worship! The search was over, God pursued me, and He won! At around five in the morning, I crawled to my phone so that I could call Jim. Dialing was difficult, the phone was covered with my tears. Jim groggily answered, "Hello?" I blurted out, "Jim, it's Ray, Jesus is inside of me". My words were broken and shaky because of my laughing and crying. Jim spoke with a great concern for me. "Ray, are you alright?, do you want me to come over?' I had all I could do to compose myself and respond, "No, no, Jesus came into my body, I'm beautiful". Jim, feeling the need to intellectually explain this, replied, "Ray, you're 'born again', The Holy Spirit lives inside of you". I could hardly communicate at this point and quietly hung up the phone. Just months before, I made fun and mockery of that term, 'born again'. I quickly recalled someone telling me that Jesus himself said that, "You must be born again".

Having not slept even a minute all night, a supernatural energy surged through me. I knew that I could ready myself to go to work. While driving to the Kasch Co., I felt like I was living in a euphoric dream. Suddenly as if transported, I found myself pulling into the employee parking lot. My emotional high was still very strong but my mind could not comprehend the magnitude of what just happened.

CHAPTER 38

LIFE N CHRIST

I must have been glowing as I drifted into the warehouse of the Kasch Company. Coworkers joked and teased, saying things like, "Are you still stoned from last night?" Or, "You must have had a good night in bed with her." I happily corrected them and openly blurted out that I let Jesus be Lord of my life. "He's real!" Most of them backed away from me, not knowing what to make of it. I just had to tell my friend, Mary Ellen, who worked in another department. There she stood, catching a glimpse of me walking over. She was always eager to receive my zany comments, but this morning she saw that I was unmistakably excited.

"Mary Ellen, I've got to tell you what happened to me!"

Taking her by the arm, I walked over to a secluded area where I could share this incredibly good news in private. Her eyes grew huge-with an anxious gaze, anticipating some amazing news.

"Mary Ellen, last night I asked Jesus to be Lord of my life.His spirit's living inside of me; I'm born again."

Mary Ellen turned deathly white. Her hands dropped cold. A terrifying shock was written throughout her face. She angrily spoke, "Ray, you've really lost it." And then she walked away.

I stood, dumbfounded, holding a deep rejection. She was one of my best friends. I could not comprehend this rejection. What a crazy thing to see your friends vehemently hate your good news!

That day, I cautiously shared my born-again experience with perhaps fifteen others. Most people had reserved, mixed reactions, though a few were genuinely happy for me, happy that I found what I was looking for. One lady's comment still rings clear to this day, a comment that I've heard many times since. "Well, if it works for you, that's great."

I immediately felt the need to correct her by saying, "Listen, it isn't that it *works* for me; anybody can have this. Jesus just isn't a positive attitude or a good feeling; He's God; He's Lord; He's the Savior; He's alive. He's the Creator!"

People didn't want to receive this. Possibly it was just too simplistic, a free gift, nothing you can do to earn it or attain to. God comes to you.

Back at home, after work, up in my loft. I sat at my round spool table, absorbing with new eyes the wealth of spiritual truth in the Bible. I was amazed over and over again at how in the past I could not understand what the Bible was saying. Now, with the Holy Spirit firmly dwelling within, what was once uninteresting and confusing ramblings now jumped off the pages as the clear revelation of God Himself. Back in Ben Lomond, I struggled to get through even the first three chapters of the gospel of John. I even thought that the New Testament was a revised version of the old. Now, all I wanted to do was read the scriptures in utter amazement. I became enthralled with this book and couldn't seem to put it down. After all my travels, here in my own backyard, God found me. What a paradox! God kept pursuing me in spite of my stubborn rejection of Him.

As I read now again with spiritual eyes, John chapter 1, these words just sing in my heart. "In the beginning was the Word (Jesus Christ) and the Word was with God and the Word was God. He was in the beginning with God."

Verse 3: "In Him was life and the life was the light of men and the light shines in the dark and the darkness did not comprehend it."

It was so true. I was in darkness and could not comprehend the light, the light that is Jesus Christ.

Verse 11: But as many as received Him to them He gave the right to become children of God, even to those who believe in His name."

Verse 14 says: "And the Word became flesh and dwelt among us and we beheld His glory, glory as of the only begotten from the Father, full of grace and truth."

John penned it so clearly, being inspired by the Holy Spirit to do so. These verses echoed in my mind. And the verse that Jim left me with, in the Book of John, Chapter 3, verse 16: "For God so loved the world that He gave His only begotten Son that whoever believes in Him should not perish but have eternal life."

I could not get enough of the Bible or of prayer. Now my prayers made sense, and they connected. I found myself anxiously looking forward to getting home from work so that I could spend two to three hours in uninterrupted prayer. It was just me and Jesus, a communion of fellowship. Shortly after coming home that day, I took a gallon and a half of Carlo Rossi's Vin Rose wine and poured it down my kitchen sink. I laughed in victory as I declared, "You don't control me anymore, Jesus does!" I was fully delivered from the bondage of alcohol. I never had the desire to drink again or even be foolish enough to toy with drugs. As the scripture confirmed to me, "When the Son sets you free, you are free indeed". Even my filthy course language was removed, I never swore again. And, the pain in my upper chest that I experienced daily, never came back! An amazing compassionate love for all people began to well up in me. Especially for those who were down and out.

The next evening, Wednesday June 6th, I went to a prayer meeting at the church that Jim attended. To my great surprise, many of my past friends were there also. This was truly a celebration. They made me aware that just two days prior at a Monday night Bible study, they prayed for me while I was meeting with Jim. Many hugs and handshakes were given.

I glanced to see the pastor walking down a side isle towards me. Briefly, I thought to myself, "He will be my spiritual teacher." As we met and shook hands, I very excitedly began to share with him all about the amazing experience that I had with Jesus just a day and a half before. Less than half way into my remarkable testimony, he turned around and walked away. I stood there in the isle somewhat in shock and left feeling very rejected. Two days later, he met with me in his office. He kindly listened while I shared a brief history of my life and expressed again, the major transforming encounter that I had with Jesus. As I remained seated, he began to explain in a rebuttal type fashion that "Ray, what you probably experienced was a nervous or emotional breakdown, or maybe because of your involvement with cults, you had some sort of manifestation of demons."

I sat there, dumbfounded and numb. He totally dismissed my testimony as being anything other than God. Well, fortunately God had other plans! Shortly thereafter, I met with several other pastors who were of a much more spiritually alive persuasion. They listened intently as I shared with them my experience with Jesus. All of them acknowledged that I was truly 'Baptized in the Spirit'. They clearly showed me through the New Testament scriptures that all the gifts and power of the early church are not only for us today, but are in full operation throughout the world. They assured me that 'Signs, wonders and miracles are for today, for all believers'. I praise Jesus daily that He has faithfully walked me into that, and that He has seen fit to reveal Himself and His Word to me.

Quite possibly the most difficult thing that I experienced at that time was the outright rejection from long-time friends and musicians. Jesus said that this would happen. But, I continued to love them with the very love and compassion of Christ that now dwelt in me. Over the years, a number of these people also received Jesus. The euphoria that I experienced initially lasted about four days. When this feeling of immense joy with laughing and crying began to subside, I at first though that Jesus had left me. Well, a firm study of His Word assured me otherwise. The Apostle Paul states in his letter to the believers in Rome, chapter 8, verses 31 to 39 that absolutely nothing could ever separate us from the love of God. Nothing can come against His believers and prevail.Uncontrollable laughter and weeping for joy continued for several more days. Even while checking out at the grocery store I began to cry. I had to assure the concerned cashier that, "I'm just very happy."

Just two days after receiving Christ, I wrote a song, a song of my testimony called "Salvation Day".

Songs began to come to me and flow faster than I could record them. They were beautiful songs, songs of joy filled with spiritual truth, songs pertaining to reality and life in Christ. Within a year's time, I had completed at least fifteen songs of great substance, and another fifteen were in the making. I was experiencing a creative surge unparalleled in my previous eighteen years engulfed in music. Even my vocal quality showed marked improvement.

For the first time since I was twelve years old, I joined a baseball team and started playing baseball again. It was like a boyish thrill to play baseball with other men on a church team.

Freedoms that were not mine to claim now were being expressed daily, like the freedom to not sin anymore. I could now choose and not only choose, but desire to do righteous acts through the prompting and empowering of the Holy Spirit: Acts of kindness and compassion, genuinely selfless deeds. They were not to gain favor with God, but to express God's love which hummed in my veins.

When the Monday morning garbage truck came down Cedar Creek Road, it took with it a paper grocery bag brimming full of dead books containing dead speculations that led the reader to a Godless eternity. As a prisoner released, I threw away the books that bound and enslaved me: occult books, mind sciences, and empty spiritual ramblings. They now were delivered to their rightful place—the garbage dump. Back to the source of their inspiration. From death to death.

For the first time in my life, a warm relationship was beginning to emerge with my father. He listened with sincerity to my testimony and buoyant enthusiasm over Jesus Christ. Sharing deeply with me, he confided that he, too, while in his late teens, had a great sense of closeness to the Lord, but that he had let the prompting of the world pull him away. Walking with Jesus is a choice, not an enforceable command.

And, Aunt Jenny received my news with gladness, making me aware that she had been praying for me for many years.

The personnel director at the Kasch Company was a professed atheist and as my bold witness continued to have a very positive affect on many of the employees, it made him extremely uneasy. So to ease his fretful condition, he laid me off just three days before Christmas, 1979.

I was ecstatic! Now I could spend weeks and months just saturated in prayer and Bible study while fostering a deep intimate relationship with my Lord Jesus. I was afforded the freedom to spend nearly seven months intensely devoted to Jesus without distraction.

Since the first days of tuning a piano in Footch Kapoot, I had a great interest in becoming experienced with not just tuning but also being adept at complete piano repair. God answered this desire (He probably gave me the desire). In the very early 80's, I started my own business, 'Ray Last Piano Tuning and Repair, (with a smile)'. I not only was able to support my family but

I also had hundreds and hundreds of opportunities to share my testimony and the pure love of Christ.

In 1985, I wrote a lengthy letter to Jesse Eagle Elk, exclaiming in depth my transformation in Christ. I sent the letter certified mail, someone received it but I never heard back from Jesse. I also wrote several elaborate and in depth letters to George Harrison. I knew that he was steeped in Hinduism but God deeply impressed upon me to openly share with George about the freedom and salvation that is found only in Jesus. As with Jesse, I never received a response back.

Also in 1985, God placed in me an overwhelming desire and urge to write this book. The great majority of this was written between the years of 1985 and 1990. As I write these ending remarks in the summer of 2015, I find myself reflecting back over the more than thirty six years of my life in Christ. I simply agree and acknowledge what my great brother the Apostle John wrote in the very last sentence of his Gospel account of the life of Jesus. "And there are many other things which Jesus did, which if they were written in detail, I suppose that even the world could not contain the books which were written." I would surely need to write volumes in an attempt to convey all the absolutely marvelous things that Jesus through His Spirit has shown, taught and brought me through. His life flows, and it flows through me.

Our destiny in Christ is found in Romans chapter 8, verse 29, that we who are in Christ would be conformed to His image, become just like Him, do the works that He did, while we are still here on Earth! Amen.

Hold on, the phones' ringin'.......... It was Aunt Jenny, she just baked some apple pies and

I need to get over there while they're still hot,

See you all later..... Ray.

CPSIA information can be obtained at www.ICGtesting.com
Printed in the USA
LVOW02s0843290915

456096LV00004B/7/P

9 781498 447010